The Legal Architecture of English Cathedrals

This original book is a comprehensive, richly documented and critical examination of laws applicable to Anglican cathedrals in England, some of the most iconic monuments in the national heritage and centres of spiritual and cultural capital. Law is the missing link in the emerging field of cathedral studies. The book fills this gap. It explores historical antecedents of modern cathedral law, traces aspects of them that still endure, and explains the law with particular reference to the recommendations of the Archbishops' Commission on Cathedrals 1994 which led to the most radical changes in the legal history of these churches since the Reformation, culminating in the Cathedrals Measure 1999 and associated later legislation. The book compares the domestic constitutions and statutes of all the cathedrals of the Church of England today – old foundations, new foundations and parish church cathedrals – as well as policies and guidelines applicable to or adopted by them. Whilst national law acts as a fundamental unifying force, there is considerable diversity between these in terms of the breadth and depth of their coverage of topics. In the socio-legal tradition, the book also explores through interviews with clergy and others, at half of the cathedrals, how laws are experienced in practice. These reveal that whilst much of the law is perceived as working well, there are equally key areas of concern. To this end, the book proposes areas for further research and debate with a view to possible reform. Taking an architectural feature of cathedrals as the starting point for each chapter, from cathedral governance through mission, ministry, music and education to cathedral property, what emerges is that law and architecture have a symbiotic relationship so that a cathedral is itself a form of juristecture.

Norman Doe DCL (Lambeth), LLD (Cambridge), Professor of Law, Cardiff University, Director of the Centre for Law and Religion, Cardiff School of Law and Politics, sometime Visiting Research Scholar, Corpus Christi College, Oxford and Chancellor of the Diocese of Bangor.

Law and Religion

The practice of religion by individuals and groups, the rise of religious diversity, and the fear of religious extremism, raise profound questions for the interaction between law and religion in society. The regulatory systems involved, the religion laws of secular government (national and international) and the religious laws of faith communities, are valuable tools for our understanding of the dynamics of mutual accommodation and the analysis and resolution of issues in such areas as: religious freedom; discrimination; the autonomy of religious organisations; doctrine, worship and religious symbols; the property and finances of religion; religion, education and public institutions; and religion, marriage and children. In this series, scholars at the forefront of law and religion contribute to the debates in this area. The books in the series are analytical with a key target audience of scholars and practitioners, including lawyers, religious leaders, and others with an interest in this rapidly developing discipline.

Series Editor: Professor Norman Doe, Director of the Centre for Law and Religion, Cardiff University, UK

Series Board:
Carmen Asiaín, Professor, University of Montevideo
Paul Babie, Professor and Associate Dean (International), Adelaide Law School
Pieter Coertzen, Chairperson, Unit for the Study of Law and Religion, University of Stellenbosch
Alison Mawhinney, Reader, Bangor University
Michael John Perry, Senior Fellow, Center for the Study of Law and Religion, Emory University

Titles in this series include:

Religious Expression in the Workplace and the Contested Role of Law
Andrew Hambler

Women's Rights and Religious Law
Domestic and International Perspectives
Fareda Banda and Lisa Fishhbayn Joffe

The Collective Dimension of Freedom of Religion
A Case Study on Turkey
Mine Yıldırım

The Legal Architecture of English Cathedrals

Norman Doe

LONDON AND NEW YORK

First published 2018
by Routledge
2 Park Square, Milton Park, Abingdon, Oxon OX14 4RN

and by Routledge
711 Third Avenue, New York, NY 10017

Routledge is an imprint of the Taylor & Francis Group, an informa business

© 2018 Norman Doe

The right of Norman Doe to be identified as author of this work has been asserted by him in accordance with sections 77 and 78 of the Copyright, Designs and Patents Act 1988.

All rights reserved. No part of this book may be reprinted or reproduced or utilised in any form or by any electronic, mechanical, or other means, now known or hereafter invented, including photocopying and recording, or in any information storage or retrieval system, without permission in writing from the publishers.

Trademark notice: Product or corporate names may be trademarks or registered trademarks, and are used only for identification and explanation without intent to infringe.

British Library Cataloguing in Publication Data
A catalogue record for this book is available from the British Library

Library of Congress Cataloging in Publication Data
Names: Doe, Norman, author.
Title: The legal architecture of English cathedrals / Norman Doe.
Description: New York : Routledge, 2017. | Series: Law and religion | Includes bibliographical references and index.
Identifiers: LCCN 2017012347 | ISBN 9781138962699 (hbk) | ISBN 9781315659268 (ebk)
Subjects: LCSH: Church buildings--Great Britain. | Church maintenance and repair (Ecclesiastical law)--Great Britain.
Classification: LCC KD8712 .D64 2017 | DDC 342.4208/5235--dc23
LC record available at https://lccn.loc.gov/2017012347

ISBN: 9781138962699 (hbk)
ISBN: 9781315659268 (ebk)

Typeset in Galliard
by Taylor & Francis Books

Printed and bound by CPI Group (UK) Ltd, Croydon, CR0 4YY

Contents

Acknowledgements viii
Abbreviations x

Introduction 1

1 The cathedral church: foundation, form and function 11
   The classification of cathedrals 11
   The purposes of a cathedral 16
   The sources of cathedral law 23
   Conclusion 35

2 The episcopal throne: the appointment and functions of the bishop 37
   The enthronement of the bishop 37
   The functions of the bishop 44
   The bishop and enforcement of cathedral care standards 52
   Conclusion 55

3 The font, altar and pulpit: sacraments, worship and mission 57
   The sacraments 57
   Worship and liturgy 67
   The ministry of preaching 74
   Conclusion 78

4 The nave and crossing: the cathedral community, hospitality and outreach 79
   The cathedral community 79
   Vergers, volunteers and visitors 87

The ministry of outreach 94
Conclusion 104

5 **The choir and presbytery: the dean, canons and musicians**   106
The dean 108
The cathedral canons 114
The musicians and cathedral music 123
Conclusion 129

6 **The chapter house: the body corporate – Council, Chapter and College of Canons**   131
The Council 133
The Chapter 139
The College of Canons 150
Conclusion 154

7 **The library and cloister: education – learning and teaching**   156
The library and archives 157
Educational work and theological study 166
The cathedral school 175
Conclusion 183

8 **The treasury: cathedral property, treasure and finance**   185
Cathedral property and the inventory 186
Treasures and other valuable objects 191
Cathedral finances 196
Conclusion 208

9 **The fabric of the cathedral church: care and conservation**   210
The Cathedrals Fabric Commission for England 213
The Fabric Advisory Committee 219
A Commission of Review 225
Conclusion 227

10 **The cathedral close: the precinct, houses and security**   229
The cathedral precinct 229
Canonical houses 238
Cathedral security 244
Conclusion 250

Conclusion: The cathedral as a normative space: conception and experience   **252**

Bibliography   258
Index   265

Acknowledgements

I am very grateful to a great many people for their support, encouragement and experiences in the production of this book which has grown out of my own interest over the years in church law. Cardiff Law School was good enough to allow me study leave in 2015–2016 to work on the book and I was the beneficiary of a generous study leave fellowship grant awarded by Cardiff University to carry out the project. Corpus Christi College Oxford elected me to the position of Visiting Research Scholar for the Michaelmas term 2015: I am deeply indebted to the (then) President, Professor Richard Cawardine, and to the Fellows, particularly Revd Canon Dr Judith Maltby, for such a stimulating and memorable time at the college which allowed access to Oxford's libraries. I also thank the Allchurches Trust for a grant to enable me to visit and conduct interviews at cathedrals. The students on the postgraduate LLM in Canon Law at Cardiff University have been a constant source of inspiration over many years.

I owe a particular debt of gratitude to numerous stakeholders who helped to design the study. Meeting the executive of the Association of English Cathedrals in 2014 was a formative moment: I am especially grateful to its chair, the Very Revd Vivienne Faull, Dean of York Minister, and co-ordinator Sarah King. As part of my time at Oxford, I had the benefit of valuable meetings at Christ Church with: Revd Canon Professor Nigel Biggar (Canon), Revd Canon Edmund Newey (Sub-Dean), Revd Canon John Paton (Precentor), Professor Stephen Darlington (Organist), and John Briggs (Cathedral Registrar). Others consulted include: Revd Canon Matthew Rushton (Precentor of Canterbury); Timothy Hone, Department of Liturgy and Music (Salisbury); Dr Ian Atherton (Keele University); and the cathedral administrators and others who supplied copies of constitutions, statutes and other documents.

Special thanks are owed to cathedral clergy from whom, by interviews and correspondence, I have learned so much about how cathedral law is experienced in practice: Very Revd Peter Atkinson (Dean of Worcester); Very Revd Dr David Hoyle (Dean of Bristol); Revd Canon Celia Thomson (Chancellor and Vice-Dean of Gloucester); Very Revd Michael Tavinor (Dean of Hereford); Very Revd Jonathan Draper (Dean of Exeter); Very Revd John Davies (Dean of Derby); Very Revd Catherine Ogle (Dean of Birmingham); Revd Canon Andrew Featherstone (Acting Dean of Wells); Revd Canon Chancellor Roland Riem (Acting Dean of

Winchester); Revd Canon Peter Howell-Jones (Vice-Dean of Chester); Very Revd Jane Osborne (Dean of Salisbury); Very Revd David Ison (Dean of St Paul's London); Revd Canon Neil Thompson (Canon Precentor, Rochester); Revd Canon Wendy Wilby and Reader Ruth Grenfell (Ripon); Very Revd Andrew Nunn (Dean of Southwark); Very Revd Mark Boyling (Dean of Carlisle); Very Revd Mark Bonney (Dean of Ely); Very Revd Pete Wilcox (Dean of Liverpool); Very Revd Jeffrey John (Dean of St Albans); and Very Revd Jonathan Greener (Dean of Wakefield). These represent half of all Anglican cathedrals of England.

Thanks are also due to Mark Hill QC, Frank Cranmer, and Robert Ombres OP, associates at the Cardiff Centre for Law and Religion, who commented so helpfully on the original book proposal, as did Stephen Slack (Director of Legal Services, Archbishops' Council, Church of England). At the law school, Sharron Alldred, Helen Calvert and Sarah Kennedy have as always provided first-class support. At Routledge, I am very grateful to Alison Kirk (commissioning editor), Olivia Manley, Alison Jones (copy-editor), and their colleagues for their faith in and patience with the project, and for the smooth production of the volume to its publication. Finally, I thank my family for their constant support – my wife Heather, our children Rachel, Elizabeth and Edward, my brother Martin, my father James (1911–2011), and my mother Julia (1925–2016), to whom I dedicate the book: it was her images of cathedrals that first stimulated my interest in them. Any errors in this book are, needless to say, my sole responsibility.

CND Cardiff Law School, Wales, January 2017

Abbreviations

ACCW	Association of Cathedral Clerk of the Works
ADCA	Association of Diocesan and Cathedral Archaeologists
AEC	Association of English Cathedrals
ARR	*Accounting and Reporting Regulations for English Anglican Cathedrals*, prepared by the Cathedrals Administration and Finance Association with the Association of English Cathedrals (2015)
Birmingham	Cathedral Church of Saint Philip Birmingham
Blackburn	Cathedral Church of Saint Mary the Virgin Blackburn
Bradford	Cathedral Church of Saint Peter Bradford
Bristol	Cathedral Church of the Holy and Undivided Trinity in Bristol
Burn	Richard Burn, *Ecclesiastical Law* (1763, 5th ed., 1788)
CAA	Cathedral Architects Association
CAFA	Cathedral Administration and Finance Association
Canons	(The) Canons Ecclesiastical of the Church of England
Canterbury	Cathedral and Metropolitical Church of Christ, Canterbury
Carlisle	Cathedral Church of the Holy and Undivided Trinity of Carlisle
CCA	Cathedral Constables Association
CCBD	Cathedral and Churches Building Division, Archbishops' Council
CCM	Care of Cathedrals Measure 2011
CCR	Care of Cathedrals Rules 2006
CCSA	Cathedral and Church Shops Association
CERC	Church of England Records Centre
CFCE	Cathedrals Fabric Commission for England
Chelmsford	Cathedral Church of Saint Mary the Virgin, Saint Peter and Saint Cedd Chelmsford
Chester	Cathedral Church of Christ and the Blessed Virgin Mary in Chester
Chi	Chichester
Chichester	Cathedral Church of the Holy Trinity in Chichester

CLAA	Cathedral Libraries and Archives Association
CM	Cathedrals Measure 1999
COA	Cathedral Organists Association
Con.	Cathedral Constitution
Coventry	Cathedral Church of Saint Michael, Coventry
CSA	Choir Schools Association
Derby	Cathedral Church of All Saints, Derby
Durham	Cathedral Church of Christ, Blessed Mary the Virgin and Saint Cuthbert of Durham
ECC	English Consistory Court
Ely	Cathedral Church of the Holy and Undivided Trinity of Ely
Exeter	Cathedral Church of Saint Peter in Exeter
Gibson	Edmund Gibson, *Codex Juris Ecclesiastici Anglicani, or, The Statutes, Constitutions, Canons, Rubrics and Articles of the Church of England* (1713)
Gloucester	Cathedral Church of Saint Peter and the Holy and Indivisible Trinity, Gloucester
Godolphin	John Godolphin, *Repertorium Canonicum or Abridgement of the Ecclesiastical Laws of this Realm* (1678)
GS	General Synod of the Church of England
Guildford	Cathedral Church of the Holy Spirit, Guildford
H&R	*Heritage and Renewal*, Report of the Archbishops' Commission on Cathedrals (1994)
Hereford	Cathedral Church of Saint Mary the Virgin and Saint Ethelbert the King in Hereford
HLE	*Halsbury's Laws of England, Volume 34,* Ecclesiastical Law (2011)
Hooker	Richard Hooker, *Of the Laws of Ecclesiastical Polity* (1593)
Int.	Interview (conducted at a cathedral)
LFCE	Norman Doe, *The Legal Framework of the Church of England* (1996)
Leicester	Cathedral Church of Saint Martin, Leicester
Lichfield	Cathedral Church of Saint Mary and Saint Chad in Lichfield
Lincoln	Cathedral Church of the Blessed Virgin Mary of Lincoln
Liverpool	Cathedral Church of Christ in Liverpool
London	Cathedral Church of Saint Paul in London
Manchester	Cathedral, Collegiate and Parish Church of Saint Mary, Saint Denys and Saint George in Manchester
Nelson	William Nelson, *The Rights of the Clergy of Great Britain* (1710)
Newcastle	Cathedral Church of Saint Nicholas Newcastle upon Tyne
Norwich	Cathedral Church of the Holy and Undivided Trinity of Norwich
Oxford	Cathedral Church of Christ in Oxford
pars.	Paragraphs

xii *Abbreviations*

Peterborough	Cathedral Church of Saint Peter, Saint Paul and Saint Andrew in Peterborough
PGN	Procedural Guidance Note of the Cathedrals Fabric Commission
Phillimore	Robert Phillimore, *Ecclesiastical Law* (1873, 2nd ed. 1895)
Portsmouth	Cathedral Church of Saint Thomas of Canterbury Portsmouth
Rec(s).	Recommendation(s)
Ripon	Cathedral Church of Saint Peter and Saint Wilfrid at Ripon
Rochester	Cathedral Church of Christ and the Blessed Virgin Mary, Rochester
s.	Section
Salisbury	Cathedral Church of the Blessed Virgin Mary of Salisbury
Sch.	Schedule
Sheffield	Cathedral Church of Saint Peter and Saint Paul, Sheffield
SO	Standing Orders
Southwark	Cathedral and Collegiate Church of Saint Saviour and Saint Mary Overy, Southwark
Southwell	Cathedral and Parish Church of the Blessed Virgin Mary (Southwell Minster)
St Albans	Cathedral and Abbey Church of Saint Alban in the City of St. Albans
St Edmundsbury	Cathedral Church of Saint James and Saint Edmund, Bury St Edmunds
Stat.	Cathedral Statute(s)
Truro	Cathedral Church of the Blessed Virgin Mary in Truro
Wakefield	Cathedral Church of All Saints Wakefield
Wells	Cathedral Church of Saint Andrew in Wells
Winchester	Cathedral Church of the Holy Trinity and of Saint Peter and Saint Paul and of Saint Swithun in Winchester
Worcester	Cathedral Church of Christ and the Blessed Mary the Virgin of Worcester
York	Cathedral and Metropolitical Church of Saint Peter in York (York Minster)

Introduction

Each Anglican cathedral in England is a landmark of cultural heritage and identity, a setting for continuing religiosity, and a mirror of national spirituality in transition. It is also a regulated sacred space. The regulatory element of cathedral life provides the normative context in which each of these three realities is played out; and cathedral law is the principal regulatory means used to facilitate and order the delicate balance between the spiritual and secular interests involved in the work of English cathedrals.

The idea for this book was stimulated in part by recent debate on the role and significance of cathedrals in national life in modern England. For example, *Spiritual Capital* (2012), a report commissioned by both the Foundation for Church Leadership and the Association of English Cathedrals, states:

> The present and future of English cathedrals lies particularly in their ability to enable and sustain a range of connections – between the tourist and the pilgrim; between people and the traditions from which modern life cuts them off; between the diverse organisations and communities that share the same social and physical space and infrastructure yet never meet; and between a people who may be less Christian than their parents but are no less spiritual, and … God.

Cathedrals 'are and will remain key institutions to deliver this "spiritual capital"'.[1] However, the report has little to say about the legal framework within which these roles are performed or its impact on those who carry them out.

This book, therefore, describes, explains, and evaluates regulatory norms applicable to cathedrals – the seat of a bishop (Anglicans have cathedrals because of the office of bishop) – and how these are perceived and experienced. First, it describes the law and associated norms, namely: national ecclesiastical law – in Measures of the General Synod of the Church of England, its legislature, principally the Cathedrals Measure 1999 and Care of Cathedrals Measure 2011, and in its national Canons; the particular instruments of each cathedral – its Constitution and Statutes, part of the ecclesiastical law of England,[2] and other domestic norms

---

1 *Spiritual Capital: The Present and Future of English Cathedrals* (2012) 62 pp.
2 *AG v Dean and Chapter of Ripon Cathedral* [1945] Ch. 239.

within a cathedral (including guidelines and policies, as well as customs, conventions, and other unwritten normative practices) reflecting the distinct history and ethos of each cathedral; and, where appropriate, the civil law relevant to aspects of cathedral activities (such as public order and finance).

Second, the book explains the background to, and the reasons for, these norms, with particular reference to the report *Heritage and Renewal*, written by the Archbishops' Commission on Cathedrals 1994, appointed 'to examine the future role in Church and nation of the cathedrals of the Church of England and to make recommendations as to how best that role could be fulfilled, including proposals for their government and support'.[3] The Commission found that the cathedrals themselves 'felt the need of a contemporary restatement of their purpose'; and it concluded there was 'scope for considerable reform and improvement of the way they are governed, staffed and manage their affairs'.[4] Recognising that the 'variety of individual cathedrals' and the circumstances facing each would preclude it from laying down 'a rigid blueprint', the Commission sought instead 'to articulate a series of principles' to help them address 'the many, often conflicting, objectives and demands' confronting them; in turn, it proposed 'a set of governance and other organisational arrangements' for 'a common framework within which longer-term planning can take place, difficult choices can be made, and greater accountability ... achieved'.[5] It also recommended establishment of a Cathedrals Commission to: advise the archbishops, bishops, and General Synod; review developments in cathedral governance, management, and finances; oversee constitutional changes following implementation of the report; and exercise limited responsibilities as to cathedral constitutions;[6] this proposal was not implemented. However, the 1994 report did lead to the enactment of the Cathedrals Measure 1999.

Third, the book evaluates the legal framework (national legislation and the domestic norms of cathedrals) by means of conversations, interviews, and correspondence with clergy and other staff at twenty-one cathedrals (one half of them).[7] Deans, acting deans, sub-deans, precentors, and other staff were interviewed (and emailed) about their own experiences of the regulatory regimes in practice – whether and how norms enable or frustrate cathedral ministry. These reveal cathedral jurisprudence: wisdom about the laws themselves, the reasons for them, and their implementation; sometimes this wisdom is satisfied, but sometimes it is critical. In this way, the book also offers, for the first time, an empirical exposition of cathedral law in the socio-legal tradition. A further theoretical theme,

---

3 H&R 1.
4 H&R 173: the Commission visited all 42 cathedrals.
5 H&R ix.
6 H&R 67–68: the Commission was not to replace the role of the Association of English Cathedrals.
7 I conducted interviews at five old foundations (Exeter, Hereford, Salisbury, St Paul's London, and Wells); three new (Rochester, Winchester, and Worcester); four Henrician (Bristol, Chester, Gloucester and Oxford); and three parish church cathedrals (Derby, Birmingham, and Ripon). I had correspondence with six cathedrals (Southwark, Carlisle, Ely, Liverpool, St Albans, and Wakefield).

addressed in the Conclusion, is the cathedral building as a normative space: how regulation both shapes and is shaped by cathedral architecture. In turn, each chapter uses as its starting point an architectural feature of the cathedral, and then moves to the norms applicable to actors and activities associated with it.

The need for the book is based on three factors. First, it will soon be 25 years since publication of *Heritage and Renewal*, and twenty since the enactment of the Cathedrals Measure 1999, enabling an objective assessment of the reception of the most wide-ranging reforms in cathedral law in the history of the English church. Second, the leading works on ecclesiastical law describe only the fundamentals of national law on cathedrals – they do not address the domestic laws of each cathedral (its constitution and statutes), consider the role of the increasing volume of quasi-legislation, policy documents, and guidelines (national and within each cathedral), or assess these in practice, how they are experienced, beyond the legal texts themselves.[8]

Third, 'cathedral studies' is an emerging field of scholarship today.[9] The field is well-served by books on cathedral architecture, which unsurprisingly do not address regulatory aspects,[10] but some scholars explore how church architecture represents images of power.[11] The book may also be located in the new area of law and the built environment; for example, a book has recently been published on the architecture of Law Courts, their design as a physical expression of our relationship with the State, society, and justice.[12] Moreover, the cathedral in modern pluralist society is increasingly studied in sociology of religion (in which law is only recently a focus).[13] The 'under-researched area' of 'cathedrals as a form of European museum', or as 'embodiments as well as carriers of memory',[14] theological perspectives on cathedrals as social phenomena,[15] and cathedrals and

---

8   E.g. Halsbury's Laws of England, Vol. 34, *Ecclesiastical Law* (London: Butterworths LexisNexis, 5th ed., 2011) pars. 343–381; M. Hill, *Ecclesiastical Law* (Oxford: Oxford University Press, 3rd ed., 2007) 281–308; T. Briden (ed.), *Moore's Introduction to English Canon Law* (London: Bloomsbury, 4th ed., 2013) 53–60; and N. Doe, *The Legal Framework of the Church of England* (Oxford: The Clarendon Press, 1996) 112, 205, 408, 446.

9   See e.g. L.J. Francis (ed.), *Anglican Cathedrals in Modern Life: The Science of Cathedral Studies* (London: Palgrave Macmillan, 2015): this uses the sociology and psychology of religion and empirical theology to explore cathedrals as a focus for church growth, and proposes new research directions.

10 E.g. M. Escott, *Round the Cloisters* (Bristol: Silver Wood Books, 2011); P. Johnson, *British Cathedrals* (London: Weidenfeld & Nicolson, 1980); and J. Harvey, *English Cathedrals* (London: B.T. Batsford, 2nd ed., 1956).

11 E.g. J.H. Kilde, *Sacred Power – Sacred Space: An Introduction to Christian Architecture and Worship* (Oxford: Oxford University Press, 2008).

12 L. Mulcahy, *Legal Architecture: Justice, Due Process and the Place of Law* (Abingdon: Routledge, 2011).

13 See R. Sandberg, *Religion, Law and Society* (Cambridge: Cambridge University Press, 2013).

14 G. Davie, *Religion in Modern Europe: A Memory Mutates* (Oxford: Oxford University Press, 2000) Ch. 9; see also S. Bruce, *Religion in the Modern World: From Cathedrals to Cults* (Oxford: Oxford University Press, 1996).

15 E.g. S. Platten and C. Lewis (eds.), *Dreaming Spires? Cathedrals in a New Age* (London: SPCK, 2006); I.M. MacKenzie (ed.), *Cathedrals Now: Their Use and Place*

4 *Introduction*

politics,[16] are all part of this growth area of cathedral studies. However, cathedral law has not yet made its mark in this new field.

Likewise, there is a vast literature on the history of cathedrals,[17] with some excellent studies on constitutional aspects of medieval secular cathedrals,[18] and the domestic rules of those associated with the religious orders.[19] However, there is still no single, landmark, study on the legal history of cathedrals of the Church of England since its establishment at the time of the Reformation in the sixteenth century and beyond, though there are some outstanding studies on cathedrals in Tudor,[20] and in Stuart,[21] England, and edited collections/studies of cathedral statutes were popular in the early twentieth century.[22] This book seeks to add a little to this academic tradition. It does so by including briefly the treatment of cathedrals in works on ecclesiastical law by such writers as Richard Hooker (1554–1600), John Godolphin (1617–1678), Edmund Gibson (1669–1748), Richard Burn (1709–1785), and Robert Phillimore (1810–1885).

In outline, in the early church a cathedral was the place where the bishop maintained his household and where there was, among other buildings, a church which contained his teaching-chair or *cathedra*. In medieval England, cathedrals were linked with the shrines of saints, and the bishop's authority was enhanced by the presence of relics; when cathedrals were entrusted to a monastic order, to guard a shrine and pray in its presence, this in part obscured their main purpose. Yet, they soon became the subject of regulation. Synods in 1070 and 1075 required the seats of bishops to be in centres of population.[23] Cathedrals related

in *Society* (Norwich: Canterbury Press, 1996); M. Kitchen, J. Halliburton and K. Walker (eds.), *Cathedrals and Society: A Theological Appraisal* (London: Tiltman Desktop Publishing, 1995); and R. Kieckhefer, *Theology in Stone: Church Architecture from Byzantium to Berkeley* (Oxford: Oxford University Press, 2004)

16 E.g. K.E. Smith, 'An old cathedral for a new Russia: the symbolic politics of the reconstructed Church of Christ the Saviour [Moscow]', 25 *Religion, State and Society* (1997) 163–175.
17 E.g. J. Backhouse (ed.), *The Medieval English Cathedral* (Donington: Harlaxton Medieval Studies, 2003).
18 E.g. K. Edwards, *The English Secular Cathedrals in the Middle Ages: A Constitutional Study with Special Reference to the Fourteenth Century* (Manchester: Manchester University Press, 1949).
19 E.g. J. Greatrex, *The English Benedictine Cathedral Priories: Rule and Practice, c. 1270–1420* (Oxford: Oxford University Press, 2011).
20 E.g. S.E. Lehmberg, author of *English Cathedrals: A History* (London: Hambledon Continuum, 2005), and 'Henry VIII, the Reformation and the cathedrals', 49 *Huntington Library Quarterly* (1986) 261.
21 E.g. I. Atherton, 'Cathedrals and the British Revolution', in M.J. Braddick and D.L. Smith (eds.), *The Experience of Revolution in Stuart Britain and Ireland* (Cambridge: University Press, 2011).
22 See e.g. A.W. Goodman and W.H. Hutton (eds.), *The Statutes Governing the Cathedral Church of Winchester* (Oxford: The Clarendon Press, 1925); and A.T. Bannister, *The Cathedral Church of Hereford: Its History and Constitution* (London: SPCK, 1924).
23 Burn I.254–265, cathedrals: I.255: 'every town which has a see of a bishop placed in it, is thereby entitled to the honour of a city'; he cites Gibson 171 and Coke I Inst. 109; see also Phillimore I.125.

to a monastic order were subject to the rule of that order, and those which were not (with their secular canons) also adopted a pattern of common life defined by rules.[24] In time, the attachment of secular functions to the episcopal office meant that the bishop was often absent (in residence at court for instance); this not only led to cathedral independence but their administration by deans and Chapters, the bishop having few rights exercisable in their own cathedrals.[25] A cathedral existing at the time of the Reformation, whether monastic or secular, was a corporation providing for regular worship (for the members of its own community), for the administration of its estates, and for the custody of any shrine within it.[26]

The Reformation left cathedrals more or less untouched: after the dissolution of the monasteries, those administered by secular canons continued (the old foundations); and those formerly under the monastic orders were secularised (becoming known as the new foundations).[27] However, the royal charters of the new foundations erected by King Henry VIII prescribed that 'they should be ruled and governed by statutes to be specified in certain indentures then after to be made by him: which statutes were accordingly made and delivered to the said churches but not indented'; therefore, an Act of Parliament of 1553 empowered Queen Mary to ordain statutes for these cathedrals – but she died before this was completed. As a result, the same power was given to Elizabeth I (by an Act of Parliament of 1558) who authorised commissioners to prepare new statutes (which were completed 1572) for royal confirmation, but 'for whatever reason' this was 'never obtained'. So, by Act of Parliament (1708), to settle disputes on their 'validity':

> [S]uch statutes as have been usually received and practised [in the time of King Charles II] shall be good and valid [unless] repugnant to or inconsistent with the constitution of the Church of England ... or the laws of the land.[28]

With regard to the statutes of the new foundations, Worcester is typical: the statutes issued by King Henry VIII in 1545, 'appointed for the government and rule'

---

24 St Osmond of Salisbury (Chancellor 1074–78) drew up model statutes dealing with e.g. the four principals: dean, precentor, chancellor and treasurer. See also Burn II.474: secular canons worked 'abroad in the world, performed spiritual offices to the laity, took upon them the cure of souls (which regulars could not without dispensation) and differed in nothing almost from common priests; save that they were under the government of some local statutes'.
25 Burn II.88: 'By degrees the dependence of the dean and chapter on the bishop, and their relation to him, grew less and less; till at last the bishop has little more left to him than the power of visiting them, and that very much limited'; see also I.255–256: exemption from archidiaconal jurisdiction.
26 H&R 189–190.
27 The dismantling of shrines took away a key purpose; attempts were made to encourage the use of cathedrals to propagate Protestant learning (e.g. the Six Preachers at Canterbury: see Chapter 3 below).
28 Burn I.264; Gibson 181. See also e.g. J. Saunders, 'The Limitations of Statutes: Elizabethan Schemes to Reform New Foundation Cathedral Statutes', *Journal of Ecclesiastical History*, 48:3 (1997) 445–467.

6   *Introduction*

of the cathedral, dealt with a wide range of matters: the officers to be maintained, from dean to cook (Chapter 1); the election, admission, and functions of the dean (Chapters 2–4); inspection and leasing of land and transfer of goods (Chapters 5–7); residence of and obedience to the dean (Chapters 8–9); as to the canons, their qualification, election, admission, oath, residence, and table (Chapters 10–12 and 14); preaching sermons (Chapter 13); remuneration of the dean and canons (Chapter 15); elections (Chapter 16); vice-dean, receiver, treasurer, precentor, minor canons, sacristan, their oaths and residence (Chapters 17–23); vergers, choristers, pupils, poor persons, junior ministers (Chapters 24–28); common table, vesture, and remuneration of all ministers, including barber and butler (Chapter 29–31); divine service (Chapters 32, 39); treasury, seal, muniments, and accounts (Chapters 33–34); discipline, alms, Chapter, and visitation (Chapters 35–39); and the school (Chapter 40).[29] The Cathedrals Commission 1559 eschewed major reform: cathedrals were to attend their duties and provide for sound theology; it was not proposed that bishops recover their earlier roles, that cathedrals become centres of diocesan life, or that they engage in parish-like pastoral ministry.[30]

In the centuries that followed, piecemeal adjustments were made to the canon law applicable to cathedrals.[31] Cathedral finance and property were the main objects of proposed/actual reform, not re-thinking the purposes of cathedrals. The Ecclesiastical Commission of 1835 (which became permanent in 1836) proposed a redistribution of church wealth and developed a scheme to use cathedral resources to provide parish clergy for the developing urban areas; the Ecclesiastical Duties and Revenues Act 1840 abolished all non-resident prebends and sinecure rectories annexed to cathedrals and restricted the number of residentiary canons to four in each cathedral.[32] However, the Cathedrals Commission 1852 saw worship as the primary purpose of a cathedral; and it recommended that each give more attention to educational work and theological training and that the neighbouring

29 Worcester: Translated from the privately printed Latin edition of 1879 by R.J.W. Bryer (1994). For the Henrician statutes of Christ Church Oxford, see J. Curthoys, *The Cardinal's College: Christ Church, Chapter and Verse* (London: Profile Books, 2012) 42–45.
30 H&R 190–191.
31 See e.g. Canons of 1571, Can. 2 and 1597, Can. 4 (on deans); Canons Ecclesiastical 1603/4, Can. 7: deans; Can. 15: litany to be read; Cans 24–25: vesture; Can. 31: ordinations at cathedrals; Can. 35: examination of ordination candidates by cathedral clergy; Can. 36: declarations to be made by cathedral clergy. See also G. Bray (ed.), *The Anglican Canons: 1529–1947* (Boydell Press: Church of England Record Society, 1998) 825 for reforms to the Canons of 1603/4 endorsed by Archbishop William Laud in 1640. For controversy over cathedral liturgy, see J. Maltby, 'Suffering and surviving: the civil wars, the Commonwealth and the formation of "Anglicanism", 1642–60', in C. Durston and J. Maltby (eds.), *Religion in Revolutionary England* (Manchester: Manchester University Press, 2006) 158–180.
32 There were exceptions: six each at Christ Church Oxford, Canterbury, Durham and Ely, and five each at Winchester and Exeter. The Act protected life interests but in due course 382 cathedral offices were abolished and thus many chapters were impoverished. But the statutes survived: H&R 192.

population should be placed under the pastoral care of the chapter; but little was done, and with no redefinition of the role of a cathedral.[33] The nineteenth century also saw the creation of parish church cathedrals to respond to the growth of urban centres, but the proposal of the Cathedrals Commission 1879–85 to set up a standing committee authorised to alter cathedral statutes came to nought.[34]

The failure to address the purposes of cathedrals continued into the next century. The Commission of 1924, reporting in 1927, dealt with property and revenues as well as how cathedrals 'might adequately fulfil their great functions in the life of the Church and people' – but these functions were not articulated. The Commission rejected the view that residentiary canons should be annexed to diocesan offices, but recognised cathedrals should be 'centres of religious learning' for their dioceses. It did not deal with the bishop's role in the cathedral, but it did recommend a permanent Cathedrals Commission, which came to nothing. Subsequently, the Cathedrals Measure 1931 addressed material concerns but left spiritual matters to private initiative: it wound up cathedral ownership of land and, crucially, laid the foundations of modern cathedral finance; the Church Commissioners compensated each cathedral for land ceded and began the practice of block grants in order to maintain cathedral dignitaries. A further Cathedrals Commission reporting in 1961 found that 'it was useless to prescribe all manner of requirements for cathedrals by Statutes, if there was no possibility that the necessary financial provision would be available'; and so, its focus, once again, was on finance: 'the cathedrals of England cannot sufficiently discharge their duties unless in some way or other their income is made to cover their work more adequately'.[35]

However, the resultant legislation went further than the Commission. Importantly, the Cathedrals Measure 1963 provided for the revision of cathedral statutes. It required certain core matters to be included in these and it empowered cathedrals to provide additions in line with local or historical uses. While no uniform arrangements were made as to the authority and functions of cathedral chapters, their property and financial transactions were to be scrutinised by the Church Commissioners.[36] Later, the Cathedrals Measure 1976 systematised the process for the revision of statutes and the Cathedral Statutes Commission was established. The growth of tourism and concern for the care of cathedrals also led to provision for English Heritage to make grants for specified and approved work to cathedral fabric, and in 1981 the General Synod established a national Cathedrals Advisory Commission.[37] In turn, the Care of Cathedrals Measure 1990 was

---

33 H&R 193–194; e.g. the founding of theological colleges was an initiative of bishops not cathedrals.
34 That was not achieved until 1976. In 1865 the Earl of Harrowby proposed without success that deans and chapters be abolished and cathedrals be run by chaplains responsible to the bishop: H&R 196.
35 H&R 198: the Commission was set up by the Church Assembly.
36 E.g. s. 38: the duty to transmit audited accounts to the Church Commissioners: H&R 199.
37 Formerly the Cathedrals Advisory Committee set up in 1949 by the Council for the Care of Churches.

8 Introduction

the result of lengthy collaboration between Church and State on the ecclesiastical exemption from listed building and associated controls; the Cathedrals Fabric Commission for England was created to authorise proposals for 'significant works' submitted by chapters and it required respect for the cathedral as the seat of the bishop and a centre of worship and mission.[38] As we have already seen, the Archbishops' Commission on Cathedrals 1994 and its report *Heritage and Renewal* stimulated both a comprehensive reappraisal of the purpose of a cathedral and best practice applicable to numerous aspects of cathedral life. As we shall see, the subsequent enactment of the Cathedrals Measure 1999, supplemented since by the Care of Cathedrals Measure 2011, introduced far-ranging reforms in cathedral law.

The legal history of a cathedral still functions as a mark of its own particular identity and continuity with the past. Several cathedrals set out in the preamble to their constitution a selective legal history of the foundation. Some are brief. Among old foundations, for example, at York:

> The Cathedral Church has been governed according to several constitutions and statutory requirements during its history, the succession of ancient and original models, first consolidated at the start of the twelfth century, each drawn up according to law and subject to the sovereigns of this Realm.[39]

Among the new foundations, at Norwich for instance, established in 1096, following the dissolution the cathedral was 're-constituted' in 1538 by royal charter; later:

> Statutes were prescribed for the Cathedral in 1620 and these remained in force until a new Constitution and Statutes were drawn up in 1941 under the Cathedrals Measures 1931 and 1934. These were repealed in 1966 and amended in 1973 under the Cathedrals Measure 1963.[40]

Among modern foundations, Guildford recites that Her Majesty in 1959 by Order in Council confirmed 'a Scheme containing the Constitution and Statutes … prepared by the Church Assembly under … the Cathedrals Measure 1931'; the cathedral was consecrated in 1961; a new scheme with a new constitution and statutes was prepared and 'confirmed by Her Majesty in Council on 14 February 1968'; the current constitution was made pursuant to the 1999 Measure.[41]

Others are more detailed. Among the new foundations, for example, at Carlisle the preamble provides that: after the dissolution of the cathedral priory of St Mary in 1540, King Henry VIII newly founded the Cathedral Church of Carlisle which

---

38 H&R 199.
39 York: Con. Preamble.
40 Norwich: Con. Preamble.
41 Guildford: Con. Preamble. For similar approaches, see the parish church cathedrals of e.g. Chelmsford: Con. Preamble and Leicester: Con. Preamble.

was rededicated to the Holy and Undivided Trinity; in 1545 he provided it with 'statutes which reflected the circumstances of the time'. Though several attempts to revise them failed, these were in force until 1936 (under the Cathedrals Measures 1931 and 1934) but they were, in turn, slightly altered by new statutes in 1968 (under the Cathedrals Measure 1963). The current constitution and statutes were drawn up by a Transitional Council under the Measure of 1999 (to reflect the recommendations of *Heritage and Renewal*) and came into force in 2001.[42] And the statutes provided by Henry VIII for Winchester were revised by Archbishop Laud and promulgated by letters patent of Charles I in 1638; during the commonwealth (from 1645) the dean and chapter was abolished, and at the Restoration (1660) the statutes were 'reinstated'; they were later revised following the Measures of 1931–1963 'retaining from the former statutes whatever provisions were still useful ... and more apt to the conditions of the time'.[43]

A particularly full legal history is found in the constitutional preamble at Manchester, a parish church cathedral; it illustrates the rich interplay between national law and local circumstances, and extended extracts are worth presenting here: 'This Collegiate Church of Manchester was first founded in 1421 by Charter and Royal Licence from King Henry V'. The College was dissolved by Act of Parliament under King Edward VI but re-founded by Queen Mary in 1553; it was again dissolved under Elizabeth I who granted it another Charter. The existing Charter was granted by King Charles I 'with the object of continuing and restoring the old College and founding it anew'; under this, the College was incorporated as 'the Warden and Fellows of the College of Christ in Manchester founded by King Charles'. The Charter also provided that there shall be 'forever in the said College two Chaplains or Vicars, being Clerks, and four men, being either Clerks or laymen, and four boys skilled in music, to perform daily prayers and Divine service in the Chapel'. The Ecclesiastical Commissioners Act 1840 enacted that the Warden and Fellows should be styled respectively Dean and Canons. However, an Order in Council 1847 provided that the Collegiate Church of Manchester 'should forever thereafter be a Cathedral Church', the seat of a bishop, and 'invested with all the honours, dignities and privileges of a Cathedral Church or Episcopal seat' and that 'the Dean and Canons ... should be the Dean and Chapter'. It continues: 'The Dean and Residentiary Canons are seized of the Rectory of the ancient Parish of Manchester', and the dean, as well as being chair of Chapter, 'is the Rector of the Residuary Parish of Manchester', and as such chairs 'the meeting of parishioners and Annual Church Parochial Meeting' which are still held 'according to ancient usage for the Residuary Parish of Manchester', and at which Church Wardens are elected annually. Finance is 'governed by the Parish of Manchester Division Act 1850 and the Parish of Manchester Revenues Measure

---

42 Carlisle: Con. Preamble. See also Liverpool: Con. Preamble: this traces the effects of the Liverpool Cathedral Act 1902, the consecration of the cathedral in 1924 and its 1931 and later statutes.
43 Winchester: Con. Preamble; the present constitution and statutes were drawn up by the Transitional Council under the Cathedrals Measure 1999 and came into effect in 2000; they were amended in 2009.

1933 and other legislation'. However, a new constitution and statutes were drawn up by a Transitional Council established under the Cathedrals Measure 1999 and these came into effect in 2002.[44]

These historical twists and turns are echoed today in the complexities of modern cathedral law as examined in this book which, it is hoped, provides a useful guide to the rules applicable to cathedrals, including how these are experienced in practice, not only for those who work at and with cathedrals, but also for worshippers and visitors (11 million in 2011)[45] in order to enhance their own encounters with cathedral churches as normative spaces which seek to meet the spiritual needs and aspirations of others.

For the purposes of this study: 'old foundations' are those cathedrals administered before the Reformation by secular canons (and which continued as such after the Reformation); 'new foundations' are both the pre-Reformation monastic cathedrals 're-founded' as secular 'new foundations' at the Reformation and the 'Henrician foundations' – though the latter are treated for the purposes of exposition as a distinct category in so far as they were not cathedrals before Henry VIII founded them *de novo* as such; and 'parish church cathedrals' are those former parish churches which acquired cathedral status in modern times (since the mid-nineteenth century) – but these do not include Liverpool and Guildford.

---

44 Manchester: Con. Preamble; see also Con. Art. I(1): 'The provisions of the Charter granted by King Charles I, in so far as they are not repugnant to the Constitution and the Statutes or to the laws of the Realm, shall continue to be observed'. See also Newcastle: Con. Preamble; Truro: Con. Preamble.
45 *Spiritual Capital: The Present and Future of English Cathedrals* (2012) 10.

1 The cathedral church: foundation, form and function

The cathedrals of the Church of England have a unique and widely admired position in terms of their architectural magnificence, aesthetic appeal, and historical significance.[1] Cathedrals also have considerable economic and social impact. In 2013, they attracted over 8.2 million visitors engaged in tourism, generating an income of around £125 million; they stimulated spending with local businesses in the order of £220 million; and they created employment, supporting over 5,000 jobs in their local economies. Socially, they engaged with the local community, in worship, pastoral care, outreach activity, and events such as concerts and ceremonies; they provided opportunities for voluntary work, with 14,000 volunteers assisting in their activities; and they offered opportunities for learning – an estimated 320,000 learners participated in organised educational activities in 2013.[2] They are also creatures of law. This chapter examines the classification of cathedrals, the purposes of a cathedral church, and the variety of legal instruments which seek to regulate the public life and activities of cathedrals.

The classification of cathedrals

Over the centuries, cathedrals have been classified in several different ways designed to reflect the chronology of their foundation and the style of their governance. At the time of the Reformation in the sixteenth century, there were two classes: old foundations and new foundations,[3] both seen as places of 'greater hospitality' and 'more respect and consequence' than other churches.[4] The old foundations were those which, before the Reformation, were under secular clergy. The new foundations were those monastic cathedrals in which, on the dissolution

---

1 Hooker VII.7.2: 'Churches Cathedral ... are as glasses wherein the face and very countenance of Apostolic antiquity remains ... notwithstanding the alterations which tract of time and the course of the world has brought'.
2 *The Economic and Social Impacts of England's Cathedrals*: A Report to the Association of English Cathedrals, written by Ecorys and commissioned by the Association and English Heritage (September 2014).
3 Godolphin 51–58.
4 Hooker V.81.8; see also VIII.6.11 for the royal confirmation of the foundation of a cathedral.

of the monasteries, the monks had been replaced by secular canons. New cathedrals founded by Henry VIII are sometimes described as of the new foundation, but this is not, in the strict sense, applicable to cathedrals of dioceses founded in more recent times.[5]

Old foundations, new foundations, and parish church cathedrals

Before the Reformation, nine cathedrals had been administered by secular clergy: Chichester, Exeter, Hereford, Lichfield, Lincoln, London (St Paul's), Salisbury, Wells, and York. Their principal dignitaries were the dean, the precentor (ranked next after the dean), the chancellor, and the treasurer; each of these had a deputy, respectively, the sub-dean, succentor, vice-chancellor, and sacrist. Their canons were 'prebendaries' whose income derived from individual endowments (prebends) of lands and the right to collect rents, fees, and tithes from parishes.[6] It is these cathedrals which at the Reformation came to be known as 'Cathedrals of the Old Foundation'.[7] Its status as such may still be part of a cathedral's legal self-identity.[8]

The other ten pre-Reformation cathedrals were monastic foundations – that is, cathedral priories administered by religious orders. Nine were Benedictine, one (Carlisle) Augustinian. They were under a prior and served by 'obedientiaries' (up to twenty-four) including the sacristan or sacrist, precentor and receiver, and subordinates such as the sub-sacrist and the succentor. Two (Bath and Coventry) were dissolved in 1539, because the Bishop of Bath and Wells (a single diocese), and the Bishop of Coventry and Lichfield (also one diocese) each had a second, secular cathedral (at Wells and Lichfield, respectively). The others were re-founded as secular cathedrals: Canterbury, Carlisle, Durham, Ely, Norwich, Rochester, Winchester, and Worcester. Six more cathedrals were founded when Henry VIII created new dioceses: Chester, Gloucester, Peterborough, and (though suppressed in 1550) Westminster, all former Benedictine abbeys, Bristol and Oxford, both Augustinian until the dissolution. These, re-founded or founded by Henry VIII, are the 'Cathedrals of the New Foundation'.[9]

There are also the modern cathedrals, founded for new dioceses by means of an Order in Council made under statutory authority, in and since the nineteenth century. Two were existing collegiate churches,[10] namely Ripon (1836) and Manchester (1847).[11] The new diocese of Truro was founded in 1877 with the

---

5 HLE pars. 165–166.
6 S. Lehmberg, *English Cathedrals: A History* (London: Hambledon Continuum, 2005) 81–84.
7 H&R 190–191.
8 See e.g. Chichester: Con. Preamble 2. See more fully the Introduction.
9 Phillimore 137.
10 That is: 'A church which is endowed for a body of canons and/or prebendaries (the "chapter"), but is not, like a cathedral, a bishop's see': F.L. Cross and E.A. Livingstone (eds.), *The Oxford Dictionary of the Christian Church* (Oxford: Oxford University Press, 3rd ed., 1997, rev. 2005) 379.
11 For a legal history of Manchester Cathedral, see Introduction above.

parish church as its cathedral (though a new cathedral church was built there later).[12] In 1877, the former Benedictine abbey at St Albans, made a parish church in 1553, became the cathedral for the new diocese of St Albans.[13] The diocese of Liverpool was founded in 1880 and a new cathedral was built (the bishop acting as dean till 1931); and Guildford was consecrated in 1961;[14] neither serves as a parish church.

A further legal distinction developed relating to the mode of governance: 'Dean and Chapter Cathedrals' and 'Parish Church Cathedrals'. Each type had a body corporate: in the dean and chapter cathedrals, the body corporate consisted of the dean and all the canons, known as the 'Dean and Chapter'; and in parish church cathedrals it was known as the 'Cathedral Chapter' comprising the provost, canons, and archdeacons (and, for some purposes, the bishop). These 'capitular bodies' were in law the body corporate for each cathedral type. In turn, a 'parish church cathedral' is both a cathedral and a parish church; the parish has an incumbent who is also dean of the cathedral by virtue of being incumbent of the parish in question. These cathedrals are as follows: Ripon, Manchester, Truro, St Albans (founded 1836–1877), Newcastle (1882), Southwell (1884), Wakefield (1888), Southwark (1905), Birmingham (1905), Sheffield (1913), St Edmundsbury (1913), Chelmsford (1914), Coventry (1918), Bradford (1919), Blackburn (1926), Derby (1927), Leicester (1927), and Portsmouth (1927).[15]

The Cathedrals Measure 1999 ended the distinction between dean and chapter cathedrals and parish church cathedrals for the purpose of their corporate governance,[16] though the category parish church cathedral survives.[17] While 'cathedral' is a legal category, of itself a cathedral has no legal personality. However, each has a body corporate with legal personality, namely: the Council, Chapter, and College of Canons;[18] each must have these three bodies,[19] which *together* constitute the 'body corporate with perpetual succession and a common seal'.[20] Those which were previously parish churches (i.e. with no body corporate known as a dean and chapter) fall within the meaning of cathedrals for the purpose of the 1999 Measure.[21] The constitution of a cathedral, therefore, must provide for the

---

12 Bishopric of Truro Act 1876; Order in Council, 9 December 1876.
13 Bishopric of St Albans Act 1875; Order in Council, 30 April 1877.
14 Liverpool Cathedral Act 1902; Guildford Cathedral Measure 1959.
15 The Diocese of Leeds, usually known as the Diocese of West Yorkshire and the Dales, was created on 20 April 2014: uniquely, it has three cathedrals, Bradford, Ripon and Wakefield.
16 H&R 179: this proposed abolition of the distinction for the purposes of cathedral governance.
17 See e.g. CM 1999, s. 36(3); Mission and Pastoral Measure 2011, ss. 6(2) and 44(1).
18 Today, however, all the various former forms and bodies of cathedral governance (with the exception of Westminster Abbey, St George's Chapel, Windsor, and Christ Church, Oxford) are now to be identified by reference to the Chapter of the cathedral: CM 1999, s. 36(1), (6).
19 CM 1999, s. 2. See also below Chapter 6.
20 CM 1999, s. 9(1)(a).
21 CM 1999, s. 35(2) and s. 36(3).

'corporation'.[22] Cathedrals themselves further distinguish the body corporate from the 'foundation'; for example, at Guildford, the 'Foundation' consists of 'those members, additional members appointed by the Bishop and others by virtue of the Constitution or Statutes. Membership of the Foundation shall not confer any rights or liabilities';[23] and Salisbury's Foundation consists of the bishop, dean, the other members of Chapter, and holders of offices designated by the bishop and the Chapter for this purpose; and: 'The purpose of the Foundation is to draw more closely into the common Christian life of the Cathedral those who are principally involved in [its] mission and administration' as well as 'to enrich that common Christian life with mutual service'.[24]

Various legal consequences flow from its corporate structure. A cathedral is an ecclesiastical corporation which exists in perpetuity and independently of its members. It may act as if it were a person and so may, for example: sue or be sued in its corporate name; buy, hold, and sell property for the benefit of the members of the corporation and their successors; have a common seal to confirm their actions; and make rules to regulate its own affairs. Moreover, a cathedral is a corporation aggregate for its spiritual purposes (see below). Importantly, the Charities Act 2011 excludes ecclesiastical corporations from its ambit; thus, a cathedral is not regulated by the Charity Commissioners as to its main activities but it is subject to its Visitor (see Chapter 2) and it qualifies as a charity for tax purposes – Her Majesty's Revenue and Customs treats a cathedral as an exempt charity, enabling it to recover sums under Gift Aid.[25]

The creation, alteration, and dissolution of a diocese are regulated by a distinct body of law which also affects cathedrals. Formerly, a diocese was created under an Act of Parliament and confirmed by Order in Council.[26] Now,[27] it may be done by or under a Measure, and by a scheme made pursuant to it.[28] If a scheme creates a new diocese, or the area in which a cathedral is situated is transferred to another diocese, the scheme must provide for the establishment of a cathedral for the diocese (or of a church to be known as the pro-cathedral of the diocese).[29] In

---

22 E.g. Ely: Con. Art. 1; Liverpool: Con. Art. 1.1; Wakefield: Con. Art. 2.1.
23 Guildford: Con. Art. 2.
24 Salisbury: Con. Preamble.
25 Charities Act 2011, s. 10: '"Ecclesiastical corporation" means any corporation in the Church of England, whether sole or aggregate, which is established for spiritual purposes'; the corporate body of a cathedral is an ecclesiastical corporation for the purposes of s. 10: Church of England (Miscellaneous Provisions) Measure 2010, s. 10(1).
26 See above nn. 12–13. Historically, see Burn I.264: 'the king has power to declare by letters patent such number of bishops, cities (sees for bishops), cathedral churches, and dioceses', 'as he thinks necessary' etc.
27 H&R 73, Rec. 13 (Ch. 6, pars. 45–48): this proposed 'a more gradual evolution of cathedral establishments'.
28 Dioceses, Pastoral and Mission Measure 2007: the Dioceses Commission recommends it to the bishop(s) who may approve and submit it to the Church Commissioners for confirmation by Her Majesty in Council; s. 56: the Commission must consult interested parties including the 'Chapter of the cathedral of every diocese affected'.
29 Pro-cathedrals are used in the Diocese in Europe: Cathedral Statutes 1997, Art. 5.

relation to a cathedral (as opposed to a pro-cathedral), the scheme must either designate an existing church as the cathedral church (whether/not it was previously a cathedral for another diocese), or provide for a new church to be the cathedral. The scheme must also: (1) provide for the establishment of a provisional council to prepare a constitution and statutes for the cathedral;[30] (2) provide for its governance, worship and administration, and, if appropriate, for the appointment of persons to hold office there and for its ownership and that of any assets belonging to or used for its purposes until the constitution and statutes take effect; (3) constitute a body consisting of the holders of such offices as the scheme must specify until a College of Canons is established;[31] (4) apply the Cathedrals Measure 1999, subject to any modifications specified in the scheme, including provision as to the coming into force of the constitution and statutes; and (5) provide as necessary for the jurisdiction of the consistory court.[32] Additional rules apply in relation to a pro-cathedral.[33] The name or the dedication of a cathedral may also be changed by means of an episcopal declaration.[34]

The cathedral interviews

As we saw in the Introduction, cathedrals with a preamble to their constitution commonly include in this a brief history of the cathedral and its domestic law, classifying the cathedral as old foundation, new foundation, Henrician foundation, or parish church cathedral. The interviews reveal that these classifications remain important for some in terms of ethos. At old foundation Hereford, the preamble reference to the cathedral's status is 'an inspiration'; such foundations (not being monastic in origin) are 'outward-looking' and their 'west fronts look towards the town deliberately';[35] this is echoed at Exeter.[36] Among new foundations, Rochester's status 'provides continuity with the past',[37] and Worcester's represents its 'Benedictine heritage' – this is a 'source of inspiration' for the cathedral as a 'school for the service of the Lord' welcoming people 'as if they were Christ'; the constitution and statutes do not mention this, 'but they should'.[38] As to Henrician foundations,

---

30 I.e. as if the provisional council was a Transitional Council under CM 1999, Sch. 1 subject to modifications as may be made by the scheme.
31 Under CM 1999, s. 5; it performs functions assigned under the Appointment of Bishops Act 1533.
32 Dioceses, Pastoral and Mission Measure 2007, Sch. 2, 4(1)-(3).
33 Dioceses, Pastoral and Mission Measure 2007, Sch. 2, 4(4)-(5).
34 E.g. the Diocese of St Edmundsbury and Ipswich was created in 1913; the Parish Church of St James in Bury St Edmunds became the cathedral; because of the resultant confusion in names, it was re-named the Cathedral Church of St James and St Edmund by Episcopal Decree 3 September 2009.
35 Hereford: Dean: Int. 5-8-2016. Compare Wells: Acting Dean: Int. 12-8-2016: the constitution has no preamble, a 20th century practice.
36 Exeter: Dean: Int. 9-8-2016: its status expresses its 'continuity' and its 'intangible spirit of looking outwards'; the cathedral's gated close was removed in the nineteenth century.
37 Rochester: Precentor: Int. 30-9-2016.
38 Worcester: Dean: Int. 28-7-2016.

Bristol has 'a strong sense of continuity', its Augustinian roots reflected in the Chapter House and quotations from the Augustinian Rule in the cloister car-park.[39] At the parish church cathedral at Derby, while its former status as collegiate church has 'almost no' practical significance today, its parish church status still 'shapes' its life and, for example, 'gives the congregation a sense of participation'; however, the parish itself is small (with about 220 parishioners) and these do not make 'much of a claim on the cathedral' (such as in terms of the rites of passage); a stronger claim is made by the congregation, most of whom live outside the parish, and by those who see the cathedral as 'Derby's parish church or as the civic centre church'.[40]

The purposes of a cathedral

As we saw in the Introduction, following the Reformation, changes in cathedral law did not address comprehensively the purposes of a cathedral; yet, historically, one idea which persisted was that a cathedral was the 'mother' church of the diocese; or else: 'The cathedral church is the parish church of the whole diocese'.[41] What follows examines the place and purposes of a cathedral under national legislation, the understandings of the role of cathedrals in the report of the Archbishops' Commission on Cathedrals 1994, and the sometimes very different ways in which cathedrals present their objects in their own cathedral constitutions.

Cathedrals in the national church and legislation

Today, each cathedral sits within the wider legal environment of the organisational structures of the Church of England. After the break with Rome at the Reformation, a new institutional church, the Church of England, was 'established by law' through a series of Acts of Parliament;[42] and the 'relationship which the state has with the Church of England is one of recognition, not one of the devolution to it of any of the powers or functions of government'.[43] The 'incidents of establishment' include a range of key legal facts. The Monarch is Supreme Governor of the Church, with significant rights of patronage, including the appointment of bishops, twenty-six of whom sit in Parliament, in the House of Lords.[44] Whilst not 'a department of State', the 'State has accepted the Church as a religious body in its opinion truly teaching the Christian faith, and given to it a certain legal position,

---

39 Bristol: Dean: Int. 3–8-2016.
40 Derby: Dean: Int. 10–8-2016: but 'the cathedral is not all about the congregation', though 'congregationalism' is a 'pressure' point at Derby as it is in the wider Church of England; Birmingham: Dean: Int. 11–8-2016: its parish status is a 'difficult' one; it is significant as to baptisms and marriages; but the parish is small – very few of its 4,000 or so residents attend.
41 Burn II.77; I.260; he cites Gibson 171. See also Phillimore I.134.
42 M. Hill, *Ecclesiastical Law* (Oxford: Oxford University Press, 3rd ed., 2007) par. 1.19.
43 *Aston Cantlow and Wilmcote with Billesley Parochial Church Council v Wallbank* [2004] 1 AC 546.
44 Can. A7; Appointment of Bishops Act 1533; Manchester Bishopric Act 1847.

and its decrees, if rendered under certain legal conditions, certain legal sanctions'.[45] The law applicable to the church – *ecclesiastical law* – is part of the general law of England, whether created by the State, the Church, or both, and whether it is enforced in State Courts or those of the Church.[46] Measures are legislation 'passed by the General Synod', with the consent of Parliament and Monarch, and have the same force and effect as Acts of Parliament; General Synod may also legislate by Canon, operative once the licence and assent of the Monarch are received.[47] This law facilitates and orders the public life of the church in its mission and witness to Christ.[48] The Church of England is also a member of the worldwide Anglican Communion, and Canterbury Cathedral is seen as the 'mother church' of the Communion.[49]

The Church of England is organised on the basis of various territorial units; each has its own structures and is subject ultimately to the jurisdiction of the national legislature of the church, the General Synod (composed of bishops, clergy, and laity). General Synod is assisted by an executive body, the Archbishops' Council, which in turn has several Boards, Councils, and Divisions.[50] Nationally, the church consists of two provinces, Canterbury and York, each the circuit of an archbishop – the former in the jurisdiction of the Archbishop of Canterbury, the latter within that of the Archbishop of York. Each province is composed of dioceses. A diocese is a territory overseen by a bishop who exercises aspects of episcopal ministry in collaboration with the Diocesan Synod (which includes clergy and laity). A diocese is divided into archdeaconries (under an archdeacon), each archdeaconry into deaneries (with a rural dean and synod), and each deanery into parishes served by a priest and governed by a Parochial Church Council; parish residents have rights, for example, to marriage and burial.[51]

Within this organisational network, each diocese has a cathedral church, itself represented in these wider church structures, the General Synod, Diocesan Synod, and Deanery Synod.[52] The cathedral contains the teaching seat or throne

---

45 *Marshall v Graham* [1907] 2 KB 112.
46 *AG v Dean and Chapter of Ripon Cathedral* [1945] Ch. 239. For church judicial bodies: Hill, op cit., Chs. 6–7.
47 Church of England Assembly (Powers) Act 1919 (measures); Synodical Government Measure 1969 (canons).
48 N. Doe, *The Legal Framework of the Church of England* (Oxford: The Clarendon Press, 1996) Ch. 1.
49 See also Canon A1: 'The Church of England, established according to the laws of this realm under the Queen's Majesty, belongs to the true and apostolic Church of Christ'. For Canterbury Cathedral, see below.
50 National Institutions Measure 1998.
51 Synodical Government Measure 1969; see Hill, op cit., Ch. 2.
52 Synodical Government Measure 1969, s. 2(1) and Sch. 2, and Canon H2: as to General Synod, its House of Clergy includes for Canterbury province three elected by and from among the deans of all cathedrals; and for York, two from among deans; Church Representation Rules: r. 30(2): the dean is *ex officio* member of Diocesan Synod; r. 27(1): a Diocesan Synod may provide by scheme for representation on a Deanery Synod of the dean, residentiary canons and other cathedral ministers, and as to a cathedral which is not a parish church, of lay persons on the cathedral community

18 *The cathedral church*

(*cathedra*) of the bishop. It is often called the mother church of the diocese,[53] as it was described in the Cathedrals Measure 1963.[54] The Cathedrals Measure 1999 recognises 'the fact that the cathedral is the seat of the bishop and a centre of worship and mission'; this it classifies as the 'cathedral's purpose', and those who exercise functions under the Measure must have regard to this fact.[55] Moreover, the Measure speaks of 'the work of the cathedral, spiritual, pastoral, evangelistic, social, and ecumenical'.[56] National law also recognises that a cathedral may be a site of 'architectural, archaeological, artistic or historical interest';[57] in point of fact, for the Cathedrals Fabric Commission for England: 'The continuity in the purpose, life and work of cathedrals from the time of their foundation … until now is part of their essential character'.[58] The constitutional status of a cathedral is one of substantial independence: it is exempt from wider diocesan administrative control and from the faculty jurisdiction of the diocesan consistory court.[59]

The Archbishops' Commission on Cathedrals

The policy underlying this legal understanding of the purpose of a cathedral was elucidated by the Archbishops' Commission on Cathedrals in 1994; but the Commission offered a far richer understanding than that appearing in national legislation. First, the 'essential purpose' of a cathedral is the organisation of the mission of the Church in the world; it 'emphatically' endorsed the idea of a cathedral as 'seat of the bishop and a centre of worship and mission'; as such, it is 'the bishop's church, the symbol of the unitary nature of Christ's mission to the world'. Second, they are: 'shrines of faith', the 'mother church' of a diocese, 'monumental representations of the truth of Christianity', 'a national reference', 'indicators of eternity', and 'the majesty of God: places of living faith'. Third, each expresses, variously: 'a perception of the holy', 'a witness to sanctity and an insight into fellowship', 'a dimension of heritage', 'an illustration of historical processes', and 'artistic and cultural achievement'; they are concerned with education, and with service that attends to social needs; they are centres of evangelism, presenting the gospel to many who would not otherwise recognise it; and they are places

    roll (required under CM 1999, s. 9), or, in the case of Christ Church Oxford, those declared by the dean as habitual worshippers there and whose names are on any parish roll.
53 HLE par. 343: it 'was originally the only church' of the diocese or *parochia*: n. 1, citing Phillimore: 123.
54 Cathedrals Measure 1963, s. 9(2).
55 CM 1999, s. 1: 'Any person or body on whom functions are conferred by or under this Measure shall, in exercising those functions, have due regard to the fact that the cathedral is the seat of the bishop and a centre of worship and mission'; see also Care of Cathedrals Measure 2011, s. 1.
56 CM 1999, s. 3(6): this category is contained in norms on the cathedral Council.
57 CCM 2011, s. 22: this is contained in e.g. norms on the Cathedrals Fabric Commission.
58 CFCE: PGN 1 (2012) 2.2.
59 See below Chapters 8 and 9.

where witness to the presence of God in the world achieves great spiritual beauty.[60]

The Commission developed its understanding of a cathedral's place in the wider Church of England in a number of ideas and recommendations. First, that a cathedral is the seat of a bishop 'does not describe an actual state of affairs except in the most removed symbolical sense'. However, it is not always clear that cathedrals regard their bishop as a major factor in forming strategy, so they should be more effectively integrated with diocesan strategy; bishops should have a voice here but not a 'determining voice' – a strategy approved by the bishop should play a crucial role in the cathedral's strategic contribution to the diocese.[61]

Second, as to the independence of cathedrals: 'specialist styles of witness require particular structures of governance appropriate to them, and a measure of practical autonomy'. So, 'The time has come for cathedral independence to be … expressed within a structure which involves more precise accountability'; their independence is important to provide space for: Christian worship; civic activities; raising issues for public debate; and encouraging the development of skills and expert practices in music and liturgy. However, their independence is not from the authority structures of the church in general, nor to offer scrutiny of episcopal stewardship. In short, cathedrals need 'to be institutionally independent in the sense that their autonomy provides space for the exercise of those functions'; but they are part of 'an integrated Christian presence in English society, and … their work should be accountable and efficient'.[62]

Third, cathedrals are called on to look outward rather than inward; thus: as centres of mission and worship, they must attend to 'their ministries of teaching, of service, of evangelism and of witness'.[63] Therefore, as to the cathedral, diocese, and parishes, good practice includes: visits by parishes to the cathedral, by Chapter members and staff to parishes (e.g. to preach), and by the cathedral choir to parishes (and *vice versa*); the appointment of a link scheme and liaison officer for each parish; attendance by the dean at parish institutions of clergy; and links with dioceses and provinces worldwide. As to the wider community, good practice includes: the dean acting as an ambassador to the local authority and business community; cathedral chaplaincy to city businesses; close involvement with local industry; and the provision of food for the homeless and unemployed.[64] Above all, therefore: 'Interdependence rather than [cathedral] independence is the key concept, not least because it reflects that mutuality of support and responsibility which should underlie all Christian relationships'.[65]

---

60 H&R 3–5.
61 H&R 5–6. For the role of the bishop in the cathedral, see below Chapter 2.
62 H&R 7–8, 14–15.
63 H&R 174.
64 H&R 251–252, Appendix 6.
65 H&R 174. See also ARR, 3.6.1: activities include the conduct of services, provision of music, charitable giving, social welfare, providing for visitors, education, fund raising, and providing services to the diocese.

The constitutions and statutes of cathedrals

The domestic laws of cathedrals also present understandings of cathedrals and their purposes. These supplement (but must not be inconsistent with) the purposes of a cathedral under the Cathedrals Measure 1999. To this extent, there is diversity amongst the cathedrals in terms of their own self-understanding. Some repeat the statutory definition, with no,[66] or little, embellishment – for example: 'the purpose of the Cathedral ... is to glorify God, to be a centre of worship and mission, and to be the seat of the bishop'.[67] By way of contrast, many offer a rich understanding of their purposes more in keeping with those of the Archbishops' Commission 1994 than the minimalism of national law – however, they do so by using different legal vehicles, namely: a constitutional preamble (non-binding) or article (binding), or statement of vision (non-binding) which may be required by a constitution or statute.

First, there are cathedrals where a constitutional preamble or article lists the cathedral objects. Among the old foundations, Hereford's constitutional preamble provides: 'The Cathedral has at the centre of its life a daily pattern of prayer which informs the work and decision-making of its community'; it is 'the mother church of the Diocese ... and has a responsibility to support and nurture the life of the Diocese as well as to serve and pray for the diocesan Bishop'; as 'a centre of mission to which people come for encouragement and education ... its resources are used to further the life and witness of the whole Christian church'; as 'a building of great antiquity' it 'attracts many tourists as well as pilgrims'; and it serves the City of Hereford and the communities of Herefordshire and South Shropshire, 'which see the Cathedral as a spiritual centre and a setting for large events'. Moreover, importantly: 'There is a precious sense of joint ownership of this historic building among those who live in the vicinity, and the Chapter and Cathedral Community are seen as guardians of this heritage'.[68]

Salisbury has a more explicitly theological approach. The cathedral is: 'a sign and symbol of the Transcendent God ... revealed in the Incarnation of Jesus Christ and whose Spirit sustains and informs the Christian Ministry of the Gospel'; and a 'sacred place' where 'the worship of God is offered every day, the word of God proclaimed, and the sacraments administered and the whole human community made welcome in the name of Jesus Christ'. It 'holds the Bishop's Chair and is the household of faith from which proceeds his Episcopal ministry and mission to the Diocese'; therefore: 'The community of Christian people in this

---

66 E.g. Portsmouth: Con. Art. 1; St Edmundsbury: Con. Art. 1; Ely: Con. Preamble; Peterborough: Con. Art. 2; Chester: Con. Art. 2; Gloucester: Con. Art. 3; Wells: Con. Art. 2.
67 St Albans: Con. Art. I. See also Rochester: Con. Art. 2.1; Preamble: it is 'a community charged with holy living, prayer and study, and the faithful ministry of Word and Sacrament, and the forwarding of the purpose of the Cathedral Church as the seat of the bishop and a centre of worship and mission'; Coventry: Con. Art. 1.1: it is 'the home of Christian faith from which the Episcopal ministry and mission to the Diocese proceed. It is a centre of worship and outreach, which exists for the glory of God.'
68 Hereford: Con. Preamble. Compare Lichfield: Con. Preamble and Art. 1.

place, lay and ordained, have a distinct vocation to support the Bishop ... with counsel, prayer and love'. In addition, Chapter must, *inter alia*:

> if so desired, set out in a statement of aims (to be reviewed, after consultation with the Bishop and the Council, every five years) the aims of the ministry and mission of the Cathedral and the role of the Cathedral in the Diocese.[69]

New foundations Winchester, Norwich, and Canterbury set out their respective purposes in a constitutional preamble. Winchester has, for example, a ministry 'to the people of the City, County and Diocese, and the wider community, to which they come in times of celebration and sorrow, aspiration and recommitment'.[70] Norwich, as 'Mother Church of the Diocese', 'maintains a daily pattern of corporate prayer and worship and shares with the parishes ... in every aspect of the mission of Christ'; and is 'the focus for the Bishop's ministry and a home of education, music and art, where hospitality is extended to people of all ages'.[71] However, Canterbury is 'a holy place of pilgrimage, founded by Saint Augustine, for the worship of ... God and in honour of Christ', seat of the Archbishop of Canterbury 'who combines ... the offices of the Bishop of the Diocese of Canterbury, Primate of All England and Primus Inter Pares of the worldwide Anglican Communion'; thus, its ministry is to the Diocese of Canterbury, the people of East Kent, the Nation, the Anglican Communion of Churches 'of which it is the Mother Church', and those who come as 'pilgrims, worshippers and tourists'.[72]

Among parish church cathedrals too, constitutional lists of objects may be highly theological. For example: Birmingham cathedral is 'a house of God' where 'the love of God for all the world is proclaimed and shared, a love supremely manifested in the life, death, resurrection and teaching' of Christ; it seeks to support the ministry of the church within the diocese under the leadership of the bishop; it is 'the central church of the Diocese'; and it ministers to those who live and work in its parish, to its regular worshippers and 'to the civic life of the City' in collaboration with the other city-centre churches.[73] Newcastle cathedral is: 'a sacred place' where the worship of God is offered daily, the word of God proclaimed, the sacraments celebrated, and 'the whole ... community made welcome' in the name of Christ.[74] Also, Derby cathedral is: to maintain a daily pattern of corporate prayer and worship, giving glory to God and holding before him the needs of the church and the world, particularly of the Diocese of Derby, the City of Derby, and the County of Derbyshire; to be a focus for the bishop's ministry, a resource to him and a place where prayer is offered for him; to preach the gospel and nurture Christian learning, in collaboration with other churches and traditions

---

69 Salisbury: Con. Preamble and Art. 6.1. Lincoln and Exeter have a similar approach.
70 Winchester: Con. Art. 1: Preamble.
71 Norwich: Con. Preamble.
72 Canterbury: Con. Preamble. Christ Church Oxford (The House) must maintain the cathedral: Stat. Preamble.
73 Birmingham: Con. Preamble.
74 Newcastle: Con. Preamble.

and 'with sensitivity to other faiths' to extend hospitality to pilgrims and visitors of every kind; to demonstrate the concern of Christ for the poor; 'to engage with the city and the county, with corporate life and institutions, in the complexities of contemporary society and culture, and to explore spiritual values with all people of goodwill'; and 'to share, as the mother church, with the parishes of the diocese in every aspect of the Church's vocation'.[75]

Second, in some cathedrals, the constitution does not list the objects; rather this is found in a separate 'statement of vision'.[76] Unusually, at St Paul's the statutes require that Chapter must, after consultation with the bishop, Council, College of Canons, Cathedral Community, and others, review, revise, or replace a statement of the vision and mission of the cathedral not less than once every five years. It must also set for annual review by Council priorities and plans coming out of the vision statement, and 'proposals for the general direction and mission of the cathedral, giving particular attention to the spiritual, pastoral, evangelistic, missionary, social and ecumenical work of the Cathedral and to the effectiveness of its governance'.[77]

The cathedral interviews

The cathedral interviews indicate various approaches to the value of statements of cathedral objects. Old foundation Hereford is seen as the 'mother church' of the diocese and it takes a great deal of work 'to make this real' in terms of hospitality, deanery functions, and prayers for the parishes;[78] Exeter's objects set out in the constitutional preamble reflect how cathedral purposes 'are expressed differently at different times'; but it is important they are reconciled in 'a single coherent approach' because they should be 'organisation-defining' and not simply 'Chapter-defining';[79] and while Salisbury's list of objects is 'never' invoked 'explicitly' in decision-making, 'everything in it informs our strategic planning' and 'its language and theological focus is how we express our values, ambitions and goals'; these are 'embedded' in cathedral life and 'we work out of its theological insights' into 'the character of God'.[80]

By way of contrast, at Wells, in the absence of a constitutional list of objects, the practice is to elucidate purposes in extra-legal documents, such as the Strategic Plan and Statement of Mission.[81] Likewise, the 'role' of St Paul's, addressed in the first article of the constitution (as seat of the bishop and centre of worship and mission), is

75 Derby: Con. Preamble. See also St Edmundsbury: Con. Mission Statement; Leicester: Con. Art. 2.2–2.3.
76 E.g. Worcester: Renewal and Development: A Strategic Vision for Worcester Cathedral 2015–20 (2015).
77 London: Stat I. See below Chapter 8 for the Annual Report (under the Accounting Regulations).
78 Hereford: Dean: Int. 5-8-2016.
79 Exeter: Dean: Int. 9-8-2016; indeed, the duty on Chapter to 'order the life of the Cathedral in accordance with the principles of the statement of purpose' (Stat. II.1) should explicitly apply to all those associated with the cathedral, not just Chapter.
80 Salisbury: Dean: Int. 20-9-2016.
81 Wells: Acting Dean: Int. 12-8-2016.

'skeletal' only, and the constitution has no preamble listing objects because: a preamble is subject to 'change' as ideas about purposes change; the constitution is 'functional', not aspirational; and 'successors may feel bound' by a statement of cathedral purposes in a constitutional preamble. So, its purposes are spelt out in the quinquennial vision statement (as we saw above) and elsewhere; this is a 'reminder' of what the cathedral is for and is sometimes invoked in decision-making. For these reasons, 'a vision of purpose is essential, but it is not essential to have it in a constitutional preamble'. Indeed, as to the quinquennial vision statement, it is right that the cathedral has a duty to have a plan, because this informs Council and so helps it fulfil its constitutional role; the vision statement 'binds' successors – it is more 'implied' than required by the Cathedrals Measure.[82]

New foundation Winchester's preamble is not invoked in discussions about the cathedral's purposes; rather, it makes sense of the various dedications of the church over the centuries; however, it does not include education or charity, but these are in practice key aspects of its ministry – 'extra-legal practices' – education because the cathedral is a 'teaching seat'.[83] At Worcester, that the cathedral is the seat of the bishop and a centre of worship and mission is 'fundamental to the character of the cathedral'.[84] The Rochester list of objects in the constitutional preamble is valuable because it provides 'common order' and 'security of common life', satisfies 'the need to know what we are for', and indicates that its purposes are 'bigger than any single personal vision'.[85] By way of contrast, the Henrician foundation at Chester has no constitutional preamble and no list of cathedral objects other than a reference to 'purpose' as including 'worship, education and mission'; this absence is not a hindrance – but a statement of purposes in the Strategic Plan is 'frequently invoked' in decision-making.[86]

At parish church cathedral Derby, the purposes in the constitutional preamble are rarely invoked; indeed, on admission to office, the Dean consulted 'the oral tradition' to ascertain those purposes rather than the preamble; the ethos adopted was to see the cathedral as a place 'to allow the diocese to come to a sense of itself'.[87] On the other hand, the objects in the Birmingham constitutional preamble have 'definitely influenced the cathedral's strategic plan, but more implicitly than explicitly', such as its charity work – but the cathedral also engages a great deal in inter-faith dialogue which is an object not listed in the preamble.[88]

The sources of cathedral law

Following the Reformation, the royal charters for new foundations required them to have a set of statutes consistent with 'the constitution of the Church of

82 London: Dean: Int. 23-9-2016.
83 Winchester: Acting Dean: Int. 16-8-2016.
84 Worcester: Dean: Int. 28-7-2016: objects are in the Strategic Vision: see above.
85 Rochester: Canon Precentor: Int. 30-9-2016.
86 Chester: Vice-Dean: Int. 19-8-2016: Con. Art. 16.
87 Derby: Dean: Int. 10-8-2016.
88 Birmingham: Dean: Int. 11-8-2016.

24 *The cathedral church*

England' and 'the laws of the land'.[89] In terms of the coverage and interpretation of statutes, in cases of doubt, recourse was to be had to the inherited (medieval) canon law.[90] Also, a Dean and Chapter could not 'alter the ancient and approved usages of their church, without consent of the bishop; and if they do, such innovations are declared void by the canon law',[91] as is a statute designed 'to bind their successors, and not themselves … forasmuch as it is not equitable that a man should lay that burden upon another, which he will not bear himself'.[92] By the nineteenth century, Chapters could of their own accord, or if required by the visitor, alter the cathedral statutes.[93]

Similarly, today, cathedrals are regulated by a variety of legal instruments; and cathedral law is part of the ecclesiastical law of England. First, as well as Acts of Parliament, there are the Measures of General Synod, forms of national law which apply, generally, to all cathedrals. The two principal pieces of primary legislation are the Cathedrals Measure 1999 and the Care of Cathedrals Measure 2011. Canons made by General Synod too contain norms applying to cathedrals, particularly as to ministry and worship.[94] General Synod may also by Measure (and Canon) authorise other bodies to legislate by way of secondary or subordinate legislation.[95] Second, each cathedral has its own domestic law: its constitution and statutes. So far as they concern the regulation of the cathedral and its services, these statutes are part of the ecclesiastical law enforced by the ecclesiastical courts;[96] and 'cathedral statutes' may include for some purposes a charter or a local Act of Parliament relating to the cathedral.[97]

The Cathedrals Measure 1999 is part of a gradual process to provide a consistent framework for cathedral governance adapted to meet individual requirements, needs, and circumstances.[98] The Measure applies to all cathedrals in England,[99] but not, except for a few specified norms, to Christ Church Oxford.[100] However, the Measure does not apply to any charity or to the property of any charity, except to the extent the Charity Commission so determines;[101] but those provisions on cathedrals which had no Dean and Chapter do apply to charities

---

89 Burn I.264: see Introduction above.
90 Burn I.257–260.
91 Burn II.88 (citing Gibson 174). The same rule is found in Phillimore I.142.
92 Burn II.89–111: cathedral statutes may be changed by 'a majority of legal votes', subject to episcopal consent. See also Phillimore I.144–159 on the history of uncertainty as to validity.
93 Phillimore I.174 citing 3&4 Vic. c. 113, s. 47.
94 See e.g. Durham: Stat. XIV.2: lay canons undertake such duties as are 'consistent with Canon Law'.
95 E.g. Care of Cathedrals Rules 2006 which continue to operate under CCM 2011.
96 *AG v Dean and Chapter of Ripon Cathedral* [1945] All ER 479; see HLE 343 n. 4.
97 Mission and Pastoral Measure 2011, s. 104(5): as to cathedral preferment: see Chapter 5.
98 HLE pars. 343–345.
99 CM 1999, s. 38(1)-(3). It does not extend to the Dioceses of Sodor and Man or Gibraltar in Europe.
100 CM 1999, s. 37.
101 CM 1999, s. 34 (as amended by the Charities Act 2006, s. 75(1), Sch. 8, par. 196).

associated with the cathedral in question.[102] As well as providing for transition to the new regime,[103] the Measure deals with the creation, content, and revision of cathedral constitution and statutes.

Cathedral constitutions and statutes

The Archbishops' Commission on Cathedrals (1994) proposed several changes with regard to constitutions and statutes. Having statutes 'recognises that each cathedral has its own life and ethos, and that a certain degree of flexibility is essential'. However, it proposed a simplified and streamlined system for approving and amending these.[104] The Commission considered that rules then in place (see the Introduction) were cumbersome, involved local initiative, the national Cathedral Statutes Commission, publication of a scheme, representations, laying it before General Synod, and confirmation by the Privy Council. The law also permitted a wide range of optional and additional material for inclusion in statutes resulting in a mass of detail on minor matters tending to obscure structures of governance. This meant that regular review and amendment were needed, the process was protracted and expensive, many sets of statutes had not been updated, and they carried out-of-date material on minor matters. The Commission recommended, therefore, a model constitution and statutes contained in a schedule to a reforming Measure which could be amended without recourse to primary legislation. Nevertheless, while new legislation was needed in some areas, in others the Commission considered its recommendations be implemented directly by 'an energetic and imaginative approach by cathedrals themselves to the running of their own affairs', open to each other's experience and willing to learn from best practice elsewhere; here, the English Cathedrals Association should encourage both mutual interdependence and independence.[105]

The Cathedrals Measure 1999, therefore, as an overriding duty, requires each body involved in the creation/revision of the constitution and statutes of a cathedral to have due regard to the fact that the cathedral is the seat of the bishop and a centre of worship and mission;[106] and every cathedral must have a constitution and statutes which comply with that Measure.[107] The Measure sets out a range of provisions which must be contained in these instruments.

102 CM 1999, s. 12, which extends to those cathedrals for which, immediately prior to the relevant date there was no body corporate known as the dean and Chapter.
103 Under the transitional provisions, for each cathedral existing on 30 June 1999, there had to be established a Transitional Council whose duty was to frame, with the consent of the bishop of the diocese in which the cathedral was situated and as soon as practicable, instruments providing for a constitution and statutes for the cathedrals in accordance with the 1999 Measure: CM 1999, ss. 29–32, 35, 38, Sch. 1. See Introduction.
104 H&R 73, Rec. 12 (Ch. 6, pars. 35–44).
105 H&R 175. CM 1999 does not contain a model constitution or statutes.
106 CM 1999, s. 1; HLE par. 346.
107 HLE pars. 344–345. The Statutes of Christ Church Oxford (The House), which require it to support the cathedral, were made within the meaning of the Universities of Oxford and Cambridge Acts 1877 and 1923.

First, the *constitution* must provide for: (a) the members of the Council, Chapter, and College of Canons to be a body corporate with perpetual succession and a common seal (the common seal of the cathedral); (b) the appointment of canons in Holy Orders, the manner of their appointment, and their tenure of office; (c) lay canons to be appointed; (d) the maximum number of residentiary canons and non-residentiary canons; (e) the appointment of an administrator of the cathedral with such functions as may be prescribed; (f) the appointment of an architect and an auditor for the cathedral; (g) the appointment of a person to supervise music; and (h) the establishment of a finance committee of Chapter to advise it in connection with its responsibilities in the field of financial and investment management, and for the membership to include persons with expertise and experience in that field.[108] A constitution which previously provided for the appointment of the dean by Her Majesty must continue to do so; in any other case (i.e. in a parish church cathedral), it must provide that the incumbent of the benefice which comprises the parish of which the cathedral is the parish church be the dean.[109] The constitution of a cathedral which is *not* a parish church must provide for the formation and maintenance of a roll of persons who are members of the cathedral community and apply to be enrolled as such.[110] The constitution *may* also contain provisions: enabling or requiring a cathedral community committee to be established, consisting of persons whose names are on the roll; and enabling or requiring committees to be established by Chapter, and for delegation of functions to them: any provision enabling/requiring such a committee to be established may provide that persons who are not Chapter members may be members of it.[111]

Second, the *statutes* must make provision (consistent with the constitution) for the good government of the cathedral and may in particular provide: (a) for the creation, continuance, abolition, suspension, or termination of suspension of any dignity, office, or body in the cathedral and for the title by which any such dignity or office is to be known; (b) that any presentations or nominations to benefices in the patronage of the cathedral must be exercised by Chapter or by a patronage committee of Chapter; (c) where a cathedral is a parish church, that part of that cathedral must be the parish church or, where part of a cathedral is a parish church, that the cathedral or any other part of it must be the parish church; and (d) for any incidental and supplementary matters (which are not defined in the 1999 Measure itself).[112]

The power to revise the constitution and statutes rests in the cathedral Council; it is validly exercised with the consent of the bishop. Whilst Council has the power of revision, it is Chapter which must keep under review the constitution and statutes and submit any proposals for their revision to Council.[113] Council must

108 CM 1999, s. 9(1)(a)-(h).
109 CM 1999, s. 9(2).
110 CM 1999, s. 9(3).
111 CM 1999, s. 10.
112 CM 1999, s. 11.
113 CM 1999, s. 4(8)(f).

consider proposals submitted by Chapter in connection with the constitution and statutes with a view to their revision.[114] The bishop too (as Visitor) may propose amendments for consideration by Council.[115] As such, Council may, with the consent of the bishop, by instrument under the common seal of the cathedral revise the constitution or statutes. Any such instrument may either provide a new constitution or statutes or may amend those in force immediately before the instrument comes into force. However, before taking any steps to revise the constitution or statutes, Council must afford Chapter an opportunity to express views on Council proposals and have regard to them.[116] Any instrument which affects any right or interest of Her Majesty may not be made without the consent of Her Majesty.[117] The statutes must: not be contrary to the Word of God, royal prerogative, and statutes of the realm as to ecclesiastical order; and be diligently observed.[118]

With regard to revision of the *constitution*, Council must prepare a draft of the instrument and a notice of the preparation of the draft instrument. The notice must set out the objects of the draft instrument and specify the place in the diocese where copies may be inspected; the notice must also state that Council will consider any written representations with respect to the instrument made before such date as may be specified.[119] The date specified must be not less than four weeks after the date of the publication or displaying of the notice.[120] Council must publish the notice in one or more publications circulating in the diocese and display the notice in a prominent position in or in the vicinity of the cathedral.[121] Council must also send a copy of the draft instrument to the Secretary-General of General Synod. After the period for representations has expired, Council, having considered such representations, may, whether as a result of them or otherwise, amend the draft instrument as it thinks expedient.[122]

The process to revise the cathedral *statutes* is similar but rather less onerous. Council must prepare a draft of the instrument and display in a prominent position in or in the vicinity of the cathedral a notice of its preparation setting out its objects, specifying the place in the diocese where copies may be inspected, and stating that Council will consider any written representations as to the draft instrument made before such date as may be specified in the notice; the date must be not less than four weeks after the date of the displaying of the notice. After the period for representations expires, Council, having considered any representations,

---

114 CM 1999, s. 3(6)(d).
115 CM 1999, s. 6(9).
116 CM 1999, s. 28(1)-(3). The College of Canons has no such authority.
117 CM 1999, s. 32.
118 Can. C21.2: the dean and residentiaries must ensure this, and that 'all other constitutions … confirmed by Her Majesty's authority, and such as shall be enjoined by the bishop of the diocese in his visitation, according to the statutes and customs of the same church, and the ecclesiastical laws of the realm, shall be diligently observed'.
119 CM 1999, s. 29(1).
120 CM 1999, s. 30(1).
121 CM 1999, s. 29(1)(a), (b).
122 CM 1999, s. 29(2)-(3).

may, as a result of them or otherwise, amend the draft instrument as it thinks expedient.[123]

After compliance with these procedures to revise the constitution and statutes, a copy of the draft instrument must be signed by the chairman of Council on its behalf or, in the case of the absence or incapacity of its chairman, by two other Council members nominated by it for that purpose. Signing the copy and affixing the cathedral common seal is conclusive evidence that the provisions as to preparation of the instrument have been complied with. A copy of must be sent to the Secretary-General of General Synod.[124] And: 'The bishop shall as Visitor hear and determine any question as to the construction of the constitution and statutes'.[125]

Cathedral constitutions/statutes often provide for the operation of the revision norms in the Measure,[126] occasionally adding to them; for example, copies of the constitution and statutes of Canterbury must be deposited in 'the Cathedral Library, Chapter Office, British Library and Archbishop's Library at Lambeth and must be available to inspect at all reasonable times'.[127]

Importantly, some constitutions and/or statutes set out their own purposes. Sometimes these are functional; at old foundation Lincoln the constitution and statutes seek to 'sustain' and 'regulate' the focus and activities of the cathedral;[128] and St Paul's constitution 'sets out the legal framework for ... governance' and the statutes 'supplement the legal requirements of the Constitution'.[129] Others are theological: new foundation Carlisle recognises that 'service of God and the law have been essentially interrelated in the Judaeo-Christian tradition'; law is not 'a constraint upon the human spirit, but the framework within which true freedom before God is discovered, known and lived'; so the Church develops its laws, and monastic founders their Rules: 'It is in this spirit that this Constitution and these Statutes ... have been revised'.[130]

Other cathedrals relate these purposes to the cathedral objects: the constitution and statutes of Gloucester 'have been made in order that worship may be continually offered in the Cathedral for the better promotion of mission and outreach', to preserve and enhance its fabric, and for all members of the cathedral community to 'perform their duties well'.[131] At Derby, the 'object' of the constitution and statutes, 'the governing instruments', is 'to secure a sound and fair basis for [its] common life, mission, administration and government';[132] and at

123 CM 1999, s. 30(1)-(2).
124 CM 1999, s. 31(1)-(2): no reason is given for this.
125 CM 1999, s. 6(4).
126 As to compliance with the Measure, see e.g. Chester: Con. Art. 21; Gloucester: Con. Art. 17.1; Wells: Con. Art. 15; York: Con. Art. XII.B; Durham: Con. Art. 1; Ripon: Con. 17(1). As to interpretation by the bishop, e.g. Ely: Con. Art. 3, Stat. 1(6); Rochester: Stat. 1(5)-(6); Bury St Edmunds: Con. Art. 3 and Stat. 1(4).
127 Canterbury: Stat. XXIX. See also Winchester: Con. Art. 2.3.
128 Lincoln: Con. Preamble.
129 London: Notes to the Constitution and Statutes.
130 Carlisle: Con. Preamble.
131 Gloucester: Con. 1: Introduction.
132 Derby: Con. Preamble.

Sheffield the constitution and statutes 'declare the rule and custom in everything pertaining to the administration and government of the Cathedral' including 'rights and responsibilities'.[133]

The normal vehicle used by a cathedral to ensure that its domestic laws bind staff is an oath, declaration, or other undertaking (as seen elsewhere in this study). York is typical:

> At the time of admission to office each member of the Chapter shall take an oath as follows: I ... do swear that I will be faithful to the Cathedral Church of York, will keep its Statutes and Customs that are agreeable to law and will to the utmost of my power defend its liberties. I will not reveal the secrets of the Chapter to which I shall be called and will fulfil all the duties which are incumbent upon me to be performed as well to the Church as to its ministers.[134]

Cathedral customs, by-laws, and other legal forms

The constitution and/or statutes may provide for the operation of other species of regulation – such as 'customs' and 'by-laws'. The canon law of the Church of England allows for the operation of cathedral customs provided they are not contrary to the Word of God or the royal prerogative.[135] However, the Archbishops' Commission 1994 had recommended abolition of by-laws because 'little use' was made of the power in national law to make them.[136] These entities are sometimes treated separately and sometimes together in constitutions or statutes.

At old foundation Chichester, 'hitherto ... governed ... by custom', the statutes make provision for governance 'within the framework of the Constitution while also allowing for the custom of the Cathedral';[137] at Salisbury, those responsible for the ordering of services 'shall observe the spirit of the liturgical traditions and usages' from time to time agreed by the bishop and Chapter;[138] and St Paul's Chapter must draw up consulting Council 'a code of practice setting out the customs of the Cathedral' as to officiating at services, preaching and appointing preachers, the role of the dean, and the responsibilities and exercise of being in residence; the working of this code must be reviewed each year by Chapter and Council; a similar code must be made on 'the rights and customs of the Bishop' when officiating in the cathedral.[139]

---

133 Sheffield: Con. Preamble.
134 York: Con. Art. VI.C.
135 Can. C21.1.
136 H&R 69: provision had been made for by-laws in the Cathedrals Measure 1963, s. 13.
137 Chichester: Con. Preamble and Stat. 1; see also Stat. 15: choristers and custom.
138 Salisbury: Stat. 1.
139 London: Stat. III.2 and IV.2. See also Stat. VIII: oaths prescribed by 'law and custom'; Stat. XI: Chapter is to agree with the College of Canons a 'code of practice' as to the expectations of prebendaries, reviewed regularly; Stat. XVII: Chapter may make by-laws 'not contrary' to the Measure, constitution and statutes.

Chichester Chapter may make by-laws, not inconsistent with the Measure, constitution, and statutes, as to: the time of divine worship, conducting it, and preaching; the care, use, and arrangement of ornaments, vessels, and other objects for worship; if not defined by statute, precedence, and Close residence; and policy statements or regulations 'amplifying legislation applicable to the cathedral'. Such 'enacted' by-laws must be recorded in the Chapter minutes and copies retained in a file.[140] Lincoln Chapter may make by-laws not being inconsistent with the Measure, constitution, or statutes 'provided that no by-law affecting the rights and privileges of any member of the College of Canons shall be made without [its] consent' and that of the bishop.[141] Lichfield Chapter may regulate by by-laws any matter within its jurisdiction as defined by the constitution/statutes or Measure including the imposition of fees and preservation of good order and cleanliness in the Cathedral Close and 'the proper control of traffic therein'.[142] Norwich Chapter may 'make, publish and enforce by-laws for the good government and regulation of the Cathedral, its property, ministers and officials'.[143] And by-laws made by the Newcastle Chapter are intended for 'the better ordering' of cathedral life.[144]

Others treat customs and by-laws together in one rule. Hereford Chapter may 'alter, add to or abolish the regulations, bye-laws and customs of the Cathedral' provided this is consistent with the constitution and statutes;[145] and at Carlisle, the statutes provide that:

> [E]xisting customs of the Cathedral in so far as they are not repugnant to the Measure, the Constitution or the Statutes, or to the laws of the Realm, shall continue to be observed unless and until they are altered by by-laws.[146]

Canterbury is of interest as to the process to make and binding effect of Chapter by-laws: 'No such by-law, nor any change in such by-law, shall be proposed unless reasonable notice of the proposal has been given in writing' to Council; the proposal must be discussed at Chapter, but no decision may be taken until the meeting after that at which the discussion takes place; the decision must be made by majority of Chapter members; the by-laws 'shall be binding upon all members

---

140 Chichester: Stat. 29; see also Con. Art. 20: Chapter may approve 'rules' made by the cathedral community.
141 Lincoln: Stat. 23. See also York: Stat. XX and Wells: Stat. 23: Chapter may make by-laws.
142 Lichfield: Con. Art. 5(10). See also Exeter: Stat. XVI: a cathedral group may make for itself a constitution (e.g. to define its purposes) 'which shall have force when approved by the Chapter'.
143 Norwich: Con. Art. VIII.5. See also Ely: Stat. Schedule A: rights and liberties.
144 Newcastle: Stat. 18.1.
145 Hereford: Con. Art. 4(4)(i); see also Stat. IV.2: customs as to enthronement of the bishop.
146 Carlisle: Stat. 30(2); 30(1): bylaws; 29(1): occupying stalls allotted to them 'in accordance with the customs of the cathedral'. See also Worcester: Stat. 20; and Ely: Stat. Sch. A: this refers to 'Ordinances'.

of the Chapter and upon all ministers and officers of the Cathedral and upon all employees of the Body Corporate'.[147] Durham too has a rule of special interest: 'Existing customs of the Cathedral, except where they conflict with the Constitution, the Statutes or the law of England, shall continue to be observed until and unless they are altered by a by-law or other competent instrument';[148] Chapter may also make Standing Orders.[149] Rochester has a Customary approved by Chapter – this deals with liturgical matters such as presidency at services, robing, weekend and weekday ceremonial; ritual, daily worship, the choirs, Holy Week and Easter Day, processions; baptisms, weddings and funerals; organ use; and broadcasts of services, concerts, and recitals.[150]

Henrician foundations also allow for the operation of custom and by-laws. For instance at Peterborough: 'The Statutes make provision for the governance of the Cathedral within the framework of the Constitution, whilst also allowing for the custom of the Cathedral'; the bishop officiating at a service there must have 'due regard to the customs of the Cathedral'; and the dean is installed 'according to the customs of the Cathedral';[151] and Bristol Chapter may make 'regulations'.[152] Similar norms exist at parish church cathedrals: St Edmundsbury's Chapter may make standing orders and by-laws not inconsistent with the Measure, constitution, and statutes; Southwark Chapter may make by-laws on 'any matter within their jurisdiction as defined by the Constitution and Statutes, not being inconsistent therewith';[153] and at Portsmouth the dean must be installed in accordance with custom, and at Coventry 'according to the usage of the Cathedral Church'.[154] Liverpool requires its Chapter to 'continue the tradition of consultation with the Bishop'.[155]

Cathedral quasi-legislation

Alongside formal law (national and local), a host of other instruments apply to cathedrals in the form of quasi-legislation – informal administrative norms in documents usually styled guidance, codes of practice, good practice, or standards, each of which may be normative in register and generate an expectation of compliance.[156] In

---

147 Canterbury: Stat. XXX.1–2.
148 Durham: Con. Art. 1.b; Winchester: Stat. 23: Chapter must have 'regard to' custom (as to e.g. precedence).
149 Durham: Stat. III.4; see also Stat. IV.6. A similar rule is found at Carlisle: Stat. 30(2).
150 Rochester: Customary (revised 2008).
151 Peterborough: Stat. 1 (and Chapter may make by-laws), 2(10) and 3(1); Stat. 2(10): custom and collections.
152 Bristol: Stat. 21(5): as to the conduct, duties and tenure of choristers.
153 Southwark: Stat. 18; St Edmundsbury: Stat. 33. See also Leicester: Stat. 14: standing orders and by-laws.
154 Portsmouth: Stat. 2; Coventry: Stat. 2.2; and App. 3: standing orders. See also Newcastle: Stat. 6: the dean is installed 'according to the customs of the Cathedral'. For customary oaths, see e.g. Leicester: Stat. 4(1).
155 Liverpool: Con. Art. 6.5.
156 For the phenomenon, see P. Colton, 'The rise of ecclesiastical quasi-legislation' in F. Cranmer, M. Hill, C. Kenny and R. Sandberg (eds.), *The Confluence of Law and*

many cathedrals, the constitution and/or statutes either require or enable their creation by Chapter: St Paul's must make and review a 'code of practice' of customs on staff roles;[157] Salisbury's must establish 'approved and effective employment policies';[158] Exeter's must issue 'a code of practice for the proper conduct of its business, including provision for consultation with other bodies';[159] and at Guildford, Chapter must 'generally formulate or modify policy in so far as it is inherent in any of its functions (after consultation with the Bishop and the Council, where required)'.[160]

Quasi-legislation may also be issued at national level by institutions under power conferred by Measure. For example, the Cathedrals Fabric Commission for England must promote, in consultation with Chapters, Fabric Advisory Committees, and such others as it thinks fit, by means of 'guidance or otherwise, standards of good practice to be observed' in relation to: e.g. the duties of cathedral architects and archaeologists; the compilation, maintenance, and dissemination of information of architectural, archaeological, artistic, and historic interest to cathedrals; and the form and content of records to be kept by Chapter.[161] Chapters must also maintain financial records 'in accordance with best professional practice and standards' specified by the Church Commissioners who may enquire into any departure from these.[162] Non-statutory bodies may also produce guidance: the Association of English Cathedrals, for example, encourages 'best practice' and provides 'guidance on issues affecting cathedrals'.[163] As we see throughout this book, other national cathedral associations also issue guidance.[164]

The cathedral interviews

These reveal various experiences of national law and the purposes and revision of cathedral constitutions, statutes, by-laws, customs, and policy documents. Among old foundations, for the Dean of Hereford, civil law in employment and in health and safety has put 'pressure' on cathedral resources; Chapter's power to make 'regulations, bye-laws and customs' is 'not used'; its power to make 'customs', as if these could be created by Chapter 'as from tomorrow', seems odd, given that

---

Religion: Interdisciplinary Reflections on the Work of Norman Doe (Cambridge: Cambridge University Press, 2016) 81–95.
157 London: Stat. III and IV.
158 Salisbury: Stat. 3.10.
159 Exeter: Stat. II.2: also, the bishop must receive notice of Chapter's agenda, minutes, and decisions.
160 Guildford: Con. Art. 9.4.9.
161 CCM 2011, s. 3(3).
162 CM 1999, s. 27(1) and (2).
163 The Association promotes cathedrals in national and church life, liaises with the church's central bodies, government departments/agencies and national ecumenical bodies (such as the Churches Legislation Advisory Service), organises conferences on cathedral ministry, and provides training for Chapters, and information.
164 E.g. the Association of Diocesan and Cathedral Archaeologists promotes 'standards of practice': Con. (2000), Art. 2; and the Church Commissioners' Bishoprics & Cathedrals Committee makes 'policy decisions'.

The cathedral church 33

custom by nature develops through long usage; yet, custom has a part to play – e.g. the Chancellor's job description is 'declaratory of the custom of the cathedral'; nevertheless: 'If you need to make law, then something has failed'; it is the same with having to take a vote in Chapter; the basic principle in the cathedral is 'governance by consent'.[165]

The revision of the constitution and statutes is taken up by the Dean of Exeter: that Council never initiates revision is 'the proper course'; proposing revision is a matter for Chapter as it is responsible for governance; revisions occur as 'infrequently as possible'; there has been an increase in policy documents and in the time and expense of implementing these – but it is important to comply with them for purposes of good practice.[166] At Wells: Chapter reviews the constitution and statutes 'as and when any issue arises'; there has been 'an increased emphasis in documenting policies agreed by Chapter'; and custom (mentioned in Statute 3) plays its part – having evening prayer on Christmas Day in the Close Chapel for the past five years may indicate a developing custom.[167] For the Dean of Salisbury, the constitution and statutes translate into action the theology contained in the constitutional preamble (on the cathedral objects): 'we are not utilitarian or transactional in our relation to law', but, rather, 'radical, pragmatic, and critical because [the law] is only as good as its roots and aspirations'; Chapter sometimes uses its power to make by-laws but it is difficult to publicise these and, therefore, to ensure compliance with them; the cathedral also has customs which are 'deep and ancient', 'unwritten', and 'mainly liturgical' (e.g. the Sarum rite and vesture colours).[168]

The Dean of St Paul's considers that 'law is like leadership' – it must be 'on the shoulder of the church, or else it imprisons or shackles' it, but not updating it 'brings the church into disrepute'. Two principles were used in recent revision of the constitution and statutes: (1) include in the constitution only those provisions the cathedral is required to include under the 1999 Measure, and include the remainder in the statutes (because the constitution is more difficult to change); and (2) do not include in statutes matters which may be addressed by a code of practice issued by Chapter – 'people tend to look at it, discuss and negotiate it, whereas they feel they have no control over the constitution and do not look at that – a code results from real collaboration'. Indeed, the Corporate Body is the legislator for the cathedral because: the bishop may propose a revision, but Council may reject it; Chapter may propose a revision, but Council may reject it; Council may propose a revision, but Chapter cannot veto it; the bishop may veto all proposals but cannot revise unilaterally; and the College of Canons has no right to propose revision. The instrument itself recites that it is 'made' by Council, consented to by bishop, and sealed by the Corporate Body (Council, Chapter, and College).[169]

165 Hereford: Dean: Int. 5-8-2016; see Con. Art. 4(4)(i) for regulations etc.
166 Exeter: Dean: Int. 9-8-2016: revision of law is often 'driven by personalities'.
167 Wells: Acting Dean: Int. 12-8-2016.
168 Salisbury: Dean: Int. 20-9-2016; Stat. 1: 'liturgical traditions and usages'.
169 St Paul's: Dean: Int. 23-9-2016: revision occurred in 2016; see above for Stat. III and IV for codes of practice issued by Chapter: for the Dean, this is an example of the cathedral using a regulatory instrument to stimulate debate and consensus. See also

34 The cathedral church

At new foundation Winchester the constitution and statutes are 'in the background', provide a 'framework within which we operate', and need to be 'as flexible as possible'; there has been a recent increase in policy documents which 'have their uses'.[170] At Rochester, having a constitution and statutes means that 'everyone knows the parameters and purposes of the common life'; while 'law may look infertile, it is merely the structure by which human lives are given order to thrive and flourish' as 'a community of grace'; moreover, it is useful to see the Foundation itself as the legislator as the constitution and statutes are made and revised 'in the name of the Foundation'; Chapter may make by-laws but it has not done so recently; however, the use of policies, which provide 'flexibility and focus', has increased recently.[171]

The Dean of Worcester reflects on the matter in these ways. A large body of law applies to the cathedral but this is 'not a hindrance'; cathedral 'life is shaped in light of all these sources'; indeed: 'It behoves the cathedral to set a good example of lawfulness in the church', not by 'slavish obedience to law', for its own sake, but by 'absorbing law into its life'; and 'law preserves the church's memory', like the building itself, the library and archives, and it helps to 'establish the character of the community'. That law has 'force' is important, as this provides 'resilience, stability, and continuity', protects 'non-negotiable' matters, such as 'the daily pattern of prayer', to counteract changes in cathedral personnel, and provides a 'picture of cathedral life'; the Henrician statutes provided great detail about the character of cathedral life.[172] It is 'difficult to state the customs of the cathedral', not least as they are unwritten, though they may be mentioned in the constitution and statutes; cathedral customs are 'over and above' what is found in written laws; the Dean wonders whether customs exist outside 'the consensus' provided by 'the minds of the dean and bishop' and 'the practice of Chapter', except when these customs are written in the laws. It is possible that the customs of the cathedral, normatively, are its very purposes: to be hospitable, to practise daily prayer, and so on – in one sense, the cathedral's objects in its strategic vision statement *are* its customs.[173]

Among Henrician foundations, for the Dean of Bristol law is no hindrance but rather part of the 'dialectic' of cathedral life; it is used 'to remind' the cathedral of the 'legal dimensions' of its activities and it is 'helpful' to have the 'support and protection' of law for decision-making; Chapter may make by-laws but it does not exercise this power; yet, it may be worth considering incorporating cathedral

---

    Stat. XVII: Chapter may make by-laws, and for the Dean, it is good to have this 'permissive power'; like codes of practice, by-laws could be susceptible to debate and negotiation – by-laws may form part of cathedral 'custom'. That the 2000 constitution and statutes were in hard-back binding is a visual statement of the idea of their 'permanence'; people generally value 'continuity'.

170 Winchester: Acting Dean: Int. 16-8-2016.
171 Rochester: Precentor: Int. 30–9-2016: there may be some 'historic bylaws' e.g. as to leases.
172 See the Introduction above for these statutes.
173 Worcester: Dean: Int. 28–7-2016.

'policies' in 'by-laws' to give them greater weight.[174] The Chancellor of Gloucester considers that the cathedral constitution and statutes are 'not too prescriptive' but sensibly 'allow some leeway'; they do not provide for Chapter to make by-laws but the cathedral has 20–30 policy documents and the impact of secular law on health and safety, charity work, and employment is keenly felt; while it is rare for the customs of the cathedral (Statute 2(2)) to be invoked in decision-making, some practices are 'customary' (e.g. the times of services which have been the same for decades, the office of Chancellor, the Canon Theologian's role, and the Canon-in-Residence serving as Vice-Dean); the category of custom 'could be useful', therefore, to explain practices if a juridical explanation is needed.[175] At Chester also the 'practice' of issuing policy documents has increased recently, and it is possible to see these 'evolving practices and policies as the new custom' of the cathedral.[176]

Among parish church cathedrals, the Dean of Birmingham considers that 'a cathedral, being a complex of communities of people, needs good order', 'most deans like good order', and the law means that 'everyone knows where they stand'; 'simple' norms are of 'value' and when they provide 'certainty and clarity' the cathedral 'works better'; the Dean also recognises a recent increase in the creation of cathedral policy documents; moreover: 'There is a sense of some urgency in the need to write policies' and making these 'helps us to focus' on good practice.[177] By way of slight contrast, for the Dean of Derby, the place of law in cathedral life is 'residual', 'interstitial', and useful to support 'instinct' or to explain a state of affairs; it is not a hindrance – rather 'the constitution and statutes are good and flexible enough to use or to work around'; however, their revision is not a priority but rather 'on the edges'.[178] Liverpool has a practice of including in the constitution a list of those articles which have been amended by instrument; they are described as 'inserted by Council': this is unusual.[179]

Conclusion

Cathedrals may be classified in various ways. The old foundations were those, before the Reformation, under secular priests. New foundations were monastic cathedrals in which, on dissolution of the monasteries, monks were replaced by

174 Bristol: Dean: Int. 3-8-2016.
175 Gloucester: Chancellor: Int. 4-8-2016.
176 Chester: Vice-Dean: Int. 19-8-2016: revision of the constitution and statutes (begun in 2010 and completed with a new edition issued in February 2016) was a difficult process; see also Stat. 9(iii): Chapter may make 'regulations for the use of the library' – none have been made.
177 Birmingham: Dean: Int. 11-8-2016: recent policies include one on the arts, and the Liturgical Plan. A similar increase in policies has occurred at: Carlisle: Dean: Email 17–1-2017; Ely: Dean: Email 17–1-2017; Southwark: Dean: Email 17–1-2017; Liverpool: Dean: Email 21–1-2017; St Albans: Dean: Email 23–1-2017; Wakefield: Dean: Email 24–1-2017.
178 Derby: Dean: Int. 10-8-2016.
179 Liverpool: Con. Art. 17.0.

secular canons. Cathedrals founded after the Reformation are sometimes described as new foundations, but this is not strictly so. A more modern classification is 'dean and chapter cathedrals' and 'parish church cathedrals'; the latter remain a legal category but all cathedrals share a governance system in which Council, Chapter, and College of Canons together constitute the corporate body. A cathedral is an ecclesiastical corporation for charity law. Historically, the foundation of cathedrals was in the keeping of the Crown, though later their foundation was under Acts of Parliament or Measures subsequently confirmed by Order in Council. Today, they may be founded by a scheme approved by the Church Commissioners and confirmed by Her Majesty in Council.

Under the Cathedrals Measure 1999, and in accordance with ancient practice and theological principle, the purpose of a cathedral church is to serve as the seat of the bishop and a centre of worship and mission for the diocese and its work is spiritual, pastoral, evangelistic, social, and ecumenical. Their domestic laws, however, offer wider understandings of the objects of cathedrals (more in keeping with those of the Archbishops' Commission on Cathedrals 1994 than Measure); they are, typically: to serve as the mother church for parishes in the diocese; to maintain a daily pattern of corporate prayer and worship; to be a focus for the bishop's ministry; to preach the gospel of Christ and nurture Christian learning; to extend hospitality to visitors; to demonstrate concern for the poor; and to engage with the city and the county.

Cathedrals are regulated by various instruments, including national legislation (particularly Measures and Canons), and their own domestic constitutions and statutes, and customs and by-laws, which must be consistent with national law. Cathedral law is also supplemented by a growing body of quasi-legislation in the forms of guidance and codes of practice. The cathedral interviews reveal, on balance, that: the ancient classification of cathedrals continues to be an inspiration to cathedrals; a statement of the objects of a cathedral is important for the purposes of the development of cathedral strategy; the law plays a valuable role at cathedrals provided it enables and orders life for the cathedral to fulfil its ministry; powers of Chapters to enact by-laws are not much used; and custom may be used to classify cathedral practice.

2 The episcopal throne: the appointment and functions of the bishop

The presence of the teaching seat or throne of the bishop defines the status of a church as a cathedral church – this is a principle of ancient canon law,[1] one which survived the English Reformation.[2] The word 'cathedral' is derived from the Latin word *cathedra* which means 'chair'. Thus, a church which contains the official chair, seat or throne of a bishop is called a cathedral. Its original position was in the centre of the apse behind the high altar, but in the medieval period it was placed in the chancel. One of the finest and most spectacular episcopal thrones in England is that in the choir at Exeter Cathedral: it is almost sixty feet in height.[3] After appointment, a new bishop is enthroned there during a service in the cathedral church. Thereafter, the relationship between bishops and their cathedrals is a close one – and when used in relation to a cathedral, 'bishop' means the bishop of the diocese in which the cathedral is situated.[4] This chapter examines the process leading to enthronement of a bishop in the cathedral, the functions of the bishop associated with the cathedral, including the jurisdiction exercised by the bishop as its visitor, and the role of the bishop in enforcing compliance with the legal standards set for the care and maintenance of the cathedral fabric.[5]

The enthronement of the bishop

The Church of England teaches that from the apostles' time there have been three orders in Christ's Church: bishops, priests and deacons; and the order of bishops is an

---

1 See C. Tracy with A. Budge, *Britain's Medieval Episcopal Thrones* (London: Oxbow Books, 2015).
2 Hooker VII.8.3: 'To note a difference of that one Church where the Bishop has his seat, and the rest which depend upon it, that one has usually been termed Cathedral ... The Church where the Bishop is set with his College of Presbyters ... we call a See; the Local compass of his authority ... a Diocese'; VII.24.19: a defence of cathedrals.
3 P. Johnson, *British Cathedrals* (London: Weidenfeld & Nicolson, 1980) 213: it is made of Devon oak and built 1312–1316; see also 8: a bishop's *cathedra* was placed on a higher level than other seats in the vicinity, such as those of the presbyters who were grouped in stalls around the bishop – some say, to reflect Revelation 4.4–5.
4 CM 1999, s. 35(1).
5 For the cathedral fabric, see below Chapter 9.

essential of Anglican identity, ministry and polity.[6] The bishop of the diocese, or diocesan bishop, is the chief pastor and principal minister of the diocese, exercises ministry under the authority of the Crown and the supervision of the archbishop, and has legal personality as a corporation sole with perpetual succession and an episcopal seal.[7] A man or a woman may become a bishop if that person is at least 30 and not more than 70 years of age, 'godly and well learned', and 'called, tried, examined, and admitted' to the order.[8] The process to admit a person as diocesan bishop is regulated by the Appointment of Bishops Act 1533,[9] and other rules, including constitutional convention, and culminates in enthronement. In the process the diocese (including the cathedral) elucidates its needs; a General Synod committee recommends a candidate; the Crown nominates; and the cathedral College of Canons elects.[10] Then follow: confirmation of the election; consecration of the bishop; and the enthronement.

A diocese becomes vacant on the avoidance of the bishopric, ordinarily by the retirement, resignation, death or translation (to another see) of the bishop. The diocesan Vacancy in See Committee, which includes the cathedral dean, prepares a statement of diocesan needs which it sends to the Crown Nominations Commission of General Synod.[11] The Commission has voting and non-voting members: the former are the Archbishops of Canterbury and York, members elected by General Synod, and members elected by the Vacancy in See Committee; non-voting members are the Prime Minister's and Archbishops' appointments secretaries.[12] The Archbishop of Canterbury is chair of the Commission and Archbishop of York vice-chair. The Commission must (a) agree on two names for submission on its behalf by the appropriate archbishop to the Prime Minister in the order decided by it; and (b) indicate a preference by a vote conducted by secret ballot supported by at least two-thirds of the votes. It must not select a name to submit to the Prime Minister unless the person presiding at the meeting is satisfied the Commission has paid due regard to the views of diocesan members and the requirements of the mission of the Church of England as a whole.[13] By constitutional convention, the Prime Minister submits the first name to the Crown for its approval; and, also by constitutional convention, the Crown must accept the advice of the Prime Minister.

---

6   Can. C1.1. See also Canon A6: church government by bishops is 'not repugnant to the Word of God'.
7   Can. C18.1 and 4; Godolphin 27: corporation sole; 23: the bishop is also called 'Ordinary' and exercises 'ordinary jurisdiction in causes ecclesiastical' in the diocese.
8   Canon C1.1–2 and C2.3; Bishops and Priests (Consecration and Ordination of Women) Measure 2014.
9   For historical antecedents, see Godolphin 29.
10 Formerly, the election was made by the Dean and Chapter: see e.g. Hooker VIII.7.1–3.
11 Vacancy in See Committee Regulation 1993 (as amended 2013): Act of Synod.
12 Standing Orders of the General Synod, SO 137: three are elected by the House of Clergy and three by the House of Laity.
13 Ibid: there are rules on the procedure of the Commission, and on archiepiscopal vacancies: SO 136–141.

Next, the Crown nominates a person and the cathedral College of Canons elects under power conferred by the 1533 Act.[14] The Crown nominates by granting to the College of Canons a licence under the Great Seal, namely, a *congé d'élire*, or permission to elect a bishop; notice of the licence is published in the London Gazette. The licence is accompanied by a 'letter missive' with the name of the person whom the Crown would have them elect.[15] The person so nominated must be elected by the College to the vacant see within 12 days of delivery to it of the licence and letter missive. The election is certified to the Crown by the College under the common seal of the cathedral: this is the certification. The person elected is styled the 'lord elect of the bishopric'.[16] The constitution of a cathedral provides for the operation of these statutory rules by stating, typically: 'In the event of a vacancy in the See, the College of Canons shall be summoned by the Dean to meet and on receiving from Her Majesty a licence under the Great Seal with a letter missive as provided by the Appointment of Bishops Act 1533 shall proceed to the election of a Bishop in the manner laid down by that Act'.[17]

That the College elects the Crown nominee may be classified as a convention. Indeed, in so doing, it expresses 'the consent of the diocese to the outcome of the process ... in which the diocese's representatives will have played a full part'.[18] If the College delays the election above 12 days after delivery of the licence and letter missive, the Crown may nominate and present such person as it thinks able and convenient, by letters patent under the Great Seal. This nomination and presentment must be made to the archbishop of the province in which the vacant see is situated, or, if the archbishopric is void, to

---

14 Burn I.179–193, citing Godolphin 29 and Gibson 117; 183: the licence has 'the name of the person which they shall elect'; Godolphin 29: 'the making of all Bishops ... shall be by Election on and after the King's Assent'.
15 Appointment of Bishops Act 1533, s. 3 (amended by CM 1999, s. 5(3)). Whether this is compulsory and for the form of *congé d'élire* and letters missive, see *R v Archbishop of Canterbury* (1848) Jebb's Report 1 at 2–4.
16 Appointment of Bishops Act 1533, ss. 3, 4 (as amended by the CM 1999, s. 5(3)). For details of the 'ceremonies', see HLE par. 183, n. 4: (1) a citatory letter to convene a meeting; (2) delivery to the dean and reading of the *congé d'élire* and letters missive; (3) return of citation by mandatory, calling over the names, assumption of directorship of the election by the dean, and pronouncement of absent members as contumacious; (4) pronouncement of members present; (5) appointment of a notary (usually the chapter clerk) and two witnesses; (6) voting, beginning with junior members; (7) on election, usually unanimous (whether a majority is sufficient seems doubtful), a decree of three certificates (to the Crown, archbishop, and bishop elect) praying acceptance; (8) decree of a proxy to three notaries to deliver the certificates; (9) publication and declaration of the election to the congregation: see *R v Archbishop of Canterbury* (1848) Jebb's Report 1.
17 E.g. London: Con. Art. 5.3; Hereford: Con. Art. 5(2); Winchester: Con. Art. 14.2; Gloucester: Con. Art. 14(2); Ely: Con. Art. 12(3); Birmingham: Con. Art. 15(2); Ripon: Con. Art. 13.
18 Bullimore Report (2012) par. 106; College is 'to give formal approval to the person selected'; 'this duty has given rise to some hand-wringing ... without leading further to effective action against the choice of nominee'.

such archbishop or metropolitan within the realm or any of the Queen's dominions as the Crown thinks fit.[19]

Next follows confirmation. The election is confirmed by the archbishop of the province or by his vicar-general on his behalf: 'It is the confirmation of the election which actually makes the person concerned the bishop of the diocese; at the end of the ceremony he is given spiritual jurisdiction over the diocese'.[20] After the election and certification of the new bishop by the College of Canons, and the taking of such oath of fealty as may be appointed,[21] the Crown must signify the election to the archbishop of the appropriate province, by mandate requiring him to confirm the election and invest and consecrate the person elected; the Crown does so, once again, by letters patent under the Great Seal.[22] The archbishop then under seal commissions the vicar-general to proceed to confirmation.[23] The vicar-general in the name of the archbishop issues a citation summoning all those who oppose the election (if any) to appear at a specified time and place to offer objections.[24] At that time and place, the proctor for the College: exhibits the royal assent and archbishop's commission to the vicar-general (who accepts them) and the College's proxy; presents the bishop-elect; returns the citation; and desires that anyone opposing be thrice publicly called and accused, and that the business may proceed, which is ordered in writing by the vicar-general. Then the proctor presents a summary petition, stating election and assent, and desiring that a time be assigned for him to prove it, which the vicar-general admits and decrees.[25] The proctor again exhibits the royal assent, the bishop-elect's assent, and the archbishop's certificate, desiring a time to be set for final sentence, which the vicar-general decrees. The proctor once more has those who oppose thrice publicly called; if none appear or oppose, they are pronounced contumacious, and a decree is made to proceed to sentence by a schedule read and subscribed by the vicar-general. The bishop then takes the oaths of allegiance to the Crown and of obedience to the archbishops, and makes the declarations of assent to the historical formularies and doctrines of the Church of England; and the vicar-general then reads and subscribes the sentence.[26]

19 Appointment of Bishops Act 1533, s. 3 (amended by CM 1999, s. 5(3)); s. 4: in such a case confirmation is not required, and the Crown nominee is to be invested and consecrated forthwith: HLE par. 184.
20 Briefing for Members of Vacancy in See Committees, issued under the Vacancy in See Committees Regulation 1993 by the Archbishops' Secretary for Appointments (December 2013) 12: i.e. 'the care, government and administration of the Spirituals' of the bishopric.
21 Appointment of Bishops Act 1533, s. 4: this refers to the taking of the oath of fealty at this stage. But it is mentioned again in s. 5 in conjunction with suing for the temporalities: HLE pars. 190, 209. In practice it seems the oath is taken on the occasion of doing homage (par. 191), usually after consecration.
22 Appointment of Bishops Act 1533, s. 4. For letters patent, see *R v Archbishop of Canterbury*, op cit., at 23.
23 HLE par. 186; citing Godolphin 25: this is the archiepiscopal *fiat confirmatio*.
24 *R v Archbishop of Canterbury* [1902] 2 KB 503 and HLE par. 188.
25 Godolphin 25.
26 Can. C13.1: allegiance; C14.1: obedience to the archbishop; C15: declarations of assent; Godolphin 25, 26: the Dean of Arches subscribes the sentence. For fitness and objections, see HLE pars. 186–188.

The 1533 Act makes no provision, at confirmation, for the archbishop to examine or question the fitness of the Crown nominee, unless this is implicit in the use of the word 'confirm'; nor is it possible to compel the archbishop to consider objections to determine their fitness.[27] A person may object on only two grounds: that the election had been defective in some manner of form; or that the individual presented is not the person on whom the Crown's choice fell. If these objections are well-founded, the archbishop may rectify the defect in form.[28] If any person has any other objection to make, or thinks the Crown's choice erroneous, that person must apply at an earlier stage than confirmation – by petitioning Her Majesty not to issue the mandate for the confirmation.[29] The archbishop may issue a citation requiring objections to be delivered to him before the confirmation to be considered at a meeting in chambers.[30] It is doubtful whether the order of these proceedings, in use since 1534, may be departed from.[31]

After confirmation, the bishop-elect is consecrated by the archbishop (or his appointee) with the assistance of two other bishops.[32] If the College of Canons refuses or fails to elect, the archbishop to whom nomination and presentment by the Crown comes must invest and consecrate the person nominated or presented: there is no confirmation.[33] Consecration must be in the statutory form – otherwise it is understood to be invalid.[34] It must be performed on some Sunday or holy day unless for weighty and urgent reasons another day is appointed.[35] After being elected, confirmed, and consecrated and having sued the temporalities of the see out of the Queen's hands in the customary manner, the bishop is installed in the bishopric.[36] The ceremony of installation, within a liturgical setting in the cathedral, is now commonly known as 'enthronement',[37] a term also used in the Canons of the Church of England.[38]

In accordance with a mandate issued by the archbishop, the bishop is introduced into the cathedral church in the presence of a public notary, and placed in the episcopal seat with the customary formula.[39] After the service designed for the

---

27 *R v Archbishop of Canterbury* [1902] 2 KB 503 at 539–540, 562: HLE, par. 187.
28 Ibid. at 510: *per* Cripps KC, Vicar-General.
29 *Dr Temple's Case* (1869) Times, 9 December, *per* Sir Travers Twiss, Vicar-General.
30 *R v Archbishop of Canterbury* [1902] 2 KB 503.
31 HLE par. 188.
32 Can. C2.1: if already in episcopal orders, i.e. for a translation, there is no consecration: Godolphin 29.
33 Appointment of Bishops Act 1533, s. 4 (amended by CM 1999, s. 5(3)).
34 HLE par. 189, n. 5.
35 Can. C2.2.
36 Appointment of Bishops Act 1533, s. 5. For suing of temporalities, see HLE par. 209.
37 HLE par. 140, n. 5: an archbishop is 'enthroned' and strictly speaking a bishop is 'installed': Godolphin 21.
38 Can. C15.2: 'Every archbishop and bishop shall, on the occasion of his enthronement in the cathedral church ... and before he is enthroned, publicly and openly make the Declaration of Assent'; see also Appointment of Bishops Act 1533, s. 5: this uses the formula 'trononysed or installed'.
39 Godolphin 26; special forms of service are designed. In the Canterbury province the mandate is issued to the archdeacon of Canterbury; there seems to be no equivalent official in the province of York: HLE par. 190, n. 3.

occasion, the bishop is conducted into the Chapter House where he receives the customary acknowledgements of canonical obedience, and the notary records the whole matter in an instrument.[40] On installation the bishop is entitled to restitution out of the Sovereign's hands of all the possessions and profits, spiritual and temporal, belonging to the bishopric, and must be obeyed in and may do and execute all such things touching his office as are customary and not contrary to the royal prerogative and the laws and customs of the realm.[41] Later, the bishop is introduced into the Sovereign's presence to do homage for the temporalities by kneeling and putting his/her hands between those of the Sovereign, who sits in a chair of state, and by taking a solemn oath to be true and faithful to Her Majesty, acknowledging that the temporalities are held of the Sovereign.[42] The same rules apply to the election and enthronement of an archbishop.[43]

Cathedral constitutions and/or statutes address enthronement in different ways. At the old foundation Chichester: 'The Bishop, so soon as is convenient after his Consecration or Confirmation, shall be solemnly placed in his Throne in the Cathedral in accordance with the custom of the Cathedral';[44] at Lichfield the bishop is similarly 'solemnly enthroned';[45] at Lincoln, the bishop at 'installation and enthronement shall make the declaration' promising to be 'a faithful pastor and priest to the people of this diocese and cathedral', 'faithfully [to] observe the statutes and customs of this cathedral church', and 'promote such works as may be properly done therein for the service of God and for the benefit of his church'.[46] The rule at Hereford is more detailed:

> Enthronement: The Bishop, as soon as is conveniently possible after his consecration or if already in episcopal orders, the confirmation of his election, shall be solemnly placed in his Throne in the Cathedral, at a Public Service in accordance with the customs of the Cathedral.

Moreover: 'Unless he otherwise elects, the Bishop, when present at services in the Cathedral, shall have the place of dignity and pre-eminence ... Two wax candles shall be lighted at his Throne in accordance with the customs of the Cathedral'.[47]

As to new foundations, for example, at Norwich:

> As soon as possible after his Consecration or (in the event of his being already in Episcopal Orders) Confirmation of his election, the Bishop shall be

---

40 Godolphin 26–27.
41 Appointment of Bishops Act 1533, s. 5.
42 Godolphin 26. See also above n. 21.
43 HLE par. 140: Appointment of Bishops Act 1533, s. 3 (as amended by CM 1999, s. 5 (3)).
44 Chichester: Stat. 5(b). Exeter has a similar formula: Stat. IV.1.
45 Lichfield: Stat. 1(2).
46 Lincoln: Stat. 1(12).
47 Hereford: Stat. IV.1–2: the bishop is conducted to the throne by the dean and the canon-in-residence.

solemnly placed on his throne according to the Custom of the Province of Canterbury and of the Cathedral Church.[48]

And at Winchester, the 'chair' of the bishop is understood as 'the symbol of the Bishop's teaching and pastoral ministry to the Diocese'.[49] As to parish church cathedrals, Manchester is typical: 'As soon as is convenient after his election, the bishop shall be solemnly placed in the bishop's seat in the cathedral church in accordance with the ceremonies of the cathedral church'.[50] By way of contrast, Guildford is untypical: 'The Bishop, as soon as may be convenient after consecration, or (in the event of the Bishop already being in Episcopal Orders) confirmation, shall be solemnly enthroned in the Cathedral'; founded in 1959, there is no reference here to the custom of the cathedral.[51]

The cathedral interviews

The cathedral interviews reveal a range of ideas about the role of the College of Canons in the appointment of the bishop. Among old foundations, for the Dean of Hereford, election by the College is designed to 'provide a positive signal to the Crown's nomination after exploration of the needs of the diocese' as well as 'greater participation in the process'; the 'language of convention' may be used 'to explain the decision of the College' militating against a refusal to elect.[52] The Dean of Exeter considers the function of the College is 'to confirm the candidate as God's elect by means of acclamation rather than by vote', and could not imagine circumstances in which it would refuse to elect.[53] The Dean of St Paul's also adopts, as it were, a 'Calvinist' approach in seeing the candidate as 'the elect'; the process is about affirming the choice and ministry of the crown nominee, an opportunity for 'education' about the whole appointment, and a useful way for the diocese to 'own' its bishop – but the ceremony of confirmation of election should be abolished.[54] However, the Dean of Salisbury could 'envisage' rejection of the crown nominee if the College considers this the right course.[55]

Among the new foundations, at Winchester it was felt that the College 'trusts the process for the Crown appointment of the bishop'.[56] At Rochester the

48 Norwich: Stat. II.2. For Durham, and permission to remove from the cathedral the Conyers Falchion (a sword) customarily used prior to enthronement of the bishop, see CFCE 191 (11) 274–20–10–2011.
49 Winchester: Con. Art. 1, Preamble; and Art. 5.1: 'The Bishop shall have the principal seat and dignity' in the cathedral; for the same rule, see e.g. London: Con. Art. 6.1; Wells: Stat. 1(1).
50 Manchester: Stat. I.4.
51 Guildford: Stat. I.2.
52 Hereford: Dean: Int. 5–8-2016: it rejected nominees in 1847 and 1917.
53 Exeter: Dean: Int. 9–8-2016: for the same view at Wells: Acting Dean: Int. 12–8-2016.
54 London: Dean: Int. 23–9-2016.
55 Salisbury: Dean: Int. 20–9-2016.
56 Winchester: Acting Dean: Int. 16–8-2016.

44 *The episcopal throne*

'expectation' is that College will elect the nominee: 'there would have to be a really morally compelling reason' not to do so. However, it would be useful to have a debate about the possible 'tension' in the process of appointment, that is, the diocesan and the cathedral aspects of the ministry of the candidate; one 'weakness' is that the process does not provide for direct consultation with the College.[57] By way of contrast, for the Dean of Worcester, the election of the bishop by the College is easy 'to smile at', given that one name is presented by the Crown. However, the function of the College must be 'taken seriously'; it comes at the end of a long process, and the College is 'called on to give assent' to the Crown's nomination. When the Dean convened the College to elect the current bishop, he charged the Canons that 'they still have a choice', that they should act 'in good conscience', and that a rejection would have 'moral force'. There is a conventional duty on the College of Canons to decide 'conscientiously'; this is important not least to provide the bishop with 'something positive' in the College's decision of the matter.[58]

At the Henrician foundation at Chester, the College would 'probably not' reject a Crown nominee; though it has a 'real role', it is 'treated as more like a ceremonial function' and, as with any law, 'if we are not using it [i.e. the power to elect or reject] it should be abolished'.[59] Among parish church cathedrals, the Dean of Derby considers that 'given all the opportunity to get the right person' appointed as bishop, 'it is hard to envisage a situation in which the College would have to reject a Crown nominee';[60] and the Dean of Birmingham considers it 'very unlikely' that the College would reject a crown nominee; there is 'hearsay' evidence that the cathedral 'enjoys the pageantry associated with the archaic convention' of election.[61]

The functions of the bishop

As has been the case since the Reformation,[62] the diocesan bishop discharges functions in relation to the cathedral, diocese, national church, and (latterly) Anglican Communion. The bishop is the chief pastor of all within the diocese, laity and clergy, as their father in God, and must teach and uphold sound doctrine, exemplify righteous and godly living, maintain quietness, love, and peace among all, and exercise jurisdiction in the diocese as its Ordinary. The bishop is also principal minister with the right (except over places and persons exempt by law or custom) to: conduct ordinations and confirmations; conduct, order, control, and authorise services; consecrate new churches, churchyards, and burial grounds; appoint clergy to parochial

57 Rochester: Canon Precentor: Int. 30-9-2016.
58 Worcester: Dean: Int. 28-7-2016.
59 Chester: Vice-Dean: Int. 19-8-2016.
60 Derby: Dean: Int. 10-8-2016.
61 Birmingham: Dean: Int. 11-8-2016.
62 Burn I.193: bishops must reside at the cathedral (except e.g. to attend parliament) and (261) on some greater feasts, and in part of lent, and officiate there on chief festivals, Sundays, and lent and advent; Phillimore I.134.

and other offices; hold visitations to obtain good knowledge of the state, sufficiency, and ability of clergy and others; preside at the diocesan synod; provide sufficient priests to minister the word and sacraments; administer discipline; and reside in the diocese, save to discharge extra-diocesan functions.[63] The bishop may also delegate functions to a suffragan or assistant bishop.[64] The bishop is a member of the House of Bishops of the General Synod and a Church Commissioner, and may be on the Archbishops' Council and in the House of Lords,[65] and be involved in the work of the institutions of the Anglican Communion.[66] The Archbishops' Commission on Cathedrals 1994 recommended a fuller involvement of the diocesan bishop in the life of the cathedral, given its place in the diocese, whilst maintaining respect for its autonomy, as well as making provision for an enhanced part to be played in cathedral life by a suffragan bishop or an assistant bishop (see Chapter 1).[67]

With regard to the cathedral, under the Cathedrals Measure 1999:

> The bishop shall have the principal seat and dignity in the cathedral. After consultation with the Chapter and subject to any provision in the statutes, he may officiate in the cathedral and use it in his work of teaching and mission, for ordinations and synods and for other diocesan occasions and purposes.[68]

Cathedral statutes repeat this and underline its significance. At Lichfield: 'all persons holding office or ministering [there] shall render to the Bishop reverent, loyal and ready service'.[69] Ely adds: 'There shall be assigned to the Bishop a chair of state in the sanctuary, the customary Stall in the Choir and the customary Stall in the Octagon'.[70] Norwich's officers or ministers must pay the bishop 'due reverence and render him loyal and ready service';[71] Canterbury echoes this rule adding that on entering and leaving the cathedral 'he shall at all times be escorted by the Dean with the Honour due to the Visitor'.[72] Similar norms exist at Henrician cathedrals,[73] and at some parish church

---

63 Can. C18.
64 A suffragan bishop is one nominated by the bishop and appointed by the Crown to assist with episcopal functions: Suffragan Bishops Act 1534.
65 See generally Hill, op cit., pars. 4.60–4.62.
66 See N. Doe, *Canon Law in the Anglican Communion* (Oxford: Clarendon Press, 1998) Ch. 12.
67 H&R 14; see now CM 1999, s. 5(2): the College of Canons includes every suffragan bishop and full-time stipendiary assistant bishop of the diocese. See e.g. Ely: Con. Art. 12(1).
68 CM 1999, s. 6(1).
69 Lichfield: Stat. 1(1). See also Lincoln: Stat. 1(1): the bishop is owed 'due reverence' and 'loyal service'.
70 Ely: Stat. 17(1). See also Birmingham: Stat. 1(1)-(2); Rochester: Stat. 1(1)-(2); Southwark: Stat. 1(1)-(2).
71 Norwich: Stat. II.
72 Canterbury: Stat. I.1. See also Worcester: Stat. 1.1.
73 Chester: Stat. 1(i): 'due reverence and ... loyal and ready service'; Gloucester: Stat. 1 (1); Bristol: Stat. 1.1.

46   *The episcopal throne*

cathedrals, such as Bradford whose bishop is owed 'due reverence and ... loyal and ready service' there.[74] Newcastle is unusual: 'The community of Christian people in this place, lay and ordained', must 'support the Bishop ... with counsel, prayer and love';[75] and the ministry of the cathedral is part of the bishop's ministry. Also: 'His seat in the Cathedral is a symbolic focus for his teaching, preaching and sacramental work'.[76] Usually, the bishop ranks first in the order of precedence in the cathedral.[77] The bishop has numerous roles in cathedral governance, the appointment, oversight and discipline of its clergy, and liturgy, and other roles explored in later chapters.

The bishop as visitor

The Archbishops' Commission 1994 recommended continuation as to cathedrals of the bishop's 'formal powers of visitation'. On the one hand, they are valuable to enable 'a comprehensive review of the functioning of the cathedral or a specific inquiry into a particular circumstance'. On the other, 'the quasi-legal nature of the visitation process may be felt to impede the desirable relationship between the bishop and dean and chapter'; however, the Commission proposed retention of the power on basis of the good experience of visitation under the Care of Cathedrals Measure 1990. Nevertheless, the bishop should be able to delegate a visitation to the Diocesan Chancellor (president of the Consistory Court), and do so 'whenever a visitation is carried out primarily for legal rather than pastoral reasons'. Whereas, in 'pastoral cases', the bishop should consider whether such review be undertaken by himself assisted by others as appropriate or by a group (consisting of for instance a bishop from another diocese, a dean and an appropriate professional person) reporting to the bishop; following such a review, recommendations might be implemented informally by agreement or become the subject (with or without modification) of an episcopal charge.[78] This distinction was not implemented in Cathedrals Measure 1999.[79]

Under the 1999 Measure the bishop serves as visitor to the cathedral; and its provisions are usually repeated in cathedral constitutions and/or statutes. Council may draw any matter to the attention of the visitor or to the Church Commissioners.[80] Chapter must from time to time consult the bishop as to the general

---

74 Bradford: Stat. 1.1. See also Southwell: Stat.1.1; but Portsmouth: Stat. 1.1 makes no reference to reverence.
75 Newcastle: Con. Preamble.
76 Newcastle: Stat.1.1.
77 E.g. Ely: Stat. 18(i): the bishop ranks first in the 'normal order'; see also e.g. Rochester: Stat. 25.
78 H&R 66–67. See more fully Chapter 1 above.
79 H&R rejected the idea of 'a regular system of inspection of cathedrals' every ten years as potentially over-centralised and bureaucratic. Historically, see e.g. Burn I.263: visitation belongs to the metropolitan of the province; and the king if the archbishopric is vacant; I.261: episcopal visitation. See also Phillimore I.166–174.
80 CM 1999, s. 3(7)(c).

direction and mission of the cathedral, and the bishop may at any time seek the advice of Chapter on any matter.[81] The constitution must provide that the bishop is the visitor of the cathedral.[82] As visitor, the bishop must hear and determine any question arising as to the construction of its constitution and statutes.[83] The bishop may hold a visitation of the cathedral when he considers it desirable or necessary or when requested by Council or Chapter.[84] During a visitation, the bishop may give such directions to Chapter, the holder of any office in the cathedral or any person employed by the cathedral as will, in the bishop's opinion, better serve the due observance of the constitution and statutes.[85] Any person/body on whom functions are conferred by or under the 1999 Measure must act in accordance with any determination or direction of the bishop under that Measure.[86] These provisions on the bishop are without prejudice to the bishop's powers under the Care of Cathedrals Measure 2011 (see below) and his powers as visitor generally.[87]

Whilst most cathedrals merely repeat the rules of the 1999 Measure,[88] some provide fuller norms on visitation and the process to be used. For example, at Carlisle: 'The Bishop shall announce to the Chapter his intention to hold the Visitation at least two months before the said Visitation and shall at the same time cause to be delivered to the Chapter written Articles of Enquiry'. All ministers, lay officers and employees, moreover:

> whose office or employment exists by virtue of the Statutes and is specifically referred to therein are subject to the jurisdiction of the Bishop as Visitor and at the Visitation shall appear, if required, before the Bishop, shall answer any enquiries which he may make and shall if they so desire make representations which he shall note and consider.

---

81 CM 1999, s. 6(2). For Chapter functions, see Chapter 6 below. For the bishop's right to seek the advice of Chapter see e.g. Rochester: Stat. 1(4); Birmingham: Stat. 1(4); St Albans: Con. Art. III; Peterborough: Stat. 2(3).
82 CM 1999, s. 6(3).
83 CM 1999, s. 6(4). See e.g. Ely: Con. Art. 3; and Stat. 1(6); York: Con. Art. III: the archbishop as visitor; Birmingham: Con. Art. 4 and Stat. 1(5); and Peterborough: Con. Art. 3 and Stat. 2(4).
84 CM 1999, s. 6(5). See e.g. Rochester: Con. Art. 4.1; St Edmundsbury: Stat. 1(5); Southwark: Stat. 1(7).
85 CM 1999, s. 6(6). See e.g. Ely: Stat. 1(8); Peterborough: Stat. 2(6); Southwark: Stat. 1(8).
86 CM 1999, s. 6(7). See also Can. C21.2: the dean and residentiaries must take care that 'any matter enjoined by the bishop in his visitation, according to the statutes and customs of the same church, and the ecclesiastical laws of the realm, must be diligently observed'. See e.g. Ely: Stat. 1(9); Birmingham: Stat. 1(8).
87 CM 1999, s. 6(8): i.e. as to matters treated in s. 6(4)-(7). See e.g. Peterborough: Stat. 2(8).
88 Chester: Con. Art. 4 and Stat. 1(v)-(x): 'The Bishop is the Visitor of the Cathedral and shall have all the powers that belong as of right to the office of Visitor'; Durham: Con. Art. 4; Canterbury: Con. Art. 9.

Others employed at the cathedral 'shall appear before the Bishop at Visitations if summoned by him and shall answer any enquiries that he may make'. At the visitation, 'the Bishop shall be accompanied by the Chancellor of the Diocese or some other person learned in the law and shall receive from the Chapter its answers to the Articles of Enquiry whether orally or in writing'. The other norms of the 1999 Measure follow these provisions as to directions, compliance, and proposing changes to the constitution and statutes.[89]

Similarly, Lichfield's bishop has 'the right to hold any Consistory Court in the Cathedral'.[90] When proposing a visitation, the bishop must issue a mandate to the Cathedral Registrar who must immediately issue and serve a summons which must (a) indicate any special issue identified by the bishop for consideration; (b) fix the date and place of it (with at least 10 days' notice unless he directs a shorter period); and (c) be served on the dean, all Chapter and Council members, all non-residentiaries, any whose conduct is to be the subject of inquiry, and any the bishop considers should attend. Anyone served 'shall so attend'. The bishop may be assisted by the Diocesan Chancellor, the Diocesan or Cathedral Registrars, or 'other legal or clerical or lay adviser' as he considers appropriate. Also: 'The Procedure at any Visitation shall be in the discretion of the Bishop', if: (a) all persons summoned must be admitted and a roll taken of those present; (b) the Cathedral Registrar must produce the mandate to the bishop and certify its execution; (c) the bishop must indicate the procedure to be adopted and identify those who must be present at any particular stage; (d) if the visitation relates to the conduct of anyone as to their office, that person is entitled to be heard before the bishop in the presence of those who attend; (e) the bishop must also hear the views of any persons summoned on the issues considered to be expressed in the presence of those attending; and: 'At the conclusion of the visitation the Bishop may deliver any ruling or direction'.[91]

Some cathedrals also provide for referral of disputes to the Visitor outside formal visitation. At Southwark, if a dispute arises between any person holding office in the cathedral and all internal procedures have been exhausted, the dispute, with the agreement of the parties, may be referred to the Visitor who either personally or by a Commissary must hear the parties and must communicate in writing to them and to Chapter, if not a party, decisions 'which shall be final and shall be binding upon the parties'.[92] Similarly, at Guildford: 'Anybody holding an appointment or office under or by virtue of the Constitution or the Statutes and every contract of employment made by the Cathedral' is subject to any procedure for the prevention and resolution of disputes that may be established and varied by Chapter in consulting the bishop; the procedure and any variation of it must not take effect until it has been approved by Council.[93] Interestingly, at Manchester, in addition to the rule in the 1999 Measure that the bishop may determine any question as to the

89 Carlisle: Stat. 1(5)-(12).
90 Lichfield: Stat. 1(7).
91 Lichfield: Stat. XI(1)-(6). See e.g. The Bishop's Visitation Charge to Peterborough Cathedral (January 2017).
92 Southwark: Stat. 1(9).
93 Guildford: Con. Art. 18.

construction of the constitution and statutes, by statute the bishop may also determine 'the lawfulness or interpretation of any by-law'.[94] The role of the bishop as to Council, Chapter and College of Canons is discussed in Chapter 6.

Cathedral ministry

As we see in Chapter 5, the bishop is involved in making appointments to various clerical offices at the cathedral, including that of the dean, residentiary and non-residentiary canons, as well as matters concerning the residence of clergy and their discipline. In addition, the bishop may remove a dean and residentiary for mental or physical incapacity.[95] If satisfied that such action is proper, the bishop may by written notice require that a special meeting of Chapter be summoned to consider and report to him whether in their opinion such dignitary is unable through disability arising from age or infirmity (whether bodily or mental) to discharge adequately their duties, and, if so, whether it is desirable that he should retire from office; a copy of the notice must be sent by the bishop to the dignitary.[96] Chapter must consider the questions put and invite the dignitary and bishop's representative, if any, to confer with it, either together or separately, and make its report in writing, answering the questions put by the bishop. The Chapter must send a copy of the report to the dignitary.[97]

If Chapter reports that it is desirable for the dignitary to retire, the bishop may, within six months of receiving the report, petition the Crown to declare the office vacant (in a cathedral where the dignitary is appointed by the Crown), or execute an instrument declaring the office vacant (when the bishop is patron).[98] If a dignity is also an incumbent of a parochial benefice, a declaration of vacation of his office as dean or archdeacon has the effect also of vacating his benefice, whether the office is annexed to the benefice or *vice versa*.[99] A dignitary who is also incumbent of a parochial benefice, and resigns his benefice or it is declared vacant under the Incumbents (Vacation of Benefices) Measure 1977 (as amended) following a finding of mental or physical incapacity, may be removed from his office as if the report of the provincial tribunal had been a report of Chapter under the Church Dignities (Retirement) Measure 1949.[100] Where an office of a dignitary is

---

94 Manchester: Stat. I.6: the 'decision of the Visitor shall be final'.
95 Church Dignitaries (Retirement) Measure 1949, s. 12. See also CM 1999, s. 7(4).
96 Church Dignitaries (Retirement) Measure 1949, s. 1(1): Chapter must also report on what additional pension provisions might be made. If a Chapter member, the dignitary cannot attend the special meeting: s. 13(5).
97 Ibid. s. 1(3): it must not report that retirement is desirable unless at least two-thirds of the members vote in favour. The dignitary may be assisted by or, in his absence, represented by a friend or adviser: s. 1(4). The bishop may appoint a Clerk in Holy Orders to represent him at the special meeting: s. 1(2).
98 Ibid. s. 2: the Crown vacates by Order in Council; the bishop must record a declaration in his registry.
99 Ibid. s. 14(1).
100 Ibid. s. 14(2): substituted by the Incumbents (Vacation of Benefices) Measure 1977, s. 20(1).

declared vacant, it may be filled in the same manner and with like incidents as if the dignitary were dead.[101]

Cathedral liturgy

Under the Cathedrals Measure 1999 the dean as chair of Chapter has primary responsibility to ensure Divine Service is duly performed in the cathedral.[102] But, as we have seen, the bishop may, after consulting Chapter and subject to any provision in the cathedral statutes, officiate in the cathedral and use it in his work of teaching and mission, for ordinations and synods and for other diocesan occasions and purposes.[103] In addition, the national Canons deal with the bishop in cathedral liturgy and ritual, such as the rule that the ordination by the bishop of priests and deacons must be in the cathedral church of the diocese subject to the discretion of the bishop.[104] Three further examples may be offered of episcopal functions in the Canons.[105]

First, the bishop may, on a request of Chapter and with the dean's consent, by written notice approve the continued use in the cathedral, for a period specified in the notice, of any form of service: (a) the use of which has ceased to be approved by General Synod due to the expiry of any prescribed period or a period of extension which has been granted; or (b) which has been discontinued. If he approves continued use, the bishop may on a request of Chapter with the dean's consent by written notice extend (on one occasion only) the period of continued use for a further period specified in the notice. The period commences on the date the use of the form of service ceases or ceased to be approved by General Synod or on the expiry of the original period of continued use. A Chapter request for continued use must not be made after twelve months following the date the use ceased to be approved by General Synod and the period for which approval is given cannot exceed three years. A request to extend a period of continued use must not be made after the expiry of the original period and the further period must not exceed the original period or two years, whichever is the less.[106]

Second, the bishop may authorise for use in the cathedral forms of service approved by the Convocations, Archbishops and Ordinary for use on occasions for which no provision is made in the Book of Common Prayer 1662 or by General Synod. The forms of service must in words and order be such as are in their opinion reverent and seemly and neither contrary to nor indicative of any departure from Church of England doctrine in any essential matter.[107]

---

101 Ibid. s. 15.
102 CM 1999, s. 7(2) and (3). See more fully below Chapter 3.
103 CM 1999, s. 6(1). See e.g. Birmingham: Stat. 1: when officiating, the bishop may 'determine the ordering ... preach or appoint the preacher and decide the object of the collection'; also London: Con. Art. 6.2.
104 Can. C3.2: or other church or chapel at the discretion of the bishop.
105 Historically, see Burn I.263 (citing Gibson 171).
106 Can. B2.
107 Can. B4.1–3: i.e. approved under Can. B2.

Third, services must ordinarily be said or sung in English. However, forms of service may also be said or sung in Latin in *inter alia* 'other places of religious and sound learning as custom allows or the bishop or other the Ordinary may permit'. This may include a cathedral. The Standing Committee of the House of Bishops of General Synod may approve translations of authorised forms of service for use when the bishop gives written permission for the use in the cathedral (whether as the whole or as part of the service in question) of such an approved translation, subject to such conditions as the bishop may specify, and with the consent of designated bodies depending on the type of cathedral in question, usually on a written application of Chapter with the consent of the dean. In relation to the cathedral church of Christ in Oxford, written application must be made by the dean and the canons.[108]

The cathedral interviews

These reveal several ideas on the role of the bishop at cathedrals, particularly visitations. At old foundation Hereford, there has been no visitation during the tenure of the present Dean who does not 'expect one' because, 'if the Council does its job, there should not be a need for' one: a visitation is a 'blunt tool' which reflects a 'bad situation'.[109] At Salisbury, there was a visitation some twenty-five years ago, but a visitation has the potential to do 'damage' and the Dean would discourage the process.[110] However, as a result of a recent visitation, the Dean of Exeter considers that the absence of norms on the conduct of a visitation in the Cathedrals Measure 1999 and in the cathedral's own constitution and statutes is 'a significant issue' and norms on the process would be 'useful'; for example, the bishop should have a duty to provide 'clear terms of reference for the visitation', give the cathedral adequate time to prepare for it, use a check-list of matters to be addressed, and appoint a panel of suitably qualified people from which visitors may be drawn to represent the bishop in the process.[111]

Among new foundations, Winchester has had no visitation recently; and, while the bishop is 'a useful sounding board', a formal visitation would suggest 'something has gone wrong'.[112] At Worcester, though the annual report provides a review of cathedral life, a visitation could make 'explicit' the jurisdiction of the bishop and point in a 'visible' way to the cathedral as the seat of the bishop – it is not 'helpful' when people claim the bishop may only enter the cathedral with the consent of the dean; but, it is important that the bishop does not intervene in cathedral life on a daily basis – the 'autonomy' of the cathedral is important.[113] But at Rochester a recent visitation

---

108 Can. B42: this also provides for Deaf Church and British Sign Language.
109 Hereford: Dean: Int. 5-8-2016. London: Dean: Int. 23-9-2016: there has been no recent visitation; one 'tends to happen' if there is something wrong.
110 Salisbury: Dean: Int. 20-9-2016: there are 'alternatives', e.g. self-evaluation.
111 Exeter: Dean: Int. 9-8-2016: as might occur in an Ofsted inspection.
112 Winchester: Acting Dean: Int. 16-8-2016: i.e. since 2005. Nor has one occurred at Carlisle: Dean: Email 17–1-2017; Ely: Dean: Email 17–1-2017: a fixed form for a visitation would not be as helpful as the Self-Evaluation Framework produced by the Association of English Cathedrals.
113 Worcester: Dean: Int. 28-7-2016.

addressing a specific issue was not a 'good experience *per se* but necessary and helpful in its outcome'; it should be a 'positive and pastoral' experience.[114]

Among the Henrician foundations, Bristol has had no visitation in the past six years; for the Dean, visitations should be avoided: 'they are a blunt instrument', 'can take a direction no-one intended', and 'give the impression of a breakdown in relations'.[115] At Gloucester, a visitation occurred in 2011 following installation of the new dean; this was an initiative of the bishop;[116] and a visitation took place at Chester in 2010: that national law is silent on the process 'potentially massively hinders the working of the cathedral'; a visitation is perceived as having a 'disruptive' effect and there should be rules to provide greater clarity about the conduct of visitations.[117] No visitation has occurred at parish church cathedral Derby during the tenure of the current Dean who considers the process a 'blunt instrument' which 'would give the impression that something was wrong' at the cathedral;[118] nor has Birmingham had one during the tenure of the current Dean for whom 'visitation happens when something is awry' but 'it would be very welcome for the bishop to adjudicate' if a serious matter arose.[119]

The bishop and enforcement of cathedral care standards

As we shall see in Chapter 9, the Care of Cathedrals Measure 2011 provides for the care of the cathedral church and associated matters. The bishop has an important role to play in this system. The primary responsibility for care rests with Chapter to ensure that necessary repairs and maintenance to the cathedral and its contents and other buildings and monuments are carried out. Chapter is accountable to Council and the bishop as visitor.[120] Applications for proposed work are made to the local Fabric Advisory Committee or to the Cathedrals Fabric Commission for England for approval. If it appears that a Chapter has implemented, or is intending to implement, a proposal without the required approval, the Measure provides a mechanism for enforcement,[121] and the Commission, on which bishops are represented, must advise the bishop and Vicar-General when sought regarding matters of enforcement.[122]

114 Rochester: Precentor: Int. 30–9-2016.
115 Bristol: Dean: Int. 3–8-2016.
116 Gloucester: Chancellor (and Vice-Dean): Int. 4–8-2016.
117 Chester: Vice-Dean: Int. 19-8-2016: visitation should not result in a confidential report.
118 Derby: Dean: Int. 10–8-2016: nor has the bishop suspended any canonry.
119 Birmingham: Dean: Int. 11–8-2016: no canonry has been suspended. Various views were provided by: Carlisle: Dean: Email 17–1-2017: there has been no visitation recently; Southwark: Dean: Email 17–1-2017: there ought not to be fixed norms on the conduct of a visitation as every situation is so different; Wakefield: Dean: Email 24–1-2017: agrees; Liverpool: Dean: Email 21–1-2017: there should be such norms; St Albans: Dean: Email 23–1-2017: there should be such norms including on presenting and handling the findings.
120 CFCE: PGN 1 (2012) 3.1.
121 CFCE: PGN 1 (2012) 8.3.
122 CCM 2011, s. 3(2).

The process involves three incremental stages, each one increasingly severe depending on the gravity of the actual, threatened or apprehended contravention and each precedes the other; thus, the 'preliminary' interview is preliminary to intervention by special visitation.[123] First, the preliminary interview regarding contravention: if it appears to the bishop, of his own motion, on the advice of the Commission, or on the basis of an allegation made by another, that Chapter may have committed, or is intending to commit, an act in contravention of restrictions on implementing proposals for works to the cathedral church or its property,[124] the bishop must, as soon as practicable and before taking any further action, afford Chapter an opportunity of being interviewed in private by him with regard to the matter in question.[125]

Second, if, after having conducted a preliminary interview with Chapter, it appears to the bishop that Chapter has or is intending to commit a breach of restrictions, the bishop must within such period as may be prescribed order a special visitation as to the cathedral church for the purpose of inquiring into the matter; and, if he does so, he must cause a written statement of his reasons for so ordering to be sent to Chapter.[126] It is not necessary for the bishop to order a special visitation if: (a) he is satisfied that Chapter intends to apply for approval of the works; or (b) Chapter has made such an application and it has not been refused; or (c) he considers that there are exceptional reasons for not doing so.[127] Without prejudice to any rule of law as to the effect of episcopal visitations, where a special visitation is ordered by a bishop, Chapter has no power to act as such with regard to the matter under inquiry without the prior approval in writing of the bishop.[128] A special visitation is not to be treated as an episcopal visitation for the purposes of any provision contained in the constitution and statutes of the cathedral church restricting the ordering of such visitations.[129]

If the bishop is satisfied, having regard to the urgency of the matter, that there is insufficient time to hold a preliminary interview, he may from time to time give such interim directions as he thinks fit to Chapter before a preliminary interview.[130] Where a bishop has ordered a special visitation he may from time to time give such directions with respect to the matter in question as he thinks fit to Chapter.[131] Without prejudice to the generality of the powers to give directions, such directions may require Chapter: (a) to take such steps as the bishop may consider necessary to avoid contravention; (b) to refrain from taking such steps as

---

123 CCM 2011, ss. 15, 17: preliminary interview; ss. 16–17: special visitation; ss. 18–20: proceedings for an injunction or restoration order in the court of the Vicar-General; see HLE par. 372.
124 I.e. in contravention of restrictions in CCM 2011, s. 2: see below Chapter 9.
125 CCM 2011, s. 15: subject to s. 17(1).
126 CCM 2011, s. 16(1).
127 CCM 2011, s. 16(2); a 'special visitation' is one under s. 16: s. 32(1).
128 CCM 2011, s. 16(3).
129 CCM 2011, s. 16(4).
130 CCM 2011, s. 17(1): i.e. contraventions of restrictions in s. 2.
131 CCM 2011, s. 17(2).

the bishop may consider likely to lead to contravention; and (c) to take such steps as the bishop may consider necessary to restore the position so far as possible to that existing before the act was committed. Before giving directions, the bishop must seek the advice of the Commission. Directions must be written unless the bishop is satisfied, having regard to the urgency of the matter, there is insufficient time to commit them to writing; if they are given orally he must as soon as practicable commit them to writing. Chapter must comply with the directions.[132]

Third, as a special visitation cannot be ordered without first attempting to resolve matters by way of preliminary private interview, judicial proceedings cannot be taken without first ordering a special visitation. If a bishop orders a special visitation and considers it necessary or expedient to take further steps as to any actual or intended contravention, he may authorise a person designated by him, either generally or in a particular case, to institute proceedings on his behalf against Chapter to obtain an injunction or restoration order or both against Chapter.[133] If a bishop proposes to authorise such proceedings, he must inform the Church Commissioners of the course proposed and the Church Commissioners must, as soon as practicable, decide whether they would be prepared to pay any costs or expenses incurred as to the proceedings and, if so, to what extent, and notify the bishop of their decision.[134]

The Court of the Vicar-General of each of the provinces of Canterbury and York has original jurisdiction to hear and determine these proceedings.[135] If in any such proceedings: (a) the vicar-general is for any reason unable to act; or (b) the cathedral is in a diocese of which the vicar-general is chancellor, then the court must be presided over by a chancellor appointed by the archbishop of the relevant province to act as deputy vicar-general; and a chancellor so appointed has all the powers and must perform all the duties of the vicar-general.[136]

In such proceedings against Chapter, the court may by special citation add as a further party to the proceedings any person who appears to the court to be or to have been concerned in furthering the alleged contravention. A special citation may require that person to attend the court at such time and place as may be specified in the citation. Where it appears to the court that Chapter intends to commit or continue to commit any act in contravention of the restrictions, the court may issue an injunction restraining Chapter or any other party to the proceedings acting in furtherance of the contravention. If it appears to the court that Chapter has committed any act in contravention, the court may make an order (a restoration order) requiring Chapter or any other party to the proceedings to take such steps as the court may consider necessary, within such time as the

---

132 CCM 2011, s. 17(3)-(6).
133 CCM 2011, s. 18(1).
134 CCM 2011, s. 18(2); i.e. prepared to pay under the Ecclesiastical Jurisdiction Measure 1963, s. 58.
135 CCM 2011, s. 19(1); HLE par. 375, n. 12: appeal is to the Arches Court Canterbury or Chancery Court York.
136 CCM 2011, s. 19(2). Proceedings are instituted and conducted in such manner as the Vicars-General of Canterbury and York, acting jointly, may direct: s. 19(3).

court may specify, to restore the position so far as possible to that which existed before the act in contravention was committed. The court may also order that the special visitation from which the proceedings ensued is to continue, on such terms as it considers just, or to cease, and make any further order as it considers just.[137]

The court must seek the Commission's advice before making a restoration order. However, the court cannot make a restoration order as to any act unless satisfied that less than six years have elapsed since the act was committed. But if there has been a deliberate concealment of any fact relevant to the institution of proceedings for the restoration order, time does not begin to run until the bishop discovers the concealment or could with reasonable diligence have done so. Deliberate commission of a breach of duty which is unlikely to be discovered for some time amounts to deliberate concealment of the facts involved in that breach of duty. Failure to comply (absent reasonable excuse) with any requirement of an injunction or restoration order constitutes contempt of court.[138] The cathedral interviews did not address any issues in relation to the special visitation of the diocesan bishop;[139] however, as we shall see in Chapter 9, the matter of the role of the Cathedrals Fabric Commission was addressed.

Conclusion

An episcopal throne, such as the extraordinary one at Exeter, is an architectural expression of the theological idea, implemented in law, that a cathedral is the seat of a bishop. This legal principle is the foundation of a body of particular norms on the admission to and functions of a bishop in a cathedral. The cathedral is directly involved in selection of a diocesan bishop. Its voice is heard on the diocesan Vacancy in See Committee, which communicates diocesan and cathedral needs to the Crown Nominations Commission, on which it is represented. The Commission recommends a candidate to Her Majesty who (by statutory authority) nominates to the College of Canons. College then elects the candidate by means of formal approval in accordance with constitutional convention. The election is confirmed by the archbishops and the process culminates in enthronement at the cathedral. This process reflects diocesan and national interests in the appointment. In and from the cathedral, the bishop discharges a range of functions, many as visitor, in areas including governance, ministry, and liturgy. But the authority of the bishop in these areas is not unlimited. Though there are major areas in which the bishop exercises unilateral discretion (as we shall see in later chapters), the norms also commonly provide for the exercise of this authority in consultation with, or with the consent of, other cathedral persons and bodies, typically the dean, Council and Chapter; and these functions are defined by Measure, Canon,

---

137 CCM 2011, s. 20(1)-(4), (10). For further powers see Ecclesiastical Jurisdiction Measure 1963, s. 81; rules for procedure may be made under the Ecclesiastical Jurisdiction Measure 1991, s. 26.
138 CCM 2011, s. 20(5)-(9).
139 Winchester: Acting Dean: Int. 16–8-2016: no recent special visitation.

and cathedral constitutions and statutes. The bishop also plays a key determinative role in relation to the enforcement of legal standards applicable to the care and maintenance of the cathedral by way of special visitation which may, ultimately, result in judicial proceedings in the court of the vicar-general of the province. The cathedral interviews reveal a range of views about the convention applying to the election of a bishop, as well as for some a desire for the conduct of an ordinary visitation by the bishop to be regulated more fully by legal rules, as occurs in a minority of cathedrals.

3 The font, altar and pulpit: sacraments, worship and mission

As we saw in Chapter 1, under the Cathedrals Measure 1999, a cathedral is understood as a 'centre of worship and mission'. Worship and mission are, in turn, central to cathedral life. The Church of England conducts its public worship in a formal manner: liturgy, the principal means by which worship is expressed and organised, consists of rites and ceremonies, or text and action.[1] Liturgical law both facilitates and orders public worship: it enables enjoyment of the spiritual benefits worship brings and imposes duties to conduct worship in accordance with prescribed forms of service (the principle of conformity); today, many liturgical texts are available for use (in contrast to the historical principle of uniformity, the use of a single Book of Common Prayer). Mission includes proclamation of the Word of God and administration of the sacraments of baptism and Holy Communion.[2] Needless to say, these all involve and express the doctrine of the church – its body of teaching about the Christian faith; and the Church of England has a complex system of rules on the proclamation of the faith, the development of doctrine, and the enforcement of doctrinal standards. In a cathedral, the sacrament of baptism is administered at the font, the Holy Communion at an altar (which may be the high altar or an altar in a side chapel), and the Word of God is proclaimed from the pulpit, lecterns and other reading desks. The font at Durham, with its towering canopy (1663), the high altar and corona at Blackburn (by John Hayward, 1963–1968) and the ornate pulpit at Canterbury (1898) are all particularly noteworthy architectural examples of these.

The sacraments

The Church of England teaches that:

> [T]he visible Church of Christ is a congregation of faithful men, in the which the pure Word of God is preached, and the Sacraments be duly ministered according to Christ's ordinance in all those things that of necessity are requisite to the same.

---

1 HLE par. 750, n. 1: citing *Martin v Mackonochie* (1868) LR 2 A&E 116 at 130.
2 Mission and Pastoral Measure 2011, s. 106: '"mission" means the whole mission of the Church of England, pastoral, evangelistic, social and ecumenical'.

The sacraments ordained by Christ are baptism and Holy Communion and the effectiveness of their administration is not dependent on the worthiness of the minister who conducts them.[3]

The administration of baptism

In 'every church' (including a cathedral) and chapel where baptism is administered, there must be a decent font with a cover (to keep it clean). It must stand as near to the principal entrance as is convenient, unless there is a custom to the contrary or the Ordinary directs otherwise, in as spacious and well-ordered surroundings as possible. The font bowl must only be used for the water at the administration of baptism and no other purpose whatsoever.[4] The nature of baptism is addressed in the multiplicity of modern baptismal rites (which assert its centrality in mission through initiation into the church), and the historical formularies: baptism is a 'sign of Regeneration or new Birth, whereby ... they that receive [it] rightly are grafted into the Church'.[5] Under canon law, by baptism the newly baptised are received 'into Christ's Church', and baptism is a pre-condition for admission to Holy Communion (normally), ordination, and various offices. The church permits infant and adult baptism.[6]

Clergy should seek out candidates for baptism. Due notice normally of at least a week must be given before a child is brought to the church to be baptised, by the parents/guardians. No minister 'shall refuse or, save for the purpose of preparing or instructing the parents or guardians or godparents, delay to baptise any infant within his cure that is brought to the church to be baptised'. If the minister refuses or unduly delays, the parents/guardians may apply to the bishop, who must, after consulting the minister, give such directions as he thinks fit. Refusal may also constitute neglect of duty for which disciplinary proceedings may be instituted. Ordinarily, a minister baptises only those children whose parents reside within his cure of souls: a minister intending to baptise an infant whose parents reside outside the boundaries of his cure must not (unless they are or one of them is on the electoral roll) proceed to the baptism without having sought the goodwill of the minister of the parish in which they reside. The minister of a parish must warn the people that without grave cause and necessity they should not have their children baptised privately at home. But in extreme cases: 'No minister being informed of the weakness or danger of death of any infant within his cure and therefore desired to go to baptise the same shall either refuse or delay to do so'.[7]

---

3 Articles of Religion (1562, confirmed 1571), Articles 19, 25 and 26.
4 Can. F1.1–3.
5 Articles of Religion, Article 27.
6 Can. B21; for baptism as prerequisite for Holy Communion, etc., see e.g. Can. B15A and Can. E.4.1.
7 LFCE 312–314; Can. B22. The duty to instruct does not apply in the case of emergency baptism; for refusals, see *Bland v Archdeacon of Cheltenham* (1972) 1 All ER 1012.

The minister must also instruct candidates 'of riper years' able to answer for themselves in the principles of the Christian religion, and exhort each to prepare 'with prayers and fasting' so they may receive the sacrament with repentance and faith; a person thus baptised must be confirmed by the bishop so soon after as conveniently may be to receive Holy Communion. Baptism is administered validly with the application of water and recital of the words 'I baptise you in the name of the Father, of the Son and of the Holy Spirit'. It is desirable that baptism, an occasional office, is administered on Sundays at public worship when most people come together and for the congregation to witness it in remembrance of their own baptism. Baptism is administered normally by a priest, or, if absent, or when required, by a deacon, and may in an emergency be administered by a lay person. There are also norms to allow conditional baptism if the validity of an earlier baptism is doubted, to regulate the number, qualifications, and responsibilities of godparents, and to register each baptism.[8]

Cathedral constitutions and statutes are generally silent on the administration of baptism,[9] though, unusually, Durham provides that members of the Cathedral Community (see Chapter 4) 'will normally be the only persons eligible to apply to the Dean for the holding of an Occasional Office in the Cathedral'.[10] However, they have 'policies' on who is eligible to be baptised in the cathedral. St Paul's has a 'rule' that Cathedral Community members may have their children baptised there and that this 'privilege is also extended to grandchildren'; moreover, members of the Order of St Michael and St George may have their children baptised in the cathedral's St Michael and St George Chapel.[11] In turn, the Rochester Customary states:

> The following may be baptized in the Cathedral: Members and family members of the Cathedral Foundation; Those who live in the Precinct; Those whose names are on the Cathedral Roll at the time of application; Chapter staff and those who have a special connection with the Cathedral, at the discretion of the Dean and the Canon Pastor.[12]

Among parish church cathedrals, Manchester's published policy provides that the 'normal place for baptism ... is in the local parish churches' where the faith is nurtured and supported: 'It is unusual, therefore, for people to be baptised in the Cathedral'. Baptism in the cathedral occurs 'normally' when the candidate (or parent of an infant candidate): lives in the Residual Parish of the Cathedral; has been a 'regular worshipper' for at least six months and considers the cathedral

---

8 Cans. B21, B23, B24, B28, B39, and B44; see also F11: registers: see HLE pars. 766–774.
9 See e.g. Derby: Stat. 1.4: 'When the Bishop is present at ... Baptism in the Cathedral, having given notice of his intention to be present, he shall normally be the president of the rite'; for a similar rule, see Leicester: Stat. 1(5).
10 Durham: Stat. VII.1.d.
11 London: Policy.
12 Rochester: Customary, 28.1.

their 'home' church; has a 'demonstrable connection' (e.g. as a staff member); or has a demonstrable connection with the Duke of Lancaster's Regiment, whose Regimental Chapel is located in the cathedral. Candidates are asked to attend baptism preparation at the cathedral, usually on a Sunday morning after the Eucharist, or at other times by arrangement; if a candidate is an infant, the parents and, if possible godparents, attend the preparation.[13]

Leicester's 'Baptism Policy and Practice' is a little different – baptism in the cathedral may be arranged for those who: live within the cathedral parish boundaries; or are regular attendees or cathedral community members; or have a strong pastoral reason which will be considered by the precentor (the dean makes the final decision), in which case an applicant is 'required to consult' the parish where they live before baptism in the cathedral is arranged. Those who do not fall into these 'criteria' are encouraged to become part of the Cathedral Community before making a formal request for baptism. There is no fee but the cathedral encourages applicants to make a generous offering in the collection during the service, using wherever possible the Gift Aid envelopes provided.[14] These two approaches are typical,[15] particularly when the cathedral is also a parish church,[16] in which case some policies properly speak of a 'right to baptism' in the church.[17] Southwark expressly provides that this also applies to the baptism of children of same sex couples.[18] It would be useful to have a debate whether the 'privileges' approach of cathedrals and the 'rights' approaches of canon law are consistent.[19]

13 Manchester: Policy: baptisms usually take place on a Sunday at the Eucharist (in line with Can. B21). See above for the baptism of those outside the boundaries of the cure of souls (under Can. B.22).
14 Leicester: baptism normally occurs on a Sunday during the main Eucharist with dates published 6 months in advance; baptism for young people and adults normally occurs as part of diocesan confirmation services.
15 E.g. Coventry: Policy: 'To be baptised [here] you need to be a worshipping member of the community or have strong pastoral reasons for desiring baptism here'.
16 E.g. Chelmsford: Policy: it 'is pleased to baptize those who live within the Cathedral parish, and members of our congregation. Those who live outside our parish should contact their own parish church'; Blackburn: Policy: it is allowed if a parent is a 'regular worshipper' there, has 'a connection', or lives in the Cathedral Parish.
17 Bradford: Policy: 'You normally have the right to baptism, wedding and funeral in the parish in which you are resident. The Cathedral is also a parish church'; if you live in its parish, 'then the Cathedral is your local church. If you live elsewhere then you need either to have some connection with the Cathedral already or to become a member of the congregation. You will also need the goodwill of your local parish priest'.
18 Southwark: Chapter Policy: 'Baptism, admission to Communion and Confirmation for children of same sex couples: The House of Bishops is clear in its guidelines that, "an unconditional welcome should be given to children in our churches, regardless of the structure of the family in which they are being brought up" (par. 24) and ... (baptism) "cannot be refused" (par. 25). Same-sex foster and adoptive parents resident in the parish and/or who are regularly worshipping in the Cathedral, or intend to make it their place of regular worship, are welcome to approach the clergy regarding their children in the same way as all other parents'.
19 The duty to baptise in Can. B22 applies to ministers with a cure of souls (typically parochial); the dean and residentiaries in non-parish church cathedrals do not have a

The administration of Holy Communion

A baptised person may also proceed to confirmation by the bishop laying hands on those who have been baptised and instructed in the faith. Candidates come to the years of discretion and able to say the Creed, Lord's Prayer, and Ten Commandments, and render an account of their faith according to the Catechism, are then presented to the bishop.[20] The Archbishops' Commission on Cathedrals 1994 considered it good practice to hold a follow-up cathedral service for all confirmation candidates six months afterwards.[21] However, cathedral constitutions and statutes are largely silent on confirmation although most provide for its administration in the cathedral at specified times, such as at Easter and Advent, as an exercise of one of the rights of the diocesan bishop.[22] Normally, a person may be admitted to the Holy Communion if baptised and confirmed, or ready and desirous of being confirmed (see below). There is a complex body of canon law on Holy Communion, much of it ancient.[23]

The Church of England teaches that the Eucharist (Holy Communion or Lord's Supper) is a sacrament instituted by Christ. No-one may consecrate and administer the sacrament unless an ordained priest.[24] If present, it is appropriate for the bishop to act as the president. There must be a sufficient quantity of bread and wine for the number of communicants – the bread, leavened or unleavened, made 'of the best and purest wheat flour' and the wine of 'fermented juice of the grape, good and wholesome'; the bread is brought to the communion table in a paten or convenient box and the wine in a convenient cruet or flagon.[25] The elements are ministered in bread and wine 'except necessity otherwise require'.[26] No-one may distribute these unless ordained; lay people may if authorised. At cathedrals, the dean may authorise a person to distribute after obtaining Chapter's consent which may specify conditions. The minister may invite a lay person to read the epistle and Gospel (unless the bishop directs otherwise); also, a minister or lay person, being baptised and a member in good standing of designated churches, may be invited to read Holy Scripture, preach, lead the intercessions, or distribute the eucharistic elements if authorised to perform a similar duty in his own church.[27]

---

general cure of souls (see Chapter 5) but may do so with regard to e.g. residents of the precincts, in which case the 'privilege' approach is questionable.
20 Can. B27.
21 H&R 251, Appendix 6.
22 See e.g. Hereford: Stat. IV.3(b): the bishop may hold confirmations 'on week-days in the Cathedral provided that the dates and times … shall have been agreed with the Dean not less than three months in advance'.
23 Burn I.262 on Canon 24 (1603). See also Phillimore I.135.
24 Articles of Religion, Articles 25 and 28; Book of Common Prayer 1662, 236. That is, in accordance with Can. C1: Can. B12.1. This includes women: Canon B4B. See also Can. C21.1A: cathedral statutes or customs cannot authorise or require a deacon to preside at or celebrate the Holy Communion or pronounce the Absolution.
25 Can. B17. Also: Can. F3; HLE pars. 775–791.
26 Sacrament Act 1547, s. 8.
27 Can. B12; Administration of Holy Communion Regulations 2015; Can. B43: ecumenical participation.

In every cathedral church, Holy Communion must be celebrated, distinctly, reverently, and in an audible voice, at least on all Sundays and other Feast Days, on Ash Wednesday, and on other days as often as may be convenient, 'according to the statutes and customs of each church'; the dean, canons residentiary, and other ministers there must all receive Holy Communion every Sunday at least, unless they have a reasonable cause not to do so.[28] Confirmed persons must receive Holy Communion regularly especially at Christmas, Easter and Whitsun; and adequate public notice must be given of its time and place on feast and fast days.[29] Prescribed classes must be admitted to Holy Communion: (a) members of the Church of England who have been confirmed in accordance with its rites or are ready or desirous to be confirmed or who have been otherwise episcopally confirmed with unction or with the laying on of hands; (b) baptised persons who are communicant members of other churches, which subscribe to the doctrine of the Holy Trinity, and in good standing in their own church; (c) any other baptised persons authorised under regulations of the General Synod; and (d) any person in immediate danger of death.[30] The 'minister shall not without a lawful cause deny the same to any person that will devoutly and humbly desire it, any law, statute, ordinance or custom contrary thereunto in any way notwithstanding'; the person must 'try and examine his own conscience before he shall receive the same'.[31] The law also provides for exclusion.[32]

Children baptised but not yet confirmed nor yet ready and desirous to be confirmed may be admitted to Holy Communion.[33] A diocesan bishop may make a direction that applications may be made in the diocese; the bishop has an 'absolute' discretion and may at any time revoke such a direction.[34] If a direction is in force, a dean of a cathedral may apply to the bishop to permit children to receive Holy Communion in the cathedral; the application must be in writing and accompanied by a copy of a resolution in support passed by Chapter.[35] Before granting it, the bishop

---

28 Can. B13.
29 Cans B15 and B7.
30 Can. B15A.1; see also B15A.3: 'Where any minister is in doubt as to the application of this Canon, he shall refer the matter to the bishop ... or other Ordinary and follow his guidance thereon'. Can. B15A.2: reception.
31 Sacrament Act 1547, s. 8. The duty to admit may be enforced at common law.
32 Can. B16: in cases of a 'notorious offender', in 'open and malicious contention with his neighbours, or other grave and open sin without repentance', the matter is referred to the bishop who directs, but, the minister 'shall not admit' if satisfied that admission will cause a 'grave and immediate scandal to the congregation'.
33 Admission of Baptized Children to Holy Communion Regulations: General Synod 2006 (made under Can. B15A.1(c)); par. 11: 'These Regulations shall apply to a cathedral as if it were a parish', but: (a) any application [under pars. 3 or 7] must be made by the dean, with a copy of a Chapter resolution in support; (b) the obligations imposed on the incumbent under pars. 8 and 9 shall be imposed on the dean of the cathedral concerned.
34 Regulations: par. 3: this is without prejudice to the validity of any permission already granted thereunder.
35 Regulations: par. 4: the children must fall into the categories listed in Regulations: par. 2.

must be satisfied the cathedral has made adequate provision for preparation and continuing nurture in the Christian life and will encourage any child admitted to be confirmed at the appropriate time. The bishop's decision is final, but refusal does not prevent further application, provided one year has elapsed since the most recent previous application was refused.[36] Any permission remains in force unless and until revoked by the bishop. The bishop must revoke it upon receipt of an application for the purpose made by the dean in writing and accompanied by a copy of a Chapter resolution in support. Otherwise, the bishop may only revoke if he considers the conditions specified are no longer being satisfactorily discharged. Before revoking, the bishop must notify the dean of his concerns in writing and afford a reasonable time to respond and, if appropriate, to take remedial action.[37]

Where permission is in force, the dean must not admit any child to Holy Communion unless satisfied that (a) the child has been baptised and (b) a person having parental responsibility for the child is content the child should be admitted. Otherwise, subject to any direction of the bishop, it is within the dean's absolute discretion to decide whether, and if so when, any child should first be admitted to Holy Communion. The dean must maintain a register of all children so admitted, and where practicable record on the child's baptismal certificate the date and place of first admission. If the certificate is not available, the dean must present the child with a separate certificate recording the same details. A child who presents evidence in the form stipulated, must be so admitted, regardless of whether or not any permission is or was in force in that place until revoked. A diocesan bishop may delegate any of his functions here (except that of issuing a direction) to a person appointed by him for the purpose.[38] Some cathedrals have policies on the matter; at Southwark, baptised children of eight or older who are regular worshippers may be admitted; and Coventry admits them 'on a regular basis'.[39]

Cathedral statutes generally provide for its celebration at the cathedral every day; Chester is typical: 'Holy Communion shall be celebrated daily in the Cathedral ... in accordance with the rites and ceremonies of the Church of England as set out in Canon Law'.[40] Provision may also exist for its celebration on Sundays,[41] Good Friday and Easter Eve;[42] and at Southwark: 'There shall in every year be a Corporate Celebration of the Holy Communion upon the Feast of the Visitation of St Mary the Blessed Virgin', unless the bishop after consulting the dean appoints otherwise; the bishop, or, if absent, the dean, or, if absent, the senior available suffragan bishop, is the celebrant; all members of Chapter, College of Canons and Council, and all cathedral ministers, officers and servants 'shall attend ... unless prevented by sickness or

36 Regulations: pars. 5 and 6.
37 Regulations: par. 7: i.e. the conditions under Regulation 5.
38 Regulations: pars. 8–12: the delegate must be a suffragan or assistant bishop or archdeacon.
39 Southwark: Baptism Policy and Practice; Coventry: Policy.
40 Chester: Stat. 21(ii) and (iv). See also Canterbury: Stat. XX.2(2).
41 E.g. Peterborough: Stat. 15(1).
42 E.g. Bristol: Stat. 23(1).

other sufficient reason'.[43] And, for admission to various posts at a cathedral,[44] an 'actual communicant' is one 'who has received Holy Communion according to the use of the Church of England, or a church in communion with it, at least three times' in the preceding year.[45]

Statutes give rights to celebrate and preside at Holy Communion in the cathedral amongst the various classes of ordained minister. First, the bishop: several approaches are used. Among old foundations, Chichester is typical: 'The Bishop shall have the right to celebrate the Holy Communion [and preach or appoint a preacher] at one of the services on Christmas Day, Easter Day and Pentecost as well as the Feast of the Translation of Saint Richard'; at other times, the bishop has the right to do so 'after consultation with the Chapter'. However, at Hereford the bishop must give eight days' written notice to the dean before celebrating Holy Communion, at one of the services on Christmas Day, Easter Day, Ascension Day, Whit Sunday and Trinity Sunday, and at least once each month at one other service held in the cathedral. And at Exeter, the bishop may celebrate Holy Communion in the cathedral on the feasts of Christmas, Easter, Ascension Day and Whitsunday; and, 'having ascertained and taken into account arrangements already made, shall also have the right ... on giving not less than eight days' notice to the Dean, to celebrate Holy Communion therein once a month'.[46]

Various approaches are also used at new foundations. In several, the bishop must give prior notice to the dean. At Durham, for example: 'After ascertaining and taking into consideration arrangements already made, the Bishop shall have the right, upon not less than one month's notice given before each occasion to the Dean (unless the Dean, for any occasion, accepts a shorter notice), to ... celebrate the Holy Communion in the Cathedral at such times as the Bishop may see fit'; and at Canterbury 'The Archbishop shall have the right, after giving reasonable notice to the Dean: to officiate, celebrate the Holy Communion and preach in the Cathedral'. However, at Bristol the bishop may do so 'on such number of occasions during each year as may from time to time be agreed between the Bishop and the Chapter'; and Chapter must ensure that the bishop has the opportunity at Christmas and at Easter.[47]

Similar variety exists at parish church cathedrals. For instance: at St Edmundsbury, after consulting the dean and Chapter, the bishop may celebrate on Christmas Day, Easter Day and Whitsunday, 'and on other occasions during each year'.[48] But at Derby, the bishop may on any principal feast 'provided he has given

---

43 Southwark: Stat. 15.
44 E.g. Winchester: Con. Art. 2.1; Canterbury: Con. Art. 1(2); Bristol: Con. Art. 1(1); Blackburn: Con. Art. 8(1).
45 E.g. Ely: Con. Interpretation. See also Chester: Con. Art. 1; Blackburn: Con. Art. 1; Coventry: Con. Art. 17.1.
46 Chichester: Stat. 5; Hereford: Stat. IV.4: this is cast as a 'right'; Exeter: Stat. IV.2 and 3.a-d.
47 Durham: Stat. I.2.a. See also Chester: Stat. 1(iii); Canterbury: Stat. 2(1); Bristol: Stat. 1(3).
48 St Edmundsbury: Stat. 1(2). See also Birmingham: Stat. 1(3); Coventry: Stat. 1.3. Compare, Southwark: Stat. 1(3): Christmas Day and Easter Day.

not less than four weeks' notice of his intention to do so'.[49] In turn, at Leicester, the bishop may celebrate at 'Christmas, Easter and Pentecost' and, 'by agreement with the Dean', at other occasions; and the bishop 'having given notice of his intention to be present ... shall normally preside'.[50] At Blackburn, the bishop, 'by arrangement with the Dean', may celebrate on Christmas, Easter, and Ascension Day, and Whitsunday and by the same arrangements, 'on such other occasions as the Bishop may desire'.[51] Provision may also be made for a suffragan bishop to celebrate as may be agreed.[52]

Second, statutes confer rights to celebrate Holy Communion on the dean and canons. As to the dean, some specify the occasion. At Rochester, subject to the rights of the bishop, 'The Dean shall have the right to preside at a celebration of the Holy Eucharist once on every Sunday'; and at Peterborough, the dean may do so at the principal Service on Easter Day, Pentecost and all Holy Days.[53] A residentiary canon may have the 'right of celebrating at the Holy Communion',[54] or the 'right of presiding regularly' at it.[55] The right is exercisable: at Canterbury, 'on such days as determined by the Chapter'; at Birmingham, on at least five Sundays in each year; at Coventry, on at least five Sundays annually; at Rochester, on the 'principal Holy Days for which other provision is not made in these Statutes'; and at Peterborough, 'Subject to the rights of the Dean, the Canon in Residence shall have the same right on Sundays'.[56] Occasionally, celebration is a 'duty' or 'obligation' of a residentiary.[57]

Third, other clergy may celebrate or preside, either in consultation with or with the consent of the dean and/or Chapter. At old foundation Hereford: 'The arrangements for the officiants at the celebration of the Holy Communion shall ... be made by the Dean in consultation with the Canon-in-Residence'; and, at Peterborough: 'It shall be the duty of the Chapter from time to time to make by-laws under which opportunity shall be afforded to the Non-Residentiary Canons of celebrating Holy Communion once in every year'.[58] In turn, an archdeacon may celebrate, for example: 'at least once a year' (Chester); 'upon occasions to be determined in consultation with the Dean' (Leicester); on two Sundays each year as arranged by the

---

49 Derby: Stat. 1.3; and Stat. 1.4: 'When the Bishop is present at the celebration of the Holy Communion ... in the Cathedral, having given notice of his intention to be present, he shall normally be the president of the rite'.
50 Leicester: Stat. 1(3)-(5): and: 'At any service at which he is present he shall normally pronounce the blessing'.
51 Blackburn: Stat. 2(2)(i).
52 E.g. St Edmundsbury: Stat. 2(4): agreed with the dean; Derby: Stat. 4.2.
53 Rochester: Stat. XIX(2); Peterborough: Stat. 15(4).
54 Bristol: Stat. 3(2); for the right, see also Durham: Stat. XIII.2.
55 Chester: Stat. 3(ii): a residentiary has the 'right of presiding regularly' (this was deleted in 2016).
56 Canterbury: Stat. X.1; Birmingham: Stat. 3; Coventry: Stat. 3; Rochester: Stat. XIX; Peterborough: Stat. 15.
57 Leicester: Stat. 3(3): duty; Southwark: Stat. 3(1): 'obligation'.
58 Hereford: Stat. V.7: subject to the rights of the bishop under Stat. IV.4; Peterborough: Stat. 15(6).

dean consulting the archdeacon (Birmingham); or on at least one Sunday annually on occasions fixed by the dean consulting the archdeacon (Coventry).[59] An honorary canon may celebrate the sacrament, typically: 'at intervals determined by the Chapter' (Chester); 'upon occasions to be determined in consultation with the Dean' (Leicester); 'on one week in every year', as agreed with the dean (St Edmundsbury); 'when invited by the Dean' (Birmingham); once annually on occasions fixed by the dean (Coventry); or if 'invited by the Dean … on or near the name day of their canonical stall or on any day agreed with the Dean' (Southwark).[60]

Responsibility to provide bread and wine in sufficient quantity for Holy Communion rests with those designated under the cathedral statutes, such as the precentor and sacrist at Bristol; at Chester, the sacrist must each week publish the names of those to preside or assist at Holy Communion, to ensure every priest has his turn in due order, and provide bread and wine in proper kind and quality; and the Chichester Chapter must appoint lay persons of sufficient age and good character to serve at Holy Communion and to assist generally at worship.[61]

The cathedral interviews

The cathedral interviews reveal general satisfaction with norms on baptism and the Holy Communion. However, they disclose that some cathedrals have published baptismal policies but others do not. Among old foundations, whilst it has no published baptismal policy, the 'practice' at Hereford is to baptise the children of, for instance, members of the Cathedral Community; the cathedral seeks to be 'inclusive' in the sense that it aims to 'protect' the parish 'as the proper place for baptism'.[62] Nor does Exeter have a published baptismal policy; but baptism is in practice open to all who come to the cathedral.[63] Wells, similarly, has no published baptismal policy but as a matter of practice 'each case is considered on its merits' – a 'sensitive' approach is used.[64] New foundation Worcester's 'policy' is to baptise in the cathedral only children of those on the Cathedral Community roll or otherwise connected to the cathedral; it is not a contentious issue.[65] Among Henrician foundations, Bristol has no 'published policy' on baptism; however, in practice, there is an 'assumption' that baptism is 'properly' administered in a parish, not in the cathedral, unless (with infants) the intention of parents is to bring up a child 'in the cathedral community'; thus, a request by a former pupil of the Cathedral School for baptism for his child, on the basis of his personal understanding of the cathedral as the 'school chapel', would be refused – the

---

59 Chester: Stat. 6; Leicester: Stat. 4(2); Birmingham: Stat. 4; Coventry: Stat. 4.
60 Chester: Stat. 7; Leicester: Stat. 5(2); St Edmundsbury: Stat. 13(4); Birmingham: Stat. 5; Coventry: Stat. 6.2; Southwark: Stat. 4(2).
61 Bristol: Stat. 7(2); Chester: Stat. 9(ii) (see also Durham: Stat. XXII); Chichester: Stat. 16.
62 Hereford: Dean: Int. 5–8-2016.
63 Exeter: Dean: Int. 9–8-2016.
64 Wells: Acting Dean: Int. 12–8-2016.
65 Worcester: Dean: Int. 28–7-2016.

proper course is to approach the parish in question.[66] As to parish church cathedrals, at Derby too, there is no published baptismal policy, but as a matter of practice the cathedral is clear that parents need to obtain a letter of support from the priest of their own parish: clergy usually grant this; but the cathedral benefits at the expense of the parish in question.[67] Nor is there a published baptismal policy at Birmingham; however, the cathedral would not take away baptisms from other parishes – in point of fact, though: 'we do not ask parish clergy to support a baptism of their parishioners in the cathedral; we do not encourage such baptisms in the cathedral'.[68]

Worship and liturgy

The liturgical law of the Church of England deals with the formation of liturgical texts, or 'forms of service', requires ministers to use only the authorised or approved forms of service, and provides for the conduct of public worship.[69] As well as for the due administration of the sacraments, there are specific canonical norms on 'Morning and Evening Prayer in cathedral churches'; in particular:

> In every cathedral church the Common Prayer shall be said or sung, distinctly, reverently, and in an audible voice, every morning and evening, and the Litany on the appointed days, the officiating ministers and others of the clergy present in choir being duly habited.[70]

This may be a vestige of the monastic heritage of the new foundations, the medieval practices of old foundations, and the collegiate past of some modern foundations.[71]

By national law, Chapter must order cathedral worship.[72] The dean as chair of Chapter has primary responsibility to ensure that divine service is duly performed in the cathedral; and the dean's consent must be obtained with respect to any alteration of the ordering of services in the cathedral.[73] The dean and the residentiary canons of every cathedral, together with the minor canons, vicars choral, and other ministers there, must provide, as far as in them lies, that during the time of divine service in the cathedral all things are done with such reverence, care, and solemnity as shall set forth the honour and glory of Almighty God.[74] In turn, a priest or deacon may officiate in

---

66 Bristol: Dean: Int. 3-8-2016.
67 Derby: Dean: Int. 10-8-2016: the 220 or so parishioners make little claim on baptism; the congregation mostly live outside the cathedral parish and these make more of a claim. As seen above, Can. B22 requires only that the goodwill of the minister with cure of souls must be sought (not obtained): Can. B22.5.
68 Birmingham: Dean: Int. 11-8-2016.
69 For a detailed description, see HLE pars. 730–765.
70 Can. B10.
71 See also: Spiritual Capital (2012) pars. 70–72.
72 CM 1999, s. 4(8)(a)-(b).
73 CM 1999, s. 7(2) and (3).
74 Can. C21.4.

68   *The font, altar and pulpit*

any place in a diocese only after receiving authority to do so from the bishop or other ordinary. However, the dean and residentiary canons may allow a minister to serve within the cathedral, for a period of not more than seven days within three months, without reference to the bishop or other ordinary; they may do so if satisfied either by personal knowledge or good and sufficient evidence that the minister is of good life and standing and qualified under canon law; a minister so allowed must sign the cathedral services register after officiating. No Chapter member is debarred from performing the duties of office and exercising ministry in the diocese merely by lack of authority from the bishop.[75]

Worship under cathedral constitutions and statutes

The Archbishops' Commission on Cathedrals 1994 recognised the centrality of worship in cathedral life, particularly Holy Communion, Morning Prayer and Choral Evensong; it also recommended that each cathedral should regularly evaluate the pattern and content of its worship, with reference to its mission, and give consideration to an imaginative approach to worship, bridging gaps between cathedral and diocese, ecumenical initiatives in worship, and stimulating the creation of new liturgical (and musical) material.[76] In turn, constitutions and statutes of cathedrals recognise the importance of worship. For example, Derby must maintain a daily pattern of corporate prayer and worship, giving glory to God and holding before him the needs of the church and the world, and particularly of the Diocese, City, and County; and at St Paul's 'worship and prayer are at the heart of the Cathedral' and 'life of the Chapter'.[77]

Cathedrals provide for administration each day of the so-called 'statutory offices' of Morning and Evening Prayer.[78] Worcester is typical:

> To the end that prayers and supplications may be offered in the Cathedral Church and that the praise of God may be celebrated with singing and music, it is hereby ordained that the Offices of Morning and Evening Prayer according to the use of the Church of England shall be performed therein daily throughout the year.[79]

At Peterborough, too, they are daily and if cathedral 'resources and other circumstances permit, shall be choral'; and at Chester these and 'all other Services

---

75 Can. C8: the rule also applies to overseas clergy with a licence/permission from the relevant archbishop.
76 H&R 1–13, 37–38, 173.
77 Derby: Con. Preamble; London: Stat. III.1–2. See also Worcester: Renewal and Development (2015) par. 14.
78 Bristol: Con. Art. 1(1): 'statutory service' means the 'daily offices of morning and evening prayer and … Holy Communion'; 'special service' means 'any other service held' there. See also Liverpool: Con. Art. 16.
79 Worcester: Stat. 19. See also Canterbury: Stat. XX.2(1); Carlisle: Stat. 26(1).

shall be conducted in accordance with the rites and ceremonies of the Church of England as set out in Canon Law'.[80]

Cathedral constitutions and/or statutes repeat the duty under the 1999 Measure of Chapter to 'order the worship' of the cathedral,[81] though Exeter adds that Chapter must ensure that a Chapter member or other responsible persons must maintain the worship 'and be available in case of emergency' and (unusually) 'make provision for a rule of life for its members which shall include a pattern of corporate attendance at public worship'.[82] Salisbury assigns such responsibilities thus: except as to matters reserved to Chapter or the precentor, responsibility for services in which the bishop participates lies with the bishop, and for other services with the dean (or if absent, the Canon in Residence); also:

> Any member of the College of Canons shall normally, when taking part in a service in the Cathedral, wear the robes appropriate to that service, and shall occupy the stall ... they have been assigned for that service, unless otherwise permitted by the dean, or in his absence the Canon in Residence.[83]

Chapter's duty under the 1999 Measure is also elaborated at new foundations and parish church cathedrals,[84] as is the rule against the alteration of the ordering of services without the dean's consent.[85]

Similarly, cathedrals often repeat the rule under national law that the primary responsibility for due performance of divine service falls on the dean, as chair of Chapter.[86] However, many embellish the rule. For instance, at Durham:

> It shall be the duty of the Dean [to] ensure that Divine Service is duly performed ... with dignity and reverence at the proper times, that sermons are preached on the appointed days and that special services are held with the approval of the Chapter whenever he may decide that they would tend to the Glory of God and the welfare of His Church.

At Bristol, the dean must 'take care that Divine Service is duly performed in the Cathedral with such reverence care and solemnity as shall set forth the honour and

---

80 Peterborough: Stat. 15(2); Chester: Stat. 21(iv). For a similar norm, see Rochester: Stat. XIX(1).
81 E.g. Chichester: Con. Art. 4e; Hereford: Con. Art. 4(3); Durham: Con. Art. 11(b)(i).
82 Exeter: Con. Art. 5.b.i and ii; and Stat. II.1.
83 Salisbury: Stat. 9.
84 E.g. Winchester: Con. Art. 10.4; Bristol: Con. Art. 10(3)(a); Blackburn: Con. Art. 9 (3); St Albans: Con. Art. V.2.a; Leicester: Con. Art. 11.1.1; Ripon: Con. Art. 9(2)(a); Coventry: Con. Art. 8.4.
85 E.g. Chichester: Stat. 3.d; Durham: Stat. III.3.c; Hereford: Con. Art. 7(4); Bristol: Stat. 16(5); Chester: Stat. 17(iv); Ely: Stat. 11; Canterbury: Con. 10(3)(a); Blackburn: Stat. 10(4); Birmingham: Stat. 8(4); Derby: Stat. 2.
86 E.g. Exeter: Con. Art. 8.b.i; Hereford: Con. Art. 7(3); Chester: Stat. 2(iii)(a); Winchester: Con. Art. 6.3.1; Birmingham: Stat. 2(3); Leicester: Stat. 2(3)(a); Southwark: Stat. 2(3)(a).

glory of Almighty God'; at Canterbury, the dean must ensure that 'at all times of Divine Service all the ministers of the Cathedral Church shall be suitably attired'; at Coventry, the dean must 'take as full a part in it as possible'; and at Hereford: 'The Dean shall be diligent in attending the daily offices in the Cathedral in so far as his other duties reasonably allow'.[87] Some statutes also explicitly incorporate the duty of the dean to uphold cathedral worship in the oath taken on his admission as dean.[88]

Residentiary canons must endeavour to strengthen the corporate worship of the cathedral,[89] and attend divine service and/or officiate. At Durham, they 'shall, unless hindered by some lawful and reasonable impediment be constant in ... attendance at the services' there, and 'be present daily at Morning and Evening Prayer';[90] Hereford requires them to be 'diligent in attendance at the daily offices in the Cathedral', and the Canon-in-Residence must attend 'all daily offices and services' and participate in 'officiating at the daily offices';[91] and at Canterbury, each one 'shall be present at Morning and Evening Prayer unless he is unwell or there is some other unavoidable reason why he should not'.[92] Parish church cathedrals are similar.[93] Provision may also exist for lay and honorary canons to attend services; Bristol is typical: 'Subject to and so far as permitted by law, a Lay Canon may take such part in the Services of the Cathedral Church as the Dean or the Canon in residence may assign to him'.[94] Moreover, regular worship is required for admission to the Cathedral Community Roll.[95]

Cathedrals repeat or embellish the rule under national law that the bishop may officiate at the cathedral. For example, at old foundation Exeter:

> After consultation with the Chapter, and subject to any provision in the Statutes, the Bishop may officiate in the Cathedral and use it in teaching and mission, for ordinations and synods and for other diocesan occasions and purposes.[96]

The bishop must give 'due notice to the dean', and at any such service, has the right 'to determine the ordering thereof' and 'to claim reasonable assistance from

---

87 Durham: Stat. XII.3; Bristol: Stat. 2(3); Canterbury: Stat. XX; Coventry: Stat. 2.3(a); Hereford: Stat. V.4.
88 E.g. Exeter: Stat. V.
89 E.g. Chester: Stat. 3(ii); Blackburn: Stat. 4(2); Leicester: Stat. 3(1); Southwark: Stat. 3(2).
90 Durham: Stat. XIII.4.b and 9.a. See also e.g. Chichester: Stat. 8.a.
91 Hereford: Con. Art. 8.A(9) and Stat. VI.3: unless excused.
92 Canterbury: Stat. IX.2: but not when serving as a Canon in Residence. See also Rochester: Stat. XIX(3).
93 Derby: Stat. 3.4(a): they must be at 'daily worship ... on a regular and frequent basis'; Leicester: Stat. 3(4)(a).
94 Bristol: Stat. 12(3). See also Durham: Stat. XIV.2: lay canons; Blackburn: Stat. 7: honorary canons.
95 E.g. Durham: Stat. VII.1.a; also Winchester: Con. Art. 20.2.1; Chester: Con. Art. 20. See below Chapter 4.
96 Exeter: Con. Art. 7.b. See also Hereford: Con. Art. 6(2).

The font, altar and pulpit 71

the Chapter and its employees'.[97] Similar provisions are found at new and Henrician foundations, such as Bristol, where such a service 'shall be agreed on each occasion' between bishop and Chapter.[98] Likewise at parish church cathedrals,[99] including Blackburn: using his right to officiate (by arrangement with the dean) and determine the ordering (consulting the dean), the bishop may have 'the reasonable assistance of the ministers, officers and staff of the Cathedral' and use vessels, ornaments and equipment, provided that 'no substantial additional expense is thereby thrown on the Cathedral revenues without consultation of the Chapter'.[100] Provision may also exist for the participation of assistant bishops and archdeacons at services held in the cathedral.[101]

By canon law, the ordinations of priests and deacons are held in the cathedral at the discretion of the bishop.[102] For example, at Hereford the bishop has the right

> to hold ordinations on not more than four Sundays in the year and to require the time ordinarily appointed for ... Holy Communion or a daily office to be varied for this purpose provided always that, before the last day of June in any year, he shall have given written notice to the Dean provisionally reserving the specific dates for such ordinations in the year commencing on the following first day of October.[103]

At Chester, the bishop must give the dean 'reasonable notice' before holding ordinations (and confirmations), and has the right to determine the order of service, preach or appoint the preacher, and decide the objects of the collection.[104] Uniquely, at Canterbury, the archbishop has the right, after giving reasonable notice to the dean: to hold ordinations and consecrations (of bishops) at convenient times as often as he thinks fit; to use the cathedral for 'special Anglican Communion, provincial or diocesan services at such times as may be arranged' after consulting Chapter; to nominate the preacher, determine the object of the collection, and require reasonable assistance of the ministers, officers and staff of the cathedral, and determine any special form of service as he thinks fit; and, after consulting Chapter, to appoint a bishop suffragan to undertake any such functions on his behalf.[105]

Chapter may assign the day-to-day administration of or preparation for public worship to a variety of offices. Cathedrals differ as to titles and roles. For example, the Precentor of Canterbury, appointed by Chapter with the dean's consent, must

---

97 Exeter: Stat. IV.2 and 3.a-d. See also York: Stat. III.
98 Bristol: Stat. 1(2). See also Ely: Stat. I(3); Winchester: Con. 5.1; Durham: Stat. I.2.c; Canterbury: Stat. I.2.
99 E.g. Birmingham: Stat. 1(2): after consulting Chapter; Leicester: Stat. 1(2); Southwark: Stat. 1(2).
100 Blackburn: Stat. 2(2)(iii).
101 E.g. St Edmundsbury: Stat. 12.
102 Can. C3.2: or other church or chapel at the discretion of the bishop.
103 Hereford: Stat. IV.3(a).
104 Chester: Stat. 1(iii). See also Carlisle: Stat. 1(3): the right of the bishop to officiate.
105 Canterbury: Stat. I.2(1) and (2).

72 *The font, altar and pulpit*

ensure that the 'statutory Services of the Cathedral Church shall never be left unserved, but that there shall always be present at [them] at least one Minor Canon'; he also has duties as to music (see Chapter 5).[106] Durham must have 'a Succentor who may also hold the office of Sacrist', appointed by Chapter,[107] to: ensure the services 'may be the more reverently and efficiently performed' and that lay clerks, choral scholars, organ scholars and choristers, 'do all things decently and in order'.[108] The sacrist must ensure the cathedral is 'kept clean and decent and in readiness for Divine Service', that other officers/servants 'fully discharge their appointed offices', and arrange 'for the safe custody of all collections until ... paid over, with an account thereof', to Chapter.[109] Bristol's precentor and sacrist (under Chapter) has charge of the books, linen, plate, ornaments and furniture used for worship, and must ensure 'the Cathedral is kept clean and decent and in readiness for the daily services', and that 'all persons engaged in the services duly and fully discharge their appointed duties'.[110] Vergers too play their part.[111]

Vesture worn at the time of divine service is also regulated. Rochester has a particularly full treatment of this. Choir habit is worn on Sundays at Matins and Evensong and on weekdays at Evensong. Bands are worn with choir habit on Sundays, at Evensong on Saturdays, on Holy Days and their Eves, and on all special or official occasions. When copes are specified, bands are not worn. When Morning Prayer and Evening Prayer are said, a cassock is worn by the Canon in Residence or other person leading the Office. At the Eucharist, the president wears a chasuble. The other sacred ministers must wear alb and stole, unless copes are specified.[112] Bradford is less detailed: the dean consulting the residentiaries determines the robes worn by members of the College of Canons (other than those in Episcopal Orders); and at Chelmsford, for example, the lay canons must 'on appropriate occasions when present at services ... wear an academic gown with blue stripe and Chapter badge on the left'.[113]

The Cathedrals Fabric Commission has also issued guidance on liturgy.[114] This encourages each Chapter to prepare a Liturgical Plan, a 'policy framework', and it will usually request a liturgical statement for large scale or complex works

---

106 Canterbury: Stat. XVIII.5. See also St Edmundsbury: Stat. 9: Canon Precentor. See below Chapter 5.
107 Chapter may appoint a lay or ordained communicant of the Church of England or of another Christian church in communion with it. See also Chester: Stat. 8(ii).
108 He may assign (subject, if Chapter so decides, to its approval) periods of duty to the Minor Canons.
109 Durham: Stat. XXII: the Sacrist also has charge of the books and robes used in Choir or elsewhere and must notify the Dean and Treasurer of requirements as to their repair and purchase of replacements.
110 Bristol: Stat. 7(2). Chester: Stat. 9: the Sacrist is to take charge of Service Books (except the music books), linen, plate, ornaments and furniture used for worship; the Precentor and Sacrist are separate offices.
111 See below Chapter 4.
112 Rochester: Customary 2.
113 Bradford: Stat. 16; Chelmsford: Stat. 6(b).
114 Guidance Note (2013): A Liturgical Plan for Cathedrals.

requiring its approval (see Chapter 9).[115] While different cathedrals will have different approaches and requirements, any Liturgical Plan should: start with general theological principles; address what Chapter considers the building should say about the nature of the Gospel and the liturgy; and state what it considers the liturgy says about the building. The Plan should be 'agreed and owned' by Chapter as a 'standing document', reviewed and updated periodically. All those involved in running the cathedral should understand the need for and central purpose of a Liturgical Plan and have the opportunity to comment and contribute to it. It should be written so as to be intelligible and inspiring to the lay professionals and craftspeople involved with cathedral projects.[116]

The cathedral interviews

These underscore the centrality of worship at cathedrals and reveal a general satisfaction with norms and the freedom they afford for the operation of liturgical custom. Among the old foundations, at Hereford, times of services and wearing vesture in quire at them are 'customary'.[117] The Dean of St Paul's sees the planned introduction of a code of practice on liturgy and the bishop's role in it as providing an opportunity 'to stimulate debate and a consensus'.[118] New foundation Winchester has a liturgical plan as recommended by the Cathedrals Fabric Commission, and a pause in the middle of a verse when a psalm is said is encouraged: this is 'our use';[119] and Rochester used to have a practice that extracts from the Rule of St Benedict would be read daily at Morning Prayer – this practice is to be re-instated in the immediate future.[120] At the Henrician foundation at Bristol, the rule under national law that Chapter cannot alter the ordering of the liturgy without the consent of the dean is not invoked in practice, though the Dean wonders what would happen if the 'Dean and Chapter squared up to one another on a matter; the law is a support here'.[121] Among the parish church cathedrals, at Birmingham the recent designing and adoption of a Liturgical Plan was 'a helpful process' in so far as it enabled the cathedral to focus on good practice;[122] and at Derby the time for the Sunday morning service was originally set to work around noise from a local power station – this has since closed, but the 'custom' would be difficult to change.[123] Prayers are also said outside the run of formal services: for example, there is a practice at Ripon for a cathedral chaplain to say prayers from

---

115 Successful schemes of work need to be underpinned by a clear and persuasive liturgical argument.
116 The Plan sits alongside other standing documents, e.g. the Conservation Plan.
117 Hereford: Dean: Int. 5–8-2016.
118 London: Dean: Int. 23–9-2016.
119 Winchester: Dean: Int. 16–8-2016.
120 Rochester: Canon Precentor: Int. 30–9-2016.
121 Bristol: Dean: Int. 3–8-2016.
122 Birmingham: Dean: Int. 11–8-2016.
123 Derby: Dean: Int. 10–8-2016.

the nave pulpit each morning and each afternoon; the texts of the prayers are provided in advance but the chaplain may vary these.[124]

The ministry of preaching

The Reformation generated a substantial body of norms on preaching at cathedrals.[125] Today, in every chapel and church (including a cathedral) there must be provided convenient desks for the reading of prayers and God's word, and, unless not required, a decent pulpit for the sermon, to be set in a convenient place; if there is a dispute, its location is determined by the ordinary – and in every church and chapel 'there shall be for the use of the minister a Bible, including the Apocrypha ... of large size' and 'a convenient Bible to be kept in the pulpit for the use of the preacher', together with a cushion or desk for use at the communion table.[126] It is from these items that the faith is proclaimed and taught by those authorised to do so. In turn, the Church of England has a complex body of national law on doctrine, grounded *inter alia* on Holy Scripture and found in the historic formularies of the church, its development (in the keeping of General Synod), sermons and catechesis, assent to doctrine and discipline.[127]

Preaching at cathedrals

For the Archbishops' Commission on Cathedrals 1994, as 'preaching is a crucial aspect of the mission of cathedrals', so they should have a policy on their preaching ministry capable of extending to public lectures and other methods to present the faith, and take opportunities to teach e.g. the young.[128] The Liturgical Plan should also address how a cathedral fulfils its teaching role.[129] Thus, as a centre of mission, a cathedral must preach the Gospel and nurture Christian learning,[130] and, by Measure, Chapter must promote the mission of the cathedral, and it must from time to time consult the bishop in respect of this missionary task.[131]

By canon law, the dean and residentiaries must preach at the cathedral the Word of God, unless they are otherwise hindered by weighty and urgent cause.[132] And any minister, with a licence from the archbishop to preach throughout the province, or throughout England from the Universities of Oxford or Cambridge, may preach in any diocese within that province or throughout England, without

124 Ripon: Ruth Grenfell, Reader and Chaplain: Int. 26–9-2016.
125 See e.g. Burn I.262: this repeats Canon 43 (1603) on preaching; and I.263 on Canon 51 (1603): preaching by strangers is not permitted without the bishop's approval; this also regulates vesture; Phillimore I.136–137.
126 Can. F6 and F9.
127 LFCE 253–280.
128 H&R 24 and 38.
129 Guidance Note (2013): A Liturgical Plan for Cathedrals.
130 E.g. Derby: Con. Preamble. See below Chapter 7 for education.
131 CM 1999, s. 6(2). See also s. 4(8)(a)-(b). These norms are repeated at e.g. Hereford: Con. Art. 4(3); Durham: Con. Art. 11(b); Leicester: Con. Art. 11.1.1.
132 Can. C21.3.

any further authority from its bishop.[133] The canonical rule that a minister must be licensed to preach by relevant authority is summed up at Carlisle:

> Only a Clerk in Holy Orders of the Church of England or of a Church in Communion therewith, a Reader of the Church of England or other person licensed by the Bishop to preach shall be allowed to preach in the Cathedral unless consent is given by the Bishop and the Chapter.[134]

Cathedral statutes assign rights and/or duties to preach to a variety of classes; and often preaching is dealt with alongside officiating. First, as a bishop may use the cathedral 'in his work of teaching and mission',[135] so cathedral statutes entitle the bishop to preach there and to appoint preachers.[136] The bishop may preach at prescribed services and times after giving notice. Among old foundations, Hereford is a good example:

> The Bishop, provided always that before the last day of June in any year he shall have given written notice to the Dean provisionally reserving specific times and dates for the exercise of such rights in the year commencing on the following first day of October, shall have [prescribed] rights.

These are: to preach at one service on each of Christmas Day, Easter Day and Whit Sunday; and to preach/appoint the preacher at the Chrism service on Maundy Thursday, at ordinations, confirmations, and synods held at the cathedral and at one service on four other Sundays each year.[137] At new foundation Norwich:

> On Christmas Day and Easter Day the Bishop or the Dean shall preach the sermon at the morning Service. On the Sunday after Ascension Day the sermon in the morning shall, according to ancient custom, be preached by the Parker Preacher appointed by Corpus Christi College, Cambridge. For the remainder of the year the Dean shall produce a rota of preachers for Chapter's approval.[138]

Parish church cathedrals use similar norms.[139]

133 Can. C8.2(c).
134 Carlisle: Stat. 26(3).
135 CM 1999, s. 6(1).
136 See e.g. Peterborough: Stat. 2(10): 'At any service or other functions which he holds in the Cathedral, the Bishop may, with due regard to the customs of the Cathedral ... appoint a preacher'; Birmingham: Stat. 1: if the bishop officiates, he may 'preach or appoint the preacher and decide the object of the collection'; for much the same formula, see also Rochester: Stat. 1(2); St Edmundsbury: Stat. 1(2)(b); Southwark: Stat. 1(2).
137 Hereford: Stat. IV.5. See also York: Stat. III; Exeter: Stat. IV.2 and IV.3.a-d; Chichester: Stat. 5.c.
138 Norwich: Stat. XX. See also Ely: Stat. 1(1)-(6), 16; Bristol: Stat. 1(3); Chester: Stat. 1(ii).
139 Leicester: Stat. 1(3)-(5); Coventry: Stat. 1.2 and 1.4; Blackburn: Stat. 2(2)(ii); Southwark: Stat. 1(3)(b).

Second, they also provide rights and/or duties for the dean and canons to preach. Chester has particularly well-developed norms: (1) 'As Holy Scripture contains all things necessary to salvation and the Word of God is a light to our feet, the Dean and Canons shall be careful to teach and expound the Word of God both in the Cathedral and elsewhere as opportunity is given'; (2) the dean must preach a sermon at one of the services on Christmas Day, Easter Day and Pentecost, and may, after consulting the Canon-in-Residence, preach at one of the services on one Sunday in any month other than a month in which one of the three Festivals occurs, or appoint a deputy to preach on any of these occasions; (3) the Canon-in-Residence is responsible for Sunday preaching during his times of residence; (4) Chapter must be careful to give opportunities of preaching, as may be convenient, to the suffragans, archdeacons, honorary canons, chaplains choral and others holding the bishop's licence to officiate in the cathedral; and (5) the consent of the bishop and Chapter must be obtained for a person to preach who is not a cleric of the Church of England or of a Church in communion with it.[140]

Norms at other cathedrals are variations on these themes. At old foundation Chichester the dean has, without prejudice to the bishop's rights, the 'right to preach at one of the services on Christmas Day, Easter Day and Pentecost' and 'to preach or nominate a preacher on two other Sundays in each year'.[141] The dean of new foundation Durham must 'personally, or by deputy appointed by him, preach a sermon at one of the services in the Cathedral on each of the Festivals of Christmas Day, Easter Day, Ascension Day, and Whit Sunday';[142] a residentiary has a 'duty of preaching',[143] and each Canon-in-Residence must personally or by deputy appointed by him with Chapter's consent preach a sermon there every Sunday (except when others like the dean may preach) during their period of close residence, but each residentiary must invite the dean to preach on one Sunday in each year during one of his close residences.[144] Parish church cathedrals have similar norms.[145] For instance, Blackburn's residentiaries have the 'duty of preaching' by arrangement with the dean.[146] Provision may also be made for suffragans, archdeacons and honorary canons to preach;[147] at Portsmouth, for

140 Chester: Stat. 22 (the reference to Holy Scripture was deleted in 2016).
141 Chichester: Stat. 6(e). See also Hereford: Stat. V.6; see also Stat. II.10: the dean may preach 12 Sundays p.a.
142 Durham: Stat. XXXII.2. See also Rochester: Stat. XX(2): the dean must preach or appoint a preacher at whichever of the two principal Eucharists on Easter Day and Christmas Day is not selected by the bishop; the dean must preach or appoint a preacher on 10 Sundays in the year.
143 Durham: Stat. XIII.2.
144 Durham: Stat. XXXII.3. See also Hereford: Stat. VI.4; Bristol: Stat. 3(2); Chester: Stat. 3(ii)
145 Coventry: Stat. 3.2: duty to preach on at least five Sundays annually; Southwark: Stat. 3(1).
146 Blackburn: Stat. 4(1). See also St Edmundsbury: Stat. 7(1); Birmingham: Stat. 3(1); Coventry: Stat. 3.2.
147 Derby: Stat. 4.2: suffragans; Leicester: Stat. 4(2): archdeacons; Chester: Stat. 6: honorary canons.

example, each archdeacon may, after consulting Chapter, preach at a service on one Sunday in each year, and the honorary canons must preach if invited to do so by the dean.[148]

Provisions on preaching at Canterbury are unique, not least for their detail. The archbishop may preach in the cathedral after giving reasonable notice to the dean or may nominate the preacher.[149] Each residentiary canon has the 'duty of preaching' on days determined by Chapter;[150] and the Canon-in-Residence must preach, or procure a substitute approved by the dean, at Sunday Eucharist, unless the statutes provide otherwise – one such Sunday sermon must be preached by the dean, if he so desires, during a period of residence. The dean must preach at the principal Morning Service on Christmas and Easter Day and Whitsunday unless the archbishop desires to do so, in which case the archbishop must preach; but if, on such occasion, the archbishop is absent, he may with the consent of the dean appoint another duly authorised bishop to preach in his stead. On Ascension Day, the Archdeacon of Canterbury must preach, either in person or by a substitute.[151] Moreover: 'There shall be six Preachers in the Cathedral Church, known as "Six Preachers", appointed by the Archbishop from among persons who have outstanding qualities as preachers'; none of them may at the same time be a residentiary or honorary canon; appointment is for five years with re-appointment for a further five-year term but no more; each is to be admitted in the same form as for installation of a residentiary canon, and must retire automatically and without the execution of any instrument of resignation the day they reach seventy.[152] Each is admitted 'according to the customs of the Cathedral', taking an oath to perform and to 'attend upon and increase the welfare and dignity of this Church' and to be 'obedient' to Chapter in all lawful directives.[153]

The cathedral interviews

The cathedral interviews did not disclose any concerns with regard to norms on preaching. Importantly, those cathedral clergy with statutory rights to preach do exercise their rights.[154] Other clergy who may preach are encouraged to – but do not assert their rights to do so.[155]

---

148 Portsmouth: Stat. 4.2 and 5.2.
149 Canterbury: Stat. I.2(2).
150 Canterbury: Stat. X.1.
151 Canterbury: Stat. XXI.
152 Canterbury: Con. Art. 13.
153 Canterbury: Stat. XV.1; XV.2: each is to 'receive a suitable sum for reimbursement of his expenses'.
154 E.g. Worcester: Dean: Int. 28–7-2016: the dean 'regularly' uses his right to do so.
155 E.g. Derby: Dean: Int. 10–8-2016: the dean invites the suffragan bishop and the archdeacons to preach; sometimes they do – but they never seek to assert their rights to do so; Winchester: Acting Dean: Int. 16–8-2016; London: Dean: Int. 23–9-2016: the historic custom was that the canons preached or invited preachers, and the dean did not; so the constitution and statutes were revised to enable the dean to do so.

Conclusion

The administration of the sacraments of baptism and Holy Communion, provision for public worship in the form of divine service (including the administration of Morning and Evening Prayer), and the promotion of the mission of the cathedral in terms of preaching, are the subject of a complex interplay of national law, particularly canon law, and the domestic laws of cathedrals. The use of quasi-legislation is also noticeable in relation to the employment of baptismal policies. As a matter of principle and practice, the administration of baptism is carried out in the parish rather than the cathedral. Holy Communion must be celebrated in the cathedral each day, and there is special provision for its administration on prescribed occasions by the bishop; ordinarily it is administered by the cathedral clergy. Morning and Evening Prayer must be administered daily, and the cathedral clergy are primarily responsible for this. Chapter is to order worship in the cathedral, but the dean has primary responsibility for implementation of this, and Chapter cannot alter the ordering of worship without the consent of the dean. The canons and other officers have particular responsibilities for the preparation and administration of cathedral worship on a day-to-day basis. The vesture designated for use in worship must be worn on prescribed occasions. The Cathedrals Fabric Commission recommends that each cathedral should have a Liturgical Plan. The bishop may use the cathedral from time to time and must in so doing comply with procedures prescribed under its domestic laws to officiate in the cathedral, including the holding of ordinations and confirmations. Reception of Holy Communion and regular attendance at worship are pre-conditions for lay people to be eligible for a variety of cathedral posts. Rights and/or duties to preach are distributed between the bishop, dean, residentiaries or others whose preaching must glorify God and edify the people. The interviews reveal that: not all cathedrals have published baptismal policies, though many cathedrals respect the parishes as the normal places for baptism; there is general satisfaction with norms on worship; not all cathedrals have a Liturgical Plan, but some that do found the creation of the plan a useful exercise; and rights to preach for clergy other than the dean and residentiaries are not greatly exercised.

4 The nave and crossing: the cathedral community, hospitality and outreach

The principal cathedral entrance is usually located in the west façade of the church. Above it, often, is a semi-circular or triangular decorative wall (tympanum), bounded by a lintel and arch which commonly depicts the last judgment: it may symbolise entry into a cathedral as a house of judgment. The nave, from the Latin *navis* (ship), an early Christian symbol, is the main body of the church that runs from the great doors at the west end to the crossing or transept, which forms wings at right angles to the nave as the central space at the meeting-point of the nave, choir (or quire) and transepts, most often lying beneath a central tower.[1] To the north and south of the nave are the aisles, walkways parallel to the nave and beyond it to the choir and sanctuary. The aisles are separated from these spaces by pillars supporting the upper walls or arcade, and, at the crossing, the quire and nave are sometimes separated by a screen or parapet. At the great west door, the visitor is first to experience the hospitality of the cathedral. In the nave people assemble for its exploration or they congregate for worship; historically, the nave was for the use of the congregation (and the chancel and sanctuary for clergy), and for liturgical processions. The crossing is often used for engagement in activities involving wider civil society. This chapter examines norms on the cathedral as a centre of mission – in service, evangelism, and witness: the cathedral community; vergers, volunteers, and visitors; and its ministry of outreach – its pastoral, social, and ecumenical engagement.

The cathedral community

The Archbishops' Commission on Cathedrals 1994 proposed that provision should be made for the cathedral community: 'all those people who are actually involved with the cathedral, not only as regular or habitual worshippers but, for example, as guides, bell-ringers, stewards or in any other regular capacity, including its employees'. They should meet annually to elect up to four representatives to participate in cathedral governance, two if need be known as Cathedral Wardens, to receive reports and raise questions on any matter which concerns the

---

1 The longest nave is that at St Albans, 84 metres (276 feet): S. Jenkins, *England's Cathedrals* (2016) 215.

80 *The nave and crossing*

cathedral; their names should be on a roll and they should have a committee.[2] Provision should also be made for the pastoral care of the cathedral community – dean and Chapter, worshippers, volunteers, and employees – because 'the cathedral community is the place of mutual ministry ... whose mission in the diocese at large will only be truly effective if within its own house there is attention to worship and an exchange of Christian service'.[3] These recommendations were implemented, in various ways, in the Cathedrals Measure 1999.

According to the Measure, each cathedral must have a 'cathedral community' which consists of persons over the age of 16 who regularly worship in the cathedral or are engaged in work or service connected with the cathedral in a regular capacity; the community may also include such other persons as may be prescribed.[4] The constitution of each cathedral that is not a parish church must provide for the formation and maintenance of a roll with the members of the cathedral community who apply to be enrolled as such.[5] The constitution may contain provision either enabling or requiring a committee, 'the Cathedral Community Committee', to be established, consisting of persons on the roll; and for Chapter to delegate functions to it. Any provision enabling or requiring a committee to be established by Chapter may provide that persons who are not Chapter members may be members of the committee.[6]

The cathedral community and cathedral community roll

Some cathedral constitutions simply repeat the Measure definition of cathedral community.[7] Others make use of the rule that the community may also include such other persons as may be prescribed; and they may differ as to who must maintain the cathedral community roll. Various approaches are used. Among old foundations, Chichester's cathedral community roll, maintained by the Cathedral Community Roll Officer appointed by Chapter, adds to the Measure list those persons resident in the Close who apply to be enrolled.[8] Hereford cathedral community consists of those over 16 who regularly worship or serve at or engage in work connected with the cathedral in a regular capacity 'whether as office holders, employees, consultants, volunteers or otherwise or who, in the opinion of the Dean, have given such service to the Cathedral as to qualify for membership'; Chapter must maintain the roll which is to 'be open to inspection at the Cathedral office during normal working hours'.[9] The Exeter roll includes the parents of choristers and pupils at the Cathedral School.[10]

2   H&R 65.
3   H&R 10–12.
4   CM 1999, s. 35(1): i.e. prescribed in the constitution and/or statutes.
5   CM 1999, s. 9(3).
6   CM 1999, s. 10(1)-(2); see HLE par. 354. See below Chapter 6 for other Chapter committees.
7   E.g. Ely: Con. Art. 14(1)-(2); Winchester: Con. Art. 20; Rochester: Con. Art. 16.
8   Chichester: Con. Art. 19. See also Lincoln: Con. Art. 22; and York: Con. Art. XI.
9   Hereford: Con. Art. 21 and 24(1). For a less detailed provision, see e.g. Wells: Con. Art. 12.
10 Exeter: Con. Art. 16. London: Con. Art. 14: there is a review of the roll every five years.

New foundation Durham's cathedral community also includes those 'who normally worship in the Cathedral but are prevented from attendance because they are currently sick or housebound', residents of the College (Durham University), employees of Chapter (including those at the Chorister School), lay clerks, choral scholars, organ scholars, bell-ringers, volunteers (including stewards), and members of the Cathedral Friends' Executive; the roll is renewed every six years with fresh applications required.[11] Canterbury adds 'residents of the Vil of Christ Church', i.e. 'the entirety of the area of land lying within the Precincts',[12] and Carlisle, those 'resident in the Abbey' – and whether someone is a community member is determined by Chapter.[13] Among Henrician foundations, similarly, Peterborough's includes those persons who are resident in the cathedral precincts,[14] and Chester's those 'who hold office linking the holder to the Cathedral';[15] and Bristol Chapter must make 'regulations' to maintain the roll including its annual revision, and prepare a new roll every six years.[16]

The position at parish church cathedrals is more complex but, in many ways, more uniform. Blackburn is typical: the 'cathedral community means persons over the age of sixteen who worship regularly in the Cathedral; or are on the Electoral Roll of the Cathedral Parish of St Mary and St Paul Blackburn; or are engaged regularly in work or service connected with the Cathedral'.[17] Other parish church cathedrals include those 'employed' rather than 'engaged' with the cathedral,[18] or those 'resident in the parish'.[19] The roll must be maintained and revised by Chapter,[20] or Chapter officer: the Cathedral Administrator of Derby must maintain the roll containing 'the names of all those lay persons entered on the Church Electoral Roll who are qualified ... by residence in the parish' or by 'habitual worship' either in the cathedral or at St Mary's Chapel on the Bridge (whether or not also resident in the parish); and those 'engaged in work or service connected with the Cathedral in a regular capacity'; each part of the roll must be revised and a new roll prepared at the same time as the church electoral roll.[21] And at

---

11 Durham: Stat. VII: however, no provision is made for a cathedral community committee.
12 Canterbury: Con. Art. 1(2) and 19: the Cathedral Community Roll is 'the roll of eligible members of the Cathedral Community established and maintained' under Art. 19(1); and Stat. XXXI: election to Council.
13 Carlisle: Con. Art. 17: there is provision for a committee.
14 Peterborough: Con. Art. 1(c).
15 Chester: Con. Art. 20(ii)(c): Chapter must maintain the roll and a new one is prepared every six years.
16 Bristol: Stat. 24(1); see also Con. Art. 14 and Stat. 5(1): Chapter must appoint a Community Roll Officer.
17 Blackburn: Con. Art. 1(1).
18 St Edmundsbury: Con. Art. 15(1); for the same formula see Birmingham: Con. Art. 1(1).
19 Coventry: Con. Art. 14.2.
20 Leicester: Con. Art. 16.1–5.
21 Derby: Con. Art. 13.1–3: these classes represent Parts 1–3 and no person may be transferred from one Part of the roll to another except at the time of annual revision; see also Coventry: Con. Art. 14.1.

Manchester the community includes those 'who hold civic or other offices which are designated for this purpose by the dean as linking the holder to the cathedral'.[22]

Cathedral norms also deal with questions arising as to eligibility for entry on the roll. At Durham: 'If any question arises as to whether a person applying to be enrolled is a member of the Cathedral community, that question shall be determined by the Dean';[23] at Peterborough it is determined by the dean 'whose decision shall be final'; at Worcester by the dean 'with a right of appeal to the Bishop as Visitor'; and at Bristol and Chester by Chapter.[24] Similar diversity is found at parish church cathedrals: any such question is determined at Leicester by the dean and at Coventry 'by the Dean who may consult with the Chapter'.[25] Newcastle, unusually, has the rule that: 'It shall be the responsibility of the Cathedral Community with the Chapter to promote the Cathedral's mission and service to the city and region and to those people who are regular or occasional worshippers or visitors within the Cathedral'.[26]

The cathedral community annual meeting and committee

Cathedral constitutions provide for the annual meeting of the cathedral community, usually chaired by the dean, in order, for example, to elect representatives to Council.[27] The provision under national law that a cathedral may enable or require the establishment of a cathedral community committee, with membership of those on the roll (and that persons who are not on the Chapter may be committee members),[28] is used by most cathedrals.[29] Various approaches are found. As to old foundations, the annual meeting of Chichester cathedral community, chaired by the dean, must 'discuss Cathedral matters and the Church at large' and elect representatives to Council and cathedral community committee. The governance of the cathedral community roll and the conduct of business at the annual meeting and at the cathedral community committee and its membership 'shall be established by a set of Rules' approved by the annual meeting and Chapter; the committee must meet not less than four times each year to advise Chapter on all matters affecting the community and undertake such functions relating to the

---

22 Manchester: Con. Art. XVI.
23 Durham: Stat. VII. See also Hereford: Con. Art. 21; Ely: Con. Art. 14(3); Winchester: Con. Art. 20.
24 Peterborough: Con. Art. 16; Worcester: Con. Art. 11.2; Bristol: Con. Art. 13; Chester: Con. Art. 20.
25 Leicester: Con. Art. 16.3; Coventry: Con. Art. 14.3.
26 Newcastle: Stat. 16; see also Con. Art. 13: the Cathedral Community Forum has 'no legal powers or responsibilities (unless such are delegated to it by Chapter)'.
27 E.g. Chester: Con. Art. 20: 'Members of the Cathedral Roll' must meet at least once each year as the Cathedral Forum which elects members to Council and Chapter: under Con. Art. 13–14 A.
28 CM 1999, s. 10(1)-(2); see HLE par. 354.
29 But there is no provision for such a committee at e.g. Lichfield: Con. Art. 14; and Winchester: Con. Art. 20.

community as Chapter may delegate.[30] Similar norms exist at new foundations: for instance Ely has ten elected by the roll for a renewable three-year term; at Worcester the committee includes one person, chosen by prescribed voluntary groups (e.g. bell-ringers, servers, voluntary choir, pastoral team, visitors' team, and stewardship team) whose name is on the cathedral community roll; and at the Henrician foundation at Peterborough the committee consists of the dean and twelve on the roll, two elected by Chapter and ten by the roll.[31]

Parish church cathedrals also provide for an annual meeting of the cathedral community and committee.[32] In some, Chapter *may* establish a committee.[33] However, in most, Chapter *must* establish one. Coventry is a good example. Immediately following the annual parochial church meeting there must be a meeting of the cathedral community; the dean convenes and presides. The meeting must elect three community members to a committee to serve for three years, and receive and discuss reports and financial statements on cathedral work in the previous year. The committee, known as St. Michael's Committee, is a committee of Chapter consisting of: the dean and residentiary canon; its lay chair; nine elected by and from the cathedral community, who hold office for three years (but are eligible for further such terms); the five cathedral churchwardens; and lay members of the Coventry North Deanery Synod, Diocesan Synod or General Synod. It must advise Chapter on matters affecting the cathedral community, and Chapter may delegate functions to it as Chapter may determine.[34] The Cathedrals Measure 1999 also provides for the cathedral community and persons with experience in connection with the work of a cathedral or the ability to reflect local, diocesan, ecumenical or national interests, to be represented on Council (see below and Chapter 6).[35]

The pastoral care of the cathedral community and others

The Cathedrals Measure 1999 requires the dean to 'secure the pastoral care of all members of the cathedral community',[36] and, whilst it does not include the provision of pastoral care amongst the duties of Chapter, it does oblige Chapter to perform such other functions as are prescribed.[37] On this basis, constitutions and/

30 Chichester: Con. Art. 20–21. See also Wells: Con. Art. 13: Committee; and Salisbury: Con. Art. 18: Forum.
31 Ely: Con. Art. 14(1)-(4); Worcester: Con. Art. 12; Peterborough: Con. Art. 16 and 17.
32 The Church Representation Rules and the Parochial Church Councils (Powers) Measure 1956 have effect in relation to the parish concerned, with modifications: CM 1999, s. 12(4), (5): HLE par. 355.
33 Blackburn: Con. Art. 11; Bradford: Con. Art. 14.
34 Coventry: Con. Art. 14.5 and Stat. 10. See also St Edmundsbury: Stat. 30; Birmingham: Con. Art. 12; Derby: Con. Art. 14.1–5; Leicester: Con. Art. 17.1–8.
35 CM 1999, s. 3(4)(f); see also s. 35(6): elected 'in the prescribed manner' includes a power for the constitution of a cathedral to specify the qualifications for membership.
36 CM 1999, s. 7(2)(d).
37 CM 1999, s. 4(8)(h).

84 *The nave and crossing*

or statutes of cathedrals contain several norms not only on the provision of pastoral care to the cathedral community, by imposing duties on the dean and/or residentiary canons,[38] but also beyond – sometimes a cathedral portrays its ministry as one to the faithful locally; at Birmingham, for example, the cathedral is 'a church which ministers to those who live and work within its parish and to its regular worshippers'.[39]

First, as to the dean, some old foundations simply repeat rule in the 1999 Measure without elaboration.[40] However: the Dean of Hereford must secure 'the pastoral care of all members of the Cathedral Community and where appropriate of visitors to the Cathedral'; the Dean of Exeter 'shall have the cure of souls within the precinct of the Close'; and the Dean of Wells has pastoral care of the cathedral community and of residents of 'the liberty of St Andrew in Wells'.[41] Similarly, some new foundations repeat national law,[42] though at their Henrician foundations the Deans of Bristol and Chester must 'preside over the Cathedral with all diligence and care, as one who watches over the flock committed to his charge' and 'secure the pastoral care of all members of the Cathedral community'.[43] The rule of the Measure is found at most parish church cathedrals,[44] though the Dean of Coventry is required merely to 'seek to secure [their] pastoral care'.[45]

Second, while some old foundations do not list pastoral care in the duties of the residentiary canons,[46] others do: one Hereford residentiary 'shall have particular responsibility for ... the pastoral care of the members of the Cathedral Community and all persons who worship in, serve or visit the Cathedral'; and the Canon-in-Residence must be 'reasonably available to assist with the pastoral care of the Cathedral Community and visitors to the Cathedral'; and Lincoln's residentiaries must 'be concerned with the pastoral care of persons worshipping, visiting or working in the cathedral'.[47] Likewise, among new and Henrician foundations, at Chester:

> The pastoral care of those who live in the precincts of the Cathedral, of those who minister therein, and of those who worship at the Cathedral, shall

---

38 Pastoral care may also be listed among the duties of Chapter; e.g. Leicester: Con. Art. 11.1.3: cathedral community and parish. For the 'cathedral congregation', see Derby: Con. Art. 7.10c; Chichester: Con. Art. 4.e.v.
39 Birmingham: Con. Preamble.
40 Chichester: Stat. 6.d.iv; Exeter: Con. Art. 8.b.iv; Salisbury: Con. Art. 3.3.
41 Hereford: Con. Art. 7(3)(d); Exeter: Stat. VI.3; Wells: Stat. 3(2).
42 Ely: Stat. 3(2)(d); Rochester: Stat. II.3(d); Winchester: Con. Art. 6.3.4; Canterbury: Con. Art. 10(2)(d).
43 Bristol: Stat. 2(1) and (3)(e); for the same formulae, see Chester: Stat. 2(ii) and (iv) (d).
44 E.g. Blackburn: Stat. 3(3); Birmingham: Stat. 2(3)(d); Leicester: Stat. 2(3)(d); Southwark: Stat. 2(3)(d).
45 Coventry: Stat. 2.3(e).
46 See e.g. Chichester: Stat. 8.
47 Hereford: Con. Art. 8.A(7); and Stat. VI.3; Lincoln: Stat. 3(2).

be committed respectively by ... Chapter to its own ordained members or some other Priest approved by the Bishop.

Canterbury residentiaries must be 'concerned' with 'the pastoral care of the Cathedral Community'; and Gloucester's residentiaries with that of 'those who live within property owned by the Cathedral and those on the Cathedral Community Roll'.[48] In parish church cathedrals, the beneficiaries include: at Blackburn the cathedral community or those 'resident or working' in the parish; at St Edmundsbury, 'the Cathedral congregation'; and at Bradford the dean with the consent of the bishop and after consulting Chapter may appoint Assistant Clergy and Honorary Chaplains with duties 'as ... Chaplain to the Cathedral Congregation or Chaplain to the City Centre'.[49]

The cathedral interviews

The cathedral interviews reveal a range of understandings as to the cathedral community, the roll, the committee (if there is one), and pastoral care. Among the old foundations, the Dean of St Paul's considers that the cathedral community roll is 'a pain in the neck' because 'it has no proper function'; the cathedral community (not the roll members) elects representatives to Council – the community has a function but the roll does not: though it serves to keep in touch with regular worshippers, it does not define the community, they are not coterminous – few cathedral staff are on the roll but they are members of the community.[50] Hereford requires the dean to provide pastoral care to the cathedral community and 'where appropriate' to visitors; in practice, the dean also gives pastoral care to residents of the Close; similarly, the residentiaries must provide it to the cathedral community and all who worship there, serve or visit: in practice a Commissioners' Canon does this; a duty chaplain has 'limited duties' to care for visitors.[51] Exeter, similarly, requires pastoral care of the cathedral community, but in practice the dean offers it to volunteers, Close residents, and other cathedral 'communities'.[52]

Among the new foundations, the Dean of Worcester explains that the rules on the cathedral community should be re-visited; the roll operates like a parish roll: 'We struggle with the idea that cathedral community embraces both the regular worshippers and the cathedral staff' (employees and volunteers), some may not be Christians – the two groups are different; the expression cathedral community, therefore, is inaccurate, but 'we are not hampered by it'; the dean has never had to determine who is qualified for the roll. The dean must provide pastoral care for those within his 'cure of souls', which 'implies something permanent and

48 Chester: Con. Art. 16(ii); Canterbury: Con. Stat. X.2(1); Gloucester: Stat. 3(2).
49 Blackburn: Stat. 4(2); St Edmundsbury: Stat. 7(2); Birmingham: Stat. 3(2); Derby: Stat. 3.2. Pastoral care is not a listed duty of residentiaries at: Leicester: Stat. 3; Southwark: Stat. 3; Bradford: Con. Art. 17.
50 London: Dean: Int. 23-9-2016.
51 Hereford: Dean: Int. 5-8-2016: see Con. Arts 7(3) and 8(7) and Stat. VI(3).
52 Exeter: Dean: Int. 9-8-2016; there is also a Canon Pastor (not in the statutes).

thorough' – that is, members of the cathedral community, including worshippers and staff, the latter on the basis that the cathedral is 'a good employer in a Christian ethos'; there is no duty on the dean to provide pastoral care for visitors, though this would be done on 'an *ad hoc* basis if a visitor were distressed' – the Canon-in-Residence (who is sometimes the dean) or day chaplain would provide visitor care.[53] Winchester has no cathedral community committee; such a committee can be a 'mixed blessing' – communication, not committees, is valued.[54] The rule at Rochester that people are not required to be baptised or communicants for admission to the cathedral community roll may reflect the general 'tolerant outlook of the Church of England' and that it should not be 'a window to the soul'.[55] Among Henrician foundations, there is no committee at Chester, but a Forum elects cathedral community members to Council annually; the statutes also provide for the pastoral care of residents of the precincts and those who minister and worship in the cathedral.[56] Bristol has a 'strong conviction' the cathedral community includes those 'who are committed to the cathedral'; there have been no cases where the dean has had to determine eligibility of a person for membership of the cathedral community roll. The dean as 'head of the foundation' has 'oversight' of all aspects of cathedral life, including pastoral care; his role therefore is 'far more than the cure of souls', but rather 'breaking open' the cathedral, which is 'not a club', so that it provides 'a glimpse of the kingdom of heaven for everybody', 'city and diocese', including cathedral visitors.[57]

Among the parish church cathedrals, the Dean of Derby considers that having both the parish electoral roll and the cathedral roll, with an annual general meeting for both constituencies, is something of 'a muddle and a palaver'; nevertheless, the dean uses the cathedral community committee as 'a sounding board' and to access the 'wisdom' of committee members; also, the dean must provide pastoral care to the cathedral community, but as a matter of practice the beneficiaries are the cathedral congregation and the parishioners.[58] And, for the Dean of Birmingham, the annual parochial church meeting is primarily 'about consulting and sharing information'; however, it is difficult for the congregation to see that the cathedral community committee has no authority to decide matters; this can generate 'misleading expectations'.[59]

---

53 Worcester: Dean: Int. 28-7-2016. Carlisle: Dean: Email 17-1-2017: the community rules do not work well; Ely: Dean: Email 17-1-2017: the rules work well 'to a degree' as 'there will always be some frustration in non-parish church cathedrals that the congregation has no place on Chapter'.
54 Winchester: Acting Dean: Int. 16–8-2016.
55 Rochester: Precentor: Int. 30-9-2016: for the roll, see Con. Art. 16; also, Stat. II deals with pastoral care; for the Precentor there is an analogy with the idea of the 'cure of souls', in so far as there is a 'mutuality of care in the community of prayer' and a duty to provide pastoral care.
56 Chester: Vice-Dean: Int. 19–8-2016; Con. Art. 20: Forum; Art. 16(ii): care.
57 Bristol: Dean: Int. 3–8-2016.
58 Derby: Dean: Int. 10–8-2016: there was also a Canon Pastor but this title was changed to Canon Missioner to reflect 'our outward-looking ethos'; the office is not in the domestic law.
59 Birmingham: Dean: Int. 11–8-2016. Southwark: Dean: Email 17–1-2017; Liverpool: Dean: Email 21-1-2017; St Albans: Dean: Email 23-1-2017; and Wakefield: Dean:

Vergers, volunteers and visitors

English cathedrals seek to offer a ministry of hospitality.[60] National law does not explicitly address this. However, their domestic instruments contain a wealth of norms associated with the ministry of welcome. Hospitality is a key feature of legal statements of their purpose. For instance: Leicester Cathedral is a place where 'strangers are given greeting, and pilgrims are spiritually nourished and satisfied'; Exeter practises 'receiving and welcoming visitors'; Winchester offers a 'Benedictine welcome', a place people 'come in times of celebration and sorrow, aspiration and recommitment'; Canterbury has a ministry 'to the many who come as pilgrims, worshippers and tourists'; and at Lincoln: 'The Cathedral as a place of pilgrimage will be vigilant to renew its hospitality and its teaching and learning as essential elements in its community life'.[61] As a result, cathedrals have developed a host of norms which assign the ministry of welcome to a variety of cathedral officers, volunteers, and employees, and which treat the management of visitors. What follows, therefore, deals mainly with vergers, volunteers and visitors;[62] some cathedrals also enable the formation of groups associated with the cathedral to further the mission of the cathedral, including its ministry of hospitality.[63]

Vergers or virgers

Traditionally, a verger (or virger), so called after the staff of office (a verge, from the Latin *virga*, or rod) is a person, usually lay, who assists in the ordering of services.[64] This ancient office has been retained. Norms deal with the office, appointment (by Chapter), functions, and terms and conditions of service. In some cathedrals the appointment is mandatory and in others permissive. At old foundation Exeter:

> Chapter shall appoint sufficient virgers to care for the security of the Cathedral and its contents and to ensure physical preparations for divine service, for concerts and for other events which [it] has decided to hold, or permit to be

---

Email 24-1-2017: the roll works well. Compare: Carlisle: Dean: Email 17-1-2107: the norms do not work well.
60 For the importance of hospitality, see *Spiritual Capital* (2012) pars. 68–69. See also L. J. Francis, J. Annis and M. Robbins, 'The spiritual revolution and the spiritual quest of cathedral visitors', Francis, L. J. (ed.), *Anglican Cathedrals in Modern Life: The Science of Cathedral Studies* (London: Palgrave Macmillan, 2015) 171–187.
61 Leicester: Con. Art. 2.3; Exeter: Con. Preamble; Winchester: Con. Art. 1; Canterbury: Con. Preamble; Lincoln: Con. Preamble.
62 See Chapter 1, introductory paragraph for statistics on cathedral staff.
63 E.g. Exeter: Stat. XVI.1–3: groups and organisations may be formed to further the cathedral's worship and mission with approval of Chapter; each may make its own constitution with 'force' if approved by Chapter.
64 Church of England Guild of Vergers: Guidance: 'Each Verger is at the forefront of the Church's ministry of hospitality, welcome, care (of people, buildings and sacred things) and outreach in one form or another'.

88 *The nave and crossing*

held, in the Cathedral. Virgers may be required to reside in the precinct of the Close in order to be able to perform their duties effectively.

Hereford Chapter may appoint a Head and Assistant Vergers 'on such terms and conditions as it thinks fit'; they have 'the duty of assisting with the mission of welcome to visitors, upholding the dignity of worship in the Cathedral, ensuring the physical preparations for the daily offices and other events [there] and caring for its security'. And Chichester's are 'subject to written agreements on such terms in respect of remuneration and duties' as Chapter determines, 'to uphold the dignity of worship in the Cathedral, to care for its security and cleanliness, as well as to welcome visitors'.[65]

New and Henrician foundations are similar. Gloucester Chapter may appoint a Head and Assistant Vergers, on terms determined by Chapter, 'to uphold the dignity of worship in the Cathedral, to care for its security and to welcome all who enter it', and to be:

> responsible to the Precentor for preparing the Cathedral for services and other events, the care of all items used in or for worship, [its] cleanliness, the provision and completion of all registers, the tolling of the bells and such other duties as the Chapter shall direct.[66]

However, Durham also has norms on the qualifications of candidates for appointment: vergers 'shall be persons of blameless character, sound health, good presence and members of the Church of England or of another Christian church'; the Head Verger and Deputy 'shall keep custody of all collections, donations and other financial charges', under the instruction of Chapter or its officers until 'paid over, with an account' to Chapter. Chapter also may appoint not more than ten Bedesmen to be present as required in the cathedral and 'to render such assistance and maintain order therein or to perform such other duties as the Chapter or its officers may think expedient'; remunerated from cathedral revenues at rates determined by Chapter, they cease serving at 75.[67]

Parish church cathedrals echo some of these norms; for instance: Southwark Chapter may appoint a Head Verger and as many Assistant Vergers as seem necessary on such terms and conditions as Chapter may determine so as to uphold the dignity of worship in the cathedral, welcome all who enter it and care for its security;[68] and St Edmundsbury's vergers 'hold their office and discharge their duties under the direction and control of the Canon Precentor'.[69]

Generally, vergers represent one category of staff discussed elsewhere; for instance: Derby Chapter may appoint suitable persons as voluntary vergers, musicians, bell-

---

65 Exeter: Stat. XIII.1–2; Hereford: Stat. IX; Chichester: Stat. 16: one serves as Sacristan.
66 Gloucester: Stat. 15.
67 Durham: Stat. XXX.1–4 and XXXI.
68 Southwark: Stat. 13. See also Blackburn: Stat. 13; Birmingham: Stat. 11; Portsmouth: Con. Art. 14.5.
69 St Edmundsbury: Stat. 23(1)-(3). See also Newcastle: Stat. 13.

ringers, servers and 'other lay helpers' holding offices and discharging duties at the 'pleasure' and 'direction' of Chapter.[70] Some parish church cathedrals also provide for cathedral churchwardens, in addition to their parish churchwardens.[71] For example, Leicester must have two cathedral wardens elected by the annual meeting of those on the cathedral community roll; they must be 'members of the Church of England who are actual communicants' and at least 21 years of age; they hold office until the conclusion of the next annual meeting but are eligible for further terms;[72] they are admitted by the dean or other Chapter member to: ensure collections are taken as agreed with the dean; promote the regular giving of money by the community; and undertake any other duties as Chapter decides after it has consulted them.[73]

Volunteers and employees

Cathedrals rely heavily on volunteers and employees. The Archbishops' Commission 1994 recognised a need for the 'rationalisation of management structures' and professionalisation; all staff should have 'clearly defined functions' within a 'structure of accountability'.[74] As to employees, the Commission recommended: job descriptions and person specifications for all heads of departments and senior staff posts; procedures to appoint and manage lay staff with contracts of employment and annual appraisal; training in specific skills and induction; and regular meetings.[75] As to volunteers: roles should be defined; they should be made aware of the spiritual aspects of their tasks; a Chapter member and appropriate department head should be involved in recruiting; training should exist for each volunteer activity; volunteers should be incorporated into the professional management of the cathedral and have appropriate lines of accountability and reporting; volunteer co-ordinators should be appointed; written instructions/guidelines for each volunteer group should be published; and all nurtured.[76]

The 1999 Measure is largely silent on these matters, beyond recognising that the cathedral community includes those engaged in work/service connected with it in a regular capacity and the Church Commissioners may make grants from their general fund for the payment of the salary or other emoluments of any lay person employed in connection with the cathedral.[77] However, some cathedrals have structure-principles within which employees or volunteers function. First, they

70 Derby: Stat. 11.2. See also Manchester: Stat. XIII.
71 E.g. Southwark: Stat. 14(1)-(4) and 17; St Edmundsbury: Con. Art. 5(1)(d); and Derby: Con. Art. 10.1(f) and 10.4: Council includes the two churchwardens of the parish; each serves for one year; and Stat. 11.3.
72 Leicester: Con. Art. 15.5 and 16.4–5; see also Art. 7.4: a Cathedral Warden, if not appointed Canon under Article 7.3, is an Honorary Canon *ex-officio* and ceases to be such on ceasing to be a Cathedral Warden.
73 Leicester: Stat. 7.
74 H&R 9; see also Chapter 7: Management Structure and Process.
75 H&R 113, Rec. 1–9 (Ch. 9, pars. 6, 9–12, 14–15, 17, 18–20, 26, 27, 32, 36–7, 40–42).
76 H&R 114: Care and Training of Volunteers (Appendix to Ch. 9).
77 CM 1999, s. 35(1); see also s. 4(8)(h) and s. 23: Chapter may carry out other prescribed activities.

encourage Christian teamwork. For example, Exeter seeks to build up 'the common life of those who work and worship at the Cathedral; encouraging all people associated with [it] to achieve their God-given potential'; Salisbury Chapter with the consent of the bishop may decide, 'in relation to employees and volunteers, which posts in the service of the Cathedral are to be filled by those who profess the Christian faith'; at Lincoln a 'volunteer' is one whose name is on 'the roll of volunteers'; and at Liverpool a 'cathedral employee' is one employed by it or by 'a company owned beneficially by the Cathedral'.[78]

Second, structures: for instance, Chichester Chapter must 'ensure a management structure in support of the Cathedral's mission which establishes clarity of purpose, responsibility, authority and accountability for all ... clergy or lay staff, paid or volunteer'.[79] It encourages volunteers to be recruited into their specific areas of expertise; the visitor services officer is responsible for their overall co-ordination;[80] and staff appointed by Chapter are listed in the statutes, Chapter making additional appointments as required.[81] As well as staff specified in the constitution (in accordance with the 1999 Measure) and statutes, Chapter may appoint 'additional staff and consultants' as required from time to time subject to written agreement upon such terms as may be determined by Chapter – these include: the chapter clerk; legal advisers; Chapter architect; consultant archaeologist; clerk of works; Chapter accountant; visitor services officer; education officer; gardeners, cleaners and maintenance staff.[82]

Third, therefore, the appointment of volunteers and employees is in the keeping of Chapter. For instance, at Winchester, as well Chapter officers prescribed under the Cathedrals Measure 1999 (see below Chapter 6): 'Chapter shall appoint such other officers, staff and voluntary helpers as necessary to assist it in the Mission and Ministry of the Cathedral'; and Chapter must consult the heads of staff and volunteer sections from time to time.[83] Similarly, at Durham:

> [T]he Chapter shall appoint and have, where necessary, the power to terminate the appointment of all ministers, officers and servants [and] determine their conditions of service in respect to emoluments, tenure and duties and may enter into written agreement with the persons so to be appointed.

Peterborough Chapter may appoint volunteers to such duties as Chapter may determine and reimburse expenses necessarily incurred in discharging those duties;

---

78 Exeter: Con. Preamble; Salisbury: Stat. 17; Lincoln: Con. Art. 1; Liverpool: Con. Art. 16.
79 Chichester: Con. Art. 4.e.ii.
80 Chichester: Stat. 22.
81 Chichester: Con. Art. 17.
82 Chichester: Stat. 21.
83 Winchester: Con. Art. 19: they are members of the Foundation; Art. 10.4.9: this mirrors Chichester.

and, unusually, Leicester Chapter must 'further the welfare' of stipendiary and voluntary staff.[84]

National guidance on volunteers has been issued by the association Cathedrals Plus. This deals with their appointment, training, functions and management, insurance, grievances, and data protection in civil law and it recommends that a cathedral has a Volunteers Handbook.[85] Gloucester, for instance has a Volunteers' Welcome Handbook that deals with the Statement of Vision, organisational structures, how the cathedral is funded, health and safety, protecting children, and confidentiality. Volunteer 'duties' include requirements to: undertake training; wear a sash, tabard, badge or robes on duty; display loyalty, dignity and respect to the cathedral, colleagues and visitors; follow cathedral procedures; and be a good ambassador and avoid conduct detrimental to its reputation and work. Volunteers may discuss issues with designated persons and they have discounts on refreshments at the cathedral coffee shop.[86]

As seen earlier, provision may also exist for representation of employees and volunteers on Council, and they are subject to the directions of the bishop at visitation.[87] Moreover, some cathedrals enable staff and others to associate in guilds,[88] or to join an order associated with the cathedral.[89] For example, at Manchester admission to the Order of William Temple is to honour long and distinguished service to the church in Manchester; it may be bestowed by the bishop 'primarily' on members of the Church of England 'although in principle, it may be open to members of any church, at the discretion of the bishop'; there are norms on induction and annual gathering, and the bishop may invite members to a special dinner or other event, if possible, annually.[90] Some cathedrals provide for their staff to come together on a named day annually in order to worship together. For example, at Carlisle, on Trinity Sunday or nearest convenient Sunday all cathedral members and officers – the dean, Chapter members, bursar and Chapter clerk, master of music, surveyor to the fabric, assistant organist, lay clerks, choral scholars, choristers and vergers, and all other salaried employees – 'shall be present at a service in the Cathedral and thereafter at a place appointed and in that place shall answer each one to his name unless for special reasons the Dean has excused his attendance'.[91]

---

84 Durham: Stat. III.1; Peterborough: Stat. 12(1)-(2); Leicester: Con. Art. 11.1.9: this repeats CM 1999, s. 6(6).
85 Cathedrals Plus: Volunteers – Standards Document (2014).
86 Gloucester: Volunteers' Welcome Handbook (2015).
87 For visitation see Chapter 2.
88 E.g. Southwark: Stat. 16: Chapter may establish guilds and delegate functions to them; the dean is a member of each; membership is approved by Chapter; its chair is appointed by Chapter after consulting guild members.
89 E.g. St Edmundsbury: Stat. 31: after consulting Chapter, the bishop may confer on anyone, whose life has demonstrated exemplary and unusual service, the Order of St Edmund.
90 Manchester: Stat. XVI.
91 Carlisle: Stat. 11(4).

92 *The nave and crossing*

Visitors and public order

The Archbishops' Commission on Cathedrals 1994 recognised the importance of 'tourism' for cathedrals. Good practice included: a visitor centre; a ministry of welcome with guides and chaplain; leaflets; tours; a bookshop (which may include the treasury); a designated area for private prayer;[92] and an enquiry centre for those wishing to know about the Christian faith staffed by trained people.[93] In turn, cathedrals should: help visitors ask questions about their experience; explain the architectural elements; demonstrate the Christian values of the community; ensure their staff are aware of the impact of their corporate service; treat tourism as 'an aspect of hospitality and witness'; and exercise professional care which as far as possible enables each visitor to make the best use of time.[94] Therefore, cathedrals should: ensure staff and volunteers are inspired to a corporate witness; introduce continuous counts of visitors; improve their marketing; review visitor facilities; appoint a visitor officer if possible; give visitor management high priority; examine the issue of charging; and provide free access to a part of the cathedral for prayer and for those who seek pastoral solace and support.[95]

National law does not address matters such as these. However, cathedrals do have hospitality norms. Salisbury Chapter must have 'such arrangements as it shall consider appropriate for the welcome, guidance and education of visitors'; at Hereford the 'needs of … visitors in terms of welcome, pastoral care, explanation and hospitality are part of the concern of the Cathedral Community'; and Chichester has a visitor services officer, a suitably qualified person (with a written agreement) responsible 'for the arrangements for visitors … as well as the co-ordination of volunteers who work for the Cathedral'.[96] Winchester Chapter must make appropriate arrangements for the provision of a 'refectory, information and other services for visitors whether in return for payment or otherwise', and for employing suitable people for these purposes; and Worcester Chapter must review the quality of welcome for visitors, level of participation available to the disabled or infirm, and guidance to those unfamiliar with services; and it must ensure the vergers' team is properly staffed, funded and resourced.[97]

The Cathedrals Measure 1999 requires the dean to 'maintain good order and proper reverence in the cathedral';[98] vergers also have duties in this regard under cathedral constitutions and statutes (see above); and, by Canon, churchwardens must maintain order and decency in the church, especially during the time of divine service, and must not suffer it to be profaned by any meeting for temporal objects inconsistent with its sanctity; and they may with reasonable force remove

92 H&R 252–253, Appendix 6.
93 H&R 31–32.
94 H&R 33–37. See above for cathedral norms on the pastoral care of visitors.
95 H&R 39, 150–151, 184. See also *Spiritual Capital* (2012), pars. 8 and 45.
96 Salisbury: Stat. 13; Hereford: Con. Preamble; Chichester: Stat. 21.g.
97 Winchester: Con. Art. 1; Stat. 19; Worcester: Renewal and Development: A Strategic Vision for Worcester Cathedral 2015–2020 (2015) pars. 18–19, 57 and 69ff.
98 CM 1999, s. 7(2)(c). This is repeated in e.g. Coventry: Stat. 2.3(d); Durham: Stat. XII.3(iii).

any person to this end.[99] It is a criminal offence: to commit riotous, violent or indecent behaviour, during divine service or any other time, in any certified place of worship, churchyard or burial ground; to molest, let, disturb, vex or trouble, or by any other unlawful means disquiet or misuse, any preacher duly authorised to preach, or any person in holy orders ministering or celebrating any sacrament or divine service, right or office; to obstruct, by threats or force, any cleric in or from celebrating divine service or officiating in a place of worship; and to strike, or offer any violence to, any cleric engaged in any of these rites or duties.[100] Cathedral security (including Cathedral Constables) is addressed in Chapter 10.

The cathedral interviews

These indicate that norms on vergers, employees, volunteers, and visitors generally work well. As seen in the previous section, cathedral constitutions, statutes, or practices provide for the pastoral care of visitors. However, various other practices are adopted.[101] Among old foundations, as to the rule at Salisbury that cathedral employees should profess the Christian faith (see above), 'we assume all [such] cathedral roles could be occupied by atheists', but the rule means that employees are asked to accept living by 'the values of compassion, integrity and accountability' – 'people respond and accept this'.[102] At new foundation Worcester the verger is employed but the functions of that office may be 'custom';[103] and at Henrician Gloucester, 'in practice' the Chancellor is responsible for the 'Visitor Experience' and provides such care for volunteers and visitors;[104] and at Chester volunteers 'must sign a volunteer agreement' which the cathedral 'enforces': 'it has dismissed volunteers who have failed to sign them or to comply with them'; the 'role description' for 'welcomers' provides that they are 'not to engage in pastoral care': they are not trained in this; visitor chaplains serve on 300 days each year; and the precinct has a priest vicar as does the congregation – these are usually retired clergy.[105]

Among the parish church cathedrals, 'daily chaplaincy' arrangements at Ripon are interesting and perhaps typical. By statute, (lay) readers may be licensed by the bishop to 'support the Cathedral clergy in preaching and in pastoral duties under the supervision of the Dean or of a person in Holy Orders nominated by the Dean'.[106] An interview with a Reader-Chaplain reveals that in practice chaplains are recruited from clergy and readers; Chapter calls for volunteers; and after

---

99 Canon E1 and F15; for removal, see HLE par. 284.
100 Ecclesiastical Courts Jurisdiction Act 1860; Offences Against the Person Act 1861, s. 36; Criminal Law Act 1967, s.1.
101 See below Chapter 7 for visitors and education.
102 Salisbury: Dean: Int. 20-9-2016.
103 Worcester: Dean: Int. 28-7-2016.
104 Gloucester: Chancellor and Vice-Dean: Int. 4-8-2016: the Chancellor was responsible for the Volunteers' Handbook (see above) which was approved by Chapter.
105 Chester: Vice-Dean: Int. 19-8-2016.
106 Ripon: Stat. VIIIB.

Disclosure Barring Service checks, they are appointed 'on an informal basis'. The chaplain provides what may be described as a ministry of 'loitering with intent'; 'we do not bowl up to people and impose ourselves; a light passing greeting usually provokes a response indicating whether a visitor would like a chat, a deeper talk or prayer, when we might remove to a side chapel'. The chaplain: is 'not to advise but to hold', 'to pick up what is important to people – sometimes they need a word'; wears a badge without a name – 'intimate anonymity' is important as a 'bridge between the lay and clerical staff'; says prayers from the pulpit at 11.00 am and 3.00 pm; serves on a rota; at the end of duty, 'writes up notes on what has happened'; uses a handbook provided, 'to know the parameters', e.g. on 'abusive visitors' or inappropriate conduct by volunteers; reports matters, exercising 'judgment', to a canon or the verger; and meets the other chaplains twice each year.[107] For the Canon who co-ordinates daily chaplaincy:

> [I]t is vital that a cathedral always offers itself as a potential place of encounter with God, as a sacred space. Our chaplains contribute to that by their presence, witnessing to a spiritual dimension as well as to the Christian faith.[108]

The ministry of outreach

Cathedrals have a long tradition of outreach to the wider community, including charitable work, civic functions, meeting need locally and regionally (e.g. supporting local agencies concerned with deprivation, day centres, and residential accommodation),[109] and ecumenical initiatives.[110] To this end, the Cathedrals Measure 1999 requires Council to further and support the evangelistic, social and ecumenical work of the cathedral, reviewing and advising on its direction and oversight by Chapter and, in particular, to consider proposals submitted to it by Chapter in connection with its mission, and to give advice on this to Chapter.[111] It is left to cathedral constitutions, statutes, policies, and guidelines to implement these provisions.

The responsibility for outreach

Outreach appears in the legal lists of cathedral objects. Parish church cathedral Coventry is 'a centre of ... outreach'; Birmingham serves 'the civic life of the City ... in close collaboration with the other city-centre churches'; Derby must

---

107 Ripon: Ruth Grenfell, Reader and Chaplain: Int. 26-9-2016; for the verger, see Stat. XI.
108 Ripon: Canon Wendy Wilby, Co-ordinator of Daily Chaplaincy at Ripon Cathedral: Email 6–10–2016.
109 H&R 29–30: examples are given, e.g. lunch clubs for older generations, and schemes for the homeless.
110 H&R 251, Appendix 6: best practice includes encouragement of ecumenical services.
111 CM 1999, s. 3(6)(a).

'engage with the city and the county, with corporate life and institutions'; and St Edmundsbury defines itself as 'an Anglican presence in the County of Suffolk and the wider community'.[112] Old foundation Hereford's ministry includes: 'Service to the City of Hereford and to the communities of Herefordshire and South Shropshire, which see the Cathedral as a spiritual centre and a setting for large events'.[113] And new foundation Winchester ministers to 'the City, County and Diocese, and the wider community', and people come to it 'in times of celebration and sorrow, aspiration and recommitment'; and, as such, Chapter must 'build relationships' with other organisations that 'share common beliefs, values and aspirations' for the 'well-being of the wider community'.[114]

Second, Chapter officers participate in outreach. At Derby, the dean must promote 'the ministry of the Cathedral in the community' and residentiaries its 'usefulness' in the diocese; Winchester's residentiaries must promote its 'engagement … in … the wider community', and Rochester's in 'civic communities'.[115] Sometimes, similar duties are assigned to lay members of Chapter.[116] A particularly interesting arrangement is found at Winchester: Chapter may appoint 'a lay person of recognised distinction as High Steward' committed to promoting cathedral welfare and willing to undertake 'an ambassadorial role both regionally and nationally in service of the Cathedral as one of the great icons of faith for the nation'; the appointment is for a renewable five-year term; the honorary office confers no vested rights.[117]

Third, honorary canons may be appointed with responsibility for mission.[118] St Albans is typical: persons who have given 'distinguished service to the Diocese or to the Cathedral' may be appointed by the bishop as honorary canons; they must contribute to the corporate life of the cathedral and promote its 'mission and work within the diocese'.[119] Exeter's honorary canons are appointed by the bishop after consulting the dean, Council and College of Canons on such terms as the bishop determines and are 'to promote the mission of the Church in Devon in partnership with the Bishop, the Diocese and the Cathedral'; they are not members of the College of Canons; the bishop determines the number after consulting the dean; however, they 'shall have no formal duties, but shall be invited to join the Cathedral Foundation at occasions designated by the Dean after consultation with the Bishop'.[120] Winchester's bishop may appoint an Extra-Diocesan Honorary Canon 'in recognition of that person holding some office/position in the Church of

112 Coventry: Con. Art. 1.1; Birmingham: Con. Preamble; Derby: Con. Preamble; St Edmundsbury: Con. Mission Statement.
113 Hereford: Con. Preamble.
114 Winchester: Const. Art. 1: Preamble; and Art. 10.4.10.
115 Derby: Stat. 2.3(a): dean; Stat. 3: residentiaries; Winchester: Stat. 6.3; Rochester: Stat. III (1).
116 Durham: Stat. XIV.2; Chester: Stat. 3(i); Peterborough: Stat. 5(2).
117 Winchester: Stat. 18: the term is renewable for a further period(s) of five years.
118 For historical antecedents, see Phillimore I.187.
119 St Albans: Con. XI.1.d; Leicester: Con. Art. 7.1: they must promote 'its mission and service' in the diocese.
120 Exeter: Con. Art. 12; Stat. IX: they are installed after taking the prescribed oath.

96 The nave and crossing

England or in a Church in communion therewith or of their being a person of distinction'; the office is held for a renewable term of five years.[121] Norwich may have up to twenty-four honorary canons appointed by the bishop after consulting Chapter from beneficed or licensed clergy with distinguished service in the diocese or cathedral; they must contribute to the cathedral's corporate life and mission.[122]

Fourth, the bishop may appoint lay canons to contribute to mission.[123] Norms differ as to the numbers permitted and qualifications required. Of parish church cathedrals, Blackburn is typical: there must be no more than 20 lay canons appointed by the bishop who have given distinguished service to the diocese or cathedral and are actual communicant members of the Church of England or of a church in communion with it; they must 'seek to contribute to the corporate life of the Cathedral and to promote its mission and service in the diocese'; they vacate office automatically and without execution of any instrument of resignation at the age of 70.[124] Old and new foundations have similar norms: at Exeter candidates must be actual communicants;[125] at Salisbury, communicant members of the Church of England (and the bishop may after consulting Chapter appoint lay (or clerical) persons, who profess the Christian faith or others as agreed by bishop and Chapter, as Sarum Canons);[126] and at Rochester the bishop may appoint consulting the dean actual communicants as lay canons.[127]

The representation of the wider community in cathedral institutions

The Cathedrals Measure 1999 provides that there may be appointed to Council not less than five nor more than ten persons appointed in the prescribed manner, being persons having experience with the work of the cathedral or the ability 'to reflect local, diocesan, ecumenical or national interests in that connection'.[128] Cathedrals implement this in various ways: Chichester Council has eight such persons appointed by the bishop and Chapter jointly; Durham has seven (ordained or lay) appointed by Council after consulting the bishop; Exeter has ten appointed by the bishop consulting Chapter, Bishop's Council, Standing Committee of

---

121 Winchester: Con. Art. 8.4–5; 8.12: the Diocesan Secretary is an additional Honorary Canon or Lay Canon.
122 Norwich: Con. Art. VI: they must vacate their position at the age of 70 (but may continue if the bishop permits) or if they lose their status as beneficed or licensed clergy. See also Canterbury: Con. Art. 12.
123 CM 1999, s. 9(1).
124 Blackburn: Con. Art. 8(1)-(3); Art. 13(1): lay canons are members of the College of Canons. See also St Edmundsbury: Con. Art. 12(1)-(2); Birmingham: Con. Art. 8(1); Derby: Con. Art. 6.5.
125 Exeter: Con. Art. 11.c and e. See also Hereford: Con. Art. 8C(1).
126 Salisbury: Con. Art. 9 and 10: they are not canons for the purpose of the CM 1999.
127 Rochester: Con. Art. 7.4–7. See also Chester: Con. Art. 8.
128 CM 1999: s. 3(4)(f). See Chapter 1 for cathedral representation on Diocesan Synod and General Synod.

Diocesan Synod and other appropriate bodies; and Peterborough has one appointed by the Bishop's Council and Standing Committee of Diocesan Synod, and one by the Diocesan Board of Finance.[129] Council may also include suffragan bishops,[130] archdeacons,[131] area deans,[132] and clergy.[133] Chapter and College too may include parish and other clergy.[134]

As to representation from civic life, some new foundations merely repeat the formula in the Measure whilst other have lists of specific appointees.[135] For example, Ely Council includes: one person with experience of local government appointed by the bishop after consulting the Lord Lieutenant of the County of Cambridgeshire and representatives of County and District Councils; and one appointed by the national church Appointments Commission. Rochester Council has one person appointed by the bishop after consulting the Lord Lieutenant of Kent, and three appointed by the bishop after consulting the Chairman of Kent County Council and Mayors of boroughs and councils in the Diocese. Chester Council has one person appointed by the bishop after consulting the leader of the Cheshire and West Chester Council, one appointed by the Trustees of the Friends of Chester Cathedral and one by the Council of the University of Chester. And the Peterborough Council includes individuals from the City of Peterborough appointed by the bishop after consultation with the Mayor of Peterborough.[136]

Parish church cathedrals are much the same. For example, Bradford Council has one person appointed by the bishop consulting the Chief Executive of the City of Bradford Metropolitan District Council, and one appointed by West Yorkshire Ecumenical Council. Manchester Council has ten persons including one appointed by the bishop after consulting the Lord Lieutenant of Greater Manchester, one after consulting the Lord Mayor of Manchester, one appointed by the Bishop's Council and Standing Committee of Diocesan Synod, one appointed by Greater Manchester Churches Together, and one elected by the Manchester Cathedral Visitor Centre Trust. Interestingly, at St Edmundsbury, the Council includes eight persons, appointed by the bishop, dean and Council chair consulting each other and Chapter 'after paying due regard to local, county and national issues, including, but not exclusively, those of an ecclesiastical, ecumenical, social, cultural, agricultural and commercial nature'.[137]

---

129 Chichester: Con. Art. 3; Durham: Con. Art. 10; Exeter: Con. Art. 4; Peterborough: Con. Art. 14.
130 E.g. Coventry: Con. Art. 7.1; Derby: Con. Art. 11.1.
131 E.g. St Albans: Con. Art. IV.1.f.
132 E.g. Birmingham: Con. Art. 14(1)(f).
133 E.g. Rochester: Con. Art. 12.1.6; Chester: Con. Art. 14(i)(g)(i): a rural dean.
134 E.g. Derby: Con. Art. 11.1: archdeacons. See more fully below Chapter 6.
135 E.g. Carlisle: Con. Art. 11(1): there is no list of episcopal appointees. See also Salisbury: Con. Art. 5.
136 Ely: Con. Art. 11(1); Rochester: Con. Art. 12.1.6; Chester: Con. Art. 14(1); Peterborough: Con. Art. 14(1).
137 Bradford: Con. Art. 15; Manchester: Con. Art. X(1); St Edmundsbury: Con. Art. 4(1)(g).

The ecumenical activity of cathedrals

As seen above, the Cathedrals Measure 1999 provides that there may be appointed to Council persons with experience in cathedral work or the ability to reflect 'ecumenical ... interests'.[138] Cathedrals use this permissive rule but they differ as to the appointing body, candidate qualifications, and constituencies from which they are drawn. The following are typical: Ely Council has one person appointed by the Cambridgeshire Ecumenical Council and resident in the diocese; Rochester has one person appointed by Chapter 'to reflect the ecumenical involvement of the Cathedral' and one by the bishop 'to reflect the ecumenical involvement of the diocese'; Canterbury has one person appointed by Churches Together in Kent; Coventry Council includes 'one person appointed by an ecumenical body covering all or part of the Diocese designated for this purpose by the Bishop'; and at Blackburn the Council includes one person who is appointed by the Council of Churches Together in Lancashire.[139]

Cathedrals also enable the appointment of ecumenical canons. Durham is a good example. The bishop, consulting Chapter, may appoint an ecumenical canon for such term of years as the bishop determines. The candidate must be 'a person of learning who shall be a lay person or a person who has been ordained to the ministry of the Word and Sacraments in a Church to which the Church of England (Ecumenical Relations) Measure 1988 applies'.[140] The ecumenical canon holds a cathedral dignity and office but not an office or a canonry for the purposes of the Cathedrals Measure 1999; the office attaches to a Chair in Anglican Studies at Durham University.[141] The person is admitted by the bishop, installed by the dean, and on admission must make the prescribed Declaration. The canonry is held during the tenancy of the university chair; if guilty of grave misconduct, negligence, or inefficiency, the bishop may remove the canon after having given that person 'sufficient opportunity of showing reason to the contrary' and having 'regard as to what is reasonable in the circumstances'.[142]

In turn, at old foundation Hereford, the bishop may with Chapter's consent appoint not more than four ecumenical companions, members of churches outside the Anglican Communion, to perform 'some function' which the bishop and Chapter believe or desire to be connected with the Cathedral and diocese. They do not occupy a stall, hold any vested interest, nor have a voice or place in Chapter (unless members of it), but must take part in such services as may lawfully

---

138 CM 1999: s. 3(4)(f).
139 Ely: Con. Art. 11(1); Rochester: Con. Art. 12.1; Canterbury: Con. Art. 5(1); Coventry: Con. Art. 7.1(j); Blackburn: Con. Art. 12(1)(f).
140 Church of England (Ecumenical Relations) Measure 1988, s. 5: the Measure applies to any Church so designated by the Archbishops of Canterbury and York acting jointly; it must be a church which subscribes to the doctrine of the Holy Trinity and administers the sacraments of baptism and Holy Communion and one to which the Sharing of Church Buildings Act 1969 applies at the time of designation.
141 Durham: Con. Art. 7(b); Stat. XV.5: it attaches to the Michael Ramsey Chair of Anglican Studies with such tenure, residence, emoluments and terms as the bishop sets with the consent of Chapter and University.
142 Durham: Stat. XV.6–8.

be agreed with and by Chapter. The appointment is a five-year term renewable by the bishop with the consent of Chapter and it ceases if they cease to perform such functions or on expiration of the term without execution of an instrument of resignation.[143] Among the Henrician foundations, for example Bristol may have not more than ten ecumenical prebendaries appointed by the bishop, after consulting Chapter, from members of churches outside the Anglican Communion, to have some office or function which in the bishop's opinion is connected with the cathedral; the title confers no vested interest and its holder is not by virtue of that title a canon under the Measure or a member of the College of Canons. The person is presented by the bishop and installed by the dean or vice-dean; an ecumenical prebendary may take such part in services as the dean or Canon-in-Residence may lawfully assign, must occupy such stall as Chapter may allot and, when occupying it, 'shall be suitably attired'.[144]

Amongst the modern foundations, Guildford is typical: 'to further ecumenical relations' the bishop, after consulting Chapter and Council, may appoint up to four ecumenical associates and may appoint such an associate as a member of the Foundation. The candidate must be a person whose appointment, in the bishop's opinion, 'is likely to contribute to the maintenance of good ecumenical relations with other churches or religious bodies or organisations' in which they must have 'good standing'; and if appointed a member of the Foundation, they may also be appointed an honorary canon; the person is appointed for 'a specified time'.[145] Liverpool makes provision for the appointment of honorary ecumenical fellows.[146] Some cathedrals also provide for the appointment of cathedral chaplains,[147] who sometimes may be drawn from churches in an ecumenical relationship with the Church of England.[148]

Liturgical functions which may be performed in a cathedral by ministers from other churches, joint ecumenical services, or the use of the cathedral for worship in accordance with the forms of service and practice of another church (on such occasions as may be specified in the approval given by the bishop), are governed by Canon. Moreover, where a local ecumenical project is set up for an area in which a cathedral is situated, the bishop may, after consulting it and such others as he considers appropriate, enter into an agreement with the appropriate authority of each participating church as to participation of that cathedral in the project.[149]

---

143 Hereford: Con. Art. 12(1)-(4). See also London: Stat. VII; and Ely: Stat. 8: the Etheldreda Canons.
144 Bristol: Stat. 14(1)-(6). See also Chester: Con. Art. 11: Canons Ecumenical; Winchester: Stat. 24.
145 Guildford: Con. Art. 7.3. See also Ripon: Con. Art. 8A; Newcastle: Con. Art. 9; Portsmouth: Con. Art. 8.1.
146 Liverpool: Con. Art. 11: they are appointed by the bishop and may attend meetings of the College of Canons.
147 E.g. Hereford: Con. Art. 9.
148 E.g. Derby: Stat. 7.1-4; St Albans: Con. Art. XIII.3.
149 Cans B43 and B44: promulgated under the Church of England (Ecumenical Relations) Measure 1988.

100 *The nave and crossing*

Marriages and funerals

The Cathedrals Measure 1999 is silent on the solemnisation of marriages and the conducting of funerals at cathedrals. Generally, cathedrals deal with these 'occasional offices' by means of 'policies' rather than statutes. Under ecclesiastical law, parishioners have a right to marry in the parish church and any person dying in a parish has a right to burial there in accordance with the rites of the Church of England;[150] these rights apply to parish church cathedrals.[151]

First, marriage: a particularly detailed policy is found at Southwark: 'Those who live in the Cathedral parish are entitled to be married here' as well as those on the cathedral electoral roll 'by virtue of having worshipped here regularly for at least six months'.[152] If one party has been married before, an interview is conducted in line with General Synod advice.[153] Enquiries are welcome from those wishing to discuss a service of thanksgiving following a civil marriage.[154] Couples proposing to enter a civil partnership may approach clergy for preparation, prayers and continuing support and counsel; while there is no service to bless a civil partnership, clergy should respond pastorally case by case.[155] In most cases, Chapter expects approaches from regular worshippers, resident parishioners and church electoral roll members. Civil partners may attend any service after civil registration of the partnership.[156]

However, at old foundation St Paul's, marriage in the cathedral is a 'privilege' and occurs in the Chapel of The Order of the British Empire (crypt), subject to a successful application for a Special Licence granted by the Archbishop of Canterbury; in addition to the weddings of members of the cathedral community, the privilege extends to members of the Order of St Michael and St George, the Order of the British Empire, holders of the British Empire Medal, members of the Imperial Society of Knights Bachelor and their children.[157] Exeter has a lengthy list of those 'welcome to ask for permission to marry in the Cathedral', including: the bishop; residents of the episcopal Palace and Precincts and their children; members (not resident in the Precincts) of Chapter, College and Council, and their children; prescribed members of cathedral staff (and their children); members of the cathedral community roll and their children; and members of

---

150 The right is also enjoyed by those with a qualifying connection to the parish church: Church of England Marriage Measure 2008, but this does not apply to cathedrals: s. 1 (11). This right does not include the marriage of same sex couples under the Marriage (Same Sex Couples) Act 2013.
151 See Cans B30–B36: marriage; and Canon B38: funerals.
152 Southwark: Policies. See also Leicester: Wedding Information Guide; Coventry: Weddings.
153 Matrimonial Causes Act 1965, s. 8(2): no cleric is compelled to solemnise the marriage of anyone whose former marriage was dissolved and whose former spouse is still living or permit such a marriage in his church.
154 Southwark: Policies.
155 Civil Partnerships: A Pastoral Statement of the House of Bishops of the Church of England (25 July 2005).
156 Southwark: Policies.
157 St Paul's London: Policy.

various regiments. Any in these categories other than those who live in the Precinct or Palace need a special licence from the Archbishop and Chapter's agreement normally given by the Canon Pastor or, if absent, by the Canon-in-Residence.[158]

Second, as to funerals, at Coventry these are 'largely' for former worshipping members of the cathedral community; others who 'qualify' include serving police, fire and other security officers, Armed Forces members; and holders of civic office in the City of Coventry and County of Warwickshire; if there are 'exceptional reasons', a funeral may be held for others: 'the decision lies entirely with the Dean'.[159] Southwark Cathedral is available for funerals of people who lived in the cathedral parish or were regular worshippers; and the cremated remains of people 'who have had a strong personal link with the Cathedral may be buried in the Cathedral Churchyard'.[160] At Leicester a funeral may take place at the cathedral if the deceased or a family member has 'a link' with it.[161] Also, Durham cathedral community 'or any immediate relative of such a person, will normally be the only persons eligible to apply to the Dean for the holding of an Occasional Office in the Cathedral';[162] and at St Edmundsbury: 'The Canon Pastor's duties shall include responsibility for the provision of pastoral care by the Cathedral and oversight of all baptisms, weddings and funerals' at it.[163]

Peterborough is unique. Its statutes provide:

> Persons resident in the precincts shall retain the right, which they have possessed from ancient times, of receiving the sacraments and other rites of the Church at the hands of the Cathedral clergy, one of whom shall be charged by the Chapter with the duty of providing these and other spiritual ministrations.

Next: 'Chapter shall provide, and shall arrange as required, for the baptism, marriage or burial of any such persons, duly registering the same in books kept for the purposes and, in the case of marriage, publishing the banns'. Moreover: 'The Bishop, the Dean and the Residentiary Canons, and those who have previously held such offices, shall have the right of burial or of having their ashes deposited in the Cathedral or in the churchyard of the Cathedral'; that of others may only be carried out with the consent of Chapter.[164] There is also national guidance on events held at times of regional or national celebration and mourning,[165] and multi-faith worship.[166]

---

158 Exeter: Policy (active July 2016): prescribed former staff members are also listed.
159 Coventry: Funerals and Memorial Services.
160 Southwark: Policies.
161 Leicester: Policies.
162 Durham: Stat. VII.
163 St Edmundsbury: Stat. 10.
164 Peterborough: Stat. 18(1)-(2).
165 Disaster and Bereavement Liturgies: The Cathedrals' Liturgy and Music Group, Occasional Paper 13 (2003).
166 Interfaith Services and Worship, Archbishops' Consultants on Interfaith Relations (1980).

102   *The nave and crossing*

The cathedral interviews

The cathedral interviews reveal different practices with regard to norms on honorary, lay, and ecumenical canons, and representation of wider society on Council. Old foundation Hereford does not specify named bodies/persons to represent wider interests on Council: such a list would be 'too prescriptive'; ecumenical companions are so styled because they do not swear an oath to Her Majesty or the bishop: the title reflects how they accompany the cathedral in the spiritual life; two such companions live in Germany and do not visit often as a result.[167] Exeter's ecumenical canons are invited to College events.[168] Wells enables appointment of lay canons but does not specify functions: this is 'flexible' and 'appointment depends on the skills required at that time'; whilst the constitution and statutes are silent on this, as a matter of 'practice' the bishop appoints ecumenical canons; the absence of a formal list of persons to represent wider interests on Council is also valued because it allows 'flexibility'.[169] St Paul's statute enabling the appointment of lay prebendaries has not been used; but it will be used in the future though not to reward service so much as 'to bring their gifts to the cathedral'.[170]

The constitution of new foundation Rochester specifies representation on Council from the wider community: this 'generally works well' – persons listed function as 'critical friends'; the provision reflects the 'outward-looking character' of the cathedral and the established position of the Church of England; such engagement also contributes to 'an open and frank exchange of moral oxygen and social inspiration' to the mutual benefit of cathedral and wider society. The constitution also enables appointment of honorary and lay canons, but does not specify the functions of honorary canons though lay canons must contribute to the corporate life of the cathedral and promote its mission; yet, the admission liturgy sets out 'expectations' applicable to honorary and lay canons; appointment is not 'just a gong' – they 'must be part of the organic life' of the community even though they are non-residentiary; their functions are agreed with Chapter; the constitution also provides for ecumenical canons of honour: this norm is used – there are two, one is Roman Catholic, the other from the United Reformed Church, who are of 'immense value' in that they preach and attend events.[171] The formal rule that Winchester Chapter must 'build relationships' with outside organisations is important as the cathedral is 'not just the congregation'; the ecumenical canons are active, preaching and attending major acts of worship; while the constitution and statutes are silent as to functions, ordained honorary, extra-

---

167 Hereford: Dean: Int. 5-8-2016.
168 Exeter: Dean: Int. 9–8-2016: the cathedral also has a 'missioner'.
169 Wells: Acting Dean: Int. 12–8-2016: a Roman Catholic was appointed. See also Salisbury: Dean: Int. 20-9-2016: a similar system affords 'flexibility'; for example, the Chaplain General of the armed forces is on the Council; also Stat. 10 (on the Sarum Canons) is used to make ecumenical appointments – e.g. there is a Lutheran Sarum Canon.
170 St Paul's: Dean: Int. 23-9-2016; also, there will be no code of practice for honorary canons as they are not members of the College of Canons.
171 Rochester: Canon Precentor: Int. 30-9-2016; Con. Arts. 7, 8 and 12.

diocesan, and lay canons, with 'roles' fixed by 'practice' and 'understanding', are not 'volunteers' nor do they have written 'role descriptions'; admission is a 'reward'; furthermore, there is a 'new tradition' that each canon has a designated stall.[172]

The constitution of Henrician foundation Gloucester enables Council to have a representative of the Mayor (for the city) and Lord Lieutenant (for the county) – as to appointment 'some bishops are more consultative than others' and some appointments have been successful, others have not: 'effective consultation is critical'; the right under its statutes to appoint ecumenical canons is used: they attend for example the installation of a new dean but beyond this 'they have no specific responsibilities'.[173] Chester's constitution, similarly, does not define the functions of honorary, lay or ecumenical canons (though Statute 7 provides for honorary canons to preach or officiate as determined by Chapter); however, their functions are defined by 'role descriptions' agreed by Chapter and the College of Canons. Ecumenical canons, appointed by the bishop after consulting Chapter, are not College members but may attend; there are two Canons Ecumenical, one Roman Catholic, the other Methodist, who occasionally attend College meetings. Council includes one person appointed by the bishop after consulting the Leader of Cheshire West and the local secular council and another appointed by Chester University; both take an 'active part' in Council meetings.[174] The Dean of Bristol appreciates the flexibility afforded by its constitution which does not name bodies or persons representing such wider interests on Council; statute provides for ecumenical prebendaries: four were appointed recently – it depends largely on the bishop's interests; their contribution has been somewhat variable, and there is no move to fill vacancies in these.[175]

Parish church cathedral Derby 'takes seriously' the provision in its constitutional preamble to collaborate with other churches and traditions: it has a Canon Missioner and it has set up a dialogue group with a neighbouring mosque in which the parties explore together theology, social issues, and the place of religion in secular society. Moreover, in order 'to demonstrate the concern of Christ for the poor', which also appears in the preamble, in collaboration with other city-centre churches the cathedral provides in the cathedral church itself beds and food for the homeless one night each week (between October and March). The cathedral also has 'additional chaplains', some of whom are ecumenical partners, who help with 'daily services' such as the lunch-time Eucharist – but the constitution does not provide for ecumenical canons as such – the Dean thinks that provision

172 Winchester: Acting Dean: Int. 16–8-2016: Con. Art. 10.4.10; Stat. 24.
173 Gloucester: Chancellor and Vice-Dean: Int. 4–8-2016: Stat. 22.
174 Chester: Vice-Dean: Int. 19–8-2016; Con. Art. 11: ecumenical canons; under Art. 12, the Benedictine Prior of Chester occupies an ancient office; each new prior 'is entitled to be installed by the dean in the place assigned to him by the Chapter' – the prior is a monk at the Roman Catholic Benedictine Monastery at Ampleforth.
175 Bristol: Dean: Int. 3–8-2016: Con. Art. 9: two people represent 'civic interests'; the ecumenical prebendaries: Roman Catholic, Methodist, URC and Black Pentecostal (appointed under Stat. 14).

should be made for these. Honorary and lay canons do not have a written agreement as to their functions (which are not spelt out in the constitution or statutes), but they are invited to attend services, seminars and other events; and the university chaplain also serves as one of the cathedral chaplains.[176] Birmingham's constitution does not list named bodies/persons to represent wider interests on Council: there must be a 'connection' between those appointed and the cathedral; for instance, the bishop appoints 'workers in the city' and this is good rather than fixed persons and entities.[177]

Conclusion

The Cathedrals Measure 1999 requires each cathedral to have a 'cathedral community' of persons over the age of sixteen who regularly worship there or are engaged in work or service connected with it in a regular capacity; the community may also include such others as may be prescribed. Many cathedrals use this latter rule by admitting e.g. residents of the cathedral precincts. A parish church cathedral community may consist of the Measure categories and/or those on the electoral roll of the parish. The constitution of a non-parish church cathedral must provide for the formation and maintenance of a roll of cathedral community members who apply to be enrolled. Cathedrals differ as to who maintains the roll and the periods after which it must be revised afresh; but any question about membership of the cathedral community is determined usually by the dean. The Measure permits a cathedral constitution to provide for a cathedral community committee consisting of persons on the roll, and for delegation by Chapter of functions to it. Some cathedrals require Chapter to set up such a committee, and others permit this. The annual meeting of the cathedral community elects persons to this committee (which is to advise Chapter on cathedral community matters), and provision exists for the community roll to be represented on Council. The Measure requires the dean to secure the pastoral care for the cathedral community; some cathedrals impose such a duty on one/more residentiaries; and some extend it to close residents and/or visitors.

Cathedral constitutions and statutes often present hospitality to visitors as a cathedral object. Vergers must welcome visitors, uphold dignity in worship, and ensure security – they are appointed by Chapter on such terms determined by it. Some parish church cathedrals also have cathedral church wardens elected at the annual meeting of the cathedral community. Many cathedrals also make provision for volunteers and employees whose appointment and functions are in the keeping of Chapter. Constitutions and statutes rarely deal with the management of visitors; but national guidance recommends cathedrals to ensure that their volunteers have clear role descriptions and training provided for by cathedral policies. It is a criminal offence, *inter alia*, to disturb the administration of divine service in the cathedral.

176 Derby: Dean: Int. 10–8-2016.
177 Birmingham: Dean: Int. 11–8-2016.

The Cathedrals Measure 1999 provides that Chapter directs mission and Council supports this work and it provides for representation of wider interests on Council, and the appointment of lay and ecumenical canons. Cathedrals in turn have various norms to enable: their clergy and honorary and/or lay canons (usually appointed by the bishop consulting Chapter) to engage in mission; representation of civic society on Council; and engagement in ecumenism (such as ecumenical representation on Council and the appointment of ecumenical canons). Some have published policies listing those who may be married or have funerals at the cathedral.

The cathedral interviews reveal some concerns about the composition and functions of the cathedral community roll and committee and the operation of rules on the annual meeting and electoral roll in parish church cathedrals. They disclose the development of practices that volunteers are given a written agreement. And they indicate general satisfaction with the use of norms in cathedrals which have them on the appointment to Council of named persons to represent the interests of wider society, and the flexibility afforded in those which do not.

5 The choir and presbytery: the dean, canons and musicians

The choir (or quire) lies immediately to the east of the crossing, and is where the offices are sung;[1] it also accommodates usually at its east end on the south side the episcopal throne (see Chapter 2). It is in the choir that the stalls of the choristers are situated on the north and south sides facing one another across a central aisle, as well as, at its west end, stalls for the dean and canons, who when in the choir at the time of divine service must wear the required vesture.[2] The choir also accommodates the organ, its case sometimes resting on a screen at the crossing which divides choir and nave. The word 'choir' is often used in a wide sense to signify the whole of the eastern area of the church and the terms 'liturgical choir' or 'ritual choir' to refer specifically to the area which accommodates the choristers, dean and canons.[3] The presbytery (or sanctuary) is to the east of the choir and accommodates the altar where the presbyters (priests) administer Holy Communion (see above Chapter 3). This chapter examines norms applicable to cathedral clergy – the dean, residentiary canons, and other clergy – and to directors of music, choristers and others associated with cathedral music. Before examining these, it is necessary to make some preliminary points about the national law applicable to the creation of cathedral offices and the appointment of persons to them.

For the Archbishops' Commission on Cathedrals 1994, appointment to cathedral posts should not be seen as 'a reward to clergy for their past service but as a means of deploying the best talents and skills available'.[4] It recommended that: (1) discussions with the Crown should take place to introduce a single system of appointment 'characterised by openness and a structured approach to consultation'; (2) advertising and interviewing are best left to be decided in relation to each

---

1 Chester: Con. Art. 1: 'Quire' means 'that part of the Cathedral building to the east of the Tower crossing that contains the ancient stalls where Divine worship is sung regularly'.
2 Peterborough: Stat. 15(3): 'No member of the Chapter or others ministering in the Cathedral shall enter the Choir during Divine Service without the accustomed habit'. See also Chelmsford: Stat. 2(d): the sanctuary.
3 M. Hislop, *How to Build A Cathedral* (London: Bloomsbury, 2012) 14, 22, 202–203.
4 H&R 174–175.

particular post; (3) some posts should be used to develop clergy who then move to senior or other posts – secondment could help; (4) freehold cathedral posts should be abolished: there should be a mix of appointments, some open-ended, some for a term of years, and all terminable after a period of notice; (5) stipend rates for all deans and canons should be set annually – expenses should be reimbursed by the cathedral; (6) ministry development review of cathedral clergy should be introduced and the bishop should see that it is in place and conduct a review with the dean, and the dean for each Chapter member (with episcopal oversight); (7) an induction and training package should be introduced for cathedral clergy; (8) arrangements to end the appointment of dean or canon due to a misdemeanour or unsuitability should be reviewed; (9) the role of suffragan bishops should be enhanced;[5] and (10) cathedral clergy should serve as confessors or spiritual directors for parochial clergy.[6]

Most of the proposals (with the notable exception of (1) above) were adopted by or following the Cathedrals Measure 1999. This requires cathedral statutes to provide: for the creation, continuance, abolition, suspension, or termination of suspension of any dignity, office, or body in the cathedral and for the title by which it is known; and any presentations or nominations to benefices in the patronage of the cathedral must be exercised by Chapter or its patronage committee.[7] The former rule is repeated in cathedral constitutions and/or statutes, such as at Exeter, where, however, the 'ancient dignities ... known as the Quattuor Personae' (i.e. Dean, Precentor, Chancellor and Treasurer) may not be abolished; Salisbury Chapter must allocate responsibilities to its members as it judges expedient but must 'normally have regard to the long established roles and responsibilities' of dean, precentor, chancellor and treasurer and other office-holders; and at Lincoln the word 'dignitary' includes the bishop, dean, precentor, chancellor, sub-dean, and suffragan bishops and archdeacons of the diocese.[8] Moreover, under national law, no person may hold a cathedral preferment with a benefice or with two or more benefices authorised to be held by a scheme/order unless the cathedral statutes so allow; if the person accepts, the office previously held is vacated; 'cathedral preferment' means the office of dean, residentiary or stipendiary canon; and 'cathedral statutes' includes a charter or a local Act relating to the cathedral.[9] Cathedral clergy must comply with the national law on ordained ministry.[10] There are also norms on the ministry of female clergy at cathedrals.[11]

---

5 H&R 99, Recs 1 to 9 (see also Ch. 8). See also *Talent and Calling*, GS 1650, 2007.
6 H&R 251, Appendix 6.
7 CM 1999, s. 11(a)-(d).
8 Exeter: Stat. X; Salisbury: Stat. 3.1; Lincoln: Con. Art. 1.
9 Mission and Pastoral Measure 2011, s. 104(1)-(5): no person shall hold cathedral preferment in more than one cathedral. See e.g. Chichester: Con. Art. 8; York: Stat. V.6.
10 See e.g. Cans C8: exercising ministry; C26: the manner of life; C27: dress; C28: occupations.
11 Bishops and Priests (Consecration and Ordination of Women) Measure 2014, s. 1.

The dean

The office of dean survived the Reformation.[12] The dean was 'an ecclesiastical governor secular, over the prebendaries, and canons in the cathedral church',[13] and could appoint a deputy.[14] The dean did not, however, possess the cure of souls.[15] The law required the dean to reside at the cathedral, preach the Word of God, exercise hospitality, maintain discipline through observance of the cathedral statutes and customs, visit the Chapter (but the ancient rule that the dean heard the confessions of the canons was abandoned), and preach in the diocese (or appoint a preacher to do so).[16] Deans of the old foundations came in by election of Chapter upon the king's licence, with the royal assent and confirmation of the bishop; deans of the new foundations came in by royal letters patent and were instituted by their bishop and installed upon a mandate directed to their chapters; it had been the case that a lay person could be appointed as dean.[17] In addition: 'The title of dean is a title of dignity; which belongs to this station as having ecclesiastical administration with jurisdiction or power annexed'; moreover:

> By which rule, no stations in the cathedral church, under the degree of a bishop, are dignities strictly speaking, besides those of the dean and archdeacon; unless where jurisdiction is annexed to any of the rest, as in some cases it is to prebends and others.[18]

A dean could also be made a bishop and simultaneously retain the office of dean.[19]

Today, under national law, no person may be appointed dean until that person has been six years complete in holy orders and is in priest's orders at the time of the appointment.[20] Where previously a cathedral constitution provided for the appointment of the dean to be by Her Majesty, the constitution must continue to so provide. In any other case, the constitution must provide that the incumbent of the benefice which comprises the parish of which the

---

12 See Burn II.77; see also Phillimore I.127.
13 Burn II.76–77. See also W. Nelson, *The Rights of the Clergy of Great Britain* (1710) 133–136.
14 Burn II.81 (citing Godolphin 55, and Watson 44). See also Phillimore I.132.
15 Burn II.78: 'Deaneries are sinecures, that is, they have not the cure of souls' (citing Godolphin 200, and Watson c. 2); therefore, by statute (13 Eliz. c. 12) a person admitted as dean need not subscribe to the Thirty-Nine Articles of Religion, but must take the other requisite oaths, declarations, etc.; Phillimore I.128.
16 Burn I.216; II.81–82: Can. 43 (1603): preaching; III.229. See also Phillimore I.130ff.
17 Burn II.78 (citing Gibson 173, and Johnson 540). See also Phillimore I.127: a dean must be ordained.
18 Burn II.79 (citing Gibson 173); II.80. See also Phillimore I.128.
19 Burn II.78 (citing Godolphin 112).
20 Can. C21.1; Phillimore I.175. See also Durham: Con. Art. 5: the candidate must also be 'distinguished by some title or proof of learning'; for an identical rule, see Guildford: Stat. II.3.

cathedral is the parish church shall be the dean.[21] Therefore, as to the latter, the bishop appoints the dean, and as to the former, the dean is appointed by the Crown, and in two cathedrals by independent trustees.[22] However, with Crown appointment, the bishop: is involved in setting the timetable; is on the selection panel; prepares a statement outlining his perspective on challenges facing the cathedral and his requirements in the next dean; gives advice on consultation within the diocese; is involved in shortlisting candidates; holds an individual meeting with the candidates; votes on selection; and makes the announcement.[23] Cathedral constitutions and/or statutes also enable appointment of a vice-dean or sub-dean.[24]

Cathedral constitutions and/or statutes deal with the admission of the dean on appointment; the dean is (normally) instituted by the bishop, received, admitted and installed by Chapter, and takes the customary oath. This is the process at old foundations,[25] and at York:

> [T]he Dean shall be admitted, invested and received by the delivery of book and bread and by the kiss of charity in the Chapter House by the Canon in Residence and shall be installed in his place in the Choir by the Canon Residentiary senior by date of appointment.[26]

In the customary oath at Hereford, the dean swears: to keep the statutes and customs of the cathedral; to promote its profit and honour; to reveal any damage or danger to Chapter; and:

> to pay respect and obedience to all ... who have authority over me in all things lawful and honest, without any appeal, citation, complaint or frivolous petition to any other judges ... except in causes which according to the statutes must rightly be referred to the Bishop of Hereford or ... Archbishop of Canterbury.[27]

---

21 CM 1999, s. 9(2). See also *Talent and Calling*, GS 1650, 2007: especially Ch. 7.
22 Bullimore Report (2012) par. 93: 28 have deans appointed by the Crown; 12 by the diocesan bishop, and 2, Bradford and Sheffield, by independent trustees; par. 96: there seems no willingness to change the system.
23 The Appointment Process for Deans: issued by the Archbishops' Secretary for Appointments on behalf of the House of Bishops (July 2011).
24 E.g. Canterbury: Stat. XII: the vice-dean (a Canon-in-Residence or residentiary) acts when the office of dean is vacant or the dean is incapacitated or absent. See also Wells: Con. Art. 6(5): sub-dean; Gloucester: Con. Art. 7: vice-dean; Manchester: Stat. VII: sub-dean; Chelmsford: Stat. 3: vice-dean.
25 Exeter: Stat. VI.1. See also Lincoln: Con. Art. 5(3); London: Con. 7.1 and Stat. VIII.1.
26 York: Stat. IV.2: the dean must take an oath to be 'faithful to the Cathedral', to 'keep its Statutes and Customs that are agreeable to law' and to 'defend its liberties' and not to reveal 'the secrets of the Chapter'.
27 Hereford: Stat. Appendix: The Customary Oath.

And at Lichfield, when the dean has been appointed by the Sovereign, the Administrator must notify Chapter, Council and College of Canons of the day for installation, 'on which day the Cathedral Registrar shall read the Royal Letters Patent for the appointment and the Dean shall make the Declaration of Fidelity' in the presence of Chapter, Council, and College; then the precentor assigns the dean to the Decanal Stall in quire at a service.[28]

Similar norms exist at new foundations. Norwich is typical: 'The Dean shall be installed according to the customs of the Cathedral and at his installation shall make such declarations and take such oaths as may be prescribed by law and by custom'.[29] At parish church cathedrals also the dean is installed 'according to the customs of the Cathedral';[30] moreover, at Chelmsford the dean's stall 'shall be the stall of St. Peter-ad-Murum and St. Cedd' and the dean has a stall in the sanctuary; at Bradford too:

> The Dean's Stall shall be the ancient Priest's Stall situated west of the Choir Stalls nearest the Nave on the south side of the Choir and [his] seat in the Sanctuary shall be situated on the north side of the Bishop's Seat.[31]

But at Sheffield the dean is installed 'according to the cathedral by-laws'.[32]

The Church Commissioners must pay out of their general fund to the dean such sums by way of stipend or other emoluments as they may determine. Chapter too may, with their consent, pay the dean such additional stipend or other emoluments as it thinks fit. A grant towards the removal expenses of a dean on appointment may also be paid by the Commissioners.[33] Ordinarily a dean holds office by common tenure,[34] and must retire at seventy – though the bishop may authorise continuation for up to a further year if the bishop considers there are special circumstances making this desirable.[35] If the office of dean is vacant, or the bishop considers the dean will be unable to discharge any or all of his functions under the Cathedrals Measure by reason of illness or absence or any other cause, the bishop must, after consulting Chapter, appoint a residentiary to carry out such

---

28 Lichfield: Stat. X: The Manner of Installation.
29 Norwich: Stat. IV.2. See also Canterbury: Con. Art. 10(4): installation follows 'customary procedures' and Stat. IV; Stat. XXVI: the dean occupies 'the first stall on the right-hand side of the entrance to the Quire'.
30 E.g. Coventry: Stat. 2.2: the dean is 'collated as Vicar by the Bishop' and 'installed by the Sub-Dean according to the usage of the Cathedral … and at installation shall take such oaths as may be prescribed by law'.
31 Chelmsford: Stat. 2; Bradford: Stat. 2.2–3.
32 Sheffield: Stat. 2(1).
33 CM 1999, ss. 21–22. See e.g. Canterbury: Stat. XXVII.
34 Ecclesiastical Offices (Terms of Service) Measure 2009, s. 1(1)(d): special provision is made for freehold.
35 Ecclesiastical Offices (Age Limit) Measure 1975, ss. 1(3), 3(1), Schedule. Cathedral constitutions/statutes generally repeat this rule. See e.g. York: Stat. XIX; Norwich: Con. Art. IV; Southwell: Con. Art. 4.2.

functions as the dean is unable to discharge during that period; whether this is justified is determined by the appropriate archbishop.[36]

The form of government of the Church of England under a dean is not repugnant to the Word of God.[37] Under the Cathedrals Measure 1999: 'The principal dignitary of the cathedral, next after the bishop, shall be known as the dean'.[38] It is 'the duty of the dean as chairman of the Chapter to govern and direct on its behalf the life and work of the cathedral and in particular', to: ensure that divine service is duly performed in the cathedral; ensure the constitution and statutes are faithfully observed;[39] maintain good order and proper reverence there;[40] secure the pastoral care of all cathedral community members; and take all decisions necessary to deal with any emergency affecting the cathedral, pending consideration of the matter by Chapter.[41] These decanal functions are repeated in cathedral constitutions and/or statutes.[42]

By Measure, no action may be taken without the dean's consent as to: any alteration of the ordering of services; settlement of the cathedral's budget; and implementation of any decision taken by Chapter in the dean's absence – but as to the latter decanal consent is deemed to have been given after the expiry of one month following the date on which the decision was taken unless, in that period, the dean requests Chapter to reconsider the decision at its next meeting – in which case the matter must be decided by a majority vote of those present and voting: the dean has a second/casting vote.[43] Constitutions/statutes repeat these provisions.[44]

The dean has a wide range of functions neatly summarised by the Association of English Cathedrals: these appear in cathedral constitutions and/or statutes, and are discussed where appropriate elsewhere in this book.[45] The dean is to share with the bishop and other senior colleagues in the oversight of mission, and is a member *ex officio* of the Bishop's Council, Bishop's Staff Meeting, and Diocesan Synod.[46] As head of the foundation and its principal dignitary after the bishop,[47] the dean is to: (1) preside over Chapter and with it direct the life and work of the cathedral;[48] (2) represent the church in public life, grow partnerships with faith and secular institutions, and contribute to the intellectual, social and theological

---

36 CM 1999, s. 7(4)-(5). See e.g. Lincoln: Stat. 2(2)-(3); Durham: Stat. XII.4–5; Southwell: Stat. 2.4–5.
37 Can. A6. This is an ancient norm: see Canons Ecclesiastical 1603/4, Can. 7.
38 CM 1999, s. 7(1). See e.g. Lincoln: Con. Art. 5(4); Durham: Stat. XII.1 and XXXIII; Chelmsford: Stat. 2(a).
39 See also Can. C21.2.
40 See also Can. C21.4.
41 CM 1999, s. 7(2). For services, see Chapter 3 and for pastoral care Chapter 4.
42 E.g. London: Con. Art. 7.2; Norwich: Stat. IV.3; Southwell: Stat. 2.3.
43 CM 1999, s. 7(3).
44 See e.g. Salisbury: Con. Art. 3.4; Winchester: Con. Art. 6.4; Derby: Stat. 2.4.
45 Dean: Responsibilities of the Role (2013).
46 Church Representation Rules, r. 30(4)(a)(ii). See below Chapter 6.
47 E.g. Salisbury: Con: Preamble; Norwich: Stat. IV.1; Rochester: Stat. II(1).
48 E.g. Exeter: Con. Art. 5.a.i; Canterbury: Con. Art. 6(1)(a); St Albans: Con. Art. V.1.

capital of the cathedral; (3) preside over the College of Canons;[49] (4) attend/participate in Council and other bodies and in collaboration with Chapter ensure sound governance;[50] (5) exercise leadership in liturgy, preaching, and pastoral care, develop teamwork, and be personally committed to its pattern of daily prayer; (6) lead cathedral outreach, including presenting and interpreting its heritage; (7) with Chapter, oversee its development and lead in obtaining funds for a secure and stable independent future; and (8) ensure its operations are properly managed (e.g. staff, finance, and care of the fabric), and its domestic norms are observed.[51]

Cathedral statutes embellish these functions in diverse ways. The Dean of Canterbury 'shall be charitable to all and especially to the poor and infirm; and in all things show himself to be honest and frugal'. Norwich's must play a role in the local community, diocese, wider church 'and beyond but this involvement must be tempered with a due regard to his responsibilities at the Cathedral'. Chichester's is Governor of the Prebendal School, and chairs the Trustees of St Mary's Hospital, Executive and Custodian Trustees of the Morse-Boycott Bursary Fund and Traditional Choir Trust. Hereford's is Visitor of two alms-houses. York's must induct, install and enthrone the archbishop and members of Chapter and College of Canons. And Wells' oversees cathedral finances subject to Chapter.[52] Some cathedrals forbid the dean to hold other preferment except with episcopal consent.[53] Rights include: to receive after installation an account from Chapter of all 'the fittings, ornaments, furniture and muniments of and in the Cathedral … with an inventory thereof';[54] to determine questions as to cathedral community membership;[55] and to be consulted over a host of matters.[56] Duties include: occupying the allotted stall;[57] providing the bishop when officiating with the assistance of ministers and officials of the cathedral;[58] attending services;[59] membership of Chapter committees;[60] and allocating seating in

49 E.g. Chichester: Con. Art. 5.a; and Stat. 4.a; Canterbury: Con. Art. 14(1); Southwell: Con. Art. 11.
50 E.g. York: Con. Art. VII.C(ii); Canterbury: Con. Art. 5(1)(b); Blackburn: Con. Art. 12(1).
51 E.g. Exeter: Con. Art. 8.f: the dean is a member of Council, Chair of Chapter, President of the College.
52 Canterbury: Stat. V.1; Norwich: Stat. IV.4; Chichester: Stat. 6.d.vi-viii; Hereford: Stat. V.5; York: Stat. IV.3 and 5: unless he decides otherwise; Wells: Stat. 3(3).
53 E.g. Newcastle: Stat. 6.5: other than that of Vicar, save with the written consent of the Bishop.
54 Hereford: Stat. V.2. See also Canterbury: Stat. V.2: the dean is responsible for the safekeeping of treasures.
55 E.g. Hereford: Con. Art. 13(5); Canterbury: Con. Art. 19.2; Norwich: Con. Art. X.
56 E.g. Chichester: Con. Art. 8: appointment of residentiary canons.
57 E.g. Ely: Stat. 17(2): 'There shall be assigned to the Dean the customary stall[s] in the Choir and … Octagon'.
58 E.g. Chichester: Stat. 5.d.
59 E.g. Hereford: Stat. V.4; York: Stat. V.8. For parish church cathedrals, see e.g. Newcastle: Stat. 6.4.
60 E.g. Hereford: Con. Art. 13(5); Canterbury: Con. Art. 8(5); Norwich: Con. Art. X; Southwell: Con. Art. 9.1.

the cathedral at services,[61] for instance, at Wakefield: 'At special services, the clerical and lay vice-presidents of the Diocesan Synod and the Rural Deans and members of the General Synod shall be allocated seats by the Dean'.[62] The dean also has rights and duties as to occupation of the deanery house.[63]

The cathedral interviews

These reveal general satisfaction with norms applicable to deans. However, they also provide a variety of understandings about and assessments of norms applicable to their appointment and authority, and the role of vice-deans/sub-deans. As to old foundation Wells at the time of the interview there was a vacancy in the office of dean (appointed by the Crown); the Acting Dean explained that the guidelines on the Appointment Process for Deans were followed: Chapter submitted a job description and person specification, and information about the challenges facing the cathedral, but took no further part in the process; also, the office of sub-dean is honorary and there is no practice at the cathedral that the sub-dean functions as acting dean.[64] The Dean of Salisbury 'takes seriously [her] position as senior priest in the diocese', attends the Bishop's Council, and preaches in the diocese on average once a month; as to functions at the cathedral: 'There are challenges with every single one of these' – for instance, no-one else wants responsibility for observance of the constitution and statutes; the dean has informal meetings with the bishop every two/three weeks.[65] The Dean of Hereford 'rarely' decides matters without Chapter in an emergency and only if they are 'not major'.[66] The Dean of St Paul's considers that he has no 'cure of souls' because the cathedral has no parish or precinct/close; he has never used the right to veto Chapter in the prescribed fields, but 'it is a helpful power … as the dean carries the can for what happens'; in terms of the legal framework, there needs to be a balance between freedom and accountability, including the need for the dean to have sufficient authority to be held to account – the balance currently is weighted against the dean, but the notion that the dean is *primus inter pares* is problematic.[67]

At new foundation Winchester, at the time of interview (like Wells), a name for a new dean had been submitted to the Crown; following identification of candidates, Chapter provided a preliminary briefing, which evolved considerably before being sent to applicants: it briefed candidates before interview, but then there was no opportunity to feedback to the interview panel (though a College member was on the panel). The authority of the dean is that of 'a brake rather than an

---

61 E.g. Coventry: Stat. 2.8: 'The Dean shall have the right to arrange the order of seating at all services'.
62 Wakefield: Stat. 11.
63 See below Chapter 10.
64 Wells: Acting Dean: Int. 12-8-2016.
65 Salisbury: Dean: Int. 20-9-2016.
66 Hereford: Dean: Int. 5-8-2016.
67 London: Dean: Int. 23-9-2016: the dean takes an oath of canonical obedience.

114 *The choir and presbytery*

accelerator'; the dean must by statute ensure that Chapter members fulfil their roles – for the Acting Dean, this function of the dean 'exhorting' is one of the 'traditions' there.[68] For the Precentor of Rochester, the office of dean may be seen as analogous to a 'cure of souls' in the cathedral: it involves a 'mutuality of care in the community of prayer'.[69]

As to Henrician foundations, the Vice-Dean of Chester considers that the oath taken by the dean (and residentiaries) has 'more than symbolic significance' because it is taken 'before God' and is about how cathedral ministry is a 'partnership'. By statute, the dean must play a role in the local community, diocese, wider church and beyond but tempered with due regard to responsibilities at the cathedral; in practice, such functions are delegated to and performed by the vice-dean.[70] At Gloucester, the functions of vice-dean are 'by custom' performed by the Canon-in-Residence but this is sometimes relaxed by the dean; in the absence of the dean, the vice-dean exercises 'jurisdiction' (e.g. chairing Chapter), is the 'first port of call for the media', and deals with routine complaints.[71] The Dean of Bristol considers that, as 'head of the foundation', he 'exercises oversight over all the various aspects of cathedral life', but he has never invoked the right to veto Chapter; also, the Deans' Conference plays an important part in the sense of 'forming a common mind' on cathedral issues; but the 'national assumption' that 'the bishop is the dean's line manager' needs debate.[72] The Dean of Derby has never vetoed Chapter.[73]

The cathedral canons

Following the Reformation, the law distinguished between a prebend, the office or stipend attaching to it, and prebendary, the one holding the office (enjoying such prebend); 'canonry' and 'canon' were also used.[74] A 'simple prebendary' had no cure and only his revenue for support; a 'dignitary prebendary' had 'jurisdiction

---

68 Winchester: Acting Dean: Int. 16-8-2016: see Stat. 3. Ely: Dean: Email 17–1-2017: the cathedral has a sufficient voice in the appointment of the dean.
69 Rochester: Precentor: Int. 3–9-2016.
70 Chester: Vice-Dean: Int. 19-8-2016: see Stat. 2(iv).
71 Gloucester: Chancellor: Int. 4–8-2016: e.g. car-parking issues during the Three Choirs Festival.
72 Bristol: Dean: Int. 3–8-2016: however, law does not feature in the training of deans.
73 Derby: Dean: Int. 10–8-2016. Southwark: Dean: Email 17–1-2017: whether the cathedral has a sufficient voice in the appointment of the dean depends on the process agreed between the Archbishop's and Prime Minister's appointment secretaries and whoever the patron is: 'I would go for greater openness personally'; Liverpool: Dean: Email 21–1-2017: the process works well if relations with the bishop are good; St Albans: Dean: Email 23–1-2017: the level of consultation with regard to St Albans is good.
74 Burn II.83: 'A prebend, is an endowment in land, or pension in money, given to a cathedral ... in *praebendum*' to maintain a secular priest or regular canon 'who was a prebendary ... supported by the said prebend'; II.84: 'A canonry also is a name of office; and a canon is the officer in like manner as a prebendary' (citing Gibson 172).

annexed' and so was called 'dignitary'; the bishop was patron of all prebends though some prebendaries were appointed by the Crown.[75] To be appointed as a prebendary, the candidate had to be a priest. Only one prebend could be held by a prebendary. A prebend had a vote in Chapter and the status of a corporation sole, but without a cure of souls at the cathedral.[76] There were also rules on residence and the functions at the cathedral of a prebendary who had a cure of souls outside the cathedral; prebendaries and canons had to preach at the cathedral when required by cathedral statutes; and on the death of a prebendary, the dean and chapter enjoyed the profits of the prebend.[77]

Today, under the Cathedrals Measure 1999, the constitution of a cathedral must: provide for the appointment of canons in Holy Orders and the manner of this and tenure of their office; enable lay canons to be appointed; and specify the maximum number of residentiary canons and non-residentiary canons.[78] Ordinarily a residentiary canon (and any other person in holy orders who holds a stipendiary office in a cathedral) holds office on the basis of common tenure.[79] The term 'residentiary canon' includes a stipendiary canon; the term 'non-residentiary' canon includes a prebendary who is not a residentiary canon; and the term 'canon' includes a lay canon and a non-residentiary canon but not a minor canon.[80] The constitutions of some cathedrals provide for the appointment of 'canons of the cathedral'.[81]

Residentiary canons

No person may be appointed as a residentiary unless in holy orders six complete years except in the case of a canonry annexed to any professorship, headship, or other office in any university; a deacon may be appointed.[82] The same rules applicable to deans as to stipends, removal expenses, retirement, and incapacity apply to residentiaries.[83] The constitution of each cathedral must provide that the holders of at least two residentiary canonries in the cathedral are to be engaged exclusively on cathedral duties. Cathedral duties means duties (whether in the

---

75 Burn II.84 (citing Godolphin 52).
76 Burn II.85–87: 'It does not appear that canons or prebends have cure of souls in any respect; they are indeed for the most part instituted, but not to the cure of souls' (citing Johnson 86); so they are not required (by 13 El. c. 12) to subscribe to the 39 Articles of Religion, but they must take 'the same oaths, and make and subscribe the same declarations, as other persons qualifying for ecclesiastical office'.
77 Burn II.86–87: he cites Godolphin 52 and Canons Ecclesiastical (1603) Cans 43–44.
78 CM 1999, s. 9(1); s. 9(4).
79 Ecclesiastical Offices (Terms of Service) Measure 2009, s. 1(1)(d): special provision is made for freehold.
80 CM 1999, s. 35(1).
81 E.g. York: Con. Art. VIII: these are 'by ancient custom styled Canons of York'; each canon holds a prebend.
82 Canon C21.1 and 1A.
83 CM 1999, s. 21(1) and s. 22; the two are commonly known as 'the Commissioners' Canons'. See above.

cathedral or diocese) which should, in the opinion of Chapter after consulting the bishop, be discharged in/from the cathedral. However, the appropriate archbishop and Church Commissioners acting jointly may in special circumstances direct that the holder of a residentiary canonry, who is normally engaged exclusively on cathedral duties, must, for such period as they may specify, be treated as so engaged for these purposes notwithstanding that he is performing duties other than cathedral duties. Any question as to whether a person is so engaged must after consulting the visitor and Chapter be determined by the Commissioners; any person dissatisfied may appeal to the appropriate archbishop whose decision is final.[84]

Constitutions and/or statutes largely repeat these rules. The residentiaries of old foundation Salisbury are appointed by the bishop after consulting dean and Chapter and must not exceed four; at least two nominated by Chapter must be engaged exclusively on cathedral duties; they vacate office automatically and without the execution of any instrument of resignation at seventy unless the bishop permits otherwise.[85] Chichester's residentiaries must not exceed six, are appointed by the bishop after consulting with others including the dean and Chapter, and the duties of each must be determined in writing by the bishop with the agreement of Chapter, having regard to the customary duties attached to the office held, provided that the bishop may in writing, with the like agreement vary such determination consulting the canon concerned.[86] Exeter has two residentiaries engaged exclusively on cathedral duties appointed by the bishop after consulting the dean and two others with duties partly diocesan and partly cathedral appointed similarly; they are collated by the bishop and installed by Chapter taking the prescribed oaths.[87] The residentiaries of York are appointed by the Archbishop of York.[88]

New foundation Canterbury must have no more than six nor fewer than four residentiaries, two appointed by the archbishop and not fewer than two nor more than four by Her Majesty (on every fourth vacancy by the archbishop); each takes the prescribed oath and is brought to the Quire for induction. Carlisle's are appointed by the bishop after affording Chapter an opportunity to express views in general and as to any specific person, and the bishop must have regard to those views. Norwich may have five, three appointed by Her Majesty and two by the bishop consulting the dean. Durham may have eight, 'godly persons ... distinguished by sound learning', appointed by the bishop consulting Chapter.

---

84 CM 1999, s. 8: during a vacancy in see, there is no duty to consult the Visitor.
85 Salisbury: Con. Art. 4; see also Art. 8: 'Canons of the Cathedral in Holy Orders' include the bishop, dean, residentiaries, area or suffragan bishops, full-time assistant bishops, archdeacons, and other clerks in holy orders beneficed or licensed and resident in the diocese appointed by the bishop after consulting Chapter.
86 Chichester: Con. Art. 8. See also Hereford: Con. Art. 8A and Stat. VI; Wells: Con. Art. 5.
87 Exeter: Con. Art. 9; Stat. VII.1.
88 York: Stat. V: four are appointed to 'the major dignities' of Chancellor, Pastor, Precentor and Theologian.

Gloucester must not exceed five, one appointed by Her Majesty, another by Her Majesty and the bishop alternately (Commissioners Canons), and three by the bishop consulting the dean (Diocesan Canons).[89]

Among parish church cathedrals, Truro is typical: two residentiary canons (funded by the Church Commissioners) must be appointed by the bishop after consulting the dean to be engaged exclusively on cathedral duties; a further two may be appointed by the bishop after similar consultation; they must be installed by Chapter making the Declaration of Assent, the oath of Allegiance, the oath of Canonical Obedience, the oath to Uphold and Observe the Cathedral Constitution and Statutes, and the Declaration of Loyalty to the Cathedral.[90] Birmingham is untypical in so far as its constitution enables one residentiary canon to be appointed by the bishop and the remaining residentiaries to be appointed by Her Majesty.[91]

Canon law prescribes the residentiaries' functions. They must: take care that the statutes and laudable customs of the cathedral are diligently observed; be resident in the cathedral for the time prescribed by law and by the cathedral statutes, and there preach the Word of God and perform all the duties of their office, except they shall be otherwise hindered by weighty and urgent cause; and, with the minor canons, vicars choral, and other ministers of the cathedral, provide, as far as in them lies, that during the time of divine service all things be done with such reverence, care, and solemnity as sets forth the honour and glory of Almighty God.[92]

Statutes supplement these national norms. Among old foundations, Chichester is typical: the two residentiaries funded by the Church Commissioners must reside in the houses allocated for at least eight months each year and attend at least one cathedral service each day; absence connected with church work without objection by the bishop, dean or Chapter counts towards this if not less than three months are spent in Close residence; up to four other residentiaries must also undertake Close residence as fixed at appointment subject to subsequent approved changes. In order to ensure a canon is in Close residence throughout the year, a periodic list of Canons-in-Residence is drawn up by mutual agreement and approved by Chapter; the canon must: daily attend all the usual services, at least Matins and Evensong; in the dean's absence, be responsible for the due performance of services; and provide a substitute from among the other residentiaries if absent; the canon may preach during residence, as agreed in the rota.[93] It may sometimes be

---

89 Canterbury: Con. Art. 11 and Stat. VIII; Carlisle: Con. Art. 5; Norwich: Con. Art. V.4; Durham: Con. Art. 6; Gloucester: Con. Art. 8.
90 Truro: Con. Art. 8; Stat. VI (the dignitaries of Chancellor, Librarian, Missioner, Pastor, Precentor and Treasurer are in the gift of the bishop and may be conferred on residentiary or Chapter canons). See also Southwell: Con. Art. 6; St Edmundsbury: Con. Art. 10(11); and Newcastle: Con. Art. 4.10.
91 Birmingham: Con. Art. 6.
92 Can. C21.
93 Chichester: Stat. 8.c. See also e.g. Exeter: Stat. VII; Hereford: Stat. VI; Salisbury: Stat. 5.2.

118 The choir and presbytery

appropriate for the non-residentiaries (or prebendaries) to act as Canons-in-Residence in order to celebrate Holy Communion and if convenient preach.[94]

New foundation Norwich's residentiaries must: celebrate the Holy Communion and preach as Chapter decides; undertake such duties as Chapter determines consulting the residentiary; endeavour to strengthen the cathedral's corporate life, worship and work and promote its usefulness in the diocese; and pursue theological reflection and research for the wider church. They must also: reside in the Close house allocated by Chapter and diligently attend services; serve such period of residence as determined by Chapter and during it ensure, consulting the precentor, that regular worship takes place as appointed; lead Morning Prayer and the intercessions at Evening Prayer daily; officiate at Evening Prayer on Sunday; be consulted by the sacrist and vergers when immediate help is required; deputise in the absence of the dean and vice-dean; and make pastoral visits to all departments of the cathedral at least once a week.[95] Parish church cathedrals have similar norms on residentiaries' rights and duties.[96]

Cathedrals also make provision (under the 1999 Measure) to suspend a canonry. If patronage vests in the diocesan, then, typically, the bishop may for financial or other reasons and after consulting with Chapter suspend or refrain from filling a vacant residentiary canonry, and after like consultation revive and appoint to it;[97] or else the bishop may suspend or revive a canonry with the consent of the dean (on behalf of Chapter) or Chapter itself.[98] By way of contrast, if a canonry is attached to the Crown, then the Crown's consent must be obtained.[99]

Non-residentiary canons

The Cathedrals Measure 1999 requires each cathedral constitution to specify the maximum number of non-residentiaries (which includes prebendaries).[100]

---

94 Chichester: Stat. 9: during this time the Dean or a Residentiary must be available in the Close.
95 Norwich: Stat. V. See also e.g. Ely: Stat. 4; Worcester: Stat. 3.2; Rochester: Stat. III (1); Winchester: Stat. 6.
96 E.g. Blackburn: Stat. 4. See also St Edmundsbury: Stat. 7; Birmingham: Stat. 3.
97 E.g. Exeter: Con. Art. 9; Lincoln: Con. Art. 7(6); Ely: Con. Art. 5(8); Durham: Con. Art. 6; Truro: Con. Art. 8(e).
98 E.g. Ripon: Con. Art. 6(1); St Albans: Con. Art. X(7); Manchester: Con. Art. VI(7).
99 E.g. Birmingham: Con. Art. 6(10): the bishop makes a representation to Her Majesty urging the necessity for the suspension and Her Majesty may 'if she thinks fit refrain from making an appointment'.
100 CM 1999, s. 9(1). See also, as to Christ Church Cathedral Oxford, the bishop may, after consulting, first, the dean and then the dean and chapter, appoint non-residentiary canons in the cathedral church of Christ in Oxford, namely: not more than 35 who are clerks in holy orders either of the Church of England or of a Church in communion with the Church of England; not more than 10 lay canons, being lay persons who are actual communicants and who, in the opinion of the bishop, have given distinguished service to the diocese of Oxford or to the cathedral church and who have an active commitment to and concern for the life of the cathedral church and its mission and service; and not more than five ecumenical canons, being persons

Cathedrals implement and supplement this rule in various ways. At old foundation Hereford, the bishop with Chapter consent may appoint one non-residentiary (an ordained person either beneficed or licensed in the diocese) on such terms in respect of remuneration, powers, duties, and conditions as the bishop and Chapter determine. No appointment may be made unless an adequate stipend (not necessarily equal to that paid to holders of residentiary canonries) can be provided from available resources. Moreover, the number of prebendaries must not exceed 27 at any one time; each must be an ordained person beneficed or licensed in the diocese or hold some office or discharge some function in connection with the diocese; the bishop appoints on such conditions as to the functions or duties of a religious, educational or administrative character as, in his opinion, are in the interests of the cathedral, diocese or church at large; each prebendary must seek to contribute to the corporate life and worship of the cathedral and to promote its mission and be ready to preach once each year if requested by Chapter.[101] Any person who holds a prebendal stall there must be 'duly habited' when occupying that stall.[102]

At new foundation Durham, there must not be more than 24 non-residentiary canons in holy orders (unless the bishop dispenses with this) ordinarily beneficed or licensed in the diocese; the bishop appoints consulting Chapter; they are collated by the bishop and installed by the dean.[103] Among parish church cathedrals, for example, at Truro, the bishop may appoint not more than 24 clergy and not more than 12 lay persons as non-residentiaries to be members of the College of Canons; the former vacate office without execution of any instrument of resignation on ceasing to be beneficed or licensed in the diocese or attaining 70; and the latter vacate on ceasing to be resident in the diocese or reaching 70;[104] they are installed by Chapter after making the prescribed declarations and oaths; clerical non-residentiaries must preach and the lay counterparts must read at a service at

    who are baptised and members in good standing of a Church (not in communion with the Church of England) which subscribes to the doctrine of the Holy Trinity; the bishop may also confer the title of canon emeritus in the cathedral church on any non-residentiary canon who vacates that office. Also: the rights and duties of non-residentiary canons and of canons emeriti in the cathedral church shall be determined from time to time by the dean and chapter of the cathedral church with the agreement of the bishop: Church of England (Miscellaneous Provisions) Measure 2010, s. 10(2) and (9).
101 Hereford: Con. Art. 11. See also Lincoln: Con. Art. 8: no more than 43 such canons from beneficed or licensed diocesan clergy may be appointed; suffragan bishops and archdeacons are non-residentiary; they are instituted by the bishop and installed by the dean; lay canons may also be appointed as non-residentiaries.
102 Hereford: Stat. VII: this also lists the Prebendal stalls; see Appendix for the customary oath. See also Lincoln: Con. Art. 11: non-residentiaries 'may occupy their stalls at any service when they shall wear the choir habit belonging to their dignities and degrees save that this provision shall not apply to lay canons'.
103 Durham: Con. Art. 8: suffragan bishops, assistant bishops, and archdeacons are non-residentiaries; Stat. XIII.
104 Truro: Con. Art. 9.

least once every three years as arranged with Chapter.[105] Norms also provide for honorary and lay canons.[106]

Cathedral constitutions and/or statutes often provide for appointment of other clergy to fulfil designated roles at the cathedral.[107] For example, Ripon Chapter may appoint minor canons 'from among the clergy or the laity' and their 'duties shall be agreed by the Chapter after consultation with them'; the dean after consulting Chapter may also appoint honorary minor canons from among the clergy or laity to 'discharge such duties within the Cathedral Benefice as may be assigned to them under the supervision of the Dean'; they are to be non-stipendiary 'but may receive expenses and housing for duty'.[108] Norms also enable the bishop to confer emeritus titles on cathedral clergy after vacation of office.[109]

Disciplinary proceedings may be instituted against any Clerk in Holy Orders who serves in a cathedral only by a person nominated by its Council, or any other person, provided that the bishop determines that such person has a proper interest in making the complaint.[110] The dean, residentiary canons and others in holy orders holding a stipendiary office in a cathedral may, moreover, be subject to additional disciplinary, capability, and grievance procedures.[111]

The cathedral interviews

These reveal general satisfaction with the norms discussed above. However, one problematic issue is the ministerial development review of clergy. At old foundation St Paul's, the Dean considers that national guidelines on appointing residentiaries are 'fine': the cathedral has an adequate voice; the statutes retain the offices of chancellor, treasurer and precentor and the practice is that each one has a 'job description'.[112] Hereford Chapter must appoint annually a precentor, chancellor and treasurer: it 'never happens'; each is a 'skilled specialist'; the duty is 'redundant' and should be 'deleted'. Residentiaries are reviewed annually by the diocese on behalf of the bishop; there is a 'case to explore review ... by the dean' rather than by the diocese; 'residence' means that the canon is 'first in line to take the services': it may not involve Close residence.[113] At Exeter, the Canon-in-

---

105 Truro: Stat. VII. For non-residentiary canons see also Chelmsford: Con. Art. 6: clerical; and Art. 7: lay.
106 See above Chapter 4.
107 See below for the clerical offices associated with cathedral music.
108 Ripon: Stat. VIII and VIIIA. See also Norwich: Stat. XVI: Chapter may appoint a cleric holding an episcopal licence as minor canon, priest vicar, and deacon; Gloucester: Stat. 12: minor canons; Wells: Stat. 14: priest vicars.
109 See, typically, e.g. Blackburn: Stat. 8.
110 Clergy Discipline Measure 2003 (as amended 2013), s. 42(2); see also Code of Practice, par. 35; see also par. 48: a complaint against cathedral clergy should be sent to the bishop.
111 Ecclesiastical Offices (Terms of Service) Measure 2009 (and the Regulations made thereunder).
112 London: Dean: Int. 23-9-2016: Stat. IX.4; there is also a canon pastor.
113 Hereford: Dean: Int. 5-8-2016; see Con. Art. 4(3)(d) on the precentor.

Residence is not physically resident in the Close, only the one who is non-stipendiary (or self-supporting); all others (i.e the residentiaries who may be on duty as Canon-in-Residence) live in the Close. The dean is not the line manager of clergy, but meets each cleric about once each six months to discuss their ministry and sometimes their professional development. The ministerial development review of clergy is conducted by the diocese; a 'formal practice' has developed, on the dean's suggestion, for the dean to be on the review panel once every three years.[114]

The rule that Wells has five principal dignitaries (dean, chancellor, precentor, treasurer and Archdeacon of Wells) is a 'historical vestige'. Under the previous bishop there were no diocesan ministerial development reviews of the precentor and chancellor, but today they occur every eighteen months as a matter of diocesan policy. There is a different reviewer for each review. But it would be 'more helpful' to have the same reviewer for each review and to have greater clarity on the 'management and pastoral' and 'appraisal and development' aspects of review. The award of a prebend under the constitution is seen to be 'honorary' and something of recognition for diocesan service; the prebendaries constitute the College.[115]

The Dean of Salisbury 'encourages' the residentiary canons to follow the diocesan policy on ministerial development review; this occurs once each year, with a senior staff peer review every three years; some residentiaries (those who have worked in the professions before ordination) see the value in having the Dean as their reviewer; others want senior staff review combined with peer review. For the Dean, 'it is silly for the dean not to carry out an annual review of cathedral clergy' but she allows colleagues to choose. In addition, all Chapter members must produce a personal plan of strategic objectives in order to deliver Chapter's priorities, and these are reviewed by the dean – 'they are meant to be every year'; and there are always informal discussions with the dean about their professional development. The statutes set out the functions of the precentor, chancellor, and treasurer, they are 'brief but deep', and clergy 'stand on these' as they represent 'the boundaries' as between the roles.[116]

None of new foundation Winchester's residentiaries is appointed by the Crown; the bishop appoints with the agreement of the dean consulting Chapter – this 'could not be better as to the form of authority which is tested in experience'. Each residentiary (an office-holder) has a written 'job description' because the statutes are silent as to functions – this is subject to an annual performance development review carried out by the dean.[117] Similarly, Rochester has an extra-statutory practice that each residentiary has a 'job description'.[118] At Henrician

---

114 Exeter: Dean: Int. 9–8-2016; also: the Dean is critical of common tenure and the Clergy Discipline Measure 2003 process: 'it is too heavy a tool'.
115 Wells: Acting Dean: Int. 12–8-2016: Con. Art. 5–6.
116 Salisbury: Dean: Int. 20–9-2016; Stat. 3.1 and 5.5–7: precentor, etc.
117 Winchester: Acting Dean: Int. 16–8-2016; see Stat. 6; the bishop has not in the past 11 years suspended a canonry. Carlisle: Dean: Email 17–1-2017: the cathedral has a sufficient voice in appointing residentiaries.
118 Rochester: Canon Precentor: Int. 30–9-2016; Stat. III is silent on the matter.

122 The choir and presbytery

foundation Chester, residentiaries' functions are set out by statute, but are supplemented by a 'role brief' determined at appointment and include 'responsibility for hospitality and welcome' and 'day-to-day oversight' of the cathedral. That the latter is the residentiaries' responsibility may be 'peculiar to Chester'.[119] At Bristol, ministerial development review of the clergy is not dealt with by the constitution/ statutes but by diocesan policy: the matter should be dealt with by the statutes and will feature in their revision; at present, a three-year review cycle has been agreed with the diocese and this has been 'signed off' by the dean.[120]

At the parish church cathedral at Derby, for appointment of residentiaries, a panel is chaired by the bishop, and the dean and Council, Chapter and College representatives sit on it. The national guidance is followed. They have common tenure: the constitution needs revising to reflect this. Annual ministerial development review is conducted by the bishop personally as cathedral clergy hold the licence of the bishop and 'deserve to have direct relatedness with the bishop' which this process provides. The dean can speak with the clergy any time about their ministry. The bishop has never suspended a canonry. Honorary canons do not have a written agreement as to their functions (on which the statutes are silent); but they are invited to attend services, seminars and other events. The cathedral has a full set of lay canons: they have no written agreement but act when invited.[121] The Dean of Birmingham explained that the constitution (Art. 6) does not require the bishop to consult the dean when appointing some residentiaries but the 'practice' is for both 'formal and informal consultation'. Ministerial development review occurs under the diocesan 'protocol': as to review of the dean, the dean has a 'prerogative' to choose a reviewer and she asks the bishop in alternate years; it is the same with residentiaries; this is a 'development review' not an appraisal; but: 'an appraisal' would also be 'helpful' to assess 'performance'. The constitution (Art. 7) does not require the bishop to consult the dean in appointing honorary or lay canons – but consultation occurs in practice. By statute honorary canons may preach and celebrate Holy Communion; there are also guidelines on their roles – a 'light touch' is adopted. Lay canons are appointed under the constitution (Art. 8): an 'expectation' has arisen among some that they are appointed for life, but the dean has had to remind them that their appointment is for five years renewable.[122] And at Ripon, one of the canons serves as co-ordinator of daily chaplaincy at the cathedral.[123]

Correspondence also suggests various assessments of as well as practices connected with the appointment of residentiaries; for example, for the Dean of St Albans, the rule there that one of the Commissioners' Canons is appointed by the bishop 'in consultation' with the dean, should rather require that the appointment is made by the bishop 'in agreement' with the dean; and the two

---

119 Chester: Vice-Dean: Int. 19-8-2016: Stat. III.
120 Bristol: Dean: Int. 3-8-2016.
121 Derby: Dean: Int. 10-8-2016.
122 Birmingham: Dean: Int. 11-8-2016; residentiaries have common tenure, so the constitution needs revising; the bishop has not suspended a canonry during the dean's tenure.
123 Ripon: Revd Canon Wendy Wilby: Email 6-10-2016.

'diocesan residentiaries', who are expected to play a part in the pastoral work of the cathedral, 'could in theory be appointed without any consultation with the Cathedral at all. In practice there is consultation, but it should be written into the rules.'[124]

The musicians and cathedral music

Following the Reformation, the Canons Ecclesiastical 1603/4 (and cathedral statutes) made provision for the conduct of cathedral music;[125] and one case decided that: 'In Cathedral Churches ... the Ordinary might compel the Dean and Chapter to erect an organ, as proper and necessary for the service usually performed in such places'.[126] Music is addressed in detail by the Archbishops' Commission on Cathedrals 1994.[127] Whilst the Commission applauded the standards of cathedral music, it also offered some criticism.[128] Examples of good practice found included: a choir school providing teaching opportunities for organists; recruitment of choristers from local schools; continued musical training of choristers after their voices have broken; organ surgeries for other churches; and having the organist on the diocesan liturgical committee.[129] It recommended that cathedrals should seek to: (1) provide chorister education for girls as well as boys; (2) where possible, establish a system of choral scholarships for altos, tenors and basses; (3) give careful consideration to the role of director of music and the musical and management expertise needed to perform the role; (4) remunerate adequately and appropriately cathedral musicians; (5) see the musical resources of the cathedral as a resource for the rest of the diocese; and (6) have regular appraisal of members of the music department and encourage in-service training.[130] The Association of English Cathedrals sees cathedrals as 'the main sustainers of the English Choral tradition', 'a unique part of English culture'; participation in it is an educational experience which develops many transferable skills; and most of the cathedrals now have girls' choirs as well as the more traditional boys' choirs.[131]

---

124 St Albans: Dean: Email 23-1-2017. Liverpool: Dean: Email 21-1-2017: the process works well if relations with the bishop are good; Wakefield: Dean: Email 24–1-2017: two elected members take part in the process.
125 Phillimore I.143. See also Canons Ecclesiastical 1603/4, Cans 24 and 42: petty canons, vicars-choral, singing men; the statute 1&2 Vic. c. 106, s. 124 included them within the meaning of 'cathedral preferment'.
126 Phillimore I.728.
127 The tradition of Choral Evensong at cathedrals, its formality and professionalism, was essentially 'a Victorian invention' of the nineteenth century: H&R 187.
128 H&R 21–23: they include: elitism (most choristers come from the higher socio-economic groups) – wider recruitment is recommended; sexism – girls should be included; it speaks only to a minority of the nation.
129 H&R 253, Appendix 6.
130 H&R 178, Recs 1 to 7 (see Ch. 5); see also 56.
131 Association of English Cathedrals: website.

124 *The choir and presbytery*

There is little national law on cathedral music,[132] though each cathedral constitution must provide for the appointment of a person to supervise music there.[133] Moreover, according to national guidance, each cathedral should have a music policy. Chapter should be responsible for its regular review and delivery. The dean has an executive overview of policy and a statutory responsibility for worship delegated to the precentor who has oversight and day-to-day responsibility for worship and overall pastoral responsibility for the music staff, lay clerks, choristers and their families. The Director of Music is responsible to Chapter through the precentor for the selection, provision and performance of music, and the principal trainer and director of the cathedral choirs, sharing pastoral oversight with and reporting to the precentor. The Assistant Director of Music is responsible to Chapter through the Director of Music for playing the organ for worship, accompanying the cathedral choirs, assisting with training and direction of the choirs and carrying out necessary administrative tasks, and reports to the Director of Music. The Organ Scholar is responsible to Chapter through the Assistant Director of Music for assisting with accompanying, training and directing the choirs, carrying out administrative tasks, and reporting to the Assistant Director of Music.[134] There is also guidance on appointments,[135] and the Association of English Cathedrals has guidance on the pastoral care of choristers.[136] The Cathedral Organists' Association is a forum for developing and supporting directors of music and disseminating 'good professional practice'.[137] And the Society of Friends of Cathedral Music exists to advance the education of the public in the art of music with special reference to the Choral Service in Cathedrals.[138]

The requirement of the Measure for a director of music, norms in the national guidance, and the good practice recommended by the Commission are implemented in various ways by the cathedrals themselves in both their constitutions and statutes. What follows are case studies from each of our cathedral types: they are offered in order to illustrate nuanced differences.

Old foundations deal with the appointment and duties of a Director of Music (various titles are used), the assistant director or organist, organist scholars, lay clerks (or vicars-choral), and choristers (which may include their musical education).[139] At Lincoln, the organist, under the supervision of the precentor, is

132 Can. B20.1: canonical norms on the appointment (and termination of appointment) of musicians, do not apply to cathedrals 'where the matter is governed by or dependent upon the statutes or customs of the same'.
133 CM 1999, s. 9(1)(g).
134 The Cathedrals' Liturgy and Music Group: Producing a Cathedral Music Policy (2006). See also Music in English Cathedrals 2001–2011 (2012).
135 The Cathedrals' Liturgy and Music Group: Suggested guidelines for appointing Directors of Music in Cathedrals (2012); and Formation for Sacramental Liturgy and Music in Cathedrals, Timothy Hone (2004).
136 Association of English Cathedrals: Pastoral Care of Choristers (2014).
137 Cathedral Organists' Association: Rules as amended 6 May 2012.
138 Con. Clauses 1–3: as well as in other churches.
139 E.g. Exeter: Stat. XI-XII: the director must be an actual communicant and duties include conducting and training the choir and care for the instruments; Chapter may

responsible to Chapter for: advising on the selection of priest vicars, lay vicars and choristers; the appointment of an assistant organist or choir director or organ scholar; training lay vicars and choristers; selecting music and submitting it to the precentor; working with the contracted school to provide a planned and systematic musical and spiritual education; contributing to the musical life of the city and diocese; and ensuring the cathedral's international ministry is advanced by music.[140] The priest vicars, appointed by Chapter on the advice of the precentor, must 'take such part in all or any of the services, choral or otherwise [as] Chapter shall determine, provided that the distribution of those duties shall be arranged by the succentor or in his absence among themselves'.[141] The precentor may with approval of Chapter appoint a succentor, normally a priest vicar, to assist him.[142] There must be sufficient stipendiary lay vicars appointed by Chapter as recommended by the precentor; the organist advises Chapter on selection and training; Chapter sets the terms as to leave, remuneration and duties, and may appoint further stipendiary lay vicars and honorary singing men according to need and availability.[143] Chapter must also make provision for: the appointment of choristers selected after a voice trial and appropriate educational test; and for their educational and spiritual welfare: to this end, Chapter may contract with a local school in return for bursaries to remit choristers' fees at such rates as Chapter must determine.[144]

The Organist of Hereford, who must be appointed by Chapter, shall be the Director of Music and is to: supervise the music; arrange and conduct the music at the daily offices and other services subject to Chapter's direction; encourage and maintain the highest standards of excellence in the performance of the choirs; care for the instruments and music owned by the cathedral; and care for the welfare and good conduct of the Lay Clerks and Choristers.[145] The former must be appointed by Chapter on such terms as to tenure, remuneration, duties, and otherwise as Chapter may determine. The principal duty of the Lay Clerks is to sing, under the direction of the Organist, at the daily offices and the Eucharist in the cathedral and elsewhere whenever required; they must maintain the highest musical standards. In turn, the Choristers, pupils attending either Hereford

> appoint priest vicars to e.g. 'assist in singing'; Salisbury: Con. Art. 7: Chapter must employ a director (on the recommendation of the precentor); it may appoint e.g. organ scholars, lay vicars or singing clerks (who have written agreements) and choristers after consulting the head of the Prebendal School and for the 'musical education' of choristers; Art. 5.5: the precentor orders the music subject to the dean; Chichester: Con. Art. 16 and Stat. 15: Chapter appoints the Organist and Master of the Choristers (who is also responsible for the 'discipline' of the choir) and e.g. an Assistant Organist. London: Con. Art. 11.4; see also Stat. IX.4, XV, XVI: the Musical Foundation includes these.

140 Lincoln: Stat. 12; see Stat. 16 for the contracted school.
141 Lincoln: Stat. 13.
142 Lincoln: Stat. 14.
143 Lincoln: Stat. 15.
144 Lincoln: Stat. 16.
145 Hereford: Con. Art. 17.

126 *The choir and presbytery*

Cathedral Junior School or Hereford Cathedral School, must sing under the direction of the Organist at such daily offices, other occasions during term time, and other times as reasonably required by the Organist.[146] The objects of the Hereford Cathedral Perpetual Trust include: the 'promotion and maintenance to a high standard of the Choral Services of the Church of England in the Cathedral' as the Board of Governors in its absolute discretion thinks fit; promoting the religious, musical and secular education of pupils attending any school where instruction in the doctrines of the Church of England is given and performance of Choral Services of the Church of England is observed; and the repair, maintenance and renewal of the cathedral organ, acquisition and maintenance of its musical books and manuscripts, and the employment of all staff including lay clerks.[147]

A similar spectrum of norms is found at new foundations.[148] Canterbury has extraordinarily detailed norms on the subject. First, there must be an Organist appointed by Chapter, on terms determined by it,[149] to: (1) diligently direct the music and where appropriate play the organ and accompany the voices; take part in special services as may be ordered by the archbishop or Chapter receiving, whenever possible, adequate notice from the dean, or, with the approval of the dean, providing a competent substitute approved by Chapter (towards whose stipend Chapter makes annual or other contribution as agreed); (2) prepare periodically consulting the Precentor for the dean's approval a list of music for the ensuing period; (3) provide for regular practices of the choir at appropriate times; (4) exercise proper supervision over the Children of the Choir and Lay Clerks and instruct them by his teaching and example that they may learn according to their ability to love sacred music as an offering acceptable to God; and (5) endeavour to promote the study of music in the City of Canterbury, diocese and elsewhere. In addition to the oath of obedience to

---

146 Hereford: Stat. VIII.1.-3.
147 Hereford Cathedral Perpetual Trust: Memorandum of Association 3.1. Also, York: Con. Art. X.F; Stat. XII.
148 E.g. Durham: Stat. XXV: Chapter must appoint as Master of Choristers and Organist a person 'of good fame and upright conversation, skilled in playing the organ, and well capable of giving instruction in singing and chanting, and ... a member of the Church of England or of another Christian church' to: ensure the organ is played at divine service; instruct the Lay Clerks, Choral Scholars and Choristers; practise with them at times the Precentor and Organist may agree; discharge such duties as Chapter may assign; consult the Precentor in all that concerns the music and the Head of the Chorister School as to choir practices and selection of Choristers, subject to the dean; Chapter may also appoint a Sub-Organist, Assistant Organist and Organ Scholar; Stat. XXVI: Lay Clerks must be 'of good character, reverent in their demeanour, skilled in singing' and members of the Church of England or other Christian church; Stat. XXVII: choral scholars from Durham University; Stat. XVIII: Chapter may appoint 22 male and 22 female choristers and make arrangements, financial or otherwise, for their education. See also Rochester: Stat. XII-XVI; Gloucester: Stat. 11, 16, 17 and 18; and Bristol: Con. Art. 12(4) and Stat. 21: Master of Choristers and Organist – and Chapter must appoint a boys' choir and a girls' choir (to serve subject to Chapter regulations); Stat. 7(1): precentor; Stat. 2: minor canons; Oxford: Stat. VII: Chapter may apply pay the stipends and salaries of e.g. the organist, lay clerks, and choristers.
149 Canterbury: Con. Art. 17.

Chapter, the Organist must on admission swear an oath to perform the duties of office and observe the statutes of the cathedral.[150]

Second, as to the Children of the Choir, there must be 16 Choristers of tender age who have both musical voices and an aptitude for singing, to serve, minister and sing in the Choir, and a sufficient number of probationers to fill the places of the Choristers when these become vacant and as Chapter thinks fit.[151] Third, there must be a sufficient number of Lay Clerks (of good character and musical ability) appointed by Chapter as members of the Choir with a written agreement setting out terms of service as to tenure, remuneration and duties; they are admitted to office according the customs of the cathedral taking an oath similar to that of the Organist, and must diligently perform singing as the Organist assigns and perform such duties and attend practices as the dean, after consulting the Precentor and Organist, may appoint.[152]

Fourth, Chapter may appoint Minor Canons and Honorary Minor Canons of good character and musical ability on such terms as Chapter determines. Each Minor Canon is admitted similarly to sing any service in the absence of the Precentor at the request of the Canon-in-Residence, and perform all such duties as Chapter may direct; if any disagreement arises the aggrieved party may appeal to the Archbishop as Visitor whose decision is final; every Minor Canon must retire from and vacate the office automatically on attaining the age of 70.[153]

Fifth, the Precentor (appointed by Chapter with the dean's consent), must: (1) maintain discipline among the singers; (2) train the Lay Clerks and Children of the Choir to behave with reverence and devotion; (3) receive due obedience from all who enter the Choir to sing; (4) act in agreement with and consult the Organist to prepare for the approval of the dean a periodic list of music, including hymns and anthems, signed by both of them; (5) ensure that the music is liturgically suitable and, with the Organist, worthy of divine worship and within the competence of the singers; (6) make provision for such special services as the Archbishop or Chapter may direct (and the Precentor and Organist must give proper notice to the dean of these); and (7) consulting the Organist, ensure that regular choir practices are held. Any disagreement between the Precentor and Organist must be referred amicably and without contention to Chapter, which must decide the issue after taking any advice it thinks fit.[154]

Norms at parish church cathedrals are generally less detailed than those at the old and new foundations.[155] St Edmundsbury and Southwark may be contrasted

150 Canterbury: Stat. XIX.1–2.
151 Canterbury: Stat. XIX.1–3.
152 Canterbury: Stat. XIX.4.
153 Canterbury: Stat. XVII.
154 Canterbury: Stat. XVIII.1–9: the Precentor also must daily record the attendance at divine service of the dean, residentiaries and choir and report, whenever Chapter requires and at the Saint Catherine's Audit, any matters affecting his office occurring during the year, and make suggestions for Chapter to consider. If absent, the Precentor must with the dean's approval appoint some other persons to perform his duties; he retires at seventy.
155 One of the most minimalistic is Coventry: Con. Art. 12.4: 'Chapter shall appoint a Director of Music to supervise the music in the Cathedral Church'.

128 *The choir and presbytery*

in terms of the depth of coverage. The Organist and Master of Choristers of St Edmundsbury, appointed by the dean on terms as to tenure, remuneration and duties determined by Chapter,[156] must: regularly consult the dean and canon precentor as to the music and the conduct of the choirs; after consulting the precentor and with the dean's approval, select the Sub-Organist (or Assistant Director of Music), who is appointed by the dean on such terms as may be determined by Chapter; and recruit, appoint and train all Choristers, Lay Clerks and other Choir members.[157]

Southwark Chapter must appoint a Director of Music on terms determined by it.[158] Subject to the general control of the dean, the Director of Music must perform such duties as the Precentor may determine. There must also be as many Assistant Organists, Lay Clerks, Chanters and Choristers as Chapter may determine. The Lay Clerks, Chanters and Choristers must be appointed by Chapter on such terms as it may determine. All, on appointment, are admitted to their offices by the dean.[159] The Precentor must, either in person or through the Succentor, and subject to the general control of the dean, have responsibility for the music performed in consultation with the Director of Music.[160] A Succentor may be appointed by Chapter, on such terms as Chapter may determine, who, in the absence of the Precentor or if the Precentor so directs, is responsible in co-operation with the Director of Music for the discipline of choir members; and who must arrange for the performance of the music for the services in the cathedral; when acting for the Precentor, the Succentor must have all the powers of the Precentor; and the Succentor has precedence over the Cathedral Chaplains.[161]

The cathedral interviews

These express general satisfaction with norms on music. However, various practices exist as to the discipline of choristers. At Hereford, while not regulated by the constitution/statutes, as a matter of practice disciplinary matters among the choristers would first be raised by the precentor and resolved by the director of music, with referral to the dean if necessary when a 'formal meeting would be held with the parents and chaired by the dean with the precentor and director present'.[162] The Salisbury constitution and statutes are also silent on the matter, but any disciplinary issue is dealt with by the Director of Music acting with the Precentor.[163]

By way of contrast, the Master of Choristers of Bristol has by statute (Stat. 21) the power of discipline over the choristers but the process is not prescribed; as a matter of practice, if there is for example a case of bullying amongst the choristers,

156 St Edmundsbury: Con. Art. 13(4).
157 St Edmundsbury: Stat. 22(1)-(3).
158 Southwark: Con. Art. XIII(4).
159 Southwark: Stat. 12(1)-(3).
160 Southwark: Stat. 3(5).
161 Southwark: Stat. 11.
162 Hereford: Dean: Int. 5–8-2016.
163 Salisbury: Dean: Int. 20–9-2016; see Con. Art. 17 and Stat. 7.2.

the dean calls and chairs a meeting consisting of the Chapter Clerk (also the safeguarding officer) and the Master of Choristers; and a case involving dismissal of a chorister is processed 'with the consent of the dean'; the dean (and not the Master of Choristers) would resolve a serious case involving a lay clerk.[164]

Finally, by statute at Gloucester, any disputes as to music are resolved on the basis of Chapter 'guidelines'; Chapter has not made any to date. Moreover, at diocesan services, when the choir is called on to perform less 'high-brow' music, in order for that music to be 'inclusive', the bishop and Chapter may encourage the choir to participate for the sake of inclusiveness. A statute also provides for a Youth Choir which includes girls; it was enacted and the choir established to give opportunities for teenage girls to sing in the cathedral. As of September 2016 a girls' choir exists for younger girls aged 7–13 and the long-term aspiration is to 'give the choir parity' with the cathedral's boys' choir and 'make it official'; 'gender' debate drove this.[165] Similarly, Rochester's statutory provision for voluntary choirs 'works well'.[166]

Conclusion

No person may be appointed dean until having completed six years in holy orders and unless a priest at the time of appointment. Some deans are appointed by the Crown, others by the bishop in consultation with Chapter, and in two cathedrals by trustees. Normally, the dean is instituted by the bishop, and received, admitted and installed by Chapter, and must make the prescribed declarations and oaths. A dean holds office on the basis of the Ecclesiastical Offices (Terms of Service) Measure 2009, must retire at seventy, and may be removed under the Church Dignitaries (Retirement) Measure 1949. The dean is the principal dignitary in the cathedral next after the bishop. As chair of Chapter, the dean is to: ensure that divine service is duly performed and that the constitution and statutes are observed; maintain good order and proper reverence in the cathedral; secure the pastoral care of the cathedral community; take all decisions necessary to deal with any emergency, pending consideration by Chapter; reside in the allotted house; preside over Chapter and College of Canons; and attend and participate in the work of Council. No action may be taken by Chapter without the consent of the dean as to: alterations in the ordering of services; settlement of the budget; and implementation of a decision taken by Chapter in the dean's absence. These rules are repeated in cathedral constitutions and/or statutes with little embellishment, with the exception of additional norms on attending divine services, preaching, and celebrating Communion at prescribed times. The interviews reveal general satisfaction with these rules, that the right to veto Chapter decisions is not used, and, in some, concern for greater openness in the appointment of deans.

By national law, the cathedral constitution must provide for appointment of canons in holy orders, the manner and tenure of appointment, and specify the

164 Bristol: Dean: Int. 3–8-2016.
165 Gloucester: Chancellor: Int. 4–8-2016: see Stat. 11(4) and 18.
166 Rochester: Precentor: Int. 30–9-2016; see Stat. XV.

number of residentiary and non-residentiary canons. No-one may be appointed as a residentiary unless they have been in holy orders for six years. The Church Commissioners must pay two residentiaries engaged exclusively on cathedral duties such stipend as they determine; and Chapter may, with their consent, pay to the residentiaries an additional stipend as it think fits. A residentiary holds office on terms similar to that of a dean. The cathedral constitution must provide that at least two residentiaries are engaged exclusively on cathedral duties; any question arising about this is determined by the Church Commissioners after consulting the Visitor and Chapter (with appeal to the archbishop). Constitutions and statutes contain elaborate norms of the duties of residentiaries, including attendance at services, preaching, celebrating the Holy Communion, strengthening cathedral life and worship, and promoting its ministry in the diocese. In most cathedrals residentiaries are appointed and collated by the bishop and installed by the dean on behalf of Chapter; in some they are appointed by the Crown. They also provide for the appointment, tenure, and functions of non-residentiaries. Complaints against cathedral clergy may be the subject of disciplinary process under the Clergy Discipline Measure 2003. Provision also exists for the creation, continuance, abolition, suspension or termination of any dignity or office in the cathedral. The interviews indicate numerous practices in relation to the ministry of cathedral canons, such as the use of 'job descriptions'; and some also propose greater clarity with regard to the ministerial development review of cathedral clergy.

Cathedrals play a unique role in the maintenance of the English choral tradition. National law, however, is largely silent on this, save that a cathedral must provide for the appointment by Chapter of a director of music to supervise music in the cathedral, and that the matter (by canon law) is regulated by cathedral statutes. Nevertheless, there is a high level of uniformity as between the cathedrals on this subject which may or may not be the result of custom, shared practice, and guidance issued at national level which provides that each cathedral should develop its own 'music policy'. A notable difference as between the cathedrals is the volume of regulation: some cathedrals employ a minimalist approach (particularly the parish church cathedrals) and many (among the cathedrals of the old and new foundations) employ a system of detailed rules. Nevertheless, several common features emerge. Chapter is responsible for music policy. The dean has executive oversight and a statutory responsibility for its use in worship. On a day-to-day basis that responsibility is delegated to the precentor, who also has pastoral responsibility for music staff, lay clerks, choristers and their families; minor canons may also be appointed in some cathedrals to assist in singing at services. The Director of Music is responsible to Chapter through the precentor for the selection, provision and performance of music, and is the principal trainer and director of the cathedral choir (sharing pastoral roles with the precentor). Cathedrals also make provision for the appointment, functions, standards, and sometimes, discipline, of lay clerks and choristers, as well as for the education of the latter in a choir school (see below Chapter 7). The cathedral interviews indicate a number of practices used in relation to the disciplining of lay clerks and choristers, as well as the introduction in recent years of choirs to include boys and/or girls.

6 The chapter house: the body corporate – Council, Chapter and College of Canons

The collegiate character of medieval cathedrals, whether secular or monastic, was nowhere better expressed than by their chapter houses in which the business of cathedral governance was transacted. They were sometimes square in ground-plan but more usually polygonal, situated either to the north or north east or south or south east of the crossing. Before the Reformation there were some 25 polygonal chapter houses in England, but more than half have been destroyed, with notable survivors at Salisbury (large at 58 feet across), Southwell (with 32 leaf-decorated stall-canopies within), and Wells (with its central clustered column of 32 branches in the decorated style); of those that are rectangular, Bristol has preserved its Norman chapter house with fine blind arcading, as has Gloucester (where William the Conqueror decreed the compilation of the Doomsday Book) and Chester with its superb set of lancet windows.[1] Today, however, the governing bodies of the cathedral do not usually meet in the chapter house but in offices in the precinct.[2] What follows examines the body corporate of the cathedral, namely: Council; Chapter; and College of Canons – their composition, functions, and relationships one to the other in the governance of the cathedral.[3] It also examines the role of officers of the Chapter, particularly that of the Administrator. The Cathedrals Measure 1999 contains a large body of rules on the subject and the constitutions and statutes of each cathedral implement and somewhat embellish these.

The Archbishops' Commission on Cathedrals 1994 recommended that cathedral governance should be supportive, effective, accountable, and responsive. As we saw in Chapter 1, the Commission proposed abolition, for the purposes of

---

1 P. Johnson, *British Cathedrals* (1980) 15, 106, 108, 113, 126, 139.
2 Oxford: Stat. I.2(b): the House must preserve the Chapter House; see also Chelmsford: Con. 12(a).
3 Burn (1788) II.75–119; II.87: 'Dean and chapter is a body corporate spiritual, consisting of many able persons in law, namely, the dean who is the chief, and his prebendaries; and they together make the corporation' (citing Godolphin 51); 'They were originally selected by the bishop from amongst his clergy, as counsel and assistants to him; but they derive their corporate capacity from the crown' (citing Godolphin 52); II.75: 'a dean has a chapter consisting of prebendaries or canons, subordinate to the bishop, as a council assistant to him in matters spiritual relating to religion; and in matters temporal relating to the temporalities of his bishopric'.

governance, of the distinction between dean and chapter cathedrals and parish church cathedrals. Rather, each cathedral should have a Greater Council, an Administrative Chapter, and a College of Canons (or Greater Chapter). The Greater Council would be chaired by the bishop, approve the statutes, advise on strategy, receive the annual budget, and approve the annual report and accounts; and it should consist of elected members of the cathedral community and College of Canons, representatives of the diocese and local community, and persons appointed by the bishop to reflect regional, national or international aspects of cathedral work. The Administrative Chapter, consisting of the dean (its executive chair) and the residentiaries, would have legal responsibility for the administration, property, and spiritual life of the cathedral – and it would be accountable to the Greater Chapter; there should also be a cathedral administrator. The College of Canons (or Greater Chapter) should consist of the residentiaries and non-residentiaries, lay and ordained, continue to have its 'purely honorific role in the election of the diocesan bishop', provide a link with parishes and wider community, and serve as an experienced forum to assist the Administrative Chapter.[4]

Under the Cathedrals Measure 1999 these bodies became the Council, Chapter, and College of Canons, but the bishop did not become chair of Council;[5] together, these three institutions became the body corporate with perpetual succession and a common seal,[6] the membership of each to be elected or chosen in the manner and with such qualifications prescribed by the cathedral's constitution.[7] Each body (Council, Chapter and College) must have due regard to the fact that the cathedral is the seat of the bishop and a centre of worship and mission.[8] As we have seen in earlier chapters, and as we shall in what follows and elsewhere, *consultation* is a key feature of these arrangements; indeed, Portsmouth's constitution provides, unusually, that:

> '[C]onsultation' means affording an opportunity to express views both in general as to an appointment or issue and specifically as to any ... appointment or ... proposed course of action and in deciding whom to appoint or on the action to be taken having regard to those views.[9]

Also, constitutions and/or statutes contain general norms on a range of procedural matters; two important principles here are that: no proceedings of the Council, Chapter or College of Canons are invalidated by any vacancy in the

---

4 H&R 57–74 (Ch. 6). See also 75–86 (Ch. 7): professionalisation of management: see above Chapter 4.
5 As to parish church cathedrals, see CM 1999, s. 12(1)-(3). See e.g. Portsmouth: Con. Art. 10.6: 'Chapter shall exercise the functions previously exercisable in relation to the Parish by the parochial church council'.
6 CM 1999, s. 2; s. 9(1)(a). See e.g. Wells: Con. Art. 2; Carlisle: Con. Art. 2; Guildford: Con. Art. 2.
7 CM 1999, s. 35(1) and (6).
8 CM 1999, s. 1; and see HLE par. 346.
9 Portsmouth: Con. Art. 16.1.

membership or any defect in the qualification of election of their members;[10] and, subject to the general law, constitution and statutes, these three bodies may regulate their own procedure.[11] Cathedrals may also have quasi-legislation applicable to cathedral governance, management and accountability (see above Chapter 4).[12]

The Council

The Cathedrals Measure 1999 requires that each cathedral constitution must provide for the establishment of a Council.[13] The Measure deals with the Council's composition, functions, and meetings. However, the Association of English Cathedrals recognised in 2016 that the role of Councils 'continues to be a challenging subject': they have minimal powers but recruit high powered individuals as members – and making full use of their talents is difficult; some cathedrals 'struggle more than others with the different governance bodies, often because of the resources required'; 'the effectiveness of a Council is dependent on its chair'; a Chapter can make good use of Council members as chairs of short-term working groups which make recommendations to Chapter; and the Council's role in revising the cathedral constitution and statutes, 'a process which is not ideal' (see Chapter 1 above), could only be considered as part of a wider review of the Measure of 1999 – but 'there is no appetite for this at present'.[14] These concerns are borne out, in various ways, in the cathedral interviews (see below).

The membership of Council

The Cathedrals Measure 1999 provides that the Council must consist of: (a) the chairman; (b) the dean; (c) a prescribed number (not less than two nor more than five) of members of the Chapter chosen by Chapter;[15] (d) two members of the College of Canons appointed by the College; (e) a prescribed number (not less than two nor more than four) of lay persons, not being Chapter members, representing the interests of the cathedral community elected in the prescribed manner;[16] and (f) a prescribed number (not less than five nor more than ten) of persons appointed in the prescribed manner, being persons having experience in connection with the work of the cathedral or the ability to reflect local, diocesan,

---

10 See e.g. Hereford: Stat. XI.1; Lincoln: Stat. 8; Manchester: Con. Art. 1(4); Southwell: Stat. 9.1.
11 See e.g. Wells: Stat. 11.
12 E.g. Salisbury: The Code of Good Governance (September 2013).
13 CM 1999, s. 3(1).
14 Executive Note on Cathedral Councils (2016): I thank the Dean of Birmingham for alerting me to this.
15 The constitution must prescribe the number: s. 35(1).
16 See above Chapter 4 for the cathedral community and the CM 1999, s. 35(1); and s. 35(6): elected 'in the prescribed manner' includes a power for the constitution to specify the qualifications for membership.

134 *The chapter house*

ecumenical or national interests in that connection.[17] The members of Council (other than the dean) hold office for a term of years to be prescribed but are eligible for membership for further terms of office.[18]

Cathedrals differ as to the number on Council of Chapter and cathedral community members, and those chosen (usually by the bishop) to represent wider interests, expertise and ability, and as to the length of their term of office. Among old foundations, for example, Lichfield Council comprises: four Chapter members; two laity representing interests of the cathedral community elected from its roll; and ten experienced in the cathedral's work or able to reflect wider interests connected with its 'spiritual, evangelistic, pastoral, educational and social work', appointed by the bishop after consulting Chapter; members serve for four years but are eligible for further terms if no more than two further terms are immediately consecutive.[19] Wells' Council has: three Chapter members; three laity on the cathedral community roll; and five persons with experience in its work and able to represent wider interests, that is: two lay communicants appointed by the Bishop's Council, and, all appointed by the bishop, one having regard to cathedral needs and particular expertise and experience; one from members of the cathedral's Fabric Advisory Committee; and one (not being a Chapter member) from the Chapter Finance Committee; office is held for a renewable three-year term.[20] Other old foundations differ as to the number of Chapter members, the number of lay persons from the cathedral community, and the number of bodies chosen by the bishop to represent the wider interests, expertise and ability, and with regard to the length of their term of office.[21]

Similar variety exists among new foundations; for instance: Norwich Council includes the High Steward (administrator); two Chapter members; three lay communicants elected by the cathedral community; and five others (at least two lay) with experience connected with the cathedral's work or able to reflect wider interests appointed by the bishop; they serve for a renewable three-year term;[22] Durham has two Chapter members; one (lay or ordained) appointed by Durham University; three laity elected by the cathedral community; and seven (lay or ordained) to represent wider interests, expertise and ability appointed by Council after consulting the bishop; they serve for a renewable three-year term.[23] However, Canterbury Council has: three Chapter members; three lay persons elected

17 CM 1999, s. 3(4). See also Chapter 4 above.
18 CM 1999, s. 3(5).
19 Lichfield: Con. Art. 6(1) and (3); (4) deals with casual vacancies; see also Art. 6(10): elections.
20 Wells: Con. Art. 9(1); and Stat. App. 3: Standing Orders.
21 See e.g. Chichester: Con. Art. 3.c: Chapter 2, cathedral community 2, wider interests 8 (appointed by the bishop and Chapter jointly); 5-year term; Exeter: Con. Art. 4: Chapter 3, cathedral community 3, wider interests 10 (appointed by the bishop after consulting Chapter, Bishop's Council and Standing Committee of the Diocesan Synod and such other bodies as the bishop deems appropriate); they hold for a renewable 3 year term.
22 Norwich: Con. Art. XI.1. See also Gloucester: Con. Art. 13.
23 Durham: Con. Art. 10.a and c.

by the cathedral community; and ten other persons: one area dean; three laity (one expert in finance) appointed by the Archbishop's Council; one appointed by the Archbishop with expertise in architectural and conservation matters and another with expertise in education; one appointed by Churches Together in Kent; one by Canterbury City Council; one by the Anglican Consultative Council (of the Anglican Communion); one by the Appointments Committee of General Synod; and one by the Canterbury Cathedral Trustees – all serve for a renewable five-year term.[24] Much the same variations are found at cathedrals of Henrician foundation,[25] and at parish church cathedrals the Councils of which too may include civic and university representatives.[26]

The functions and meetings of Council

Under the Cathedrals Measure 1999, the Council has numerous duties and powers. First, Council must further and support the work of the cathedral – spiritual, pastoral, evangelistic, social and ecumenical – reviewing and advising on its direction and oversight by Chapter, and in particular it must: (a) consider proposals submitted by Chapter in connection with the general direction and mission of the cathedral and give advice on them to Chapter; (b) receive and consider the annual budget of the cathedral; (c) receive and consider the annual report and audited accounts; (d) consider proposals submitted by Chapter in connection with the constitution and statutes with a view to their revision; and (e) perform such other functions as may be prescribed.[27] Second, Council may: (a) request reports from Chapter on any matter concerning the cathedral; (b) discuss and declare its opinion on any such matter; and (c) draw any matter to the attention of the bishop as Visitor or the Church Commissioners.[28]

Cathedrals repeat these norms, sometimes making use of the power to add functions as prescribed. Among old foundations,[29] for example, at Wells, Council must 'perform such other tasks as from time to time it shall be called upon by the Chapter or the Bishop' to perform;[30] Salisbury Council must carry out such other functions 'as may be agreed by the Chapter after consultation with the Bishop';[31] and Chichester Council must perform such other functions as are determined by Council, Chapter and bishop jointly.[32] Similarly, among the new and Henrician

---

24 Canterbury: Con. Art. 5(1).
25 E.g. Bristol: Con. Art. 9(1): Chapter 5; cathedral community, 4 laity, and 7 other persons to reflect wider interests appointed variously by the Bishop's Council and bishop for a renewable 4-year term; Chester: Con. Art. 14.
26 E.g. Blackburn: Con. Art. 12: Chapter 3, cathedral community 3 (including 2 from the parish electoral roll), 8 serving wider interests for a renewable 5 year term.
27 CM 1999, s. 3(6); see also s. 35(1): prescribed by the constitution.
28 CM 1999, s. 3(7).
29 The CM 1999 list is repeated at e.g. York: Con. Art. VII.D: duties; VII.K: powers.
30 Wells: Con. Art. 9(6)(e).
31 Salisbury: Con. Art. 5.1(5): duties; 5.5: powers (the article repeats the Measure list).
32 Chichester: Con. Art. 3.c.

foundations, most merely repeat the list in the Cathedrals Measure 1999,[33] as do parish church cathedrals, but some may add 'educational' work to their list.[34]

The Cathedrals Measure 1999 requires the bishop to appoint a lay person, not being a Chapter member, as Council chair, but: (a) before doing so must afford to Chapter an opportunity to express views both in general as to the appointment and as to any specific person proposed by the bishop; and (b) in deciding whom to appoint the bishop must have regard to the views of Chapter.[35] Constitutions repeat these rules and sometimes add to them: for instance, the chair of Lichfield Council serves for four years but is eligible for further terms if no more than two are immediately consecutive; at other cathedrals the term may be for three or five years.[36]

The Cathedrals Measure 1999 requires Council to meet at least twice each calendar year.[37] Cathedrals have norms on the calling of and notice for meetings, quorum, chair, and the right of non-members to attend and speak but not vote at meetings. Lichfield Council must meet at least three times each year; Chapter members must be given notice of these and may attend and (at the chair's direction) speak but not vote; Council may invite any person to attend and speak but not vote.[38] Meetings must be called by the chair in accordance with a resolution of Council, on the chair's own motion or on the written request of at least one third of Council members; quorum is seven; each member has one vote; and if the chair is absent, Council must elect a member to chair that meeting.[39] Wells Council meetings are similarly called by the chair on a Council resolution, his own motion, or the written request of at least eight Council members; quorum is eight (but for revision of the constitution or statutes, two thirds of members must be present); if the chair is absent, the dean may invite a Council member to preside.[40] Chichester Council must have at least two annual meetings; quorum is one third of members (at least two must be clerical); a meeting may be requested by at least six members; and in the absence of the chair Council must elect one of

---

33 E.g. Durham: Con. Art. 10; Norwich: Con. Art. XI.6–7; Bristol: Con. Art. 9(7)-(8); Chester: Con. Art. 14(ii). See, however, Worcester: Con. Art. 6.6: 'It shall be the duty of the Council to further and support the work of the Cathedral, spiritual, pastoral, evangelistic, social, ecumenical, educational and prophetic'.
34 E.g. Manchester: Con. Art. X(5)-(6); Newcastle: Con. Art. 11.6–7; Southwell: Con. Art. 10.6–7.
35 CM 1999, s. 3(3). Bullimore Report (2012) par. 85: a response from one cathedral indicated that 'there was insufficient consultation by the bishop with the Council before the chair was appointed'.
36 Lichfield: Con. Art. 6(3). See also Hereford: Con. Art. 3(2): 5 years; Bradford: Con. Art. 15.3: 3 years.
37 CM 1999, s. 3(8). See e.g. Chichester: Con. Art. 3.g: twice each year; Exeter: Con. Art. 4.g.
38 Lichfield: Con. Art. 6(7) and (9)(d). See also Wells: Con. Art. 9(5).
39 Lichfield: Stat. V.
40 Wells: Stat. 9: Council must appoint a secretary (who need not be a Council member).

its members to preside.[41] Other old foundations have similar norms,[42] as do new foundations,[43] and parish church cathedrals.[44]

By Measure, the bishop may be present and speak, but not vote, at Council meetings.[45] This rule too is repeated in the constitutions and/or statutes of the old foundations,[46] the new foundations,[47] the Henrician foundations,[48] and parish church cathedrals.[49] It is uncommon for the constitutions or statutes of cathedrals to prescribe the venue for meetings of the Council; however, at Guildford: 'The Council shall be entitled to meet in the Cathedral'.[50]

The cathedral interviews

These disclose a variety of understandings and practices in respect of the Council (in addition to those set out in Chapter 4 as to the representation on it of the interests of wider society). The Dean of Hereford considers Council a 'good backstop': it is a 'critical friend' to Chapter, provides a culture of 'discipline for clergy', and helps 'talk up the cathedral in the diocese'; but its powers under the constitution (Art. 3) to request reports from or draw matters to the attention of Chapter are 'never used'.[51] By way of contrast, Exeter Council does 'declare its opinion on everything' but 'it does not decide on anything'; Council 'cannot tell Chapter what to do'; yet it 'wants to have more authority than it has'; this is 'sometimes divisive' and its chair works hard to prevent it; the Dean has sometimes asked Council as a 'critical friend' to request reports from Chapter; and the bishop has on several occasions recently used his right to attend Council (latterly, to prepare for a visitation).[52] The Acting Dean of Wells considers Council as 'useful' in providing 'fresh perspectives' on the basis that its members have 'varied backgrounds'; its power to refer a matter to the visitor or Church Commissioners has not been used

41 Chichester: Stat. 2.
42 See e.g. Exeter: Stat. 1; Hereford: Stat. I; Lincoln: Stat. 6; York: Stat. II.
43 Canterbury: Con. Art. 5(5); Stat. II; Norwich: Con. Art. XI.5; Durham: Stat. II; Peterborough: Stat. 14.
44 Blackburn: Stat. 9(1)-(2): called by the dean; quorum of one third; in the dean's absence, Council elects a chair; Manchester: Stat. IV; Newcastle: Stat. 4; Southwell: Stat. 7.
45 CM 1999, s. 3(2). See also the Bullimore Report (2012) par. 84: 'the practice of the bishop in attending and involving himself in Council meetings varies somewhat from diocese to diocese. It seems to me that it would give a higher profile to the Council's work and to the importance of what individual Council members were doing, if the bishop were present at *some* of its meetings'.
46 E.g. Wells: Con. Art. 9(4); Salisbury: Con. Art. 5.4; London: Con. Art. 3.6.
47 E.g. Ely: Con. Art. 11(4); Rochester: Con. Art. 12.4; Norwich: Con. Art. XI.4.
48 E.g. Bristol: Con. Art. 9(5); Chester: Con. Art. 14(viii).
49 E.g. Manchester: Con. Art. X(3); St Albans: Con. Art. IV.4; St Edmundsbury: Con. Art. 4(5).
50 Guildford: Stat. V: this also deals with calling, quorum, and the chairman at meetings.
51 Hereford: Dean: Int. 5-8-2016.
52 Exeter: Dean: Int. 9-8-2016; Con. Art. 4: the bishop may attend Council.

during the incumbency of the Acting Dean.[53] Similarly, for the Dean of Salisbury, Council is not 'intrusive' or 'directive', though its introduction was originally seen as 'a bit of a pain'. However: 'we work hard on relations and for Council to be involved'; it has had considerable 'impact for good' and engages in 'robust' conversations. The Dean is 'grateful Council is there for governance'; but 'governance would not be massively weakened if there were no Council' – indeed: 'every failure of mission is a failure of governance'.[54] And St Paul's Council does not intrude into the work of Chapter; it has 'never invoked' its powers which are 'justified and needed'; they are not used because the Dean 'proactively but informally involves Council' in cathedral life; the bishop does not attend Council meetings.[55]

At the new foundation at Winchester the view was expressed that Council, which should be a 'workable size' without too many episcopal appointees, functions as a 'critical friend' to Chapter not 'as a director', and the bishop does attend Council and 'studiously contributes when asked'.[56] At Rochester, in practice there is a 'good interchange between Council and Chapter'.[57] However, among the Henrician foundations the view was expressed at Gloucester that Council lacks 'power', and, as a result, Council is 'seeking a meaningful role for itself'.[58] There is at Chester a 'perception' amongst Council members that they have authority to direct Chapter and they do from time to time 'dabble in management which they should not do'; Council has never in the past five years used its powers (e.g. request reports); and the bishop exercises the right to attend its meetings 'occasionally'.[59] Indeed, Bristol's domestic law does not forbid an atheist to be a Council member; having an atheist on Council urging a broad public agenda and seeing faith as a hindrance would generate a complicated conversation in Council; as such there is a good case 'to change the law to require a member of Council to be a communicant'; as to its functions, the strategic advice of Council is appreciated, but Chapter is the 'engine'; the bishop offers from time to time to attend Council 'if needed' but in practice has not attended recently.[60]

At the parish church cathedral of Derby, the Dean considers that Council has no authority to direct Chapter – it advises only but does sometimes use its powers under the constitution; however, there are 'questions to be asked over an institution [i.e. Council] which meets only twice a year'; and the bishop never

---

53 Wells: Acting Dean: 12–8-2016; Con. Art. 9.
54 Salisbury: Dean: Int. 20–9-2016; Con. Art. 4.
55 London: Dean: Int. 23–9-2016; Con. Art. 3.3.
56 Winchester: Acting Dean: Int. 16–8-2016. Ely: Dean: Email 17–1-2017: 'Council can be a committee seeking a reason for its existence'; it should not have 'executive powers' but 'should operate as perhaps an assessor of risk', and 'having some audit role might be helpful'; Carlisle: Dean: Email 17–1-2017: Council's role is clear.
57 Rochester: Precentor: Int. 30–9-2016: Council is a 'critical friend'.
58 Gloucester: Chancellor and Vice-Dean: Int. 4–8-2016.
59 Chester: Vice-Dean: Int. 19–8-2016: Con. Art. 14(iii) and (vii).
60 Bristol: Dean: Int. 3–8-2016.

attends its meetings: but this is 'a good sign'.[61] Similarly, Birmingham Council does not use all its powers: 'this is a good sign'; before 2010 Council would bring some matters (such as finance) to the attention of the Visitor, but this power has not been used since, though the Dean does sometimes remind Council of its powers. Indeed, in light of the AEC Executive Note on Cathedral Councils 2016 (see above), the Dean of Birmingham is concerned about recruiting 'high powered individuals' and then not giving them something substantial to do; it is more useful and manageable to recruit people active 'on the ground' in the city who can offer wisdom/intelligence about the city, and region – 'practical advice'.[62]

The Chapter

Following the Reformation, a large body of ecclesiastical law developed around Chapters:

> A chapter ... consists of persons ecclesiastical, canons and prebendaries, whereof the dean is chief, all subordinate to the bishop to whom they are as assistants in matters relating to the church, for the better ordering and disposing the things thereof, and for the confirmation of such leases of the temporalities and offices relating to the bishopric, as the bishop from time to time shall happen to make.[63]

Moreover: 'they are all termed by the canonists *capitulum*, being a kind of head, instituted not only to assist the bishop ... but also anciently to rule and govern the diocese in the time of vacation'.[64] Today, Chapter is seen as 'the administrative powerhouse' of a cathedral.[65] A cathedral constitution must provide for its establishment.[66] No person may be a Chapter member if disqualified from being a charity trustee; anyone so disqualified must cease to be a member.[67] However, the archbishop may, on the application of any person so disqualified, waive the disqualification in respect of that Chapter; the waiver must be notified in writing to the person concerned.[68] Constitutions repeat these norms.[69]

---

61 Derby: Dean: Int. 10–8-2016; see Con. Art. 10.12: powers. Southwark: Dean: Email 17-1-2017: the role of Council and its relation to Chapter are insufficiently well-defined; compare Liverpool: Dean: Email 21–1-2017; and Wakefield: Dean: Email 24–1-2017: Council's role and relation to Chapter are sufficiently well-defined.
62 Birmingham: Dean: Int. 11–8-2016; Con. Art. 14: Council.
63 Burn II.82 (citing Gibson 58). See also Phillimore I.137 for the same approach.
64 Burn II.82 (citing Godolphin 56).
65 HLE par. 348.
66 CM 1999, s. 4(1); see also ss. 36(1) and 38(2)-(3); and CCM 2011: s. 33, Sch. 3.
67 CM 1999, s. 4(4); i.e. disqualified under the Charities Act 1993, s. 72(1) (as amended by the Charities Act 2011, s. 178).
68 CM 1999, s. 4(5).
69 E.g. Wells: Con. Art. 7(1); Lincoln: Con. Art. 9(1).

The composition of Chapter

Under the Cathedrals Measure 1999, the membership must consist of: (a) the dean and all the residentiary canons of the cathedral; and (b) a prescribed number (not less than two or more than seven) of others, at least two-thirds of whom must be lay, chosen in the prescribed manner,[70] who hold office for three years but are eligible for further terms of office.[71] The dean must be: (a) the chair and must have a second/casting vote; and (b) a member of every Chapter committee.[72] Cathedrals differ as to those other than the dean and residentiaries. Old foundation Lichfield Chapter has at least five but no more than seven such persons: the first five are appointed by the bishop, after consulting the dean and residentiaries; any further member, up to two, may be appointed by and at the discretion of Chapter, after consulting the bishop, each having particular expertise to fulfil a specific function; all lay members must be 'confirmed and practising communicants of the Church of England'.[73] Wells' Chapter includes the Cathedral Administrator and two laity (actual communicants) appointed by the bishop.[74] And Chichester Chapter includes one College member elected by it, no fewer than two to six appointed by bishop and Chapter jointly, and the Communar (administrator).[75]

The new foundations follow suit. Durham Chapter has two, three or four lay communicants, appointed by the bishop after consulting the dean and the other Chapter members.[76] Norwich Chapter has an honorary canon appointed by the bishop and three lay actual communicants, resident in the diocese or on a parish electoral roll, appointed by the bishop after consulting the dean and Council chair.[77] Canterbury Chapter includes the administrator (Receiver General) and four appointed by the archbishop consulting Chapter and the Archbishop's Council (one must be ordained, and lay members, actual communicants).[78] Parish church cathedrals have similar patterns; some enable the appointment of ecumenical partners.[79]

---

70 CM 1999, s. 4(2). See below for s. 4(3): a constitution may provide for the Administrator to be a member.
71 CM 1999, s. 4(7); i.e. those mentioned in s. 4(2)(b).
72 CM 1999, s. 4(6).
73 Lichfield: Con. Art. 5(1)-(3). See also London: Con. Art. 4: 4 additional persons, at least 2/3 lay, appointed by the bishop with agreement of the dean after consulting Chapter; they may be 'paid reasonable compensation' for loss of earnings.
74 Wells: Con. Art. 7(1); see also Stat. 2(7): Chapter members between them hold the offices of Keeper of the Fabric, Overseer of the Estate, President of the Guild of St Andrew with such duties as Chapter may decide.
75 Chichester: Con. Art. 4: 4 of the 6 must be lay.
76 Durham: Con. Art. 11.a.
77 Norwich: Con. Art. VIII.1. See also e.g. Bristol: Con. Art. 10(1); Chester: Con. Art. 15(1).
78 Canterbury: Con. Art. 6(1); see also Stat. III.1: the 10 others must make a Declaration of Acceptance of Office containing an undertaking to be bound by the constitution and statutes.
79 E.g. Blackburn: Con. Art. 9(1)-(2): 1 honorary canon; 2 laity appointed by the bishop after consulting the dean, 1 active in the cathedral community; 2 laity elected by the

The functions of Chapter

The Cathedrals Measure 1999 requires Chapter to direct and oversee the administration of the affairs of the cathedral and in particular to: (a) order its worship and promote its mission; (b) formulate, after consulting the bishop, proposals in connection with the general direction and mission of the cathedral and submit them to the Council for its advice; (c) prepare an annual budget for the cathedral; (d) submit to Council the annual report and audited accounts prepared by Chapter and such other reports as may be requested by Council on any matter concerning the cathedral;[80] (e) submit to the College of Canons the annual report and audited accounts prepared similarly; (f) keep under review the constitution and statutes of the cathedral and submit proposals for their revision to Council; (g) manage all property vested in the cathedral and income accruing from it and, in particular, ensure that necessary repairs and maintenance in respect of the cathedral and its contents and other buildings and monuments are carried out; and (h) perform such other functions as may be prescribed.[81] Chapter must exercise any rights of patronage which may be vested in it (as to presentations or nominations to benefices in the diocese), in accordance with the Patronage of Benefices Measure 1986.[82] Moreover, where the guardianship of the spiritualities of a province or bishopric belonged to the dean and chapter of a cathedral, it shall belong to the corporate body of the cathedral and be exercisable on behalf of that body by the Chapter.[83] Chapter functions as to property and finance are considered more fully in later chapters.

Most cathedral constitutions and/or statutes merely repeat these functions,[84] but some add to them. Old foundation Lichfield Chapter functions include 'nurturing the faithful', consulting the bishop on the general direction and mission of the cathedral, and if requested by him advising the bishop; Wells' Chapter, subject to the constitution, statutes and Measure, 'shall possess and enjoy all rights, powers and privileges previously enjoyed by the Dean and Chapter'; and Chichester Chapter must elect members to its Finance Committee, Governors of the Prebendal School, and trustees of the Chichester

> cathedral parochial church meeting (from those on the parish electoral roll); 2 actual communicant members of the Church of England or of a church in communion with it resident in the diocese or on a parish electoral roll appointed by the Bishop's Council and Standing Committee of Diocesan Synod.

80 That is, prepared by Chapter in accordance with CM 1999, s. 27.
81 CM 1999, s. 4(8).
82 E.g. Chichester: Con. Art. 4 and Stat. 14: after consulting the College; Lincoln: Stat. 9; York: Stat. I.5; Canterbury: Stat. III.4; and Oxford: Stat. I.5 and V; Chelmsford: Stat. 13. See also CM 1999, s. 11(b): this stipulates that cathedral statutes may provide that any presentations or nominations to benefices in the patronage of the cathedral shall be exercised by the Chapter or by a patronage committee of the Chapter.
83 Church of England (Miscellaneous Provisions) Measure 2014, s. 14 (amending CM 1999, s. 36, and inserting s. 36(1B)).
84 E.g. Lincoln: Con. Art. 10(1); York: Con. Art. VI.D; London: Con. Art. 4.

Cathedral Friends.[85] Exeter Chapter must: ensure one of its members or other responsible person maintains cathedral worship and is available in case of emergency; consult the bishop at least twice each year as to the direction and mission of the cathedral; order its life 'in accordance with the principles of the statement of purpose of the Cathedral'; make 'a rule of life for its members which shall include a pattern of corporate attendance at public worship'; draw up a 'code of practice' for the proper conduct of its business; establish an Operations Committee to co-ordinate day-to-day implementation of its policy and decisions and report to Chapter on its work; and appoint such staff and officers as required and such other staff as it may determine; and Chapter may: provide for the establishment of limited companies to support the cathedral; maintain a school to educate its choristers; and allocate a house for the dean.[86] Hereford too has a list of additional roles; for example it must appoint annually a Precentor, Chancellor, Treasurer, and ensure the maintenance of records; and its powers include allocation of residences and stalls, appointment of prescribed officers, formation of companies, maintenance of a school, and exercising 'all the powers lawfully exercisable by the Ordinary in relation to the Cathedral'.[87]

New and Henrician foundations,[88] and parish church cathedrals,[89] largely repeat the functions in the Measure, but some add powers such as appointing officers, ministers and servants,[90] and incorporating companies;[91] at Carlisle, the bishop and Chapter must 'take counsel together regularly and frequently for the common good';[92] and at Liverpool, unusually:

> In furtherance of collaborative ministry between the Bishop and the Chapter, the Bishop shall be invited to meet the Chapter at least once a year and to conduct a review of the life and work of the Cathedral every five years.[93]

Winchester is also unusual in that it provides how Chapter must exercise its functions: 'The primary responsibility for discerning and ordering the mission and ministry of the Cathedral rests with the Chapter, subject to the accountability noted in the Constitution and Statutes'; in fulfilling these roles:

> [I]t should be attentive to the suggestions and wisdom of those who share with them in this mission and ministry, conscious that the guidance of the

---

85 Lichfield: Con. Art. 5(4)(a) and (6); Wells: Con. Art. 7(3) and (6); Chichester: Con. Art. 4.e.
86 Exeter: Con. Art. 5.b; and Stat. II.1–3.
87 Hereford: Con. Art. 4(3): duties; (4) powers. For a similar comprehensive list, see Salisbury: Con. Art. 6.1.
88 E.g. Norwich: Con. Art. VIII.2; Bristol: Con. Art. 10(3); Chester: Con. Art. 15(iv)-(v).
89 E.g. Newcastle: Con. Art. 5.3; Blackburn: Con. Art. 9(3).
90 E.g. Canterbury: Con. Art. 7(1); Stat. III.2; Durham: Stat. III.e.
91 E.g. Durham: Con. Art. 11: duties; 15: companies. See also Guildford: Con. Art. 9.4; Stat. VI.2: companies.
92 Carlisle: Stat. 1(1).
93 Liverpool: Stat. 1.6.

Spirit is to be discerned in the community of those who serve [there], though the responsibility and accountability lies with the Chapter.[94]

Chapter may also set up its own committees.[95] Lichfield is typical: Chapter may establish such committees as it may determine, and may delegate functions, powers and duties to them. The dean must be a member of each such committee; persons who are not Chapter members may also be committee members; and Chapter may invite anyone to attend and speak at any meeting of such a committee but not to vote.[96] This rule is commonplace at other cathedral types.[97] However, as seen in Chapter 5, by Measure, Chapter must not, without the consent of the dean, make decisions with regard to alteration of the ordering of services, settlement of the cathedral's budget, or implementation of any decision taken by Chapter in the dean's absence – but the dean's consent is deemed to have been given after the expiry of one month following the date on which the decision was taken unless, within that period, the dean asks Chapter to reconsider the decision at the next Chapter meeting, when the matter must be decided by a majority vote of those present and voting; the dean has a second/casting vote.[98]

Meetings of Chapter: procedure

The Cathedrals Measure 1999 requires Chapter to meet on at least nine occasions in each calendar year; the dean presides and has a casting vote.[99] Constitutions and/or statutes of cathedrals are much the same as to the calling of meetings and the transaction of business. Differences are minor. Four cathedrals may be offered by way of illustration. Lichfield designates one such meeting as the 'Principal Chapter' and prescribes its business (e.g. reviewing the cathedral's work, and appointing members of its Finance Committee). This and other meetings are called by the dean, on the dean's own motion or on the written request of at least four members of Chapter. The quorum is half the members at least one of whom must be a lay person. Each member has one vote (except the dean who has a casting vote). The dean presides but in his absence the Canon-in-Residence serves as chairperson but without a casting vote. Any member with a conflict of interest arising from an item of business must declare it and withdraw from the meeting

---

94 Winchester: Stat. 1.4; see also Con. Art. 10.4: functions in general.
95 This power seems to be implied in CM 1999, s. 4(6).
96 Lichfield: Con. Art. 5(12). See also London: Con. Art. 13; Wells: Con. Art. 8; Exeter: Con. Art. 19; Chichester: Con. Art. 23; Hereford: Con. Art. 13(4)-(6); Winchester: Con. Art. 12.
97 E.g. Lincoln: Con. Art. 12; Peterborough: Con. Art. 11; Leicester: Con. Art. 13; Ripon: Con. Art. 11.
98 CM 1999, ss. 4(11) and 7(3). See e.g. York: Stat. I.4; Durham: Stat. III.3.c; Norwich: Stat. X.6; Blackburn: Stat. 10(4).
99 CM 1999, s. 4(12). See e.g. Wells: Con. Art. 7(4); Exeter: Con. Art. 5.f.

during discussion and/or determination of that item. Chapter may invite any person to attend and speak at any Chapter meeting but not to vote.[100]

Wells' Chapter must meet in the Chapter Room or elsewhere on the first day each month or on the nearest convenient day. Meetings are called in the same way as at Lichfield but may be called on the written request of four Chapter members of whom at least one must be a lay person. The Administrator must send each member at least eight days beforehand a written notice and agenda, 'unless the Dean, with the consent of the majority of other members of the Chapter, decides to dispense with such notice'. Quorum is four (with at least one lay person). In the absence of the dean, the president is the senior residentiary present (but with no casting vote).[101] At Chichester, in addition to planned meetings, the dean must convene a meeting either on his own motion or within two weeks of receiving a request from any two Chapter members. Quorum is four (and at least two must be dignitaries). If on any issue there is no consensus, the decision must be made by a simple majority, the dean having a casting vote. Chapter may invite 'relevant persons' to appear before it 'to account for their stewardship' and offer suggestions as to their area of responsibility; the Communar acts as secretary.[102]

Hereford Chapter must meet at least nine times each year as agreed by Chapter and in default of such agreement, by the dean. A special meeting may be called by the dean at any time and must be called if requested by any two Chapter members; notice must be given. The dean is chairman and has a casting vote (or in his absence the Canon-in-Residence); the administrator (also chapter clerk) takes the minutes (to be entered in the Chapter Minute Book); quorum is three members. Decision-making is on a show of hands by the majority of those present and voting; a member must declare any material interest of his own, a partner, parent or child in any contract, arrangement or proposal under consideration at a meeting. The dean may invite any person to attend and speak but not vote. The cathedral may indemnify any member of Chapter against liability and purchase and maintain insurance for any member.[103] Similar norms exist at new foundations,[104] Henrician foundations,[105] and parish church cathedrals.[106] Interestingly, Wakefield expressly provides: 'The Bishop may attend meetings of the Chapter after giving due notice and may have a matter of his choosing included on the agenda'.[107]

100 Lichfield: Con. Art. 5; Stat. IV. See also London: Con. Art. 4.8: it meets 9 times each year.
101 Wells: Stat. 2(1)-(6). The Chapter Room is not the same as the Chapter House.
102 Chichester: Stat. 3: the Communar is the cathedral administrator: see below.
103 Hereford: Stat. II.1–10 and 13. See also Lincoln: Stat. 7; York: Stat. I.
104 E.g. Canterbury: Con. Art. 7(2); Durham: Stat. III.2; Norwich: Stat. X; Winchester: Stat. 3.
105 E.g. Bristol: Stat. 16; Chester: Stat. 17; Peterborough: Stat. 9.
106 E.g. Blackburn: Con. Art. 9(4): meetings; (8): power to make standing orders; Stat. 10: it is called by the dean on a Chapter resolution, on his own motion, on request by at least 5 members; quorum is at least 5; in the dean's absence, Chapter elects one of its own to serve as chair (with no casting vote); Manchester: Stat. V.
107 Wakefield: Stat. 1.10.

The officers of Chapter and the cathedral: the administrator

The Cathedrals Measure 1999 requires a cathedral constitution to provide for the appointment of a cathedral architect, auditor, and supervisor of music in the cathedral (each dealt with elsewhere in this volume).[108] It must also provide for an administrator of the cathedral with such functions as may be prescribed,[109] and may provide for the administrator to be a Chapter member.[110] Constitutions and/or statutes differ as to the appointment process, title of office, term of office, remuneration, and functions of the administrator as Chapter may determine. The office of administrator is linked with the historic office of Chapter Clerk;[111] and in some cathedrals, the offices of administrator and chapter clerk are separate, in others merged; in some, the chapter clerk is mandatory, in others permitted; some may also have a registrar. Cathedrals also differ in terms of the breadth and depth of their rules on Chapter officers.

Various approaches are found among the old foundations. Some cathedrals separate the offices of administrator and chapter clerk. The Administrator of Chichester, known as the Communar, must be appointed by Chapter, subject to a written agreement, upon such terms as to tenure, remuneration and statutory and other duties as Chapter decides.[112] The person appointed must be an actual communicant member of the Church of England or of a church in communion with it and is a Chapter member. The Communar must: (1) administer reserves, act as receiver, and ensure an annual budget and audited accounts are submitted for approval to Chapter; (2) give directions as to fabric repairs; (3) oversee personnel management; and (4) refer matters requiring professional legal advice to Chapter's Legal Advisers.[113] It may also appoint a Chapter Clerk, with a written agreement, who is legally qualified and an actual communicant member of the Church of England or a church in communion with it, to assist, advise, and undertake formal/ceremonial duties required by Council, Chapter or College; if absent, these are performed by 'a suitably qualified person'.[114]

By way of contrast, Wells' Cathedral Administrator must be a lay actual communicant of the Church of England, appointed by Chapter after consulting the bishop on such terms in respect of tenure, remuneration and duties as Chapter may determine.[115] The administrator is 'Chief Executive Officer of the Cathedral' who, in carrying out their duties, must have regard to any job description which may have been agreed by Chapter, and who in discharging those duties is responsible to Chapter. Chapter must also appoint a Chapter Clerk and a Registrar, both on the same terms as the Administrator.[116] York's Administrator, or

---

108 For the architect, see Chapter 9; the auditor, Chapter 8; and for supervision of music, above, Chapter 5.
109 CM 1999, s. 9(1)(e).
110 CM 1999, s. 4(3): that is, an additional member.
111 The administrator was formerly known as the chapter clerk: CM 1999, s. 36(1A).
112 Chichester: Con. Art. 12.
113 Chichester: Stat. 20; the Communar sits on the Finance Committee: Con. Art. 18.b.
114 Chichester: Con. Art. 13; Stat. 21.a.
115 Wells: Con. Art. 11(1).
116 Wells: Stat. 5–7.

Chapter Steward, with a written agreement and such remuneration and conditions of service as Chapter determines, is responsible for: the cathedral's 'overall administration and commercial enterprises'; acting as senior lay adviser to Chapter; and providing 'any necessary liaison between the various departments of the cathedral's domestic operations'. Chapter must also appoint a Chapter Clerk, with a written agreement and remuneration and conditions of service as it determines, whose duties include attending meetings of Chapter, Council and College 'unless dispensed from attendance by the Dean' and keeping their minutes and those of Chapter committees.[117]

However, at Salisbury, Hereford and Lincoln, the offices of Administrator and Chapter Clerk are merged. The Salisbury Administrator is appointed on 'conditions of employment' set by Chapter, and is responsible to Chapter for the financial and administrative management of the cathedral, its fabric, properties, possessions, investments, income, and all who work for it and within its precinct; acting as clerk to Chapter and its committees; preparation and retention of Chapter minutes; maintenance and safe-keeping of cathedral and Chapter records; custody of the common seal; subject to Chapter-imposed restrictions, making and terminating contracts including contracts of employment; and acting as clerk to Council and College.[118] Hereford's Administrator, appointed by Chapter on such terms as to tenure, remuneration, duties and otherwise as Chapter may determine, serves as Secretary to Council and Chapter Clerk; the duties of office include: the efficient administration of the cathedral, including its office, finance and other departments; supervision of such of its paid servants and volunteers as determined by Chapter; and maintenance of records of income and expenditure, assets and liabilities of the Cathedral.[119] The Lincoln Administrator (called Chapter Clerk) who is 'the senior officer' of Chapter and responsible in the first instance to the dean as Chapter chair, must attend all Chapter and College meetings and be responsible for day-to-day management of cathedral affairs, in line with Chapter 'policies', and for 'implementing its decisions'.[120]

New foundations also may separate or merge the offices of Administrator and Chapter Clerk; and some do not have a Chapter Clerk. Durham merges the two offices, and its administrator is not a member of Chapter but must attend its meetings and may speak but not vote,[121] and acts as secretary to both Chapter and College.[122] The person appointed as Administrator and Chapter Clerk must be a

---

117 York: Con. X.A-B. London: Con. Art. 11: the Administrator, also known as the Registrar, is 'senior administrative officer'; Surveyor of the Fabric, Auditor, Director of Music, Head of School, and Solicitor.
118 Salisbury: Con. Art. 13.1.
119 Hereford: Con. Art. 15; see also Stat. II.5: 'The Administrator shall be the Chapter Clerk' and 'shall cause a minute of each resolution passed to be entered in the Chapter Minute Book'.
120 Lincoln: Con. Art. 15; and Stat. 17. See also Exeter: Con. Art. 13: the administrator is responsible for 'the efficient administration of the Cathedral, supervision of the staff, co-ordination of activities, and other such duties as the Chapter may from time to time require'.
121 Durham: Con. Art. 17; see also Stat. XXIV.1. See also Peterborough: Con. Art. 12(1).
122 Durham: Con. Art. 12.b and Stat. II.9.

member of the Church of England or 'another Christian church'; the duties of office are: on the dean's instructions, to summon meetings of Chapter and College; to attend such meetings unless reasonably prevented; to keep minutes; to perform any other duties as Chapter determines; to transact with the assistance of such other officers as Chapter may appoint all the general business of Chapter, and to advise on this; to be responsible under the Treasurer's supervision for keeping the accounts; to act as Deputy Treasurer; and as instructed by Council's chair, to summon Council meetings, attend these, keep the minutes, and perform such other duties as Council may from time to time 'reasonably determine'.[123]

Chester separates the two offices, both mandatory. The Administrator, appointed on such terms as Chapter determines,[124] must: have charge of the common seal and inventory; be responsible for personnel management under Chapter direction; prepare the annual budget for presentation to Chapter; monitor cathedral income and expenditure against the budget and report to each Chapter meeting; be responsible for collection of all rents and other moneys, including alms, fees, charges, and gifts as may be presented to the cathedral and pay them into its bank account; keep the cathedral diary bringing all requests for events to Chapter for decision; and oversight of cathedral communications (internal and external).[125] Chapter must also appoint a Cathedral Clerk on such terms as to tenure, remuneration and duties as Chapter may determine; the duties are: on the instructions of the dean or relevant chair, to summon meetings of Council, Chapter, or College of Canons, to attend, if required, these meetings and keep the minutes, and to perform any other duties Chapter may determine.[126] By way of contrast, Ely Chapter must appoint an Administrator,[127] but may appoint as officers a Chapter Clerk, High Bailiff, Chapter Steward, and Chapter Registrar on such terms and conditions as Chapter decides; such appointments are honorary unless agreed in writing by Chapter; these officers may also attend and speak but not vote at meetings of the College of Canons.[128] Norwich's administrator is known as Chapter Steward, Worcester's as Steward (who must also be an actual communicant), and Winchester's and Canterbury's as Receiver General.[129]

There is considerably less variety amongst parish church cathedrals. As to appointment, St Albans is typical: 'There shall be a Cathedral Administrator, who shall be appointed by Chapter on such terms in respect of tenure, remuneration and duties as the Chapter shall determine'.[130] As to functions, St Edmundsbury is

---

[123] Durham: Stat. XXIV.1–4. See also Rochester: Con. Art. 14.1; see also Stat. X(1)-(2): the terms of reference, remuneration and conditions of service of 'the Chapter Clerk and Administrator will be in the form of a contract agreed with the Chapter'.
[124] Chester: Con. Art. 15(vii).
[125] Chester: Stat. 11.
[126] Chester: Con. Art. 15(viii); Stat. 10. The offices were merged in 2016: Con. Art. 16.
[127] Ely: Con. Art. 13(1); see also Bristol: Con. Art. 12(1).
[128] Ely: Stat. 7.
[129] Norwich: Con. Art. XIII.1; Stat. XIV; Worcester: Con. Art. 10.1 (and Gloucester: Con. Art. 15); Winchester: Con. Art. 9 and Stat. 8; Canterbury: Con. Art. 15.
[130] St Albans: Con. Art. XII.1. Also Blackburn: Con. Art. 14(1); St Edmundsbury: Con. Art. 13(1); Birmingham: Con. Art. 16(1); Leicester: Con. Art. 15.1; Manchester: Con. Art. XV(1); Coventry: Con. Art. 12.1.

148 *The chapter house*

typical: the Cathedral Administrator must prepare the agendas for and attend Council and Chapter meetings, and may speak but not vote at these; keep or procure to be kept the minutes of the proceedings of all meetings of Chapter and Council and, under the direction of the dean, summon and forward agendas to Council and Chapter members.[131] Titles vary; for example: Truro's Administrator is Chief Executive and responsible to Chapter for all such administrative, financial, commercial, planning and personnel matters as may be decided by Chapter.[132] Derby's Administrator serves as Clerk to Chapter,[133] but Southwark separates the offices of Administrator and Chapter Clerk (and the latter must be a solicitor or barrister and serves as legal adviser to the cathedral).[134] Guildford Chapter must appoint a Director of Operations, 'the senior lay officer', who serves as Executive Secretary of Chapter and is responsible for 'efficient execution' of its decisions.[135]

Some cathedrals also provide for the appointment of legal advisers distinct from the office of Chapter Clerk. At old foundation Chichester, Chapter 'shall appoint a firm of solicitors as their Legal Advisers … entitled to charge fees for work undertaken'; the Chapter Clerk is a member of that firm and Chapter, and nothing prevents the firm of Legal Advisers charging fees and the Chapter Clerk, if a partner, from sharing in them.[136] At new foundation Winchester, Chapter may appoint a barrister or solicitor as 'Counsellor' who is to 'perform such functions in the course of Divine Service and otherwise' as Chapter may assign and which may lawfully be performed by the person appointed; the office is honorary and confers no vested rights; appointment is for five years but may be renewed for further periods of five years;[137] and Chapter must appoint a Clerk at Law to participate in ceremonies and advise on their legal content; appointment is for five years renewable for further five-year periods.[138] At parish church cathedral St Edmundsbury, Chapter may appoint a solicitor or a barrister to serve as Clerk to Chapter and to Council upon such terms as Chapter may determine.[139]

The cathedral interviews

These indicate general satisfaction with norms applicable to Chapter. However, they also disclose a variety of understandings, and practices in the discharge, of its

---

131 St Edmundsbury: Stat. 28; see also Con. Art. 6.
132 Truro: Stat. IX; the constitution does not deal with the office.
133 Derby: Con. Art. 12.1. For the Administrator as Chapter Clerk, see also Ripon: Con. Art. 9(1) and (6).
134 Southwark: Con. Art. XIII(5): this is a separate office to that of Administrator: Art. XIII(1).
135 Guildford: Con. Art. 14.1 and Stat. XI. See also Liverpool: Con. Art. 13: the offices are separate.
136 Chichester: Stat. 21.b.
137 Winchester: Stat. 13.
138 Winchester: Stat. 17. See also Canterbury: Stat. XIV: a Seneschal may be appointed by Chapter to assist it with financial and secular counsel and advice on matters pertaining to the cathedral.
139 St Edmundsbury: Stat. 27. See also Leicester: Con. Art. 15.6.

functions. The constitution of old foundation Salisbury requires Chapter to consult the bishop from time to time as to the direction and mission of the cathedral; the Dean explained that the bishop is 'guest of Chapter at lunch once a year' and meets with the dean informally every two to three weeks. The statutes provide for Chapter business to be transacted by way of consensus but vest in the dean the right to a casting vote: the Dean has never used this; the cathedral has a policy document on governance (with operational principles) which is 'very important' for cathedral practice.[140] This may be compared with Exeter: as to the constitutional rule that Chapter must consult the bishop twice annually, as a matter of 'practice', the previous bishop and the dean met 'informally' each four–six weeks; currently, such meetings are less frequent but would be good.[141] The Dean of Hereford considers the rule that Chapter is 'to exercise all the powers lawfully exercisable by the Ordinary in relation to the Cathedral' as 'unclear'.[142]

St Paul's has a 'practice' that Council, Chapter and College of Canons meet together (in the past four years, on three occasions) as the Corporate Body.[143] The bishop rarely seeks Chapter's advice, but by 'custom' attends one Chapter meeting each year which fulfils the constitutional duty of Chapter to consult the bishop. Chapter's practice is to seek consensus, but there have been votes against proposed decisions which are recorded in the minutes – the dean has never used a casting vote.[144] Wells requires Chapter to consult the bishop on the general direction of the cathedral; this rule is followed as a matter of good practice; in turn, Chapter transacts its business on the basis of consensus, and a vote is 'hardly ever' taken.[145]

At the new foundation Winchester, a key principle (used in the constitution and statutes) is that the bishop makes decisions (e.g. as to appointments) with the consent of the dean and in consultation with Chapter – that this is enshrined in law (though it may be the practice in other cathedrals) is 'comforting' and provides a system of 'checks and balances' enabling the cathedral to have its 'own life'. The cathedral is not an agent of the diocese and the bishop in practice 'respects its autonomy' while encouraging and expecting collaboration in mission. Within this context, some are members of Chapter by virtue of the fact that they are diocesan officers, on the understanding that the canonry is vacated on termination of the diocesan post – this is made 'absolutely clear in the job description'. Chapter consults the bishop and *vice versa*: the dean has regular one-to-one meetings with the bishop and is on the bishop's staff which meets monthly. It is important for the Receiver General (the administrator) to be on Chapter: this gives a sense of co-responsibility for the cathedral's welfare and integration of its

---

140 Salisbury: Dean: Int. 20-9-2016; Con. Arts. 2 and 6: consultation and the bishop; and Stat. 3.6: consensus and casting vote in Chapter; the document is entitled Good Governance (2013).
141 Exeter: Dean: 9-8-2016; Con. Art. 5.b.
142 Hereford: Dean: Int. 5-8-2016: Con. Art. 4(4)(h).
143 See below for Bradford.
144 London: Dean: Int. 23-9-2016; Con. Art. 6.3: duty to consult the bishop.
145 Wells: Acting Dean: Int. 12-8-2016; Con. Art. 7(3)(b): consultation.

150 *The chapter house*

operations and mission. The most challenging duty for Chapter is designing a sustainable strategic plan. That Chapter must be 'attentive to the suggestions and wisdom' of all who share in cathedral ministry (under Statute 1.4) expresses a 'tradition' which reflects 'a strong sense of our own integrity as a cathedral, not as an arm of the diocese'. Chapter members see themselves as 'fiduciary trustees'.[146] For the Precentor of Rochester, the themes which most exercise Chapter are: 'maintenance of the family through the fabric and money'; 'engaging with the world in mission' as part of the diocese; and operating on the 'national stage'.[147]

At the Henrician foundation at Chester, the 'tenor' of governance is that the bishop exercises authority after consulting the dean and/or Chapter – this can be 'challenging'; two further practices are that Chapter seeks consensus but its members 'more often vote on a decision'.[148]

At the parish church cathedral at Derby, as a matter of practice Chapter does not vote on issues (unless required e.g. for a funding application) – the style of business is consensual; Chapter 'rarely consults the bishop'; but the dean does 'as a matter of course' – they are 'on the same page'; and Chapter invites the Council chair and vice-chair to Chapter meetings: 'this is really useful'.[149] The Birmingham Chapter consults the bishop 'regularly', through the dean, on strategic matters; this is 'very useful', and is a good example of following a rule in the constitution because of the utility of the reason underlying that rule: 'good practice'.[150]

The College of Canons

The Cathedrals Measure 1999 requires the constitution of each cathedral to provide for the establishment of the College of Canons.[151] Its membership must consist of: (a) the dean; (b) every suffragan bishop of the diocese; (c) every full-time stipendiary assistant bishop of the diocese; (d) every canon of the cathedral, and (e) every archdeacon of the diocese.[152] Many old foundations merely repeat this provision.[153] Others elaborate: for example, voting members of Lichfield's College are: the dean, each residentiary, each non-residentiary, and each lay canon; an ecumenical canon is a member of College but has no right to vote; when any member vacates office and retires, the bishop may confer on that person an emeritus title but such person is not by virtue of that title a member of the

---

146 Winchester: Acting Dean: Int. 16–8-2016; Con. Art. 5.3: consultation.
147 Rochester: Canon Precentor: Int. 30–9-2016; Con. Art. 9.3: Chapter duties.
148 Chester: Vice-Dean: Int. 19–8-2016.
149 Derby: Dean: Int. 10–8-2016.
150 Birmingham: Dean: Int. 11–8-2016: Con. Art. 10.
151 CM 1999, s. 5(1).
152 CM 1999, s. 5(2); s. 35(1): 'canon' includes a lay canon and a non-residentiary canon but not a minor canon.
153 E.g. Hereford: Con. Art. 5(1); Lincoln: Con. Art. 14(1); Salisbury: Con. Art. 7.2; York: Con. Art. IX.

College but may be appropriately vested at any service attended in that capacity; unless 'unavoidably prevented', the non-residentiaries must attend any meeting of the College of Canons.[154] Most new foundations and Henrician cathedrals simply repeat the membership list in the Measure,[155] as do parish church cathedrals.[156]

The 1999 Measure requires the College of Canons to: (a) receive and consider the annual report and audited accounts; (b) discuss such matters concerning the cathedral as may be raised by any of its members; and (c) perform such other functions as may be prescribed.[157] It must also perform the functions conferred by statute as to the election of the diocesan bishop (see Chapter 2).[158] Some old foundations merely repeat these functions.[159] Others add to them. Salisbury College meets for corporate worship and prayer, expresses through its members the integral relationship between the cathedral and diocese, and performs such other functions as may be requested by the bishop after consulting Chapter.[160] At Chichester, the bishop may call upon College, as part of its 'diocesan functions', 'to aid him in his work by its counsel and ... help maintain the regular worship of ... God in his Cathedral'; as such, it is 'a Council or Senate', over which the bishop may preside, to be consulted and offer advice 'on weighty matters affecting the diocese even though its consent is not required'.[161] Again, some new foundations merely repeat the Measure list, as do parish church cathedrals.[162]

However, Bradford adds to them: College members must 'endeavour under the guidance of the Bishop and Dean to extend the influence of the Cathedral throughout the Diocese', have 'the right and duty of attendance at the Cathedral at all major diocesan services and events' and 'should seek opportunities from time to time to join in [its] ordinary worship'; members who serve on Chapter or Council or any other bodies connected with the cathedral 'shall regard this work as of high importance'; the Canon Theologian must after consulting the dean lead study in theology at one College meeting at least of its three meetings each year;[163] and, unusually, the College, Chapter and Council must meet jointly on

---

154 Lichfield: Con. Art. 8(1)-(2); Stat. VI(1).
155 E.g. Canterbury: Con. Art. 14(1); Durham: Con. Art. 16; Norwich: Con. Art. XII.1; Bristol: Con. Art. 11.
156 E.g. Manchester: Con. Art. XII; Newcastle: Con. Art. 8.1; Southwell: Con. Art. 11.1.
157 CM 1999, s. 5(4).
158 CM 1999, s. 5(3).
159 E.g. Lichfield: Con. Art. 8(3); Wells: Con. Art. 10(2)-(3); Carlisle: Con. Art. 12; York: Con. Art. IX.B and C.
160 Salisbury: Con. Art. 7.1. See also London: Con. Art. 5.1.
161 Chichester: Con. Art. 5: in which case: 'Of the College of Canons when acting in this capacity the Bishop is the Head, *Principale Caput*'. For advice to the bishop, see also Hereford: Con. Art. 5(3) and Stat. III.2.
162 E.g. Durham: Con. Art. 16; Norwich: Con. Art. XII.3-4; Bristol: Con. Art. 11; Blackburn: Con. Art. 13.
163 Bradford: Stat. 6.

one occasion each year, on a date determined by the dean in order to review the Mission and Vision of the Cathedral.[164]

The Cathedrals Measure 1999 is silent on the frequency and procedure of College meetings. Instead these matters are regulated by the cathedrals themselves. At Chichester, College must meet at least once annually (as near as possible to the Feast of All Saints). The bishop may attend and speak but not vote. It is summoned by the dean after giving reasonable notice whenever: the bishop desires its counsel or advice on any matter; the dean deems it desirable; it must make an election; or if requested by no less than two-thirds of the total number of the canons. The dean has a casting vote; and the Communar is secretary.[165] Lichfield College may invite any person to attend and speak but not to vote.[166] Exeter's must meet at least twice each year; the bishop may attend and speak but not vote; the dean presides (or if absent, the senior residentiary). It is summoned by the dean (with notice), but it must meet whenever: an election falls to be made; dignitaries, residentiaries, prebendaries, and lay and Chapter canons are installed; the dean considers it necessary or desirable; the bishop seeks its counsel and advice; or a request is made by no less than ten members. The quorum is half the members; decisions are made by a majority of votes of those present.[167] Similar norms exist at other old foundations,[168] new foundations and parish church cathedrals.[169] For example at Manchester, the College may make standing orders to regulate procedure at meetings;[170] and, unusually, the Common Seal, in the custody of Chapter, must not be affixed to any document except on a formal resolution of Chapter or, in the case of a matter relating to the jurisdiction of the College of Canons or Council, on a formal resolution of either of these two bodies.[171] Similar but special provisions apply to Christ Church Oxford: 'There shall be a college of canons of the cathedral church' consisting of: the dean, every suffragan bishop of the diocese, every full-time stipendiary assistant bishop of the diocese, every canon (including any lay canon), and every archdeacon of the diocese; the College must receive and consider any report of the dean and chapter relating to the management and activities of the cathedral church, including any financial statement, and discuss such matters concerning the cathedral church as may be raised by any of the members.[172]

---

164 Bradford: Stat. 12. See also Guildford: Stat. VIII: College must give counsel to the bishop whenever sought.
165 Chichester: Con. Art. 5 and Stat. 4. See also Exeter: Con. Art. 6: the College must 'give such advice and counsel as requested by the Bishop or the Chapter'.
166 Lichfield: Con. Art. 8(4).
167 Exeter: Con. Art. 6 and Stat. III.
168 Hereford: Stat. III: it must meet at least once a year; Salisbury: Con. Art. 7.4: it must meet twice each year.
169 Durham: Con. Art. 16: it must meet at least once a year 'normally at Michaelmas'; Stat. IV: it may make standing orders; Norwich: Con. XII.2: it meets at least once a year; Chester: Stat. 18; Peterborough: Stat. 13.
170 Manchester: Con. Art. XII.
171 Manchester: Stat. V.7. See also e.g. Coventry: Stat. App. 4: Standing Orders applicable to the College.
172 Church of England (Miscellaneous Provisions) Measure 2010, s. 10(7)-(8).

The cathedral interviews

As was the case in relation to the part it plays in the election of a bishop (see Chapter 2), and with respect to honorary, lay and ecumenical canons (see Chapter 4), the cathedral interviews suggest various understandings and practices about the role of the College of Canons.[173] At old foundation Exeter, the 'ethos' is that the College represents the cathedral to the diocese, and the diocese to the cathedral. This is not reflected in the domestic law of the cathedral. But the College has 'no power'. As a matter of practice, Chapter sends a representative to an installation of a cleric in a parish under the cathedral's patronage; this should be the College's function or else one shared with Chapter.[174] Whilst the constitution and statutes of Wells are silent on the matter, there is an 'aspiration' that the College engages in theological reflection and it has done so with the bishop on a 'one off' basis.[175] St Paul's College functions are limited in the constitution to those in the Cathedrals Measure 1999, but a code of practice will be produced to spell out more fully the expectations applicable to its members. However, it is difficult to assemble the whole College (given their number) and so they are not good at attending. Moreover, unlike at Salisbury (where it works well), the bishop is not a member *ex officio* of the College; having him as such might seem contrary to the principle of the bishop as visitor, but in reality bishops exercise multiple roles as pastor and disciplinarian.[176] Salisbury Chapter's constitutional right to consult College for its view *is* used, as is the right of the bishop to request College to perform tasks after the bishop has consulted Chapter.[177]

At new foundation Rochester, the Precentor expressed the view that, outside election of the bishop, the College may be understood as the bishop's forum, but this is not so in practice.[178] At Henrician foundation Chester, the constitution requires College to further and support the cathedral's 'educational work', but in practice, it does not engage in this.[179] Bristol's College meets twice each year, at Bristol and at Swindon where the members engage in 'theological reflection' to 'build community'; and the bishop has attended such meetings.[180] The custom at Gloucester is for the bishop to attend the two annual College meetings.[181] At the parish church cathedral at Derby, the constitution requires College to promote theological learning in the cathedral and diocese: it does so through for example

---

173 See also the Bullimore Report (2012) pars. 106–110: this found that for some deans the College has no clear purpose, that its diocesan role is limited, but that its inclusion of lay and honorary canons is valued.
174 Exeter: Dean: Int. 9-8-2016.
175 Wells: Acting Dean: Int. 12-8-2016.
176 London: Dean: Int. 23-9-2016; Con. Art. 5.
177 Salisbury: Dean: Int. 20-9-2016.
178 Rochester: Precentor: Int. 30-9-2016: this 'facility' is not used thus. Ely: Dean: Email 17-1-2017: as to whether the College of Canons contributes to the ministry of the cathedral: 'I probably tend towards "no"'; Carlisle agrees: Dean: Email 17-1-2017.
179 Chester: Vice-Dean: Int. 19-8-2016; Con. Art. 19(ii).
180 Bristol: Dean: Int. 3-8-2016.
181 Gloucester: Chancellor and Vice-Dean: Int. 4-8-2016.

seminars held at the cathedral.[182] However, the Dean of Birmingham explained that the College of Canons there is not used to promote theological learning at the cathedral, but the possibility is worth exploring.[183] Several other deans were critical as to whether College contributes to cathedral ministry.[184]

Conclusion

Under the Cathedrals Measure 1999 the Council, Chapter and College of Canons constitute the corporate body of a cathedral. The Measure prescribes the membership of Council and cathedral constitutions and/or canons differ as to the persons who are to be members of it to reflect wider interests as do their term of office within the ranges prescribed by the Measure. The Measure assigns to Council duties and powers as to the spiritual, pastoral, evangelistic, social and ecumenical work of the cathedral, reviewing and advising on the direction and oversight of that work by Chapter. The constitutions and/or statutes repeat but sometimes add to these duties/powers. The Measure requires a lay chair and twice yearly meetings at least. It is though the constitutions and/or statutes of cathedrals which regulate procedure. The interviews reveal that Council is a good critical friend to Chapter, particularly in terms of strategy, and members provide varied experiences which are valuable. However, sometimes there is a perception that Councils have greater authority to direct Chapter than exists in law, but its powers to request reports from Chapter or to refer matters to the visitor are rarely used.

The Measure provides for the membership of Chapter and requires the dean to preside, with a casting vote, and to be a member of every Chapter committee. The duties and powers of Chapter as prescribed in the Measure are merely repeated in most cathedral constitutions but some add to and elaborate upon them. The Measure requires Chapter to meet at least nine times each year. Constitutions and/or statutes contain norms on the frequency and calling of meetings (by the dean on a Chapter resolution, on his own motion, or on the requisition of a prescribed number of Chapter members), quorum at, presidency in the absence of the dean by a member elected by Chapter, and the declaration of personal interests at, its meetings. By Measure, the constitution of each cathedral must provide for the appointment of a cathedral architect, an auditor, a person to supervise music (each dealt with elsewhere in this volume), and an administrator of the cathedral, having such functions as may be prescribed. Cathedral constitutions and/or statutes differ somewhat as to the appointment, title and term of office, remuneration, rights and duties of the administrator as these are determined by

---

182 Derby: Dean: Int. 10–8-2016; Con. 11.4.
183 Birmingham: Dean: Int. 11–8-2016.
184 Southwark: Dean: Email 17–1-2017: 'No to be perfectly honest'; Liverpool: Dean: Email 21–1-2017: 'No: but it works fine if expectations are mutually low-key'; St Albans: Dean: Email 24–1-2017: 'No: but I blame this more on lack of imagination than the statutes'; Wakefield: Dean: Email 23–1-2017: 'Not in general, but they are always extremely supportive individuals'.

Chapter. In some cathedrals the administrator serves as Chapter Clerk; in others they are separate offices. The interviews found that in practice Chapter and bishop meet periodically, Chapter business is transacted on the basis of consensus (and deans rarely use their casting vote), and in a small number of cathedrals Council, Chapter and College meet together each year as a single body.

The Measure requires each cathedral constitution to provide for establishment of the College of Canons consisting of a prescribed membership. Cathedrals differ as to the qualifications, numbers, titles, and appointment of canons. As the Measure is silent on the frequency and procedure of its meetings, so cathedral constitutions and/or statutes typically provide that College is to meet at least twice each year; the bishop may attend and speak but not vote; the dean presides (and in his absence the senior residentiary); and they provide for: summoning it; its use by the bishop as a forum for counsel; its role in electing the bishop (see Chapter 2); and its place in the diocese. However, the interviews found broad agreement that there are questions over the actual contribution of the College to the life of the cathedral and diocese.

7 The library and cloister: education – learning and teaching

Historically, English cathedrals have been important centres of learning (traditionally the responsibility of the cathedral chancellor), centred on the cathedral library, cathedral school, preparation of ordination candidates, and the scholarship of cathedral clergy.[1] Educational work, including its cultural aspects, continues today as an invaluable part of their functions and ministry.[2] Many cathedrals still have fine libraries: that at Rochester, formed in 1082, has the *Textus Roffensis*, a copy made in the 1120s of an early code of English law; Hereford has its famous chained books and the *Mappa Mundi*; Salisbury houses an original of *Magna Carta* 1215; by 1500 Canterbury had some 9,000 manuscripts bound in 2,000 codices; and while York's was dispersed at the Reformation, today it is one of the most active cathedral libraries in England (with over 65,000 books); and in the nave the 'Chancellor's Window' (c. 1330) depicts Chancellor Ripplington instructing scholars.[3] Cloisters too, for the monastic cathedrals, were places where the monks studied; and several secular cathedrals added them (though York and Lichfield did not); perhaps the finest among the former monastic cloisters are at Gloucester and among the old foundations, those at Salisbury.[4] Today, several cathedrals include education in their legal objects; for example, Lincoln 'will be vigilant to renew … its teaching and learning as essential elements in its community life'.[5] Moreover, the Cathedrals Fabric Commission has duties to assist Chapters by participating in educational and research projects which in its view

---

1 H&R 187: their long association with education was fairly residual until the Endowed Schools Act of 1869 obliged Chapters or the trustees of the ancient schoolrooms to turn them into 'proper educational institutions'.
2 O. Edwards and T. ap Siôn, 'Cathedral engagement with young people', in L.J. Francis (ed.), *Anglican Cathedrals in Modern Life: The Science of Cathedral Studies* (2013) 29–49.
3 P. Johnson, *British Cathedrals* (1980) 48, 190, 221–224; see 196 for York's 'Chancellor's Window' (c. 1330).
4 A. Clifton-Taylor, *The Cathedrals of England* (London: Book Club Associates, 1967) 136.
5 Lincoln: Con. Preamble. See also e.g. Lichfield: Con. Art. 1(2): learning; Hereford: Con. Preamble: education; Southwell: Con. Preamble: the cathedral is to enhance 'the education of those using the Cathedral facilities'; Coventry: Preamble: it must 'nurture Christian learning'.

promote the care, conservation, repair or development of cathedral churches and ancillary buildings; it must also maintain, jointly with the Church Buildings Council, a library of books, plans, drawings, photographs and other material relating to cathedrals and objects within them, and give advice on storing records.[6] This Chapter explores: the regulation of the cathedral library and archives; the educational work of cathedrals, particularly school visits; and the relationship between the cathedral and the cathedral/choir school as treated in cathedral constitutions and statutes.[7] Norms on libraries and schools are more evident in old and new foundations than parish church cathedrals.

The library and archives

The Archbishops' Commission on Cathedrals 1994 recognised the importance of cathedral libraries in providing 'a basis for theological reading', found that in some cathedrals money received from admission charges was earmarked for book purchase, and recommended introducing facilities for academic research in the library and an 'adopt a book' scheme.[8] However, the Cathedrals Measure 1999 does not require the constitution or statutes of a cathedral to make provision for a cathedral library or the appointment of a cathedral librarian. As a result, cathedrals differ. Some have norms expressly devoted to the library, others do not. Some impose a duty on Chapter to maintain a library, others do not. Some provide for the appointment of a librarian and/or archivist, others do not. Some provide for oversight of the library, if there is one, by the chancellor, or other Chapter officer (though in some the chancellor has functions only with regard to education (see below)). And there are, in turn, differences as between the classes of cathedral as well as in terms of the breadth and depth of their coverage of these matters. There is also a substantial body of national guidance on the management of cathedral libraries and archives issued by the Cathedral Libraries and Archives Association and the Church of England Record Centre. Cathedral records and the inventory, as they relate to cathedral property and its maintenance, are treated in Chapter 8.

Old foundations

Some old foundations do not include provision for a librarian in their constitutions or statutes among the cathedral officers. Surprisingly, this is the case at Wells. Among the canon residentiaries: 'It belongs to the Chancellor ... to have oversight of the library and archives', who is responsible to Chapter for this; in carrying out this duty the chancellor 'shall have regard to any job description which may have been agreed by the Chapter'; if there is a vacancy in the office of Chancellor,

---

6 CCM 2011, s. 3(2). See below Chapters 8 and 9.
7 See below Chapter 8 for the display of treasure and access by the public: CCR 2006, Sch. 1 par. 4(1).
8 H&R 24–28 and 252.

the duties attaching to that office must be carried out by Chapter members in such way as Chapter may decide;[9] also:

> In consideration of the ancient connection between the Cathedral and Wells Cathedral School ... such privileges in ... the Library of St Andrew shall be granted to the Head Teacher, teachers and scholars of the school as the Chapter may from time to time determine.[10]

However, most provide for the office of librarian, sometimes subject to supervision by the chancellor. Lincoln has a rather minimalist approach: 'There shall be a librarian who shall be appointed by the Chapter' and who 'under the supervision of the chancellor, [is] responsible to the Chapter for maintaining the library in an efficient condition'.[11] Likewise Chichester: 'There shall be a member of the Chapter who shall have responsibility for the Library'; and Chapter 'shall appoint a suitably qualified Librarian, subject to a written agreement', on such terms as to tenure, remuneration and duties as Chapter may determine;[12] and the Librarian is a member of the Foundation.[13]

Other old foundations impose an explicit duty on Chapter to maintain a library, and in turn they too may provide for the office of librarian. For example, Exeter Chapter 'shall maintain the Cathedral Library and Archives', and it may 'arrange for outside bodies to manage these institutions on its behalf', such as Exeter University and Devon Record Office; however: 'the books, manuscripts and other artefacts within the library and archive shall remain the property of the Cathedral'; Chapter may also appoint 'a Librarian, Assistant Librarians, an Archivist and Assistant Archivists as may be ... necessary'; provision exists for the office of chancellor – but no mention is made of library oversight in connection with that office.[14]

Hereford has a more detailed approach: 'From the earliest times the Library [has] been an integral part of the Foundation of the Cathedral';[15] therefore: 'Chapter shall maintain the Cathedral Library, the Chained Library and the Cathedral archives'. To this end, it must appoint 'a Librarian and an Archivist on such terms in respect of tenure, remuneration, duties and otherwise as the Chapter may determine'. The librarian's duties include: maintaining an inventory of books and manuscripts of the cathedral; advising Chapter on 'the preservation and maintenance' of these and supervising all works thereon; and advising on the affording of facilities for research and study of these and all day-to-day

---

9 Wells: Stat. 4(6), (8) and (9).
10 Wells: Stat. 22.
11 Lincoln: Con. Art. 20; Stat. 20; there seems to be no treatment of the chancellor (who does not appear in the order of precedence in Stat. 24).
12 Chichester: Stat. 18: The Librarian.
13 Chichester: Stat. 23.
14 Exeter: Stat. XV; Stat. X.2: the chancellor.
15 Hereford: Con. Preamble.

management of such facilities.[16] The librarian and archivist both appear in the order of precedence at cathedral services.[17]

Salisbury provides for the chancellor's oversight, librarian's duties and, in somewhat wider terms than Wells (see above), for access to the library. The chancellor has 'general oversight of the Library and Muniments'.[18] However: 'There shall be a Librarian and Keeper of the Muniments, who shall be appointed by the Chapter on such conditions of employment as [it] may determine'. As to functions, 'in accordance with the requirements laid down from time to time by the Chapter, and subject to the overall supervision of the Chancellor', the librarian is responsible for: the maintenance and safe-keeping of the Library and Muniments; making available the books, manuscripts and other documents there to clergy of the diocese, scholars, students and other research workers at such times and on conditions determined by Chapter; and performance of such other duties as may be assigned by Chapter.[19] By way of contrast, Lichfield's statutes name only the non-residentiaries as being 'entitled to have access to the Cathedral Libraries' subject to regulations made by Chapter; no chancellor is mentioned.[20]

York is untypical: its statutes do not seem to provide for a librarian, but a statute on 'The Cathedral Library' provides that: 'Chapter shall maintain a Library whose purpose shall include the promotion of sacred learning'; the Canon Theologian has 'general responsibility' for the Library and Archives and must be assisted by 'such qualified persons' as Chapter may determine; like Exeter, Chapter may enter into agreements with the University of York or other institutions of Higher Education concerning the Library such as may be 'mutually advantageous', in policy and staffing, and the maintenance and use of the Chapter Archives.[21]

New foundations

These too differ as to whether Chapter must maintain a library, whether the office of librarian is mandatory or permissive, whether regulations are to be made as to use, and whether provision is made for the office of chancellor to have library oversight.[22] In Norwich, the librarian is a member of the Foundation and one of 'the officers of the Cathedral', and Chapter may appoint an Archivist – but there are no norms in either constitution or statutes which deal with their appointment, tenure or duties.[23] However, there is a statute on the 'Archives and Library',

---

16 Hereford: Con. Art. 20(1)-(3).
17 Hereford: Stat. XII. See below under the cathedral interviews for the practice of the chancellor serving as canon librarian.
18 Salisbury: Stat. 5.6.
19 Salisbury: Stat. 8; see also Annex to Stat. 9, Annex (4): the chancellor in the order of precedence.
20 Lichfield: Stat. VI(2); see also Stat. Schedule II: order of precedence: no chancellor is listed.
21 York: Stat. XV.1–3.
22 Rochester has no norms on the library in its statutes.
23 Norwich: Stat. I: foundation (as is the chancellor); XV.1: officer; Stat. XVII: archivist.

160 *The library and cloister*

which includes 'all the muniments, charters, books, manuscripts, documents and records (including matters of illustration or record however produced) and all other things of a like nature belonging to the Cathedral'. Moreover, and this is unusual, Chapter must ensure 'the safe custody, maintenance, repair, preservation, access, loan and storage of the archives and library either in the Cathedral or elsewhere as it shall think fit'.[24]

The librarian at Carlisle must be a Chapter member: Chapter must at its first meeting after 1 November each year appoint from amongst its members a librarian,[25] who 'shall hold office for a term of three years and shall be eligible for re-election' with 'special oversight of all charters, deeds, documents, books and manuscripts belonging to the Cathedral whether in the Library or elsewhere' except only those that concern the accounts of the cathedral and the service books in regular use it. The librarian must:

> prepare and maintain a full and correct catalogue of the same and shall render a yearly report upon all matters relating to the Library and its expenses at the first meeting of the Chapter held after 1 November in each year.[26]

Similarly, by statute at Durham: 'There shall be a Librarian ... responsible to the Chapter for the organisation of the Library and the proper custody and cataloguing of its books'. The librarian must: arrange for the purchase of new books after such communication with Chapter as it must direct; report from time to time to Chapter concerning 'the repairs that are needed to the Library or to [its] books'; and, at the Chapter's meeting next before Advent, 'make a special report on the Library'. Moreover, Chapter must make 'regulations for the use of the Library by members of the Chapter, the clergy or laity of the Diocese and others, under such conditions as may from time to time be deemed appropriate'; and, unusually, the Librarian must 'be assisted in all the duties aforesaid by such staff as the Chapter may determine'.[27]

Three contrasting minimalist approaches are used at Ely, Canterbury and Winchester. The Ely statutes merely provide that: 'There shall be an Archivist who shall be responsible for the Chapter Archives ... and those deposited or on loan at the Cambridge University Library and elsewhere'.[28] Canterbury Chapter must maintain the cathedral Archive and Library and devote such sums and employ such persons (including an Archivist and a Librarian) as it thinks fit for 'the care of the archives, books, manuscripts and other muniments and chattels therein'; as at Exeter and York, Chapter may enter such agreements as it thinks fit for their better maintenance with experts/institutions including but not

24 Norwich: Stat. XXI.1–2.
25 Carlisle: Stat. 15.
26 Carlisle: Stat. 18.
27 Durham: Stat. XX.1–3; no chancellor is listed in the order of precedence under Stat. XXXII.2.
28 Ely: Con. Art. 13(5): this does not deal with appointment, tenure, or duties.

limited to Kent County Council and the University of Kent; and must annually appoint one of the residentiaries as Canon Librarian 'to oversee the Archive and Library'.[29] However, at Winchester, provision for the appointment of a librarian is implicit rather than explicit: 'The Chapter has a duty of care in respect of the conservation of the Cathedral Library, Archive and Collection and shall meet this duty by making appointments on such terms as shall be determined by the Chapter'.[30]

At Henrician foundation Bristol, appointment of a librarian is mandatory: at its first meeting each year, Chapter must appoint a librarian from members of the Chapter who has 'charge of the Library of the Cathedral and of all muniments, writings and documents which are not the responsibility of the Keeper of the Fabric'.[31] By way of contrast, at Peterborough, appointing a librarian is permissive: Chapter 'may appoint one or more persons (whether members of the Chapter or not) to any of the offices of Chancellor, Librarian and Keeper of the Muniments' for such period(s) and on such terms as Chapter decides.[32] Moreover: Chapter must 'maintain the Cathedral Library', take 'all reasonable measures for the preservation against loss or damage by fire, decay or theft' of its contents and all muniments, records, and other documents belonging to the cathedral; and 'frame rules under which scholars and others may have access to the books, as well as to all documents of historical interest, in its possession'.[33]

Chester, where Chapter must appoint 'a person suitably qualified as a Librarian', is of interest in so far as its statutes spell out the purposes of the library:

> Seeing that the possession and use of good books, and other means of storing information, promote sound learning and wisdom, it is ordained that the Cathedral Library in Chester shall be made a special subject of consideration by the Chapter each year, and that the Librarian shall then make a written report of the condition thereof; [and] that new books and other resources shall be purchased for the library from time to time by the Librarian with the approval of the Chapter.

To this end, in relation to access, and like old foundation Lichfield and new foundation Durham and Henrician foundation Peterborough: 'Chapter shall make regulations for the use of the Library and its resources by the Canons, the clergy of the diocese and others'. The librarian must report from time to time to Chapter concerning 'the repairs and improvements that are needed in the library'.[34]

---

29 Canterbury: Stat. XXIV.1–3.
30 Winchester: Stat. 16; see also Stat. 6.5: library oversight does not appear in the chancellor's duties.
31 Bristol: Stat. 5(1) and 10; see Stat. 9(3) for documents under the responsibility of the Keeper of the Fabric.
32 Peterborough: Stat. 9(7).
33 Peterborough: Stat. 17.
34 Chester: Stat. 9.

Parish church cathedrals

Most parish church cathedrals do not make explicit provision for a library or a librarian.[35] However, the canon theologian (see below) of St Edmundsbury has responsibility for 'oversight of ... the Chapter Library'; and: 'The Chapter may appoint an Archivist/Librarian upon such terms in respect of tenure, remuneration and duties as may be determined by the Chapter' with 'the oversight of all charters, deeds, documents, books, manuscripts and other retrievable information (including films, computer discs, etc.) of the Chapter other than those which are in the custody of the Clerk to the Chapter'; also: 'The Archivist/Librarian may, subject to any direction given by the Chapter, make regulations for the use of and access to the Library and Cathedral Archives'.[36] At some parish church cathedrals, provision is made for appointment of a Chancellor, but domestic laws are silent as to the duties of the office.[37]

The Cathedral Libraries and Archives Association

The aims of the Association are to advance education by the promotion, preservation and protection of cathedral libraries and archives, and provision of appropriate access to them. It also facilitates the use of guidance issued by the Church of England Record Centre (drawing on expert advice from the National Archives, Local Record Offices and wider archive profession) to help 'cathedrals develop a consistent and best practice approach to the treatment of Church records in their care whether paper or electronic'. The two bodies have jointly issued guidance to support cathedral staff in managing their records from the point of creation through to destruction or permanent retention as an archive record. And if a cathedral holds parish, episcopal or diocesan records as well those of cathedral bodies, including papers generated by the bishop 'as a consequence of the cathedral being his seat', or parish registers kept by a parish church cathedral, these should be managed distinctly.[38]

Each cathedral should appoint one trained member of staff to co-ordinate the management of records created by cathedral administration in order: to enable it to meet its operational needs; to provide a testimony of its 'continuing witness'; to provide accountability to wider society; to reflect the diversity of its activities; and to recognise that records are subject to external regulation (e.g. by the Charity Commission, and Office of the Information Commissioner).[39]

35 See e.g. Blackburn, Manchester, Newcastle, Southwell, Chelmsford, Truro, and (which seems surprising given its excellent library) Southwark. For the Parochial Libraries Act 1708, see Hill, par. 7.117.
36 St Edmundsbury: Stat. 11: canon theologian; and Stat. 26: archivist/librarian.
37 Derby: Stat. 12(b): this mentions the chancellor in the order of precedence.
38 Chapter and Verse: The Care of Cathedral Records, Church of England Record Centre, Records Management Guide No. 4 (2013), Section 1, Introduction.
39 Chapter and Verse, Section 2.

The cathedral *must keep* records which it is legally required to maintain either permanently or for a minimum period. The cathedral *should keep* records which it is not legally required to maintain permanently or for a minimum period but *should keep* as 'good practice'. In both cases, records of historical value for research or business continuity should be transferred to the archives if not required for current administrative purposes. The cathedral *may keep* records it has no legal obligation to retain after they cease to be required for administrative purposes, but which have a continuing historical value for research; it should consult the archives before disposing of these. And the cathedral *should destroy* records, which, at the end of their administrative life no longer have statutory or historical value. The cathedral should develop a retention schedule for all records (electronic/paper) which clearly states the period of retention for each category. Moreover, there should be two records appraisals: one undertaken by staff to assess their business value; and another by the archivist or local record office to assess their historical value. These should be made together as a joint exercise by the administrators and archives staff prior to transfer to the archives.[40] The guidance places records in ten categories and within these those which must, should or may be kept, or destroyed. The categories indicate well the extraordinary range of activities carried out at cathedrals.

First, the cathedral must keep core records which relate to its foundation, regulation and management. These include: statutes and letters patent, to be kept in secure storage in suitable conditions; minutes and related papers of Council, Chapter, College, and Fabric Advisory Committee, to be bound and transferred to the archives or maintained in secure office storage;[41] minutes of the principal Chapter committees (and supporting papers), to be retained permanently;[42] and reports and formal documents created by the visitor which should be kept, but correspondence as to visitations should be reviewed. The cathedral may keep, for example: minutes of short-term Chapter committees; papers as to Council, Chapter, College, Fabric Advisory Committee, and principal Chapter committee business not presented at meetings. It should destroy: duplicate minutes and papers (unless significantly annotated as part of record keeping); routine files; and minutes of minor committees/bodies.[43]

Second, as to finance, the cathedral must keep annual audited accounts and insurance register. It may keep subsidiary accounting records, e.g. cash books, payroll summaries, and records of charitable income (including fundraising accounts). It should destroy, after the statutory retention period has expired, for

---

40 Chapter and Verse, Section 3.1–2. The CCM 2011 requires each cathedral to draw up and maintain an inventory of cathedral property, in particular identifying objects of outstanding interest: see below Chapter 8.
41 For minutes held electronically, safeguards should ensure authentication, preservation and accessibility.
42 Those on matters of more short-term interest, e.g. catering or car parking, may be destroyed after review.
43 Chapter and Verse, Section 3.3.1.

example: bank statements, cheque books, invoices, delivery notes, orders, receipts, expired insurance policies, budgets and periodic financial reports.[44]

Third, as to administrative and personnel records,[45] the cathedral should keep correspondence and papers relating to major developments and events (such as policy files). It may keep these records as to less important developments and events (including outreach), liaison with the media, and personnel (clergy/lay staff) and disciplinary files of long-term research interest; but it should destroy these after the relevant statutory retention period has expired.[46] Fourth, as to services and ministry: it should keep: registers of baptisms, confirmations, marriages, interments and burials; registers of services, such as decanal installations, enthronements of bishops, and major memorial services; plans of burials in the cathedral and/or churchyard. It may keep, for example: registers of banns, marriage blessings and funerals; orders of service; sermons; and community magazines. It should destroy, for instance: baptism and marriage certificate counterfoils, copies of burial and cremation certificates, applications for banns, baptisms, marriages and funerals; and special or other marriage licences (after expiry of a recommended retention period).[47] Fifth, as to music establishment records, the cathedral should keep music lists, choir calendars or fixture lists, and choir audio-visual recordings. It may keep voice trial records, concert programmes, files on external choir engagements (such as tours), and choir photographs, noting dates and names of those in any of these pictures.[48]

Sixth, with regard to buildings and property records, the cathedral must keep: major project files including contracts, specifications, reports and correspondence (selected after appraisal); files on projects resulting in alterations to the cathedral fabric; the quinquennial reports of the architect; archaeological, conservation and historic building consent reports; and inventories and terriers. It should keep, for instance: plans relating to major projects and alterations to buildings; building files on significant alterations or repairs; photographs of buildings and projects (all selected after appraisal); rentals and surveys; organ specifications, contracts, and maintenance files. It should destroy, for example: files on minor projects (e.g. specifications, tenders, and correspondence); and major projects which have been rejected (after appraisal).[49]

Seventh, as to legal records, the cathedral should keep: title deeds, including conveyances and long-term leases; legal opinions, rulings and court papers about significant legal matters; and charity foundation documents, orders

---

44 Chapter and Verse, Section 3.3.2.
45 See also Personal Files Relating to Clergy: Guidance for Bishops and Their Staff (2013).
46 Chapter and Verse, Section 3.3.3: clergy files and lay staff files of personnel in contact with children and disciplinary files not selected for research have long statutory retention periods; see the retention schedule.
47 Chapter and Verse, Section 3.3.4.
48 Chapter and Verse, Section 3.3.5.
49 Chapter and Verse, Section 3.3.6. See Chapter 8.

and schemes. It should destroy conveyancing files and legal papers of minor significance.[50] Eighth, records relating to the Library and Archives, which under the Care of Cathedrals Measure 2011 must be listed collectively in the inventory with reference to library and archive catalogues which itemise the collections (see Chapter 8), the cathedral must keep: catalogues of archives and rare books; accession registers recording terms of accession (e.g. transfer, gift, and loan) and source of acquisition; and conservation registers or records. It may keep exhibition files and should destroy routine enquiries files.[51]

Ninth, there are education,[52] and outreach records; the cathedral must keep official minutes and papers of the Cathedral/Choir School Board of Governors (if held by the cathedral); should keep records of events held there; may keep a copy of Board minutes and papers (where official records are held elsewhere), samples of publicity material, learning resources, and event programmes; and should destroy records of enquiries and individual visits.[53] Tenth, fundraising records; it must keep securely and then destroy sensitive personal data about benefactors; it must keep administrative files relating to major appeals and campaigns; and it may keep samples of publicity materials produced, for example, for special appeals.[54]

When separate organisations are employed to run ancillary enterprises connected with the cathedral, such as shops, marketing, catering and conference centres, they are responsible for their own records and should maintain them in accordance with the relevant legislation and good practice. Friends' organisations should also keep their own records in accordance with Data Protection and other legislation. However, in the case of Friends' organisations, their committee minutes and newsletters may be of long-term interest to the cathedral and, if possible, should be offered to the cathedral's archives once no longer of administrative use.[55]

---

50 Chapter and Verse, Section 3.3.7.
51 Chapter and Verse, Section 3.3.8.
52 Records relating to the education of choristers in the cathedral/choir school or other establishment are the responsibility of the school; they are not covered in this guide. However, if Chapter is represented on the board of governors and committees, copies of minutes of these bodies may be held in the Chapter Office or offices of Chapter members. Where the official records of the governing body (e.g. signed minutes) are held by the Chapter Office, these must be kept but reference copies may be destroyed.
53 Chapter and Verse, Section 3.3.9.
54 Chapter and Verse, Section 3.3.10; see also the Data Protection Act 1998 (as amended).
55 Chapter and Verse, Section 3.3.11. Section 4 sets out the retention advice; Section 5 deals with what to do when senior staff leave the cathedral; Section 6 addresses electronic records; Section 7 is on the storage, conservation, repair, access and use of records; Section 8: the Church of England is not defined as a public body for the purposes of the Freedom of Information Act which therefore does not apply to it; Section 9: copyright; Section 10: contracts and agreements with Record Offices; and Section 11 contains a glossary.

The cathedral interviews

These disclose several extra-legal practices in relation to cathedral libraries. Hereford has a practice under which the Chancellor is styled Canon Librarian and the person appointed to manage the library is a professional librarian. Salisbury's statutory librarian is a member of the Foundation, though the statutes do not expressly provide for this. At Gloucester, which has 'a modest library', the statutes do not provide for appointment of a Canon Librarian but as a matter of practice there is a part-time Archivist who is also the librarian. The rule at Chester that Chapter must make regulations for access to the library has not been used.[56]

Educational work and theological study

The Archbishops' Commission on Cathedrals 1994 understood that the preaching ministry of cathedrals was an integral part of their educational role; however, 'the area least developed in the preaching role is in teaching offered to the casual visitor'.[57] As a result, the Commission recommended that a cathedral should: allocate a trained member of Chapter, or a full-time professional educator, to oversee, develop, and promote cathedral involvement in education; develop links with schools; provide for teachers' and students' guide packs and materials linked to the National Curriculum; and set up an education centre and workshops for school visits. The cathedral should also: engage with theological colleges and the local university; exchange education resources, materials, and ideas with each other; create education priorities in liaison with diocesan authorities; extend preaching ministry to public lectures, theological seminars, and other vehicles designed to present the faith; and create joint Chapter/university theological posts.[58] Today, the Association of English Cathedrals also acknowledges that 'cathedrals are immensely rich learning resources': they offer facilities for visits by schools; most employ education officers who work within national curriculum guidelines to provide tours, trails, and workshops which supplement classroom learning; and they give opportunities for adult learning, with guided tours and openings to develop skills through volunteering.[59] Whilst the Cathedrals Measure 1999 did not incorporate these recommendations in its own provisions, cathedral constitutions and/or statutes do so in a number of different ways.

---

56 Hereford: Dean: Int. 5–8-2016: see Con. Art. 20 and Stat. XII; Salisbury: Dean: Int. 20–9-2016: see Stat. 9 Annex for 'members of the Foundation' in the order of precedence at services: but there is no members' list; Gloucester: Chancellor and Vice-Dean: Int. 4–8-2016; and Chester: Vice Dean: Int. 19–8-2016.
57 H&R 24–28 and 38: at the Reformation, the principal form of teaching was the lecture and the sermon.
58 H&R 49 and 178, Recs. 1 to 7 (Chap. 4), 252, Appendix 6.
59 AEC: www.englishcathedrals.co.uk.

Theological study and canons theologian

Cathedrals often provide for theological study at the cathedral; and typically the chancellor and/or a canon theologian is to engage in and/or promote this. However, they vary as to whether these positions are mandatory or permissive, as well as in relation to the process of appointment, tenure, and, importantly, the duties of office. Whilst some do not specify the educational roles of the chancellor,[60] others do. For example, Wells' chancellor (who must be a residentiary) is by statute 'to promote theological study'. In terms of policy, education is key to cathedral mission and based on a 'creative relationship between faith and study'; the Chancellor is responsible for the 'Theology in Wells' programme which uses 'a wide range of educational methods to attract different people at different levels'; it includes a lecture series, regular residential theological conference, and short summer series of lectures for a local audience. Its aim is to provide: stimulating and challenging events for those longing for the church to grapple with world issues; intellectual and spiritual support for an intelligent and critical faith; and a forum for those on the fringes of faith to engage in issues facing the church.[61] Similarly, Salisbury's chancellor must 'seek to promote religious and theological education and have oversight of the ministry to visitors within the Cathedral';[62] at Hereford, the bishop may attach to a prebendary such 'educational' duties as are, in his opinion, in the interests of the cathedral, the diocese or the church at large;[63] and York has a theologian.[64]

With regard to those cathedrals which have a canon theologian, at old foundation Chichester the office is mandatory: among non-residentiaries, four named prebends must be designated as theological canonries and lectureships attached to named prebends. As to their duties: 'Theological Canons and Lecturers shall be expected to contribute to the educational life of the Cathedral and diocese in accordance with the statutes', and hold office for a five-year term renewable at the discretion of the bishop and Chapter acting jointly.[65] The prebends must be 'persons of sound learning and distinction who shall represent a range of theological disciplines' and are expected to give 'such courses of lectures concerning theology' as are agreed by Chapter.[66] Moreover, if the bishop considers that

---

60 See e.g. York: Stat. V.5: the four residentiaries include the chancellor who is 'to represent and interpret the Chapter's policy and in accordance with that policy to administer, as appropriate, such departments in the cathedral Church as the Chapter from time to time determines'.
61 Wells: Stat. 4(6): the chancellor also acts as the secretary to Chapter if need so requires.
62 Salisbury: Stat. 5.6; see also Con. Art. 12.2: the chancellor has a named stall.
63 Hereford: Con. Art. 11(4).
64 York: Stat. V.5: the four residentiary canons include the Theologian who is 'to represent and interpret the Chapter's policy and in accordance with that policy to administer, as appropriate, such departments in the cathedral Church as the Chapter from time to time determines'.
65 Chichester: Con. Art. 9.
66 Chichester: Stat. 10; see also Stat. 23: Theological Canons and Lecturers are members of the Foundation.

168 *The library and cloister*

'insufficient funds' are being used towards the promotion of learning and education through the Theological Canons and Lecturers, the bishop may, after consulting Chapter, and if satisfied that funds are available, require Chapter to allocate the necessary funds (from prebend income) for those purposes.[67]

However, at Exeter the office of canon theologian is permissive and the role is diocesan and not (as at Chichester) cathedral *and* diocesan. The bishop may, after consulting the dean, appoint not more than two additional College members with the title of canon theologian – they must be actual communicants but need not be clergy beneficed, licensed or resident in the diocese; appointment is for a five-year term but may be renewed by the bishop, after consulting the dean, for a further term(s) not exceeding three years. The canon must fulfil 'a particular role in contributing to the theological life of the Diocese' as agreed by the bishop,[68] is installed by Chapter after the requisite oaths,[69] and appears in the order of precedence.[70]

Among the new foundations, Winchester (and the same applies to Henrician foundation Gloucester) operates a permissive and minimalist approach: the bishop may appoint after consulting the dean one additional honorary or lay canon as canon theologian for a term of five years renewable similarly for a further term(s) not exceeding three years; the statutes are silent as to functions.[71] By way of contrast, Durham is more comprehensive: the bishop in consultation with Chapter may appoint not more than two canons theologian for such term as the bishop may determine; a person appointed need not be ordinarily resident in the diocese but must be a person of 'learning' ordained in the Church of England or of a church in communion with it; the appointee becomes a supernumerary non-residentiary and so holds a dignity in the cathedral but not an office.[72] The bishop may attach to the dignity a research fellowship or other academic post in the University of Durham or any other English university under such conditions as to tenure, residence, emoluments, and terms of service as the bishop may determine if the consent of the Chapter and of the university concerned is obtained. A canon theologian is admitted by the bishop and installed by the dean, and must make the prescribed declaration. If the person at the date of appointment to the canonry at the same time held an academic post at Durham University or elsewhere, and was appointed to the canonry on the understanding that the canonry would be held only so long as the university post was held, the canon on ceasing to do so automatically and without execution of any instrument of resignation must vacate the canonry. Moreover, if guilty of any grave misconduct, negligence, or inefficiency in the discharge of duties, the bishop may remove the canon after giving sufficient opportunity of showing reason to the contrary and regarding what is reasonable in the circumstances.[73]

67 Chichester: Stat. 26.h.
68 Exeter: Con. Art. 11.b and d.
69 Exeter: Stat. VIII.1.
70 Exeter: Stat. XVII.ix.
71 Winchester: Con. Art. 8.10; Gloucester: Con. Art. 9(7).
72 Durham: Con. Art. 7(a).
73 Durham: Stat. XV.1–4.

Similar diversity exists among parish church cathedrals with regard to the number of canons theologian who may be appointed, their qualifications for appointment, and their educational functions within and/or beyond the cathedral. At Coventry there must not be more than four canons theologian, lay or ordained; the candidates, who must be 'people of learning', are appointed by the bishop after consulting the dean and hold office for five years renewable for further such terms. Each is admitted by the bishop and installed by the dean, takes the prescribed oaths, and must 'contribute to the teaching ministry of the diocese and promote its mission and service'; but functions are not set out.[74] At Birmingham the bishop may appoint up to two additional honorary or lay canons as canons theologian; the former need not be beneficed/licensed in the diocese; appointment is for a five-year term renewable similarly for a further term(s) not exceeding five years.[75] However, duties of office are not set out, as is also the case at Truro, which allows its bishop to appoint, for a renewable five-year term, one additional ordained or lay canon as the canon theologian occupying the stall of St Samson.[76]

However at St Edmundsbury, it is the dean who may, after consulting bishop and Chapter appoint one residentiary as canon theologian with responsibility for 'the theological and educational life of the Cathedral and oversight of the Discovery Centre'.[77] Interestingly, at Leicester, to be appointed as canon theologian a person must be of 'good standing in sacred learning'; at Manchester one canon at least must be appointed with 'especial competence in theological learning'; and Bradford provides for a canon theologian but neither qualification nor functions is set out in the statutes.[78] Some parish church cathedrals also provide for the office of chancellor but without elaborating functions or involvement in educational work.[79]

The education officers and policy of the cathedral

There is a substantial body of national guidance on engaging young people in education and learning at cathedrals.[80] It recommends that each cathedral should have an Education Officer accountable for achieving the highest possible standards in this area and able to forge positive professional relations with educational establishments.[81] The officer must: (1) set high expectations which inspire, motivate and challenge young people; establish a safe stimulating environment rooted

---

74 Coventry: Con. Art. 6: each must retire at seventy; Stat. 7; Stat. 14.1(1): precedence.
75 Birmingham: Con. Art. 9.
76 Truro: Con. Art. 9(d).
77 St Edmundsbury: Con. Art. 10(7), and Stat. 11. Sheffield in 2016 ran a programme 'Religion and Law'.
78 Leicester: Con. Art. 8; Stat. 5(1); Manchester: Con. Art. VI.8; Bradford: Con. Art. 9.
79 E.g. Southwark: Stat. 3(3). See also Liverpool: Con. Art. 9.6: canon theologian; 10.1: cathedral lecturer.
80 Cathedrals Plus: Engaging Visitors in Places of Christian Worship: Standards for those Working with Young People in Education and Learning (2014): hereafter Standards.
81 Standards (2014), Introduction.

in mutual respect; and demonstrate consistently the positive attitudes, values and behaviour expected of young people;[82] (2) guide the young people to reflect on their visit, and encourage them to take a responsible and conscientious attitude to their own learning;[83] (3) demonstrate knowledge of the curriculum relevant to topics covered during a visit, current approaches to teaching/learning, and how to include opportunities for spiritual development within this;[84] (4) plan and deliver structured visits to promote, e.g. a desire to learn and enquire about the cathedral, and reflect systematically on and evaluate all visits;[85] (5) adapt the visit so that it responds to the different strengths and needs of those involved;[86] (6) use formative and summative assessment to secure progress during a visit, give regular oral feedback and encourage responses;[87] (7) manage behaviour effectively to ensure a good and safe learning environment, with clear rules/routines for behaviour, sharing responsibility with visiting teachers for this, and establishing discipline with a range of strategies, using praise, sanctions and rewards consistently and fairly, and exercising appropriate authority;[88] (8) fulfil professional responsibilities, e.g. making a positive contribution to the cathedral, developing professional relations with colleagues, deploying/training volunteers, engaging in professional development, communicating with schools, and managing a budget efficiently.[89] The education officer is also expected to demonstrate consistently high standards of personal–professional conduct, uphold public trust and high standards of ethics and behaviour in and outside the cathedral (e.g. by not undermining the cathedral's Christian values, and ensuring personal beliefs do not exploit the vulnerability of others), and uphold the cathedral's aims.[90]

In turn, cathedrals in their own constitutions, statutes, and policy documents, address aspects of issues treated in the national guidance. We have already seen how the bishop and clergy exercise a preaching ministry at the cathedral,[91] and how it may list education, learning and teaching among its objects; and many provide for inclusion on Council of persons with expertise in education: for example, at Rochester one person must be appointed by Chapter to Council 'after consultation with the principals of one or more of the institutions of higher education in the Diocese'.[92] In addition, among the old foundations, Salisbury

82 Standards (2014), Part, 1, Section 1.
83 Standards (2014), Part 1, Section 2.
84 Standards (2014), Part 1, Section 3.
85 Standards (2014), Part 1, Section 4.
86 Standards (2014), Part 1, Section 5.
87 Standards (2014), Part 1, Section 6.
88 Standards (2014), Part 1, Section 7.
89 Standards (2014), Part 1, Section 8.
90 Standards (2014), Part 2.
91 See above, Chapters 2, 3 and 5. See also CFCE 190(11): Exeter: approval for education rooms in the cloister.
92 Rochester: Con. Art. 12.1.6. See also e.g. Chester: Con. Art. 14: one person appointed by the University of Chester; Guildford: Con. Art. 1.1.10: one appointed by the bishop after consulting the University of Surrey; Derby: Con. Art. 10.1(f): one representative from the University of Derby; Lincoln: Con. Art. 13(1)(f)(v): 'education'

Chapter must arrange for 'the Christian education of those who worship and visit the Cathedral', and, if it considers appropriate and with the bishop's written consent, it may make provision for 'the study of theology, sacred music, ecclesiastical art or other branch of sacred learning';[93] and Chichester Chapter may appoint, as additional staff and with a written agreement on terms it determines, an Education Officer who 'shall be a suitably qualified person ... responsible for undertaking those tasks'.[94] Similarly, among new foundations, Norwich Chapter may appoint a 'Schools' Officer';[95] and Winchester's must make arrangements it considers appropriate for the 'education' and 'information' of visitors 'whether in return for payment or otherwise'.[96]

Among the Henrician cathedrals, Chester is exceptional: Chapter must appoint, on such terms and conditions of service as it may determine, 'a person suitably qualified as a Chancellor', to 'oversee, promote and develop the educational work of the Cathedral', with its agreement, to promote and sustain links between the cathedral and appropriate educational establishments; and to 'encourage patronage of the contemporary arts promoting and supporting discussion of particular schemes' in Chapter.[97] Similarly, among parish church cathedrals Newcastle and Derby are untypical: Newcastle Chapter must make 'suitable arrangements for the Christian education' of adults and children who worship at and visit the cathedral;[98] and Derby's College of Canons must promote 'sound theological learning' in the cathedral and diocese.[99]

In terms of policy documents, Guildford has a very well-developed 'Education Policy'.[100] It provides that: 'Education is a central aspect of the Cathedral's mission' which seeks 'to offer opportunities for Christian learning and ... cultivate wisdom through engagement in the public sphere'. The policy is the responsibility and under the direction of the Canon for Education who is accountable to Chapter.[101] The scheme has three strands: congregational programmes; diocesan-based lectures; and public engagement with faith – the aim of each is to deepen understanding, facilitate dialogue, and contribute to flourishing relationships. First, as to cathedral education: 'The Cathedral is committed to developing opportunities for people of all ages to learn about the Christian faith in order to foster Christ-like relationships and to equip people to fulfil their potential as disciples'. Activities include Sunday schools, working with young people (e.g. confirmation preparation), Lenten lectures, study groups and adult confirmation

and 'the arts'; Southwark: Con. Art. VIII(1)(iii); Southwell: Con. 10.1: persons able to support the cathedral 'as a Centre of ... Education'.
93 Salisbury: Con. Art. 6.1(10) and (17).
94 Chichester: Stat. 21.h.
95 Norwich: Stat. XVII.2.
96 Winchester: Stat. 19.1.1–2: this also applies to provision of a 'refectory'.
97 Chester: Stat. 8: the Chancellor may be on Chapter.
98 Newcastle: Stat. 10.
99 Derby: Con. Art. 11.4(b).
100 Guildford: Education Policy: Pursuing the Spirit's Gift of Wisdom.
101 Chapter decided to appoint a Canon for Education rather than a Canon Pastor.

classes, and encouraging clergy to develop research interests. The cathedral's Schools' Department (managed by the Canon for Education): offers a programme of visits and workshops; has a Schools' Officer to develop an activity strategy; and provides for the recruitment and training of volunteers. Second, as to diocesan education, the cathedral is committed to developing its teaching ministry in order to support the work of clergy and parishes, finding opportunities to collaborate with the diocese as 'a theological and educational resource'. Activities include: an annual lecture given by the canon theologian; with the diocese, an annual summer school; housing a library developing acquisitions through the Library Committee; support for the ministry of parishes, deaneries and diocesan groups (e.g. leading talks); and facilitating theological reflection on the arts in conjunction with the Canon responsible for the cathedral Arts Policy. As to public education, the cathedral is committed to engaging with issues of faith in the public sphere through collaboration with other institutions and facilitating dialogue.[102] Activities include: collaborating with Surrey University Chaplaincy 'to contribute to multi-faith work', and seeking ways to engage with issues emerging from the public sector, including social responsibility, science, and ethics.[103]

Cultural events at cathedrals

The Archbishops' Commission on Cathedrals 1994 recognised the importance of cathedrals for culture and the arts, and it found as examples of good practice: holding an annual festival of music; the patronage of contemporary arts; and making cathedral vestments.[104] Indeed, the Canons of the Church of England provide that when any church is used for plays, concerts, and exhibitions of films and pictures, the minister must take care that the words, music and pictures befit the House of God, are consonant with sound doctrine, and make for edifying the people; the minister must obey any general directions as to such use issued from time to time by the bishop or other ordinary. No such event may be held unless the minister first consults the local or other authority concerned with precautions against fire and other dangers legally required for performances of plays, concerts, or exhibitions of cinematograph films, and these authorities must have signified that the proposed arrangements comply sufficiently with any relevant regulations in force. If any doubt arises as to the manner in which these norms are to be observed, the minister must refer the matter to the bishop or other ordinary, and obey his directions.[105] However, the constitutions and/or statutes of cathedrals only occasionally deal specifically with such events; Coventry is untypical: 'When the Cathedral is to be used for any major theatrical, musical production or

---

102 The cathedral shares a site for this purpose with the University of Surrey and the Diocesan Education Centre.
103 The policy also addresses how the commitment to education should be reflected in the cathedral budget and how a culture of research among cathedral clergy might be developed. See also the Annual Reports.
104 H&R 252, Appendix 6.
105 Can. F16.1–4. See below Chapters 8 and 9.

similar event, all details must normally be approved in advance by the Senior Staff Team or someone nominated by it'.[106]

The Cathedrals Fabric Commission has issued national policy on new art in cathedrals.[107] This strongly encourages all Chapters to develop an Arts Policy, as to the installation of all new works and the development of specific proposals, which 'should be reviewed and updated on a regular basis'; and 'any application for approval of a new art work should make reference to this Policy'; temporary installations do not require approval.[108] A proposal to install a new work of art should be assessed by Chapter against its Liturgical Plan (see above Chapter 3) and the Conservation Management Plan where the cathedral has one. In the absence of the latter, the Cathedral Architect and Archaeologist should provide a statement on the nature and significance of those parts of the cathedral or its fabric to be affected by the installation and the likely impact of the work. When installation of a new work of art, in any medium, is proposed, it is subject to the same procedures and assessment of its effect on the cathedral's character and fabric, whether it is a gift to Chapter or work purchased or specially commissioned by it. The installation of a new work of art (sculpture, painting, object, new media installation etc) is usually considered by the Commission to comprise the permanent addition to the cathedral of an object which would materially affect its character. As such, an application for its approval would usually be made to the Fabric Advisory Committee.[109]

The cathedral interviews

These disclose a variety of understandings of and practices associated with the educational work of cathedrals, and those responsible for it. The functions of the chancellor of Hereford are not spelt out in the constitution/statutes but 'the practice' is that the chancellor serves in the 'education' field 'stimulating theological reflection and life-long learning'; it is most likely that these functions are 'customary' and so the chancellor's 'job description' is declaratory of custom.[110] At Exeter, where the canon theologian is appointed by the bishop, the cathedral is currently thinking about a job description for the role 'to help with the

---

106 Coventry: Stat. Appendix 3: Standing Orders: B. Topic Standing Orders 2(a).
107 New Art in Cathedrals: A Cathedrals Fabric Commission Policy and Practice Note (2012): 'The Commission considers all applications on their own merits and in accordance with the procedures outlined in the Care of Cathedrals Measure 2011 and the Care of Cathedrals Rules 2006. This Policy and Practice Note sets out its expectations of an application and some of the considerations it will bring to bear on its decision-making'.
108 'Temporary' is usually held to be a period of 6 months and not more than 12 months. Chapter should take advice on any such installation from the Fabric Advisory Committee. However, if a 'temporary' installation will necessitate work that will have a material effect on the cathedral fabric, such that it would fall under the CCM 2011, s. 2(1)(a)(i), an application for approval should be made.
109 CCM 2011, s. 2(1)(d). See below Chapters 8 and 9.
110 Hereford: Dean: Int. 5-8-2016.

programme of adult learning', 'to include looking out to debate publicly the Christian faith', and 'to nurture public theology within the communities of the cathedral'; the post is not remunerated.[111] St Paul's has no canon theologian: the chancellor performs this function.[112]

At new foundation Winchester, the canon theologian preaches and runs study days for the College of Canons.[113] At Henrician foundation Gloucester, the view was expressed that it is surprising that the preamble to the constitution does not mention the educational role of the cathedral. However, the constitution enables the bishop to appoint, consulting the dean, an additional honorary or lay canon as canon theologian, but functions are not spelt out in the statutes. Nevertheless, it is a 'custom' that the canon theologian preaches once or twice each year – but invitations to do so are sometimes not taken up by the canon theologian – in this sense, one might say that the 'customary duties' of the canon theologian are 'dormant'. However, the Diocesan Director of Mission and Ministry is responsible for 'Christian education for adults' and is a residentiary. As a matter of custom, the canon chancellor oversees the cathedral Education Centre, but as the constitution and statutes are silent, it is a 'customary office'.[114] At Bristol, neither constitution nor statutes mention an office of canon theologian; but this title has recently been attached to a new honorary canon (a university professor) whose brief is 'to build up theological reflection and conversation with civic and social justice and ethical issues'; there is a 'job description' and the canon is 'effectively a residentiary', delivering lectures throughout the year. Provision in the constitution or statutes for such an office would have been useful, given that theological learning is part of the 'vocation' of a cathedral.[115]

The interplay of law and practice is particularly interesting at Chester. First, the constitution enables the bishop to appoint after consulting Chapter one or more additional honorary or lay canons as canon theologian for five-years renewable by the bishop; they are not members of College of Canons but may be invited to meetings (Art. 10); in practice, roles are agreed between Chapter and the canon who gives two lectures each year for the cathedral (not for the College). Second, by statute Chapter must appoint on terms it may determine a suitably qualified person as chancellor, who may be a Chapter member, to oversee, promote, and develop the cathedral's educational work, with its agreement, promote and sustain links between the cathedral and appropriate educational establishments, encourage patronage of the contemporary arts, and promote discussion of schemes in Chapter (Stat. 8). In practice, the chancellor organises sixth-form study, pilgrimages, and lectures thrice each year. Inclusion of the office in the statutes was an initiative of the bishop.[116] Third, by statute each residentiary must endeavour to pursue theological reflection and research for the benefit of the

111 Exeter: Dean: Int. 9–8-2016.
112 London: Dean: Int. 23–9-2016.
113 Winchester: Acting Dean: Int. 16–8-2016.
114 Gloucester: Chancellor and Vice Dean: Int. 4–8-2016; Con. Art. 9(7).
115 Bristol: Dean: Int. 3–8-2016
116 Chester: Vice-Dean: Int. 19–8-2016.

wider church (Stat. 3(ii)); this does not occur formally: all cathedral ministry represents 'engagement in practical or applied theology'.[117] At the parish church cathedral at Derby the canon theologian gives lectures and works with interfaith dialogue; and Birmingham has two canons theologian who preach twice each year but do not provide adult education in the faith; and it would be worth exploring engaging the College of Canons in theological education.[118]

The cathedral school

Historically, cathedral schools were founded in part to educate choristers and potential clerics;[119] and legal rules developed with regard to a cathedral's rights over them.[120] In turn, the Archbishops' Commission on Cathedrals 1994 recommended that a cathedral should have creative relations with its choir school (if it has one), consider its future governance, and address potential conflicts of interest between Chapter and school (particularly in the areas of finance and property).[121] Today, many cathedrals are still associated with a particular school; the relationship between cathedral and school differs as between cathedrals, as does the breadth and depth of norms. For convenience, this section also deals with child protection.

The relationship between cathedral and school

The Cathedrals Measure 1999 does not address cathedral schools.[122] The resultant freedom means that various approaches are used by cathedrals in their constitutions and/or statutes. Some have a duty to maintain a school, others have a power to do so; at several, the school's head teacher and/or staff are appointed by the cathedral, and they have stalls in it, while at others this is not the case; in some, provision is also made for cathedral scholarships; in several, the dean and/or residentiary canons may be members of the school's governing body; and in some the statutes make express provision for the use of the cathedral by the school. The diversity of approaches is best elucidated on the basis of the various cathedral types.[123]

---

117 Derby: Dean: Int. 10–8-2016.
118 Birmingham: Dean: Int. 11–8-2016.
119 H&R 24–28.
120 Phillimore I.130: e.g. the right of the dean and Chapter to remove a cathedral school master (subject to appeal to the visitor); *R v Dean of Rochester* (1851) 17 QB 1.
121 H&R 49 and 178.
122 They (and their various types) are subject to the civil education law for which see generally M. Hill, R. Sandberg and N. Doe, *Religion and Law in the United Kingdom* (Hague: Wolters Kluwer, 2nd ed., 2014) 184–189. The Choir Schools Association, founded in 1918, represents 44 schools attached to cathedrals, churches and college chapels in Great Britain and elsewhere. The majority of members are fee-paying independent schools, but some are state schools; some cathedrals without choir schools are also members.
123 See also Chapter 5 above for references to the school in norms on cathedral choristers. There are also national regulations on cathedral accounting in matters relating to a choir or related school: ARR, 3.11.

As to old foundations, St Paul's has a high degree of control over its school. Chapter must appoint as Headmaster of the Cathedral School a suitably qualified person 'who shall be charged with the leadership and management of the School within the policy guidelines laid down by the Chapter'.[124] Chapter must provide an education there to enable the choristers to play their full part in the liturgical and musical life of the cathedral,[125] and 'for such other pupils between the ages of four and thirteen years as can be properly accommodated from time to time within the School'. Chapter must also establish a committee to govern the school, the Governing Body, to which it 'shall devolve by an Instrument of Delegation all appropriate and necessary powers for the direct governance of the School'; the dean, precentor, and three other Chapter members appointed by Chapter are *ex officio* members of the Governing Body; and:

> Chapter reserves the power by virtue of the Constitution and the Statutes of the Cathedral after consultation with the Governing Body to amend, withdraw or replace the Instrument of Delegation at its absolute discretion provided that any amendment, withdrawal or replacement is notified to the Governing Body in writing.

The appointment of the Headmaster must be made by Chapter in consultation with the full Governing Body.[126]

By way of contrast, Chichester provides for an independent governing body: 'The Prebendal School is a financially independent charity and incorporated company for the advancement of education and religion of its pupils who shall continue to include the Choristers of the Cathedral'; it is a preparatory school, which may include a pre-preparatory department, and is open to both boys and girls. The 'management and control of the ... School, including the accounts and appointment of the Head Master and other staff, is undertaken by a body known as the Governors of the Prebendal School (the Governing Body)'; and the governors are the company directors and trustees of the charity.[127] The College of Canons must elect as representatives among its members such Governors as are prescribed in the school's own constitution.[128] The dean is a governor.[129] Further, Chapter must consult the Head Master (and the Organist) in appointing choristers, and it must ensure that provision is made for their education and upbringing;[130] the Head Master is also a member of the Foundation of the cathedral.[131] Moreover, in appointing to a named prebend, Chapter must have regard 'to the traditional

---

124 London: Con. Art. 11.5.
125 London: Stat. XV.4.
126 London: Stat. XVI.1–5.
127 Chichester: Stat. 27: as such, the governors have 'control of the Charity and its property and funds'.
128 Chichester: Con. Art. 5(e).
129 Chichester: Stat. 6.d.vi.
130 Chichester: Stat. 15.d.
131 Chichester: Stat. 23.

connection' with the School;[132] indeed, for so long as it remains an independent School, the income of the Highleigh Prebend at the cathedral must be paid to the School.[133]

Variations on these themes are played out at other old foundations. At Wells: 'the ancient connection between the Cathedral and Wells Cathedral School' is maintained by provision in the School's Memorandum of Association for the training and instruction of choristers and in its Articles of Association for representation of the cathedral on the School's governing body. Moreover: 'such privileges in the Cathedral and the Library of St Andrew shall be granted to the Head Teacher, teachers and scholars of the school' as Chapter may determine;[134] and the Head Teacher appears in the order of precedence at cathedral services.[135] Exeter Chapter: may 'maintain a school at which choristers are educated',[136] or else 'children from among whose numbers choristers may be drawn'; and it must determine 'the method of governance of the Cathedral School and ... select and appoint the head teacher'.[137] Hereford recognizes that: 'From the earliest times ... the Cathedral School, from which the choristers are drawn', has been 'an integral part of the Foundation of the Cathedral';[138] thus Chapter may: 'Maintain a school or schools for the primary purpose of educating choristers and others';[139] also, one of the objects of the Hereford Cathedral Trust is to promote the religious and secular education of pupils attending any school in which instruction in the doctrines of the Church of England is given.[140] Salisbury Chapter must in so far as it may consider appropriate, 'make provision for the Salisbury Cathedral School and the education or maintenance of Choristers'.[141] And at Lichfield: 'So long as there is a Cathedral School the Choristers shall be educated there according to the terms prescribed by any Service Agreement made between the Cathedral and the ... School'; Chapter may use its income for the education, remuneration and maintenance of choristers; and the Head of the School has a stall in the quire, is a member of the Choral Foundation, and must be consulted about the number of boy and girl choristers.[142]

There is a particularly full treatment of the subject at York: the Minster School is 'under the jurisdiction of the Chapter', but Chapter must 'delegate all day to day matters of finance and management to the Board of Management appointed by the Chapter'. The school is under the direction of a Headteacher, 'by custom called "The Master of the Minster School"' and must 'provide an education for

132 Chichester: Stat. 10.b: i.e. the Prebend of Highleigh.
133 Chichester: Stat. 26.g.
134 Wells: Stat. 22.
135 Wells: Stat. 21(1): unless the dean determines otherwise.
136 Exeter: Stat. II.8.b.
137 Exeter: Stat. XIV; see also Stat. XVII.xviii: the head teacher appears in the order of precedence.
138 Hereford: Con. Preamble.
139 Hereford: Con. Art. 4(4)(g).
140 Hereford Cathedral Perpetual Trust: Memorandum of Association, 3.1.
141 Salisbury: Con. Art. 6.1(16).
142 Lichfield: Stat. VII(1)(d), (4) and (5); see (6) for meetings of the Choral Foundation.

children consonant with the principles of the Christian religion as received and taught by the Church of England'. The composition of the Board must be laid down in a Chapter by-law: it must be chaired by the dean or if absent a person recognised by both Chapter and the Board as having an 'adequate knowledge of modern educational uses'. Chapter must require the Board to submit to Chapter an annual report, budgets and audited accounts, such other reports as may be requested by Chapter, and all matters of strategic planning for approval prior to implementation. The Master must be: appointed by Chapter consulting the Board; assisted by 'a staff of duly qualified teachers'; and hold office under a written agreement. Probationers and Choristers are subject to the Master's 'authority ... for all educational purposes'. Moreover: 'It shall be a priority of the School to have places for Probationers and Choristers ... who shall be educated in religion and general subjects'; but according to 'availability of places the School shall also admit boys and girls other than Probationers and Choristers'. Fees must be fixed by the Board after consulting the Master.[143]

New foundations Norwich and Ely have few norms. The Headmaster of The Norwich School is a Foundation member.[144] The Head and King's and Queen's Scholars of the King's School at Ely must make on admission the appropriate declaration as prescribed by statute, and the Head appears in the order of precedence.[145] However, by way of contrast, Rochester, Durham, and Canterbury have fuller though miscellaneous norms. The 'King's School Rochester is the Cathedral School and worships in the cathedral'; the residentiaries or their nominees 'shall be the Governors' with the dean as *ex officio* chair. The consent of the dean and residentiaries is required to appoint the Head. While clergy (licensed by the bishop) on the staff of the School are *ex officio* Priest Vicars at the cathedral, such appointments do 'not necessarily involve any duties in the Cathedral other than those required by the School'. King's Scholars may be appointed by the Head and admitted by the dean. The Foundation includes the Head and King's scholars. Chapter (or its delegate) must choose, in consultation with the School, no fewer than 12 and no more than 18 boy choristers as pupils.[146]

Durham Chapter must provide 'efficiently for the general education of the Choristers and the Probationers at the Chorister School under such conditions, financial or otherwise, as it may from time to time determine'; Chapter must appoint its Head Teacher, ordained or lay, who must be a member of the Church of England or another Christian church; the Head must receive such emoluments as Chapter may determine, and must be assisted by such assistant teachers as Chapter, after taking the advice of the Head, may appoint. Chapter may admit other pupils to the School besides Choristers. If the school's Governing Body ceases to be either Chapter or a body on which its members form a majority, Chapter may make other convenient arrangements for the general education of

---

143 York: Stat. XIV.1–6.
144 Norwich: Stat. I.
145 Ely: Con. Art. 2; Stat. 2: the declaration; Stat. 18(xvi): order of precedence.
146 Rochester: Stat. XVI, XVII and XIV.1.

the Choristers and Probationers.[147] The Precentor (as *custos puerorum*) must act 'in concert' with the Head Teacher for the welfare of the children educated at the school and advise Chapter on matters concerning the school.[148] Chapter may also allocate a house free of rent or at a reduced rent (as it may determine) to the Head Teacher as may be required for the better performance of the duties of the Head.[149]

The King's School, Canterbury, is 'an integral part of the Cathedral Community', and a chartered corporation called 'The Governors, the Head Master and the Lower Master of the King's School of the Cathedral Church of Canterbury in the City of Canterbury'.[150] The Head Master, Lower Master and King's Scholars are admitted 'in the accustomed form to the foundation of the Cathedral' by the dean on behalf of Chapter; each master and scholar must also make 'the profession of obedience' to Chapter, and is 'assigned a seat in the Quire'; the Head Master and Lower Master 'shall occupy the stalls customarily assigned to them on the south and north sides of the Quire respectively and next to the stalls assigned to the Minor Canons, behind the Lay Clerks'. Chapter may also from time to time assign 'some of the Chapels or other parts of the Cathedral to be used for services for the King's School', that is, at other times than those for which special provision is made in the cathedral Statutes.[151]

Henrician foundations have few constitutional/statutory rules on the subject.[152] For instance, the Head of King's School Gloucester is a member of the cathedral community; Chapter may appoint three of its members to its Governing Body 'for so long as that is provided for by or not inconsistent with the provisions ... in the separate Constitution of the School'; and: 'In accordance with custom the Head ... shall be assigned a stall in the Quire' on appointment.[153]

Needless to say, Christ Church Oxford is a special case. First, the Schoolteacher is a member of the Foundation and the dean and Chapter must make 'arrangements for the education (under the supervision of the Schoolteacher) of the Choristers'. The Governing Body must set aside a Chapter Fund which may be applied to pay stipends or salaries to the Schoolteacher; and it may at its discretion from time to time and on such terms as it decides provide buildings and/or land for the use of any school in which the Choristers are educated, and contribute (having regard to the funds at its disposal) such a sum as it considers

147 Durham: Stat. XXXIV.1–4.
148 Durham: Stat. XXI.2.
149 Durham: Stat. XXXVI.6.a: the same applies to the Chapter Clerk, Organist, Sub-Organist, and Head Verger.
150 Canterbury: Con. Preamble and Art. 1(2).
151 Canterbury: Stat. XXVI: Stat. XII: this sets out the accustomed forms of admission and obedience.
152 Peterborough: Stat. 19: 'The King's School in Peterborough having been part of the original foundation of the Cathedral as established by King Henry VIII, the Head Teacher of the school shall have the right at all times to occupy a stall assigned to his office in the Choir of the Cathedral'.
153 Gloucester: Con. Art. 16(2) and Stat. 20; for the cathedral community roll, see Stat. 19.

requisite for maintenance of the Choir School and buildings provided to the school by the Governing Body.[154] Second, three residentiary canonries must be annexed respectively to the university Regius Professorships of Divinity, Moral and Pastoral Theology, and Lady Margaret Professorship of Divinity; and the Regius Professor of Ecclesiastical History holds a residentiary or a lay canonry. The House objects include 'the advancement of religion, education and learning', in particular but not exclusively by the provision, support, conduct and maintenance of Christ Church as a college in the University of Oxford; research in any branch of learning; and the advancement of the arts, culture, heritage and science, in particular but not exclusively by preserving or conserving collections of articles of historical, aesthetic or scientific interest.[155]

The protection of children, young people and vulnerable adults

The Church of England, in a wide range of policy statements and guidance documents, accepts, endorses and will implement 'the principle enshrined in the Children Act 1989 (and subsequent legislation and guidance) that the welfare of the child is paramount'; as such it will: (1) foster and encourage best practice by setting standards for working with children and young people and by supporting parents in the care of their children; (2) work with statutory bodies, voluntary agencies, and other faith communities to promote the safety and wellbeing of children and young people; (3) act promptly whenever a concern is raised about a child or young person or about the behaviour of an adult; and (4) work with the appropriate statutory bodies when an investigation into child abuse is necessary. These documents have norms on such areas as: recruitment and risk assessment for those who may pose a risk to children and adults; the maintenance of safeguarding records; and responding to serious safeguarding concerns. In turn, each diocese has a safeguarding policy designed to implement the national policy.[156] Moreover, the Safeguarding and Discipline Measure 2016 is designed to provide a

154 Oxford: Christ Church: Stat. I.1(a) and 6(b); Stat. VII.1 and 2.
155 Oxford: Christ Church: Stat. I.1–2: see also the Church of England (Miscellaneous Provisions) Measure 2014, s. 19: notwithstanding the Ecclesiastical Commissioners Act 1840 ss. 5 and 6, which annexed two canonries in the Chapter of the Cathedral Church of Christ in Oxford to the Lady Margaret's professorship of divinity and the regius professorship of ecclesiastical history, those professorships may be held either by residentiary canons in the Chapter or by lay canons duly appointed.
156 Child Protection Policy Statement of the Church of England – Promoting a Safe Church: Safeguarding Policy for Adults (2006); Protecting All God's Children: Policy for Safeguarding Children and Young People in the Church of England (4th ed., 2010); Responding to Domestic Abuse: Guidelines for those with Pastoral Responsibility (2006); Responding Well: Policy and Guidance (2011); Learning and Development Practice Guidance: Responding to Serious Safeguarding Situations (2015); Risk Assessment for Individuals who may pose a risk to Children or Adults (2015); Safer Recruitment (2015); Safeguarding in Religious Communities (2015); Safeguarding Records: Joint Practice Guidance for the Church of England and the Methodist Church (2015); and Safeguarding Guidance for Single Congregations in Local Ecumenical Partnerships (2015).

national statutory framework to make the church a safer place for children and young adults by making the disciplinary processes under the Clergy Discipline Measure 2003 more effective where safeguarding issues arise and to reduce the risk of abuse taking place. Canon law requires bishops to appoint diocesan safeguarding advisers, create new powers to require clergy to undergo a risk assessment (to be conducted in accordance with regulations to be made by the House of Bishops and approved by General Synod), and impose a duty on all clergy authorised to administer in a diocese to participate in safeguarding training.[157] Within these national and diocesan frameworks, cathedrals too have their own policies. Two particularly well-developed examples are found at Guildford and St Paul's.

Guildford Chapter's policy commits the cathedral community: to support, nurture, protect and safeguard all, especially the young and vulnerable at risk of harm; to act in accordance within current legislation, guidance, national and diocesan safeguarding procedures; to work in an open, transparent and accountable way in partnership with the Diocesan Safeguarding Adviser, Children and Adult Social Care Services, Police, Probation Services and others; and to 'assist in bringing to justice anyone who has committed an offence' against such persons. Therefore, Chapter will: (1) ensure checks are made for the safe selection and recruitment of ministers, employees and volunteers; (2) provide the supervision, support and training for them to fulfil their roles effectively; (3) respond without delay to every concern raised that a child, young person or vulnerable adult may have been harmed or be at risk of harm, or about their behaviour; (4) cooperate with the diocese and appropriate agencies during an investigation into abuse, including allegations made against a Cathedral Community member; (5) ensure pastoral care is available to children, vulnerable adults and their families and Cathedral Community members against whom an allegation is made; (6) ensure care and supervision for any Cathedral Community member known to have offended against a child or vulnerable adult or to pose a risk to them; and (7) review the safeguarding policy annually.[158]

St Paul's Policy Statement illustrates the distribution of functions. Chapter 'endorses fully' the national policy of the Church of England, and recognises that all staff (paid or volunteers) must protect children and vulnerable adults from abuse, neglect, and exploitation in the cathedral.[159] The aim of Chapter is to:

157 Canon C30.
158 Guildford: Policy Statement for the Safeguarding of Children and Adults at Risk of Harm (2016). See also e.g. Canterbury: Policy of Child Protection; and Safeguarding Public Policy.
159 London: Safeguarding (Child Protection) Policy and Procedures (2015): Section 1; 1.4 repeats Protecting All God's Children (2010) par. 6.19: 'relevant information may be disclosed in the ... context of confession'; Can. 113 of the Canons of 1603/4 'constrains a priest from disclosing details of any crime or offence ... revealed in ... formal confession; however, there is some doubt as to whether this absolute privilege is consistent with the civil law'; if behaviour is at issue, the priest 'should ... urge the person to report it to the police or ... local authority children's social care', if appropriate, may 'withhold absolution', consider it necessary 'to alert the bishop ... to

ensure safe recruitment in checking the suitability of staff and volunteers to work with children and vulnerable adults; raise awareness of child protection issues at induction and regularly thereafter for all staff; recognise the risks of abuse and indicators of harm and train its staff appropriately; ensure all staff are made aware of their responsibilities; and implement procedures to identify and report cases or suspected cases of abuse to the local authority children's service.[160] Chapter appoints one of its own members as Cathedral Safeguarding (Child Protection) Officer to: provide support, advice and expertise; monitor implementation of the procedures; decide whether to make a referral to the statutory bodies and liaise with them; undertake training; ensure all staff have access to the policy and procedures; ensure appropriate staff have regular training (and record this); and keep written records of all concerns about child protection in a locked location. In turn, all staff and volunteers have a responsibility to: raise concerns about the welfare of a child or vulnerable adult; contribute to assess the needs of a child or vulnerable adult and take action to meet those needs; behave professionally in contact with children and vulnerable adults; and not enter a 'special relationship' with them nor accept invitations to become their 'friend' (e.g. on Facebook) without referral to their line manager or the Safeguarding Officer.[161] The Chapter has adopted procedures with regard to: safe recruitment; existing staff; induction and training; and dealing with concerns, disclosures and allegations about staff;[162] and there is guidance on school visits which applies to the cathedral Schools and Families Department.[163]

The cathedral interviews

The interviews reveal several practices and issues as to cathedral schools. At old foundation Exeter, the cathedral has a 'service agreement' with the school; a third stipendiary canon works as a priest to the school – but this is a recent innovation and needs to be assessed; and the cathedral adopts national and diocesan safeguarding policies.[164] The Wells statute on the cathedral school, an independent school specialising in music, is brief (see above), but the relationship with the cathedral is 'very significant'.[165] For the Dean of Salisbury, the relation between cathedrals and cathedral schools is 'an issue' today; cathedrals share 'the same experiences in terms of issues and difficulties', but are 'trying to resolve them

---

safeguard' that priest and seek advice (but 'the penitent's details would not be shared without their permission'), and 'judge it appropriate to encourage the penitent to speak personally to the bishop'.

160 London: Safeguarding (Child Protection) Policy and Procedures (2015): Section 2.
161 Ibid. Section 4.
162 Ibid. Section 5; 6: safe recruitment; 7: existing staff; 8: induction and training; 9: procedure for dealing with a suspicion or concern; 10: disclosures; 11: confidentiality.
163 Additional Safeguarding Procedures Pertaining to the Schools and Families Department (2014); see also: Additional Safeguarding (Child Protection) Procedures Pertaining to the Music Department (2014).
164 Exeter: Dean: Int. 9-8-2016.
165 Wells: Acting Dean: Int. 12-8-2016; Stat. 22.

differently'; some schools want independence; the head of Salisbury cathedral school is not a member of the Foundation but should be; Chapter is the charitable company which runs the school.[166]

New foundation Winchester's cathedral school (which is independent) is dealt with primarily by its Memorandum and Articles of Association and is not mentioned in the constitution or statutes but it should be; the cathedral owns the land of the school and the dean is the head of governors – though there is currently discussion about reducing this role as it is so very time consuming.[167] As to the Rochester statute on the King's School, there is currently a debate as to whether the whole Chapter should be the Governors of the school; and the statute needs revision as the dean is no longer *ex officio* chair of Governors. The corporate body of the cathedral owns some school premises, the school head lives in a cathedral-owned house, the old deanery is used by the school, and the cathedral serves as the 'chapel of the school'.[168]

At the Henrician foundation at Gloucester, the statutes provide for Chapter members to sit on the school governing body, but this does not reflect fully the relationship between cathedral and school. A former dean stepped down as Chair of Governors in 2009 in order to enable a lay governor to chair the governing body and to avoid any potential conflicts of interest. As a matter of practice, the school holds a daily assembly in the cathedral, carol services, concerts, and speech days. Cathedral and other clergy preside at school services of Holy Communion celebrated in the cathedral.[169] At parish church cathedral Derby, neither the constitution nor statutes provide for a school; but the cathedral and Diocesan Board of Education have applied to government for the establishment of a Derby Cathedral School with free school status.[170]

Conclusion

The Cathedrals Measure 1999 does not require cathedrals to make provision with respect to a cathedral library or to appointment of a librarian. Instead the matter is dealt with by the constitutions and/or statutes of cathedrals. Few parish church cathedrals have norms on the subject. However, old and new foundations do – and many of their libraries are ancient. Yet, there are profound differences. Some have norms expressly devoted to the cathedral library, others do not; some require Chapter to maintain a library, others do not; some provide for the appointment and functions of a librarian and/or archivist, others do not; and some provide for oversight of the library, if it has one, by the chancellor, or other officer designated usually by Chapter. Typically, the librarian and/or archivist have responsibility for the day-to-day running of the library and/or archives; and in some cases these

---

166 Salisbury: Dean: Int. 20-9-2016; Con. Art. 6.1(16).
167 Winchester: Acting Dean: Int. 16-8-2016.
168 Rochester: Precentor: Int. 30-9-2016; Stat. XVII.
169 Gloucester: Chancellor and Vice-Dean: Int. 4-8-2016; Stat. 19–20.
170 Derby: Dean: Int. 10-8-2016.

may be authorised to make regulations, such as on access and use. However, there is also a substantial body of detailed national guidance issued by the Cathedral Libraries and Archives Association and the Church of England Record Centre on which records must/may be kept and which destroyed; but there is national law on the inventory and records as they relate to property (see Chapter 8).

Similarly, there is little General Synod law on the wider educational work of cathedrals. Yet, the Association of English Cathedrals considers a cathedral to be a centre of education, and many recommendations of the Archbishops' Commission on Cathedrals 1994 as they relate to education have been implemented in cathedral constitutions and/or statutes. First, many provide for the appointment of canons theologian (often appointed by the bishop) who (and in some cathedrals alongside the chancellor) promotes theological education at the cathedral and/or in the diocese. In some cathedrals the appointment is mandatory, in others permissive. Few cathedrals spell out qualifications necessary for such an appointment. Second, there is national guidance on the appointment of cathedral education officers, with a wide range of functions relating to the education of visitors. In turn, cathedrals list education, teaching and learning as amongst their objects; many include on Council persons with expertise in education; some require Chapter to make arrangements for the Christian education of those who worship and visit the cathedral; and some provide for appointment of an education or schools' officer (a function sometimes assigned to the chancellor). Education policies are common. By way of contrast, whilst the Canons of General Synod require cultural events held there to befit the cathedral as a church, few cathedrals have laws on this matter. The introduction of new art into a cathedral, however, is regulated by policy issued by the Cathedrals Fabric Commission which recommends that each cathedral has its own arts policy (and special norms apply when such installation affects the cathedral fabric). The cathedral interviews reveal several practices which supplement the formal laws of cathedrals, such as the use of job descriptions for those involved in cathedral educational work and the provision of educational programmes to stimulate public debate about theological and associated issues.

As the Cathedrals Measure 1999 does not address cathedral schools, so there is some variety in the approaches of cathedrals to this subject; it is difficult to induce common principles. The degree of control which a cathedral exercises over the school differs from cathedral to cathedral. In some cathedrals there is a duty to maintain a school, in others a power to do so. In many cathedrals the head teacher, and sometimes staff, are appointed by the cathedral, and have stalls in it; in others this is not the case. In some provision is also made for scholars. In many the dean and residentiaries may be members of the school governing body. Often express provision is made for admission of pupils other than choristers. And provision also exists for the use of the cathedral (or designated parts within it) by the school. In any event, there is extensive national guidance on the protection of children and young people (and vulnerable adults) at cathedrals; individual cathedrals also operate policies which provide for the appointment of safeguarding officers, standards for cathedral staff and volunteers working with children, and procedures to report and investigate cases. The interviews reveal that the relationship between the cathedral and its school, and what this entails, is ripe for debate.

8 The treasury: cathedral property, treasure and finance

In a recent case the Consistory Court of the Diocese of Chichester granted a faculty to permit a figure of Christ, originally part of a medieval crucifix made in Limoges, and 'an item of exquisite craftsmanship' held at a parish church in the diocese, 'to be the subject of a long-term loan to Chichester Cathedral so that it may be securely housed in its treasury and therefore available for public viewing'. Chancellor Hill considered that: a long-term loan would provide security and allow the public extensive access to view it; 'the connection with the mother church of the diocese is a weighty factor'; the item could be displayed alongside another sacred piece of Limoges work; and the decision to deposit it in the cathedral treasury could be revisited any time, the faculty amended and an alternative solution found. However, the Chancellor imposed conditions including: the loan would be for ten years but renewable for successive ten-year periods on terms agreed between the cathedral and priest-in-charge and churchwardens of the parish from which it came; the figure would continue to be under the faculty jurisdiction and must not be moved permanently or temporarily, altered in any way, or be subjected to scientific or other investigation without the court's prior permission; the figure should be 'available for public viewing at the cathedral treasury during normal public opening times'; and Chapter must provide there 'an explanatory note describing its provenance and subsequent history' and 'maintain adequate insurance' for it. Importantly, the Chancellor concluded that the scheme afforded the cathedral 'an excellent and timely opportunity to capitalise on its new acquisition as part of the cathedral's educational function which it discharges to such good effect'.[1] The judgment illustrates well the interplay between the topics discussed here: the acquisition, ownership and disposal of property, including maintenance of the cathedral inventory and other records pertaining to cathedral property; cathedral treasures and objects of architectural, archaeological, artistic and historic interest; and the regulation of finance, the cathedral

---

1 *In the Matter of Coombes Parish Church* [2016] ECC Chi 5: the crucifix was known as the 'corpus'.

Finance Committee, accounting, the auditor and the treasurer.[2] In 2013, English cathedrals generated an income of around £125 million.[3]

Cathedral property and the inventory

As already seen, a cathedral's corporate body (Council, Chapter, and College of Canons) has the legal capacity to own property;[4] the historical antecedents of this rule had been the subject of much discussion.[5] Property includes a thing in action and any interest in real or personal property, and land includes corporeal or incorporeal hereditaments of any nature.[6] Moreover, the Church Commissioners with the consent of Chapter may prepare a scheme for the transfer of property by the Commissioners to the cathedral. The scheme may amend or repeal any other scheme made under any Act or Measure as to the property of the cathedral concerned, but not that cathedral's constitution or statutes, and contain such incidental, consequential, or supplementary provisions necessary or expedient in order to give full effect to the scheme.[7]

Chapter, in turn, has power to acquire and dispose of property on behalf of the corporate body of the cathedral, and holds the common seal of the cathedral which it must affix if required in any relevant property transaction.[8] This power of Chapter comprises a power both to acquire property for any purpose connected with the cathedral and to acquire property by gift *inter vivos* or by will.[9] Before it acquires or disposes of *land*, Chapter must obtain the consent of the Church Commissioners; and if it involves disposal of a house of residence: (a) the consent

---

2 Hooker VIII.23.8: the 'Office [of Treasurer] in Churches Cathedral remains even till this day, albeit the use thereof be not altogether so large now as heretofore'. In 1291, York's Treasurer received £233.6s.8d. p.a.
3 *The Economic and Social Impacts of England's Cathedrals*: A Report to the Association of English Cathedrals, written by Ecorys and commissioned by the Association and English Heritage (2014).
4 See above Chapter 6. See also CM 1999, s. 13: property vested prior to the Measure in the dean and chapter or cathedral chapter, by operation of law, without any conveyance, assignment, transfer or other assurance, now vests in the cathedral along with, in the case of land, any easements, rights or other privileges annexed thereto. Vesting under this rule does not affect any previously existing trust, contract, mortgage or other charge affecting the property. The cathedral here means the corporate body established by s. 9(1)(a): s. 35(5).
5 E.g. Burn II.83: 'A chapter of itself, is not capable to take by purchase, or gift, without the dean, who is the head of it'; II.89: this describes the rule (abolished in 2000 with the repeal of Can. C19) that the dean and chapter are 'guardians of the spiritualities of the bishopric during the vacation, although the archbishop now usually has that right by prescription or composition'. See also Phillimore I.129: the possessions of deaneries.
6 CM 1999, s. 35(1).
7 CM 1999, s. 14.
8 CM 1999, s. 4(9)-(10); provided that moneys which form part of the endowment of the cathedral must not be invested or used except as provided by s. 16: see below.
9 CM 1999, s. 35(4).

of the dean or residentiary canon who normally occupies the house, except during a vacancy in these offices, and (b) where the house is allocated for the use of the holder of a dignity, the right of presentation to which is vested in Her Majesty, the consent of Her Majesty.[10]

However, Chapter is not required to obtain the Church Commissioners' consent for: (i) the grant of a lease to a cleric holding office in the cathedral or a person employed in connection with the cathedral; or (ii) the acquisition of land by a gift *inter vivos* or by will; or (iii) any transaction for which an order is required under the Charities Act;[11] or (iv) any transaction relating to land which immediately before the relevant date is held by the dean and chapter of St Paul's London as part of the Tillingham estate.[12] But the Church Commissioners may by order except from these rules transactions about land forming part of an estate specified in the order, or transactions of a class so specified. The sealing by the Church Commissioners of any document is conclusive evidence that all the requirements with respect to the transaction (to which the document relates) have been complied with. A statement in a document sealed by Chapter that the consent of the Church Commissioners is not required is sufficient evidence of that fact. Chapter's power to acquire or dispose of property may be exercised notwithstanding that the consideration for any transaction may not be the full consideration.[13]

Moreover, Chapter must manage all property vested in the cathedral and the income accruing from it and, in particular, it must ensure that necessary repairs and maintenance in respect of the cathedral and its contents and other buildings and monuments are carried out.[14] In turn, Chapter must arrange for an architect or surveyor to carry out an inspection every five years of all property (other than the cathedral church) and any ancillary building which Chapter is liable to repair and maintain, and the architect or surveyor must report to Chapter any necessary works and the degree of urgency to carry them out (see below for inspections).[15]

The Care of Cathedrals Measure 2011 provides for the care and conservation of cathedrals. It requires a local Fabric Advisory Committee for each cathedral and it establishes a Cathedrals Fabric Commission for England.[16] No work may be carried out on the cathedral that would materially affect its architectural, archaeological, artistic or historic character, nor may any object of architectural, archaeological or artistic interest be sold, lent or disposed of without the approval of either the Fabric Advisory Committee or the Commission (see below and Chapter 9). The Cathedrals Fabric Commission has a duty, *inter alia*: to give

---

10 CM 1999, s. 15(1)(a) and (b).
11 I.e. Charities Act 1993 (as amended), s. 35.
12 CM 1999, s. 15(1), proviso.
13 CM 1999, s. 15(2)-(5).
14 CM 1999, s. 4(8)(g).
15 CM 1999, s. 20(1) (amended by the Care of Cathedrals (Amendment) Measure 2005, Sch. 3 para. 8). A similar duty relates to the cathedral church itself: see CCM 2011, s. 14 (see HLE par. 371).
16 For the Fabric Advisory Committee, see e.g. Lichfield: Con. Art. 13; Hereford: Con. Art. 14.

advice to Chapter and the cathedral Fabric Advisory Committee, on the care, conservation, repair or development of any objects vested in the corporate body of the cathedral or of which it has possession or custody or to which it is otherwise entitled; to promote, in consultation with Chapters, Fabric Advisory Committees, and such other persons or organisations as it thinks fit, by means of guidance or otherwise, standards of good practice to be observed as to the compilation, maintenance and dissemination of information of architectural, archaeological, artistic, and historic interest concerning cathedral churches and their objects, and as to the form and content of the mandatory records (that is, those Chapter is required to keep).[17]

The cathedral inventory

Under national law, Chapter must compile and maintain an inventory of all objects the property in which is vested in the corporate body, or which are in the possession or custody of the corporate body, or to whose possession or custody the corporate body is entitled, which the cathedral Fabric Advisory Committee considers to be of architectural, archaeological, artistic, or historic interest.[18] The inventory must be completed within such period as the Cathedrals Fabric Commission determines, after consulting Chapter and the Fabric Advisory Committee. The period must be one which the Commission considers reasonable, having regard to the particular circumstances of each case. The Commission may specify different periods for different parts of the inventory. Chapter must make an annual report to the Fabric Advisory Committee on the contents of the inventory (or on progress made in compiling it). The report must certify the accuracy of the inventory and describe alterations made to it during the twelve months preceding the report. The Fabric Advisory Committee must designate those objects in the inventory which the committee considers, after consulting the Commission, to be of *outstanding* architectural, archaeological, artistic, or historic interest.[19]

The purpose of the inventory is to: (a) identify and record any object the Fabric Advisory Committee considers to be of architectural, archaeological, artistic or historic interest which is owned or possessed by or in the custody of the corporate body (or to whose possession or custody the corporate body is entitled, whether or not the object is for the time being in the possession or custody of another person or body); (b) note the designation by the Committee, after consulting the Commission, of objects considered to be of outstanding architectural, etc., interest; (c) record new acquisitions the Committee considers of architectural, etc., interest, and note any designation of the object; (d) aid the proper care, conservation, and security of such objects; and (e) record their loan, sale, disposal, or

---

17 CCM 2011, s. 3(1)-(3); i.e. objects covered by s. 2(1); s. 27: records. See also CFCE: PGN 7 (2012) IV.5.1.
18 CCM 2011, s. 24(1); see also CCR 2006, r. 28; and CFCE: PGN 7 (2012) IV.1.1, and PGN 4 (2001).
19 CCM 2011, s. 24(2)-(4).

loss. It must include such movable/removable items as ornaments, furnishings, fittings, books, manuscripts, displaced architectural or archaeological materials, musical instruments, and other artefacts.[20]

In the interest of security, where an inventory is compiled in electronic form, all relevant files or other records of information in electronic form that are prepared in connection with the compilation or maintenance of the inventory – including updating, amendment, or new recording – must be securely stored in accordance with advice which may be published by the Commission. As the inventory is an important cathedral record (whether or not electronic), two written copies must be made and maintained in securely bound volumes; both must be kept in a secure place, one within and the other outside the precinct, approved by Chapter.[21]

When information in the inventory requires updating or amendment, this must as soon as reasonably practicable be done in identical terms: in both copies of the relevant volume; and, where the inventory is in electronic form, in that inventory. A photographic record of objects recorded in the inventory must be bound into or retained in a loose leaf collection in conjunction with the inventory unless in a particular case the Fabric Advisory Committee informs Chapter in writing that it considers it unreasonable to require such a record. All entries in an inventory must be made in accordance with such general or special directions as may be issued by the Commission; and Chapter must have regard to any advice as to the form of the inventory issued by the Commission. Access to the inventory or part of it is limited to those expressly authorised in writing by Chapter who at the time of its inspection provide authorisation and documentary evidence of personal identification as Chapter may require.[22]

Inspections, reports and records

Under national law, Chapter must arrange every five years for its architect or surveyor of the fabric, consulting the archaeologist,[23] to make a written report to Chapter on: (a) any works which the architect or surveyor considers need to be carried out as to the cathedral church and any ancillary building; and (b) on the urgency with which the architect or surveyor considers that they should be carried out; Chapter must send a copy of the report to the Commission.[24] The reports must be based on an inspection of the fabric of the cathedral church and ancillary buildings which the architect or surveyor considers necessary to enable them to

---

20 CCR 2006, r. 28(1)-(2). See also ARR, Appendix 2.
21 CCR 2006, r. 28(4)-(5).
22 CCR 2006, r. 28(6)-(9). See above Chapter 7 for archives.
23 I.e. the architect or surveyor appointed under CM 1999, s. 9(1)(f) and archaeologist under CCM 2011, s. 23(2).
24 CCM 2011, s. 26(1); s. 26(6): 'ancillary building' means any building which Chapter may specify, being a building attached to or adjacent to the cathedral church and used for purposes ancillary to the use of the cathedral, but excluding any building used wholly or mainly for residential purposes.

190 *The treasury*

fulfil these requirements.[25] As to property in the precinct, the report must be compiled in consultation with the archaeologist; Chapter must send a copy of it to both Committee and Commission.[26]

Second, the architect or surveyor of the fabric, and the archaeologist, must advise, in the annual report which they must make to Chapter,[27] as to works carried out in the previous year of which a permanent record should in the opinion of the architect, surveyor, or archaeologist be maintained; Chapter must have regard to that advice and, pursuant to it, make and maintain appropriate permanent records of such works; and every five years it must make a written report to the Fabric Advisory Committee about such records, make arrangements to maintain those records, and send a copy of the report to the Cathedrals Fabric Commission.[28]

Third, Chapter must arrange for the archaeologist: to assess matters of archaeological interest relating to the cathedral church and its precinct, including precinct buildings and remains in or under the cathedral church or within its precinct; and, consulting the architect or surveyor, report in writing to Chapter with recommendations on how those matters should be managed and on the compilation and maintenance of archaeological records relating to them. The archaeologist must report annually to Chapter on progress in fulfilling any recommendations and other matters the archaeologist considers relevant. These written reports must be made in consultation with the architect or surveyor, and a copy must be sent to the Commission.[29]

The cathedral interviews, constitutions and statutes

These reveal that the absence of rules in national law requiring cathedrals to incorporate in their constitutions and/or statutes norms on the inventory, reports and records, explains the general absence of such norms in these domestic instruments. National laws apply directly without the need for such incorporation.[30] Nevertheless, there is a practice at some cathedrals to legislate by statute on these matters, of which the following are examples. The Canon Treasurer of Canterbury must ensure an inventory is made of all movable property and that it is reviewed annually; an account of property is also given to a new dean on appointment.[31] At

25 CCM 2011, s. 26(2): i.e. the requirements in s. 26(1); s. 26 also deals with first and subsequent reports.
26 CCM 2011, s. 32(2); CM 1999, s. 20(2).
27 Under CCM 2011, ss. 26(5) or 28(3).
28 CCM 2011, s. 27.
29 CCM 2011, s. 28: or the architect or surveyor appointed to inspect property other than the cathedral under the above-mentioned provisions, if different. See also below Chapter 9.
30 Also: discussion of property matters takes up a great deal of time at Chapter meetings: e.g. Wells: Acting Dean: Int. 12-8-2016; Rochester: Precentor: Int. 26–9-2016; Winchester: Acting Dean: Int. 16-8-2016.
31 See e.g. Canterbury: Stat. VI.3: 'Any person who has any effects belonging to the Body Corporate in his custody shall account for them in writing to the new Dean or

Worcester, Chapter Registers, Minute Books, Financial Accounts, Cathedral Inventory, Constitution and Statutes, Deeds and Documents which relate to 'the estates, possessions, rights, responsibilities and privileges of the Cathedral', must 'be kept in safe custody and care'; care must be taken that none be removed from its place without the permission of the officer to whose charge they have been committed by Chapter; and upon any authorised removal a record must be kept of what is taken out, when and by whom, and the date it is returned.[32] Durham Chapter must 'keep the muniments and other objects of great value and importance and the keys in safe custody in some fit and secure place under the charge of the Chapter Clerk'; there must be an annual visitation of the muniments 'to ensure their proper care and custody and to receive a report from their custodians'; and the dean may at any time call for the production and checking of the inventory.[33] Carlisle has much the same rules, and its inventory, which includes 'cathedral plate, ornaments and keys', must be checked at the first meeting of Chapter after 1 November each year; and an inventory of property in the residences of the dean and residentiaries or elsewhere in the Abbey must be deposited with the Bursar and Chapter Clerk and checked by him on behalf of Chapter as Chapter directs.[34]

Treasures and other valuable objects

The Cathedrals Fabric Commission recognises that Chapters regularly wish to loan objects in their collections to other institutions, often for public exhibition, or as part of a fundraising or awareness-raising initiative. Many such objects are of national/international significance and are irreplaceable. The same applies to the sale, loan, or other disposal of such valuable objects, and to proposals requiring approval include carrying out work on, or the permanent addition of, an object which might affect its architectural, archaeological, artistic, or historic character. National law requires approval for such initiatives. However, the requirement for approval does not apply to anything done by Chapter in carrying out its duties under the cathedral's constitution and statutes as to ordering of services or to further its mission, if what is done is temporary in nature and does not materially affect the cathedral church's fabric.[35]

The sale, loan or other disposal of valuable objects

Chapter must apply for approval of a proposal involving the sale, loan, or other disposal of an object: (a) to the Cathedrals Fabric Commission, if the object is

   to the Canon Treasurer within one month after the installation of the new Dean'. See also the Canterbury Records Management Policy.
32 Worcester: Stat. 17 and 18. See also Salisbury: Stat. 8: Keeper of the Muniments.
33 Durham: Stat. IX; see also Stat. VI.1–2 and XIII.4: inventory.
34 Carlisle: Stat. 27. See above Chapter 7 for the archives.
35 CFCE: Policy and Practice Note (2012): 'temporary' means up to 6 or, at most, 12 months.

designated by the Fabric Advisory Committee as being of *outstanding* architectural, archaeological, artistic or historic interest; or (b) to the Fabric Advisory Committee, if the object has *not* been so designated, but it is of architectural, archaeological, artistic or historic interest.[36] Similarly, if Chapter proposes work to an object which would materially affect its architectural, archaeological, artistic, or historic interest, it must apply (a) to the Commission, if the object has been designated by the Fabric Advisory Committee as of outstanding architectural, archaeological, artistic, or historic interest; and (b) to the Fabric Advisory Committee, if the object is not so designated.[37] Provision is made for the public display by the cathedral administrator of such proposals.[38] The Commission may require that it is to determine the application if it declares in writing that the proposal gives rise to considerations of such special architectural, archaeological, artistic, or historic interest that the application should be determined by it.[39] The Commission must also determine an application to approve works on such objects which have already been implemented in contravention of the requirement to obtain approval.[40]

The Cathedrals Fabric Commission has issued guidance on applications for the sale, loan, or disposal of objects of 'outstanding' interest. First, in an application to loan such object for *temporary exhibition*, the Commission expects the information supporting the application to include: (i) a description of the object (a copy of the inventory entry and photograph are appropriate); (ii) details of the location, duration, aims, and scope of the exhibition for which the loan is requested; (iii) details of proposed arrangements for insurance, transport, handling, security, and environmental control and monitoring, during the exhibition and in transit; (iv) information on the condition of the object and its conservation requirements, together with an assessment of foreseeable risks to it that might be incurred if it were to be moved from its context in the cathedral; and (v) details of any proposals for the conservation of the object.[41]

Second, if an application concerns *the sale, the long-term loan*, or other disposal of such an object the Commission expects supporting information to include: (i) a description of the object (the inventory entry and photograph are appropriate); (ii) an assessment of its historic association with the cathedral and importance to its collections; (iii) a statement of reasons for the proposal; (iv) a statement of reasons why Chapter could not continue to look after the object; and (v) if sale is proposed, a statement as to: the method of sale; how the proceeds of sale would be used; if it is to be funded, how the project fits strategically in the cathedral's work; and the consequences if the sale did not go ahead.[42] The Commission may request Chapter to consult Council, if it has not done so, and inform the

36 CCM 2011, s. 6(1)(a)(iv); CCR 2006, r. 12.
37 CCM 2011, s. 24; see also s. 6; CCR 2006, r. 13.
38 CFCE: PGN 8 (2012) 4.7–10; and PGN 2 (2012) I.5.3.
39 CCM 2011, s. 6(1)(a) and (b).
40 CCM 2011, ss. 2(3), 6(11), 9(8).
41 CFCE: PGN 6 (2012) II.4.11.
42 CFCE: PGN 6 (2012) II.4.12.

Commission of its views, and may consult the Church Commissioners on financial matters (other than the object's value).[43]

Third, where an application concerns *carrying out works* to such an object, the Commission expects supporting information to include: (i) a description of the object; (ii) a statement of the works proposed and reasons for them; and (iii) such reports or assessments made by experts to support or describe the work. In these instances, such information should be proportionate in scope to the project and provide a full understanding of what is proposed.[44] The application process and the powers of the Commission are examined below in Chapter 9.

An object of treasure

National law also deals with the discovery, display, sale, loan or other disposal of, or carrying out of works to, any object which is treasure within the meaning of the Treasure Act 1996.[45] First, if any object which would, but for an order under the Treasure Act, be treasure within the meaning of that Act, is found in or under a cathedral church (or within its precinct), special considerations apply.[46] A cathedral administrator, who becomes aware that such an object has been discovered, must: (a) within 14 days in writing notify the Cathedrals Fabric Commission; and (b) arrange for the object to be recorded and designated as treasure in the inventory in accordance with directions issued by the Commission. The Commission secretary must also report the discovery to the Secretary of State and the Vicar General.[47]

Second, if such an object is discovered in the precincts, the cathedral administrator must notify the cathedral archaeologist (if not already aware of it), and ensure such information as the latter may advise is recorded; the archaeologist, after examining it and taking any advice he thinks necessary, must notify Chapter and administrator in writing whether in his opinion the object is potential treasure.[48] The administrator must as soon as reasonably practicable obtain expert advice as to the conditions appropriate to preserve the object, and ensure it is kept in secure and appropriate conditions having regard to that advice.[49] The

---

43 CFCE: PGN 6 (2012) II.4.13; see also 7.5: if the object is a fixture or fitting the local planning authority should be satisfied on the grounds that its removal would constitute a permanent alteration to the fabric; see also CCM 2011, s. 32(2) and CCR 2006 r. 14.
44 CFCE: PGN 6 (2012) II.4.14. See also CCM 2011, s. 2(1)(c)-(d) for carrying out such works.
45 CCM 2011, s. 24 (1): i.e. objects under CCM 2011 s. 2(1)(b) and s. 7.
46 CCM 2011, s. 7(1): i.e. under an order under the Treasure Act 1996 s. 2(2); CCR 2006, Pt. 7 (rr. 12–16).
47 CCM 2011, s. 7(2)-(3): or to such a person or body as may be designated by the Secretary of State.
48 CCR 2006, Sch. 1, par. 2(1); par. 2(2): Chapter must ensure that these requirements are complied with. See also par. 1(1): 'object of treasure' is an object declared by the Vicar-General as such (under par. 3); 'potential treasure object' means an object which appears to be or there is a reasonable possibility of its being treasure.
49 CCR 2006, Sch. 1, par. 2(3).

Commission must also be notified in writing and on doing so report the discovery to the Vicar-General and the Secretary of State.[50] In order to ascertain whether a potential treasure object is treasure, the administrator must: within 28 days after receiving notification from the archaeologist, seek written expert advice from the British Museum (and if Chapter thinks fit, others suitably qualified) as to its nature, age and other relevant matters; and within seven days of receiving it send the advice, the information recorded, and a written copy of any other information the archaeologist advises, to the Vicar-General to determine whether the object is treasure; the administrator must also send the Commission copies of documents sent to the Vicar-General. The Vicar-General may direct Chapter to supply further information and/or expert advice. The administrator must send the Commission copies of any directions the Vicar-General may issue, and any information or advice supplied by Chapter to the Vicar-General in response to those directions. The Vicar-General must, when satisfied Chapter has done so, make a written declaration, having regard to that information and advice, that the object is or is not treasure, and send copies of it to the administrator and Commission. When the Commission receives the declaration, its secretary must send a copy to the Secretary of State. Chapter must ensure that as soon as reasonably practicable any amendments necessary or appropriate in consequence of a declaration by the Vicar-General are made in the appropriate inventory.[51]

Third, if reasonably practicable to do so, Chapter must ensure that any treasure discovered within the precinct is made available for view by the public in conditions that are secure and appropriate for its preservation. Any inspection of the object by members of the public on an individual basis must be limited to those who have been expressly authorised in writing by Chapter and provide such documentary evidence of personal identification as Chapter may reasonably require. 'Member of the public' means a person other than a cathedral officer or other person carrying out work for the cathedral (whether or not on a paid basis) who seeks to view or inspect the treasure in connection with the functions of that office or that work.[52]

Fourth, there must be no sale, loan, or disposal of an object of treasure unless approved by the Cathedrals Fabric Commission; and before its sale or other disposal (other than a loan), Chapter must supply the British Museum, or any registered museum nominated by it, an opportunity to purchase the object.[53] Chapter must consult the Fabric Advisory Committee, supply the British Museum or its nominated museum with photographs and a description of the object, and request it to state in writing whether it is interested in acquiring the object.[54]

50 CCR 2006, Sch. 1, par. 2(4).
51 CCR 2006, Sch. 1, par. 3.
52 CCR 2006, Sch. 1, par. 4(1)-(3).
53 CCM 2011, ss. 6 and 7; 'registered museum' is defined in the Code of Practice issued under the Treasure Act 1996, s. 11 or as the Secretary of State may specify: s. 7(6); CCR 2006, Sch. 1, par. 6(1).
54 CCR 2006, Sch. 1, par. 6.

The treasury 195

Whilst the Commission may 'call-in' any proposal of special interest it considers should be determined by it,[55] an application to it must: be made in the prescribed form particularising the proposed sale, loan or other disposal; be accompanied by photographs and a detailed description of its size, features, history (if known) and significance; and be accompanied by copies of correspondence between Chapter and British Museum as to which is to be the specified museum, and between Chapter and that museum as to the interest of that museum in purchasing or acquiring the object if the Commission were to approve the Chapter proposal.[56]

Provision exists for the public notice of the proposals and consequent written representations and consideration of them by the Commission.[57] If the Commission decides to approve a proposal for the sale or other disposal of an object of treasure (other than a loan or a disposal to the specified museum on terms already agreed with it), then, unless that museum confirms in writing it has no interest in purchase, the Commission must (a) specify a reasonable period (not less than four months after the price has been determined) to give the museum an opportunity to purchase the object at that price; and (b) direct that, on expiry of the period without a purchase having taken place (or on the museum confirming in writing it does not wish to purchase it, if sooner), the object may be sold in accordance with the proposal approved by the Commission subject to conditions it specifies. If the Commission approves the proposal, with regard to the purchase price: (a) Chapter and the museum may each obtain written valuations from an independent valuer(s) with experience of the market nationally and internationally; (b) Chapter and the museum must jointly request a valuation from any independent panel of experts approved by the Secretary of State to establish the market value of objects (under the Treasure Act 1996, s. 10) and supply to the panel copies of valuations obtained; (c) if it provides one, the panel valuation must be the purchase price. However, if there is no panel or such panel declines to provide a valuation, or it provides such a valuation but within 14 days of receiving it Chapter or the museum or both declare in writing their wish for the matter to be referred to the Vicar-General, then Chapter and museum (or, in the case of reference whichever has declared a wish for such reference) must refer the determination of the purchase price to the Vicar-General. On a reference to the Vicar-General: (i) Chapter and the museum must submit to the Vicar-General any valuations obtained; (ii) the Vicar-General may issue directions; and (iii) when satisfied that he has sufficient information, the Vicar-General must determine the purchase price and notify it in writing to Chapter, museum, and Commission. On receiving notification of the determination as to purchase price, the Commission secretary must send a copy to the Secretary of State or his designated person.[58] Some cathedrals also have norms on the use of specific objects within the cathedral, such as bells; for example, at Sheffield:

---

55 CCM 2011, s. 6(1)(b).
56 CCR 2006, Sch. 1, par. 6(4).
57 CCR 2006, Sch. 1, pars. 6 and 7.
58 CCR 2006, Sch. 1, par. 8.

The Dean shall maintain all usages and relationships hitherto existing from ancient time between the Vicar and the Sheffield Cathedral Company of Change Ringers ... granting to them the use of the belfry and according to them all the privileges established by custom.[59]

The cathedral interviews

These did not disclose problems with respect to the administration of these norms in practice. However, they did provide an assessment of the role of the Commission generally and as to applications for works on the fabric of the cathedral. These are discussed in Chapter 9 below.

Cathedral finances

As we have seen, historically, cathedral finances were the focus of most reforms in cathedral law.[60] The Archbishops' Commission on Cathedrals 1994 made various proposals with regard to finance. It recommended that each cathedral should: appoint a qualified accountant as head of finance; set up a Finance and Property Committee and a Finance and Investment Advisory Committee; introduce clear-cut management structures to be kept under constant review; prepare, audit and publish its accounts in accordance with best current practice; issue annual budgets, long-term projections and monthly management accounts; exercise the highest standards of financial management; agree a balance of payments statement and decide what should be contributed to the diocese; increase professionalism in managing its trading activities; and have a policy on collaborative purchasing for its shop; also, the Association of English Cathedrals should offer resources to aid efficiency, effectiveness and economy.[61]

The Cathedrals Measure 1999 deals with some of these matters and the domestic instruments of cathedrals with others. The Measure requires Chapter to: (1) prepare an annual budget for the cathedral; (2) submit to Council an annual report and audited accounts prepared by the Chapter and such other reports as may be requested by Council; and (3) submit to the College of Canons the annual report and audited accounts.[62] In turn, Council and College of Canons must receive and consider the annual budget, annual report and audited accounts.[63] These provisions are repeated in cathedral constitutions.[64] Moreover, under the

---

59 Sheffield: Stat. 17: the company 'shall be responsible to the Dean, and shall in all things act in accordance with his wishes'.
60 See Introduction. See also e.g. Burn I.255: cathedral revenues which may be applied to the repair of the cathedral included funds acquired by means of forfeiture for the 'unfaithful execution of wills; for extorting undue fees for the probate of wills; [and] for undue administration of penance'.
61 H&R 86, 134, 172 and 183.
62 CM 1999, s. 4(8)(c)-(f): accounts must be prepared in accordance with s. 27.
63 CM 1999, s. 3(6)(b)-(c): Council; s. 5(4): College. See also HLE par. 379.
64 See above Chapter 6.

1999 Measure, the constitution of each cathedral must provide for the establishment of a Finance Committee of Chapter to advise Chapter in connection with its responsibilities in the field of financial and investment management, and for the committee's membership to include persons with expertise and experience in that field.[65] Again, cathedral constitutions repeat these rules.[66]

Chapter must also maintain proper records of income and expenditure, assets and liabilities, and its annual report and accounts must show a true and fair view of transactions throughout the year and of the position at the year's end in accordance with best professional practice and standards. Those accounts must be audited by a person who may audit the accounts of a charity. The Church Commissioners may specify what constitutes best professional practice and standards relating to the report and accounts, and it may enquire into any departure from those practices and standards. A copy of the annual report and audited accounts prepared by Chapter must be sent to the Church Commissioners and any other person who requests it, and be displayed in a prominent position in or in the vicinity of the cathedral.[67] Money forming part of the cathedral endowment must not be invested or used except as may be provided.[68] Also, Chapter may borrow money for any purpose connected with the cathedral; but if the purpose for which money is to be borrowed is such that the use of moneys forming part of the endowment of the cathedral for that purpose would require the consent of the Church Commissioners, then the Church Commissioners' consent is required to borrow that money.[69]

The Church Commissioners must pay from their general fund the dean and two residentiary canons, who are engaged exclusively on cathedral duties, such sums by way of stipend or other emoluments as the Commissioners may determine; and, with the Commissioners' consent, Chapter may pay the dean or a residentiary canon, to whom the Commissioners are required to make a payment, such additional stipend or other emoluments as they think fit.[70] Where any person is appointed dean of a cathedral or a residentiary canon whose stipend is to be paid by the Commissioners, the Commissioners may also make out of their general fund a grant towards removal expenses incurred by the person so appointed.[71]

---

65 CM 1999, s. 9(1)(h).
66 E.g. Worcester: Con. Art. 8: the committee consists of the dean (chair), a Chapter member (nominated by it), the Cathedral Steward (administrator), and at least two others appointed by Chapter (not being members of it), with expertise in property, investment and taxation matters; Carlisle: Con. Art. 9: the committee includes the Bursar and Chapter Treasurer. See also e.g. Norwich: Con. Art. IX; Lincoln: Con. Art. 11; York: Con. Art. VI.G-H; Chester: Con. Art. 17; Bradford: Con. Art. 12; Southwell: Con. Art. 8; Chelmsford: Con. Art. 11.
67 CM 1999, s. 27; the person must be qualified to do so under the Charities Act 1993, s. 43 (as amended).
68 CM 1999, s. 4(9). As to money forming part of the endowment, see also s. 16 (and below).
69 CM 1999, s. 26.
70 CM 1999, s. 21.
71 CM 1999, s. 22.

The Commissioners may also make out of their general fund grants, as they may determine: (1) to pay the stipend or other emoluments of any clerk in Holy Orders holding office in the cathedral (other than a dean or residentiary) and the salary or other emoluments of any lay person employed in connection with the cathedral;[72] (2) to secure better provision of houses for clerks in Holy Orders who hold office in the cathedral;[73] and (3) to repair any chancel, other than that of the cathedral, which that body is wholly or partly liable to repair.[74] The Cathedrals Fabric Commission also administers a number of funds for the benefit of English cathedrals.[75]

Clergy pensions are covered by two schemes. First, the Church of England Pensions Scheme, funded by the Church Commissioners, relates to pensions arising from service up until 31 December 1997; no charge for that past service pension is made on cathedrals which thus are not required to account for any aspect of the scheme. Second, the Church of England Funded Pensions Scheme relates to pensions as to service from 1 January 1998; it is a contributory scheme: contributions are paid by those who pay the members' stipends; when cathedrals are responsible for paying stipends, they make contributions to the scheme and must account for this.[76] Pension arrangements for lay employees vary between cathedrals: some participate in the Church Workers Pension Fund; others have separate third party provision.[77] In turn, cathedrals may regulate pay, expenses, benefits, and pensions in their domestic instruments.[78]

The constitution and/or statutes may also make provision for the establishment of companies; for example, at Guildford, Chapter has power:

> to form companies for a purpose which may advance the mission or management of the Cathedral, including the provision or maintenance of shops and a refectory provided that the Chapter shall at all times have complete control over any such company. Any staff, as may be necessary for its efficient management, shall be employed by the company.

And Chapter may grant franchises for business purposes.[79]

---

72 CM 1999, s. 23.
73 CM 1999, s. 24.
74 CM 1999, s. 25.
75 CFCE: PGN 6 (2012) I.8.1–3. The Cathedral Amenities Fund exists to assist with the preservation and improvement of the visual amenity of ancient cathedrals; and the English Cathedrals Repair Fund assists with the care and conservation of the Church of England's cathedrals in England.
76 Contribution rates to the scheme will vary according to actuarial review, normally undertaken every 3 years.
77 ARR, Appendix 3.
78 E.g. Carlisle: Stat. 5: Stipends and Expenses of the Dean and Canons; Canterbury: Stat. XXVII: Emoluments and Remuneration Committee; Durham: Stat. XXXV; Exeter: Staff Handbook (2015): Section 7.
79 Guildford: Con. Art. 9.4 and Stat. VI.2.1–2.2. See also e.g. Durham: Con. Art. 15.

Cathedral funds

Cathedrals operate various funds. Unrestricted funds are applied at the discretion of Chapter to further cathedral ministry and supplement expenditure from restricted funds. Chapter may set aside part of unrestricted funds for future purposes; these are called 'designated funds'. The designation is administrative only, and does not restrict Chapter's discretion to reallocate such funds to unrestricted funds. Funds held on specific trusts under charity law are classed restricted funds; the trusts establish the purpose for which the cathedral may use the restricted funds as declared by the donor or the terms of an appeal for funds. A cathedral may have several individual restricted funds, each for a particular purpose. Restricted funds fall into two classes: restricted income funds or endowment funds; the former to be applied within a reasonable period from their receipt for a specific purpose of the cathedral; as to the latter, trust law requires a cathedral to invest the assets of an endowment, or retain them for the cathedral's use in furtherance of its charitable purposes, rather than apply or spend them as income.[80] In maintaining accounting records (see below), cathedrals must separately identify each restricted fund and income received and expenditure made from each restricted fund.[81]

A capital fund, where there is no power to convert the capital into income, is known as a permanent endowment fund: generally, it must be held indefinitely. Permanent endowment cannot be used as if it were income. However, certain payments may be made out of the endowment, such as for investment management fees relating to investments held within the endowment. Where assets held in a permanent endowment fund are exchanged, their place in the fund must be taken by the assets which are received in exchange; and exchange may mean a change of investment or the application of the proceeds of sale of freehold land in the purchase or improvement of freehold property. Income from investing capital (endowment) funds may be applied for the general purposes of the cathedral (unrestricted income) unless a specific purpose has been declared for the application of the income from the capital fund. Such income may be applied for that purpose as restricted income. Any expenses incurred in the administration, or protection of endowment investments should be charged to capital.[82]

The statutes of some cathedrals provide lists of their funds; for instance, at Carlisle: cathedral revenues comprise all monies accruing to the cathedral from any source except benefactions, alms, offerings and donations given for special purposes other than the objects on which the cathedral revenues may be expended; they must be divided into such funds as Chapter thinks fit. Moreover:

> The cathedral revenues shall under the direction and control of the Chapter be expended solely for the purposes of the Cathedral as set forth in the Constitution and Statutes which purposes may include charitable donations and

---

80 ARR, Appendix 1.1–3.
81 ARR, Appendix 1.3.
82 ARR, Appendix 1.4. See above for CM 1999, ss. 16–19.

200 *The treasury*

shall include the insurance of the fabric of the Cathedral and Abbey buildings [and] the fees of any architect employed on work to the fabric.

For example, the cost of structural repairs or external and internal (re)decoration of the houses and other buildings in the Abbey (except the Deanery) or houses of residence of residentiaries, the council tax, water charges, and the cost of their insurance, must be met from cathedral revenues if there is a legal obligation to so do or if Chapter so determines.[83]

As seen in Chapter 3, cathedral statutes may permit the bishop to decide on the distribution of money collected at a service in the cathedral which the bishop holds or officiates at. Norms differ: Lichfield's bishop may decide unilaterally; Worcester's may decide 'subject to the condition that … costs and expenses incurred … are defrayed under arrangements agreed between the Bishop and Chapter'; Newcastle's decides if 'there is no additional expense … unless this has been authorised in advance' by Chapter; and Blackburn's if 'no substantial additional expense is … thrown on the Cathedral revenues' without consulting Chapter.[84]

The cathedral auditor

The Cathedrals Measure 1999 requires a cathedral constitution to provide for the appointment of an auditor for the cathedral,[85] that is, an individual (or firm) who may under the Charities Act 2011 (s. 114(2)) audit the accounts of a charity. A partner or employee of the auditor should not be a member of any body comprising the corporate body. Terms of engagement should be agreed in writing with Chapter at least every three years.[86] Constitutions repeat these rules and provide for functions of the auditor. For example, at Hereford, an auditor, 'a person professionally qualified as defined by legislation pertaining thereto who is authorised to audit the accounts of a charity' must be appointed by Chapter on such terms in respect of tenure and remuneration as Chapter determines; moreover: 'It shall be the duty of the Auditor to audit the accounts of the Cathedral in accordance with the provisions of the Measure', to present them in 'a timely fashion' to Chapter and, where necessary, to make proposals to Chapter for improving financial management.[87] Chichester also has a Chapter Accountant.[88]

---

83 Carlisle: Stat. 6(1)-(3). See also e.g. Durham: Stat. XXXVI; Canterbury: Gifts and Donations Policy.
84 Lichfield: Stat. 1(3); Worcester: Stat. 1(2); Newcastle: Stat.1.3; Blackburn: Stat. 2(2)(iii).
85 CM 1999, s. 9(1)(f).
86 ARR, 2.7. The constitutions and/or statutes of most cathedrals still refer to s. 43 of the Charities Act 1993: these should be amended and refer to the Charities Act 2011, s. 114(2).
87 Hereford: Con. Art. 16. See also: London: Con. Art. 11.3; St Albans: Con. Art. XII.4; Birmingham: Con. Art. 16(3); Coventry: Con. Art. 12.3; Derby: Con. Art. 12.3; Leicester: Con. Art. 15.3; Ripon: Con. Art. 14(3).
88 Chichester: Stat. 21.f. See also Salisbury: Con. Art. 16.

Cathedral constitutions and/or statutes may also provide for the office of treasurer.[89] For example, at Durham: 'There shall be a Treasurer' who is to: chair the Resources Committee; keep Chapter informed of its financial position and present the accounts to Chapter; make disbursements as may from time to time be ordered by Chapter; have 'financial and general responsibility for all the Cathedral's lands and tenements, including the collection of all rents and other moneys', arrange for 'timely aid with necessary repairs to the dilapidations of all its buildings'; advise Chapter on any financial matters concerning the Chorister School; and be assisted 'in all the duties by such staff as the Chapter may determine'.[90] Canterbury's Canon Treasurer is principal financial officer of the cathedral.[91] And the Bristol Treasurer must: have 'charge of all moneys due to the Cathedral'; ensure that they are 'promptly paid into an account at a Bank or other institution' in the cathedral's name; ensure payment of salaries and other expenses on the cathedral's behalf; be responsible for submission to Chapter of drafts of an annual budget and accounts; and have charge of the common seal on behalf of Chapter.[92]

The cathedral accounts

Accounting and Reporting Regulations for English Anglican Cathedrals, prepared by the Cathedrals Administration and Finance Association in conjunction with the Association of English Cathedrals, are issued by the Church Commissioners under the Cathedrals Measure 1999; the regulations provide 'best professional practice and standards' relating to the report and accounts of cathedrals to which the Measure applies.[93] Under these, Chapter must prepare accounts (incorporating an annual report) giving a true and fair view of the affairs of the cathedral and its connected entities at the end of its financial year and financial activities for that year. The accounts must comply with these regulations and state (in their notes) that they so comply or describe which requirements have not been met giving reasons.[94] The regulations apply to corporate property held for ecclesiastical purposes. However, to the extent that Chapter controls other property for the cathedral's benefit (falling under the Charities Acts or other legislation), accounts

---

89 This is an ancient office: see above n. 2.
90 Durham: Stat. XIX, III.1 and VIII.2: Resources Committee. See also e.g. York: Con. Art. VI.G: Treasurer; X.C: Bursar (Chief Accountant); Stat. XI: the Treasurer, assisted by the Chapter Steward, is responsible for 'the administration of all ... revenues and expenditure, investments, property and any other financial business'.
91 Canterbury: Stat. XIII.
92 Bristol: Stat. 8.
93 Accounting and Reporting Regulations for English Anglican Cathedrals, prepared by the Cathedrals Administration and Finance Association in conjunction with the Association of English Cathedrals, and specified by the Church Commissioners under s. 27 of the Cathedrals Measure 1999 (Feb 2015) (ARR).
94 ARR: Preface provides a brief history of the regime; see also par. 1.2.3: Charities Act 2011, s. 10(2).

relating to that property must be prepared in accordance with that legislation and relevant Statement of Recommended Practice (SORP).[95]

The annual report and accounts must contain the: annual report; auditor report; consolidated Statement of Financial Activities (SOFA); consolidated balance sheet; entity only balance sheet; cash flow statement; accounting policies; and account notes. The auditor must present a management letter to Chapter at the conclusion of each year's audit or confirm that none is required. The accounts must be approved by Chapter and balance sheet signed and dated by the dean and one other authorised Chapter member. The annual report must also be dated and signed. Both must be published within seven months of the end of the financial year.[96]

To give a comprehensive picture of all the resources available to Chapter in its running of the cathedral, the accounts must deal with the 'cathedral entity' and other entities analogous to subsidiaries and associates of a commercial company – the 'connected entities' – namely: trusts, companies or other entities which are controlled by Chapter or, if not so controlled, function for the benefit of the cathedral (such as associates and joint ventures). Such entities must be regarded as part of the cathedral entity and included in restricted funds in the entity only and consolidated accounts.[97] Therefore, where appropriate, shops, restaurants, and other non-charitable trading entities, and charitable entities (which benefit the cathedral and are controlled by Chapter), should be consolidated in the SOFA. Control by Chapter over a connected entity means its ability to govern the financial and operating policies of that entity in order to benefit from it. Benefit to the cathedral ministry means 'direct or indirect benefit of the physical fabric of the cathedral or its community or any of the activities normally and usually carried out by a cathedral'. If such an entity is a special trust, its results must be included in restricted funds in the cathedral's entity only and consolidated accounts. Other entities should be consolidated.[98] A discretionary benefit arises when the extent to which the trust or fund benefitting the cathedral is entirely within Chapter's discretion. Some entities controlled by Chapter may not be of benefit to the cathedral (e.g. alms-houses, or schools); separate accounts should be prepared for such entities which should be listed in a note.[99]

The format of the accounts: income and expenditure

The accounts must: state the sources and applications of funds, assets and liabilities; describe the accounting policies used; and state whether they were prepared

---

95 ARR, 1.3.2.
96 ARR, 2. See above for publicising them and access to them under CM 1999, s. 27.
97 See Charities Act 2011, s.12: such as an appeal fund for e.g. cathedral restoration administered by Chapter or their appointees, whether or not it is registered with the Charity Commission.
98 E.g. conduct of services, charitable giving, social welfare, providing for visitors, education, fund raising and providing services to the diocese; for 'special trusts', see 3.2; see ARR, 3.6.2 for 'partial benefit'.
99 ARR, 3.

in accordance with the regulations and applicable accounting standards. A cathedral should have accounting policies on, for example, funds, donated assets, legacies, investments, grants, and governance costs.[100]

The consolidated Statement of Financial Activities (SOFA) must show all in- and out-flows to and from the entities included in the cathedral consolidated accounts and transfers to and from funds. That is, the SOFA must be a comprehensive account of all resources receivable and payable by the cathedral during the year. Income is recognised when a transaction or other event results in an increase in assets or a reduction in liabilities. It may include income and receipt of endowment from: donations and legacies (e.g. congregational collections and giving, income from appeals, tax recoverable under Gift Aid); legacies; grants (from e.g. the Church Commissioners or Heritage Lottery Fund); charges and fees arising from e.g. fees for marriages and funerals; gross income of the choir school; trading and fundraising activities; charges to visitors; lettings of cathedral or other buildings; gross income from the shop, refectory and other trading; income from investment property; and insurance.[101]

Only expenditure actually incurred on repairs, restoration and maintenance should be charged to the SOFA. Any amount retained for future expenditure should be carried forward as part of the unrestricted or designated funds. Expenditure accounted for should include the costs of: (1) raising funds: welcome ministry (e.g. administration associated with visitors); shop, refectory and other trading activities; marketing costs (e.g. advertising); appeals; investment property costs (e.g. rent payable, insurance, repairs and maintenance); (2) ministry: clergy stipends and working expenses, and housing and support costs (e.g. training); services and music (e.g. music staff and choir costs); verger costs; (3) cathedral insurance; (4) precincts, security, and gardens upkeep (e.g. gardeners, security officers, and their equipment); (5) education and outreach: choir school costs; grants and scholarships (e.g. grants to ordinands); educational activities (e.g. education centres, courses and seminars); and archives and library costs; and (6) community, parish and congregation: e.g. maintenance of the Cathedral Community Roll and committee costs; and, for those cathedrals which have such costs, the parish share, youth work, and parish or congregational groups and their activities.[102]

The account notes should disclose for example: cathedral funds; staff numbers; staff costs; pensions; investing activities, including the acquisition or disposal of investments; the acquisition or disposal of tangible fixed assets including property, plant, and equipment; the remuneration of those Chapter members entitled to it; expenses of Chapter members, i.e. the amount of expenses reimbursed, their nature (e.g. travel, entertainment) and the number of persons reimbursed; the remuneration of the cathedral auditor; and investment property.[103]

100 ARR, 5.
101 ARR, 6.
102 ARR, 6.
103 ARR, 8–11.

The annual report

The annual report must contain both a review of activities and a commentary on the accounts, providing an objective analysis explaining the main features which underlie the financial position.[104] The report is a chance for Chapter to explain in simple terms what has happened over the year, future plans, and resources needed. It is intended to enable users to understand how the cathedral fulfils its legal purpose, the activities it undertakes, and what it has achieved, setting out the mission statement, steps to implement it and priorities for the year.

First, the review of the cathedral's activities must deal with all entities appearing in the consolidated accounts, including those related to: ministry; cathedral and precincts upkeep; education and outreach; community, parish and congregation work; and additions to cathedral buildings and inventory, and disposals from it. Within these categories, it may be appropriate to comment on: cathedral events; diocesan events; the number attending services; the number and type of services and other events; the numbers of visitors; diocesan and extra-cathedral activities undertaken by cathedral clergy and staff; and the use and contribution of volunteers. It should also describe how success is assessed, and this should be quantified if appropriate.

Second, the report must review the financial position of the cathedral and the other entities consolidated with it. Matters to be covered include: a statement of the cathedral's policies on reserves held in unrestricted funds and their purposes; a comparison of the level of reserves with the policy and an explanation of steps being taken to bring the reserves into line; if funds are in deficit, an explanation of the reasons for this and steps taken to eliminate the deficit; and, if relevant, an explanation of the financial effects of significant events. The report must also describe the principal risks and uncertainties facing the cathedral and its subsidiary undertakings, as identified by Chapter, and a summary of its plans to manage those risks. Further items on which it may be appropriate to comment include: the level of voluntary income, from the congregation and other gifts; major sources of finance; the results of trading operations; property; the extent of any material donated assets, goods or services, and how they have been dealt with in the accounts; and the date of the last and next quinquennial.[105]

Third, it must summarise plans for the future: the aims, objectives, and activities planned to achieve them; and it should explain Chapter's position on the future direction of the cathedral and, where relevant, how experiences from past activities have influenced future plans and decisions about allocating resources to their best effect. With regard to structure, governance and management, the report must describe: the nature and date(s) of the cathedral's statute(s); the status of the cathedral as an ecclesiastical corporation; its role in the diocese; its organisation

---

104 CM 1999, s. 4(8): the annual report by Chapter is mandatory.
105 See above Chapter 7 for the quinquennial.

(i.e. the corporate body, Finance Committee, and the role of the bishop); the relationships between the cathedral and other organisations with which it cooperates; the methods used to appoint members of Chapter; policies and procedures for the induction and training of Chapter members; how decisions are made (e.g. which are taken by Chapter and which are delegated); changes in senior clerical and lay appointments; arrangements to set the remuneration of senior staff and benchmarks, parameters or criteria used; the responsibilities of Chapter; a summary of investment powers; and the cathedral's legal titles and officers.[106]

Cathedral investments

The Cathedrals Measure 1999 empowers Chapter to invest moneys forming part of the cathedral endowment, or otherwise vested in the cathedral or Church Commissioners on its behalf,[107] in: (a) the acquisition of land, including participation in any collective investment scheme operated for these purposes by the Church Commissioners; (b) any investment fund or deposit fund constituted under the Church Funds Investment Measure 1958; and (c) any investments in which trustees may invest pursuant to their general power of investment under the Trustee Act 2000;[108] and (d) it may use such moneys for the improvement or development of any property vested in the cathedral.[109] Before investing in the acquisition of land, the Chapter must obtain the necessary consents.[110] Moneys which form part of the cathedral endowment may not be used to: (a) improve/develop the cathedral or certain other specified buildings – and Chapter must obtain the consent of the Church Commissioners before using them to do so; or (b) repair property – unless Chapter is satisfied an emergency justifies their expenditure to repair the cathedral/buildings to which the ecclesiastical exemption applies.[111]

If any property which forms part of the cathedral endowment is disposed of, the proceeds of the disposal (including money received by way of loan on a mortgage or charge on land or premium on the grant of a lease) must be treated as part of the cathedral endowment. Where the Church Commissioners hold on behalf of the cathedral moneys which form part of its endowment, the Commissioners may, if Chapter requests them to do so, make payments out of those moneys to enable

---

106 ARR, 4.
107 CM 1999, s. 35(1): 'moneys' includes any stock, share or other security. The Church of England (Miscellaneous Provisions) Measure 2014 amended the CM 1999 to allow cathedrals to adopt a total return approach to permanent endowment funds.
108 Trustee Act 2000, s. 3 (as restricted by ss. 4 and 5).
109 CM 1999, s. 16(1), subject to s. 16(3).
110 CM 1999, s. 16(2); the consents are those required by s. 15: see above.
111 CM 1999, s. 16(3): see below Chapter 9 for Ecclesiastical Exemption; it may, with the Church Commissioners' consent, incur that expenditure and the sum expended must be replaced by Chapter within such period and in such manner as may be agreed between them and Chapter: CM 1999, s. 16(4), proviso.

206 *The treasury*

Chapter to exercise its powers of investment.[112] There are special accounting rules which apply to the annual report in its treatment of cathedral investments.[113]

The Cathedrals Administration and Finance Association

The Association is a charity and limited liability company.[114] Its objects are to advance the mission of the Church of England and the Christian religion for the benefit of the public in accordance with the doctrines of the Church of England by: (1) supporting English Anglican cathedrals (which are members of the Charity) by considering, debating and recommending on matters affecting their administration or financial arrangements; (2) working with the Association of English Cathedrals to assist its charitable objects; (3) working with the National Church Institutions and other Church of England bodies to further cathedral work, in particular advising the Church Commissioners on accounting regulations for cathedrals; (4) working with the Churches' Legislative Advisory Service and other such ecumenical bodies to further cathedral mission and work; (5) working with the Government and its agencies to represent cathedral interests as to administration and finance; (6) proposing policies affecting their administration or finance, including their role in advancing education, community development, arts, culture and heritage, and environmental protection and improvement; and (7) encouraging the development and sharing of best practice between cathedrals.[115] The Association is overseen by a Board of Directors (the Executive Committee) elected by the members, which meets three or four times each year to further the work of the Association.[116]

The Charity has power *inter alia* to: raise funds; buy, take on lease, hire or otherwise acquire property; sell, lease or otherwise dispose of its property; borrow; co-operate with or support other charities, voluntary bodies and statutory authorities; acquire, merge with or enter into any partnership or joint venture with any other Charity; employ or remunerate a director; and deposit or invest funds.[117] Its income and property must be applied solely to promote its objects.[118] Membership is open to Anglican cathedrals in England, and provision is made for classes, rights, duties and termination of membership, an annual general meeting, annual subscriptions, the representation of members at meetings, and appointment and functions of directors.[119] The directors may make such reasonable and proper rules or by-laws as they deem necessary or expedient for the proper conduct and

---

112 CM 1999, s. 17.
113 ARR, Appendix 4.11–12.
114 CAFA: Articles of Association (2012), Art. 2 and 3.
115 CAFA: Articles (2012), Art. 4.
116 CAFA: Articles (2012): Art. 1. It is assisted by the Association of English Cathedrals' part-time Coordinator.
117 CAFA: Articles (2012), Art. 5. In so doing comply with the Charities Act 2011, ss. 117, 119–126, 189.
118 CAFA: Articles (2012), Art. 6: this also deals with the rights and duties of the director.
119 CAFA: Articles (2012), Arts. 7–52.

management of the Charity, e.g. as to member rights and 'all such matters as are commonly the subject matter of company rules'.[120]

The cathedral interviews

There is general satisfaction with norms on cathedral finance. For the Dean of Exeter, it is critical for Chapter to have people with 'particular skills' in 'management and accountancy', and Chapter has its own published ethical investment policy; Exeter Cathedral Enterprises is a company which runs the cathedral shop, café, and car park.[121] At Wells, the Finance and Investment Advisory Committee, which meets twice a year, is a 'professional group', 'highly skilled' and 'supportive but firm', 'pulling no punches'; the cathedral runs two companies for catering and the shops.[122] Similarly, the finance committee at Salisbury is 'very rigorous'; its chair is a lay canon and Chapter member; the chair of the Chapter Remunerations Committee is also a lay canon.[123] At St Paul's, formerly, the constitution enabled Chapter to employ its members; this was revised to avoid potential conflicts of interest and to enable Chapter to compensate lost earnings and cover the expenses of members engaged on Chapter business; the legal rules on the finance committee are 'sound'; the treasurer has a 'job description'.[124]

At new foundation Worcester, the requirements on the annual report are valuable not only in the maintenance of accountability but also in monitoring progress as to implementation of the strategic vision of the cathedral.[125] Winchester 'tries not to set up independent trusts', though Winchester Cathedral Enterprises is a company with charitable status; there is a trust for the housing of lay clerks; that the Receiver General (administrator) is a Chapter member gives a sense of co-responsibility for the welfare of the cathedral and the integration of its operations and mission.[126] And 'money' is a constant theme which exercises the Rochester Chapter.[127]

The Bristol Chapter finance committee is 'very good', offers a 'critical' outlook and 'real interrogation of the accounts and the assumptions behind them', and helps 'to drive Chapter strategy'.[128] At the parish church cathedral at Derby, the finance committee 'works well'; it is the 'favourite' committee of the Dean;[129] and

---

120 The charity in general meeting may alter, add to or repeal the rules and by-laws. The rules or by-laws 'are binding on all members', but cannot repeal anything in the Articles: CAFA: Articles (2012), Art. 59. Provision is also made for the dissolution of the CAFA and the application of its assets on dissolution: Art. 60.
121 Exeter: Dean: Int. 9-8-2016.
122 Wells: Acting Dean: Int. 12-8-2016; Con. Art. 8: the committee.
123 Salisbury: Dean: Int. 20-9-2016: the committee is 'fantastic'.
124 London: Dean: Int. 23-9-2016.
125 Worcester: Dean: Int. 28-7-2016.
126 Winchester: Acting Dean: Int. 16-8-2016.
127 Rochester: Canon Precentor: Int. 30-9-2016.
128 Bristol: Dean: Int. 3-8-2016: the Cathedral Trust controls a large part of the cathedral's historical assets and e.g. the Choral Foundation funds are restricted to music.
129 Derby: Dean: Int. 10-8-2016.

at Birmingham, where the turnover of the cathedral is 'small' (c. £1,000,000 p.a.), before 2010 Council would exercise its power to bring matters, including finance, to the attention of the visitor; this has not been used since.[130]

Conclusion

The corporate body (Council, Chapter, and College) has the legal capacity to own property. Chapter may acquire and dispose of property on behalf of it; in prescribed cases, the consent of the Church Commissioners is required. Chapter must manage all property vested in the cathedral and income from it and ensure that repairs and maintenance of the cathedral, its contents and other buildings are carried out. Each cathedral must have a Fabric Advisory Committee and no work may be carried out on the cathedral that materially affects its architectural, archaeological, artistic or historic character, nor may any object of architectural, archaeological, artistic or historic interest be sold, lent or disposed of without the approval of either the Fabric Advisory Committee or the Cathedrals Fabric Commission. Chapter must compile and maintain an inventory of all cathedral property and of objects which the Fabric Advisory Committee considers to be of architectural, archaeological, artistic, or historic interest; and the committee must designate those objects in the inventory which it considers, after consulting the Commission, to be of outstanding architectural, archaeological, artistic or historic interest.

There are elaborate rules on the inspection of cathedral property and on reports associated with that inspection. Chapter must make an application for approval of a proposal involving the sale, loan or other disposal of, or work on, an object to the Cathedrals Fabric Commission if the object is designated by the Fabric Advisory Committee as being of outstanding architectural, archaeological, artistic, or historic interest, or to the Committee if it has not been so designated, but it is of the same interest. The Commission may call in the application if it considers that the proposal raises considerations of special architectural, archaeological, artistic or historic interest so that it should determine it. Special rules apply to the discovery, designation, preservation, display, sale, loan, or other disposal of items classified as treasures.

Chapter must prepare an annual budget for the cathedral, and submit to Council and College an annual report and audited accounts. The cathedral constitution must provide for a Chapter Finance Committee to advise it on its responsibilities in the field of financial and investment management; and committee members must include persons expert and experienced in that field. Chapter must maintain proper records of income and expenditure, assets and liabilities, and its annual report and accounts must show a true and fair view of transactions and the position at the end of the year in accordance with best professional practice and standards. The accounts must be audited. The Church Commissioners may specify what constitutes best professional practice and standards relating to the report and account. There are very detailed national accounting regulations

130 Birmingham: Dean: Int. 11–8-2016.

applicable to cathedrals and the Church Commissioners may enquire into any departure from them. The annual report and audited accounts must be sent to the Church Commissioners and any person who requests it, and displayed at the cathedral. Chapter may invest moneys forming part of the cathedral endowment in a range of prescribed ventures and it may also borrow money for any purpose connected with the cathedral. The interviews indicate that cathedrals value norms on and work of the Finance Committee, the expertise and vigilance of its members, and the rigour this brings in terms of accountability.

9 The fabric of the cathedral church: care and conservation

Historically, cathedrals have fallen outside the faculty jurisdiction of the consistory court of the diocese: a faculty is a permissive right to effect an alteration to a church building or its contents; instead, authority was vested in the dean and chapter.[1] However, the Care of Cathedrals Measure 1990 established a national body, the Cathedrals Fabric Commission for England; it required the appointment of a local Fabric Advisory Committee for each cathedral; and it instituted a system of controls over the cathedral and ancillary buildings. The Archbishops' Commission 1994 examined the system;[2] it recommended that: local Faculty Advisory Committees should have as high a degree of decision-making as is compatible with the Care of Cathedrals Measure 1990; cathedrals should establish clear management structures and define the roles of those concerned in the care and conservation of the fabric (particularly the role of the cathedral architect); the Cathedrals Fabric Commission should continue to play a national role so as to provide public confidence in the operation of the regime, and as such should not be under-funded; and an 'audit of objectives' with plans of a developmental nature and a fabric report for cathedral and Close properties should be prepared every five years.[3]

Legislation followed,[4] including the Care of Cathedral Rules 2006,[5] secondary legislation, and the earlier Care of Cathedrals Measure 1990 was itself revised by

---

1 See e.g. Phillimore I.133; II.1420. A parish church cathedral could have decided, under the Care of Cathedrals Measure 1990, s. 18, to be subject to the faculty jurisdiction of the consistory court; this power was ended under the Care of Cathedrals (Amendment) Measure 2005, s. 16.
2 H&R 253, Appendix 6.
3 H&R 127, Recs. 1 to 7 (Ch. 10). For the quinquennial report, see above Chapter 8.
4 As well as being followed by the Cathedrals Measure 1999, the Care of Cathedrals Measure 1990 was followed by Care of Cathedrals (Supplementary Provisions) Measure 1994, Care of Cathedrals (Amendment) Measure 2005, and Church of England (Miscellaneous Provisions) Measure 2010, s. 10(3).
5 Care of Cathedrals Rules 2006 (SI 2006/1941): these revoked and replaced the Care of Cathedrals Rules 1990. For the purposes of CCM 2011, Rules may be made by the rule committee under the Care of Churches and Ecclesiastical Jurisdiction Measure 1991, ss. 25–27. The Commission (hereafter CFCE) also issues Guidance Notes (GN), Procedural Guides (PG), Procedural Guidance Notes (PGN), Directions and Advisory Guidelines (DAG), and Advisory Notes (AN): HLE par. 356.

the Care of Cathedrals Measure 2011.[6] The 2011 Measure sets out which works require formal approval from the national Commission and/or the local Committee; it also requires each cathedral to maintain an inventory (see Chapter 8), and regulates the cathedral precinct (see Chapter 10). Most cathedral churches are Grade I listed buildings, and so exempt from secular listed building and scheduled monument control; but scheduled monument and listed building consent are required for prescribed works to monuments and buildings located in the cathedral precinct.[7]

Chapter must ensure that necessary repairs and maintenance in respect of the cathedral and other buildings and monuments are carried out.[8] Approval is required for four categories of work.[9] Subject to certain exemptions,[10] Chapter must not, without approval from the relevant body, implement or consent to the implementation of any proposal: (a) to carry out works, including repair or maintenance, on, above or below land the fee simple in which vests in the corporate body of the cathedral – being works which would *materially* affect: (i) the architectural, archaeological, artistic, or historic character of the cathedral church or any building within the precinct being used for ecclesiastical purposes, or (ii) the immediate setting of the cathedral church, or (iii) any archaeological remains in or under the cathedral church or within its precinct, or (iv) any human remains in or under the cathedral or within its precinct (for the sake of convenience, Category 1); or (b) for the sale, loan, or other disposal of any object vested in the corporate body or which is in its possession or custody or to whose possession or custody it is entitled, being an object of architectural, archaeological, artistic, or historic interest (Category 2); or (c) to carry out work to such object which would materially affect its architectural, archaeological, artistic or historic character (Category 3); or (d) to add permanently any object which would materially affect the architectural, archaeological, artistic or historic character of the cathedral

---

6 CCM 2011 consolidates, corrects and improves the legislation set out in n. 4 above.
7 Ecclesiastical Exemption (Listed Buildings and Conservation Areas) Order 2010, under the Planning (Listed Buildings and Conservation Areas) Act 1990, s. 60: CFCE: PGN 1 (2012) 1 and 2: it applies because Government is satisfied that the Church of England gives protection equivalent to secular controls compatible with its Guidance: The Operation of the Ecclesiastical Exemption and Related Planning Matters for Places of Worship in England (Department for Culture, Media and Sport, July 2010). The exemption from listed building control applies to the cathedral church and ancillary buildings in ecclesiastical use; churches in use cannot be scheduled as ancient monuments so scheduled monument control does not apply to the cathedral church, but it is possible for land around or under a cathedral to be scheduled and, if so, scheduled monument control will apply to that land. Cathedrals are covered by normal development controls (e.g. Planning Permission); CCR, r. 11.
8 CM 1999, s. 4(8)(g). See e.g. Exeter: Con. Art. 5b; Carlisle: Con. Art. 8(4); Norwich: Stat. 15: Fabric.
9 See CFCE: PGN 1 (2012) 3.1 and 4.1; and PGN 2 (2012) I.1.1
10 See below for CCM 2011, s. 2(2) and ss. 5 and 6. Where a proposal has been implemented in contravention of s. 2, anything done in connection with that implementation may be approved under the Measure and, in that event, is deemed to have been done in compliance with this section: CCM 2011, s. 2(3): see Chapter 2.

(Category 4).[11] This chapter deals in the main with works proposed by Chapter in Category 1 (for works in Categories 2–4, see Chapter 8) and with the procedures applicable to an application for a proposal in relation to such works.

However, these rules which require approval do not apply to anything which: (a) is done by Chapter in pursuance of its duties under the cathedral constitution and statutes with respect to the ordering of services or otherwise in furtherance of the mission of the cathedral; (b) is of a temporary nature; and (c) does not materially affect the fabric of the cathedral church itself.[12]

For the purposes of these rules, in terms of definition, 'building' includes any monument or other structure/erection and any part of a building; 'fabric' must be construed accordingly; a building is treated as used for ecclesiastical purposes if it would be so used but for any works proposed; 'precinct' means the precinct indicated on the plan required for that cathedral; any object or structure permanently situated in or affixed to a cathedral or any precinct building must be treated as part of that cathedral church or building or its fabric; and 'archaeological remains' means the remains of any building, work or artefact, including a trace or sign of it.[13]

Depending on the nature of the work in question, the relevant body from which approval is required will be either the local Fabric Advisory Committee or the national Cathedrals Fabric Commission, which may also call in some matters for its own approval, and determine appeals against refusal to grant permission by the Committee. Refusals by the Commission may in turn be reviewed by a national Commission of Review, whose decision is final; and, as seen in Chapter 2, the system may also be enforced by the bishop as visitor in prescribed cases of contravention or in urgent cases needed for intervention. The approvals required are in addition to, and do not dispense with consent/approval required under, the constitution and statutes of a cathedral.[14] In the exercise of their functions, the Committee, Commission and Commission of Review must have regard to the fact that the cathedral is the seat of the bishop and a centre of worship and mission, and to the desirability of preserving: (a) the fabric of the cathedral church and any of its features of architectural, archaeological, artistic, or historic interest; (b) the immediate setting of the cathedral church; (c) any building within the precinct of architectural, archaeological, artistic, or historic interest; (d) any archaeological or human remains in/under the cathedral church or within its precinct; and (e) any objects.[15]

---

11 CCM 2011, s. 2(1)(a)-(d). See also CFCE: PGN 2 (2012) I.1.6.
12 CCM 2011, s. 2(2). 'Temporary' is interpreted by the Commission as meaning up to 6 or, at most, 12 months, and the work must not materially affect the fabric of the cathedral church etc: CFCE: PGN 2 (2012) I.1.7.
13 CCM 2011, s. 32.
14 CCM 2011, s. 31: i.e. for anything done by the Chapter of that cathedral church; CFCE: PGN 7 (2012).
15 CCM 2011, s. 22: as to objects, that is, those objects listed in s. 2(1)(b). See also CFCE: PGN 1 (2012) 6.1.

The Cathedrals Fabric Commission for England

National law distinguishes those works which must be approved by the national Cathedrals Fabric Commission and those to be approved by the local Fabric Advisory Committee.[16]

The functions, composition, and procedure of the Commission

The Cathedrals Fabric Commission for England, established by Measure,[17] has six functions: (1) to advise Chapter and the Fabric Advisory Committee on the care, conservation, repair or development of the cathedral church, any archaeological or human remains in/under the church or within its precinct, any buildings within its precinct, the landscape and environment in which the cathedral church is situated, and any objects vested in it, of which it has possession or custody or to which it is entitled; (2) to give advice to bishops and the Vicar-General's court when sought as to matters of enforcement; (3) to consider and determine applications made to it by Chapter; (4) to promote co-operation between the Commission and organisations concerned with the care and study of buildings of architectural, archaeological, artistic, or historic interest in England; (5) to assist Chapters by participating in educational and research projects which in the Commission's view promote the care, conservation, repair or development of cathedral churches and their ancillary buildings; and (6) to maintain jointly with the Church Buildings Council a library of books, plans, drawings, photographs, and other material relating to cathedrals and objects in them.[18] It must also promote, consulting Chapters, Fabric Advisory Committees and such other persons or organisations as it thinks fit, by means of guidance or otherwise, standards of good practice to be observed in the: care, conservation, repair and development of the cathedral, archaeological and human remains, objects, buildings and landscape; roles of cathedral architects, surveyors, and archaeologists; compilation, maintenance and dissemination of information of architectural, archaeological, artistic and historic interest about cathedrals, archaeological remains in/under them or within their precincts and objects; and the form and content of mandatory records kept by Chapter.[19]

The Commission consists of the chairperson, vice-chairperson and twenty-two others.[20] The Chair must be a lay person appointed by the Archbishops of Canterbury and York after consulting the relevant Secretary of State; the Vice-Chair

---

16 CFCE: PGN 1 (2012) 5.1 and 7.2; PGN 2 (2012); PGN 6 (2012); and PGN 7 (2012).
17 CCM 2011, s. 3(1). See also CFCE: PGN 1 (2012) 3.4.
18 CCM 2011, s. 3(2).
19 CCM 2011, s. 3(3); as to mandatory records, that is, those required to be kept under s. 27. See also s. 3(4): Schedule 1 of the Measure has effect with respect to the Commission.
20 CCM 2011, Sch. 1, par. 1. Schedule 2 contains Forms for use as to different types of application.

is appointed by the Archbishops after consulting the Archbishops' Council and such organisations as may appear to the Archbishops representative of the deans of cathedrals.[21] Seventeen of the members must be appointed by the Archbishops of Canterbury and York: one nominated by the House of Bishops from its members; two by any organisation appearing to the two Archbishops to represent cathedral deans (of whom at least one must be a dean); three by the Church Buildings Council (two selected from its members or committees); two cathedral architects or surveyors of the fabric (one, after consulting the President of the Royal Institute of British Architects and the other after consulting that President and that of the Royal Institution of Chartered Surveyors), one an architect or chartered building surveyor after consulting the President of the Ecclesiastical Architects and Surveyors Association, and one a chartered engineer after consulting the President of the Institution of Structural Engineers and the President of the Institution of Civil Engineers (experienced in the care of historic buildings); one, a painter, sculptor or other artist, experienced in work for cathedrals or other churches, appointed after consulting the President of the Royal Academy of Art; and six appointed as follows: one after consulting the Secretary of State; one after consulting English Heritage's chair; one after consulting the President, the Council for British Archaeology and President, the Society of Antiquaries of London; two after consulting the Chair of the Liturgical Commission; and one after consulting the Director of the Royal School of Church Music.[22]

Of these seventeen members, except the House of Bishops' nominee, all must be persons who between them have special knowledge of archaeology, architecture, archives, art, the care and conservation of books, manuscripts, and other historic objects, history (including the history of art and architecture) and liturgy (including church music).[23] Five members, of whom at least one must be on a cathedral Chapter, are elected by the General Synod from its members, each one so elected with knowledge of the ways in which cathedrals are currently used and of their contribution to the work of the Church of England.[24] No member of any Chapter or Fabric Advisory Committee or relevant committee of any designated organisation may be appointed as Chair or Vice-Chair.[25] Members hold office for a renewable five-year term.[26] If a casual vacancy occurs among members appointed by the Archbishops of Canterbury and York, the

---

21 CCM 2011, Sch. 1, par. 2. The relevant Secretary of State is currently that for Culture, Media and Sport: Secretary of State for Culture, Media and Sport Order 1997 (SI 1997/1744) art. 2.
22 CCM 2011, Sch. 1, par. 3. See also CFCE: PGN 8 (2012).
23 CCM 2011, Sch. 1, par. 4.
24 CCM 2011, Sch. 1, par. 5.
25 CCM 2011, Sch. 1, par. 6; par. 22: the Archbishops acting jointly may designate the organisations which are to be 'designated organisations' for the purpose of pars. 6 and 13 and specify their 'relevant committees'.
26 CCM 2011, Sch. 1, par. 7; see also pars. 8–9 for those not re-elected to General Synod.

Archbishops, after such consultation as appears to them appropriate having regard to the knowledge or experience of the person to be replaced, may appoint a person to fill the vacancy;[27] if it occurs among members elected by General Synod, Synod may elect one of its members to fill the vacancy.[28] Anyone appointed or elected to fill a casual vacancy holds office only for the unexpired portion of the term of office of the person whom they replace, but is eligible for re-appointment or re-election.[29] The Commission must appoint a secretary (not a member/officer of a Chapter, Fabric Advisory Committee or relevant committee of a designated organisation),[30] and may appoint such committees as it considers expedient.[31]

The quorum is eight members. Business must be decided by a majority of members present and voting and the chair has a second/casting vote. Subject to quorum, the Commission may act notwithstanding any vacancy in membership. It may hold a public hearing for any matter considered by it, in order to receive oral representations from the public, and it may appoint a panel of not less than three members for such a hearing who then report on that matter to the Commission. In an appeal to it, no Commission member who is also a member of the Fabric Advisory Committee against whom the appeal is brought may participate in the proceedings. It may regulate its own procedure,[32] and the chair (or member authorised to so act), may give directions as to procedure, whether or not anyone has made an application for directions.[33]

The Commission must keep a register of applications for approval made to it held in the custody of the Commission secretary and available for inspection by any person free of charge by prior arrangement. On prior application by telephone or otherwise a person must be supplied with one or more extracts of that part of the register relating to a particular application; and on prior application by telephone or otherwise a person may be supplied with parts of the register additional to such extracts or a copy or copies of the whole register.[34]

---

27 CCM 2011, Sch. 1, par. 10.
28 CCM 2011, Sch. 1, par. 11: i.e. a person with the knowledge prescribed in par. 5.
29 CCM 2011, Sch. 1, par. 12: i.e. for one further term of office, and if the Archbishops of Canterbury and York so direct, for re-appointment or re-election for a second further term.
30 CCM 2011, Sch. 1, par. 13.
31 CCM 2011, Sch. 1, par. 14; see also par. 15: non-Commission members may be appointed to any Commission committee, but their number must be less than half the total number of that committee's members.
32 CCM 2011, Sch. 1, pars. 16–21: subject to the preceding Schedule rules and any directions on procedure given by General Synod. See also CCR 2006, r. 23(3): casting vote of the chair; 23(4): public notice must be given.
33 CCR 2006, r. 23(1); see also r. 23(2): where the Commission considers a request under r. 6 or an appeal under r. 8 or r. 9 no Commission member who is also a member of the Fabric Advisory Committee against whose decision or non-determination the appeal is brought may participate in the proceedings.
34 CCM 2011, s. 13; CCR 2006, r. 27(4); r. 27(3) applies to the Commission as to fees for applications.

Works requiring applications for approval of the Commission

An application must be made to the Commission in three cases. First, where the proposal would involve: (a) works, including repair or maintenance, which would permanently alter the fabric of the cathedral church or any building within the precinct used for ecclesiastical purposes; (b) demolition of any part of the church or building; (c) disturbance or destruction of archaeological or human remains in/under the cathedral or within its precinct; and (d) the sale, loan, or other disposal of or work to any object designated as an object of outstanding architectural, archaeological, artistic, or historic interest.[35] Second, an application must be made if the Commission declares in writing that the proposal gives rise to considerations of such special architectural, archaeological, artistic, or historic interest such that the application should be determined by it.[36] Third, an application must be made for the approval of works already implemented in contravention of the legal requirement to obtain approval.[37] Any application for approval for any other proposal must be made to the local Committee.[38]

If Chapter or Committee wish to have it determined whether an application is required to be made to the Committee or to the Commission, the Commission may determine that matter.[39] However, even when a proposal is for works otherwise requiring referral to the Commission, if the Commission considers it does not give rise to considerations of sufficient importance to require an application to it, the Commission may make a declaration in writing to that effect and any application for approval must be made instead to the Fabric Advisory Committee.[40]

The Commission may also determine that proposals otherwise to be considered by it should be left to the relevant Committee if those proposals are within a class or description specified by it as to cathedrals generally or to particular cathedrals so specified.[41] Before deciding, the Commission must consult the relevant Chapter and Committee, English Heritage, the national amenity societies (or appointees) and, as to works which would materially affect the cathedral church or its precincts, any relevant local planning authority.[42] Any application for approval of a

---

35 CCM 2011, s. 6(1)(a): i.e. under s. 24(4); CCR, rr. 12–16; and CFCE: PGN 2 (2012) I.2.1.
36 CCM 2011, s. 6(1)(b).
37 CCM 2011, s. 2(3), 6(11), 9(8): see HLE par. 358. For retrospective approval, see CFCE: PGN 1 (2012) 8.4.
38 CCM 2011, s. 6(1); however, see also s. 7(4) as to valuable objects, for which see above Chapter 8.
39 CCM 2011, s. 6(2); for the procedure see CCR 2006, r. 3.
40 CCM 2011, s. 6(3); i.e. the proposal falls within s. 6(1)(a).
41 CCM 2011, s. 6(4); see also CCR 2006, r. 3.
42 CCM 2011, s. 6(5): English Heritage is the Historic Buildings and Monuments Commission for England; 'national amenity societies' means the Ancient Monuments Society, Council for British Archaeology, Georgian Group, Society for the Protection of Ancient Buildings (SPAB), Twentieth Century Society, and Victorian Society and any other body designated by the Dean of the Arches and Auditor as a national amenity society; the 'local planning authority' is that under the Town and Country Planning Act 1990, Part I; CCM 2011, s. 32(1).

proposal specified in the determination must be made instead to the local Committee.[43]

In addition, following a written request from Chapter, the Commission, after consulting the local planning authority, Committee and English Heritage, may make a declaration that no approval is required. It may do so if satisfied that: (a) the proposal involves the immediate setting of the cathedral church or any archaeological remains in or under it or within its precinct but does not involve human remains; or (b) the proposal does not relate to the cathedral church or a building within its precinct used for ecclesiastical purposes; or (c) planning permission, listed building consent or scheduled monument consent is required; and (d) any considerations relevant to preserving that setting and remains will be adequately taken into account by the person/body responsible for granting the permission or consent.[44]

Chapter requests for such a declaration must be written and accompanied by plans, drawings, specifications or other documents describing the proposal. Before making its declaration, the Commission must be satisfied that any considerations relevant to preserving the immediate setting of the cathedral church or any archaeological remains within the precinct will be or have been adequately taken into account by the person/body responsible for granting the planning permission or consent. The secretary must ask each body specified to reply to the consultation within 28 days; if no reply is so received from one or more of those bodies, the Commission may proceed to decide whether to make a declaration that no approval is required. Within 28 days from the expiry of the period for replying, the Commission must decide on whether or not to make the declaration, and its secretary must notify Chapter.[45]

Moreover, the Commission must consider applications for approval where the application has correctly been made in the first instance to the Fabric Advisory Committee but where at least three members of that committee determine that the proposal gives rise to considerations of such special architectural, archaeological, artistic or historical interest that the application should be determined by the Commission; in such a case, the secretary of the Committee must refer the application to the Commission and must notify Chapter accordingly.[46] Also, if a proposal has been implemented in contravention of the rules on approval, anything done in connection with that implementation may be approved and, in that event, must be deemed to have been done in compliance with the relevant rules.[47]

---

43 CCM 2011, s. 6(6)-(7): i.e. a proposal under s. 6(4). The Commission may revoke/vary its determination.
44 CCM 2011, s. 6(8): i.e. under the Town and Country Planning Act 1990, s. 336(1); Planning (Listed Buildings and Conservation Areas) Act 1990, s. 8(7); Ancient Monuments and Archaeological Areas Act 1979, s. 2(3)(a): CCM 2011, s. 6(9); see also CCR 2006, r. 4(1)-(3).
45 CCR 2006, r. 4(4)-(7).
46 CCM 2011, s. 6(10): s. 9 then applies to that application; see also CCR 2006, r. 5(4): in that event the procedure applicable to applications to the Cathedrals Fabric Commission applies.
47 CCM 2011, s. 2(3). Any application under 2(3) must be made to the Commission: CCM 2011, s. 6(11). All applications under the above provisions are to be made in accordance with CCR 2006: CCM 2011, s. 6(12).

Subject to all of the foregoing, all applications for approval are made to the Fabric Advisory Committee in the first instance.[48]

The process of applying to the Commission

When Chapter makes an application to the Commission, the cathedral administrator must display and send to the Fabric Advisory Committee, English Heritage, and national amenity societies (or their joint appointees), a notice in the prescribed form. This must specify where details of the proposal are available to inspect and state that written representations may be sent to the Commission secretary before a specified date; if the application relates to works above/below ground, the administrator must also send the notice to the local planning authority.[49] The notice must be displayed for twenty-eight days inside and outside the cathedral, readily visible to the public, giving particulars of the proposal and stating representations must arrive with the Commission secretary no later than twenty-eight days from the notice date.[50] After receipt of the notice, the Committee secretary must inform the Commission in writing whether the Committee has considered the proposal and, if it has, about its views.[51] The Commission may discuss the proposal with Chapter; if a meeting is arranged for this, the administrator must notify the Committee secretary and its representatives may attend.[52]

Immediately after expiry of twenty-eight days following display of the public notice, the administrator must complete the certificate of publication and send it to the Commission secretary.[53] After receiving the certificate and within three months after the date for written representations and the holding of a public hearing, if any, the Commission must consider all the representations and determine whether to give its approval, either unconditionally or subject to such conditions as it may specify, or refuse to give its approval; its decision must be in writing, and if approval is refused or given subject to conditions, written reasons must be given for that decision.[54]

Within ten days of the decision, the Commission secretary must send/deliver a notice of the decision to the Chapter, Fabric Advisory Committee, English Heritage, national amenity societies (or their joint appointees), and, where appropriate, the local planning authority.[55] The cathedral administrator must within seven days

---

48 CCM 2011, s. 6(1). See also CFCE: PGN 2 (2012) II.4.
49 CCM 2011, s. 9(1); see also s. 30. The application must be in writing and be accompanied by such detailed plans, drawings, specifications and other documents as describe the proposal or the Commission requires.
50 CCR 2006, r. 7(1)-(4). For the relevant Forms, see Schedule 2. See also r. 8: the prescribed periods for public display are similar to those applicable to the Fabric Advisory Committee: see below.
51 CCM 2011, s. 9(2); CRR 2006, r. 7(5): this must be done within fourteen days of receiving notice.
52 CCM 20011, s. 9(6); CCR 2006, r. 7(6): 14 days' notice of the date of the meeting must be given.
53 CCR 2006, r. 7(7).
54 CCM 2011, s. 9(3); CCR 2006, r. 7(8).
55 CCM 2011, s. 9(7); CCR 2006, r. 7(9) (and r. 8); and r. 7(9)(f).

of receipt of the notice display a copy of it inside and outside the cathedral, readily visible to the public, for not less than 28 days.[56]

The cathedral interviews

These reveal a variety of approaches to these rules and the practices of the Cathedrals Fabric Commission: some consider that the rules are 'useful',[57] or they explain that contact is made with the Commission 'as and when appropriate';[58] others consider the rules 'can generate an adversarial culture' or tend towards 'bureaucracy', and that sometimes it appears as if the Commission sees itself as 'expert and safe' but deans as 'unsafe and inexpert'.[59] In practice, the Commission has used a range of its powers in recent years. The following may be offered by way of example. As to a proposal from York to remove nineteenth-century glass from a window, the Commission decided that a new application should be pursued.[60] Canterbury's proposal to repair the great south window was approved subject to the conditions *inter alia* that: a detailed design should be submitted; old stonework should be removed and retained for future study; a method to support the window frame should be submitted for Commission approval; and a photographic and documentary record should be made of fabric affected.[61] The Commission decided as to a withdrawn application to visit Chester to offer guidance on access facilities.[62] The Commission determined that Coventry Chapter was entitled to install a new statue in the ruins as a temporary work for six months, but that at the end of the period, it should submit a new application to the Commission.[63] A Salisbury proposal to develop the area between the Chapter House and south transept, known as Little Paradise, to provide lavatories, storage and plant room was approved.[64] But a proposal from Chichester to install by way of suspension a piece of new art was refused because, *inter alia*, this would have 'an unacceptably detrimental impact on the architectural character of the Cathedral interior'.[65]

The Fabric Advisory Committee

National laws regulating the local Fabric Advisory Committee mirror those applicable to the national Cathedrals Fabric Commission but, broadly, they are a little less complicated.[66] The constitutions and/or statutes of only a minority of

56 CCR 2006, r. 7(10).
57 Winchester: Dean: Int. 16-8-2016.
58 Wells: Acting Dean: Int. 12-8-2016.
59 Bristol: Dean: Int. 3-8-2016.
60 CFCE 192 (11) 310.
61 CFCE 192 (11) 311.
62 CFCE 192 (11) 312.
63 CFCE 192 (11) 313.
64 CFCE 192 (11) 316.
65 CFCE 192 (11) 315.
66 CFCE: PGN 7 (2012). See also PGN 1 (2012) 3.3 and 7.2–7.7.

220 *The fabric of the cathedral church*

cathedrals mention the Committee.[67] The legal relationship between Chapter, Fabric Advisory Committee and Commission is close.[68]

The functions, composition and procedure of the Committee

The Chapter of a cathedral and the Commission must jointly establish for the cathedral of that Chapter a Fabric Advisory Committee. It is the duty of the Committee to give advice to Chapter on the care, conservation, repair or development of the cathedral church, and on archaeological or human remains in/under the cathedral church or within its precinct, precinct buildings, the landscape and environment in which the cathedral church is situated and its architectural, archaeological, artistic, or historic objects or treasure; and consider and determine applications made to it by Chapter.[69] The Committee has power: if requested by Chapter, to determine whether an application for approval of a proposal by Chapter is required; and after consulting Chapter and with the Commission's agreement, to determine that the requirement for approval does not apply to proposals of a class or description specified by the Committee, and it may vary or revoke such determination. If the Chapter desires this, the Committee also may so determine. Moreover, where the Commission has made a determination in relation to any matter, the Committee must not make a determination in relation to the same matter.[70]

The Committee consists of: not less than three nor more than five members appointed by Chapter after consulting the Commission – these must not be a Chapter member or employee or paid office-holder of the cathedral; and not less than three nor more than five members appointed by the Commission after consulting Chapter – i.e. persons with special knowledge of the care and maintenance of buildings of outstanding architectural or historic interest and having a particular interest in the cathedral concerned. The Committee must appoint a chair from its members. The dean, administrator, and such other members of Chapter as Chapter, after consulting the Committee, considers appropriate, may attend and speak at Committee meetings or at such of its meetings as Chapter may specify; but no

---

67 E.g. Lichfield: Con. Art. 13; Hereford: Con. Art. 14; Durham: Stat. IX; Bristol: Con. Art. 15; Chester: Art. 16.iv(h); Guildford: Stat. XV.4; Truro: Stat. X.4; see also Chelmsford: Con. Art. 12: Works Committee.
68 E.g. Chapter must consult the Commission as to: its appointments to the Committee (CRR, Sch. 2, par. 4): appointing an architect (CCM 2011, s. 9(1A) and s. 23(1)) and archaeologist (ibid. s. 23(2)); the inventory must accord with Commission directions (CRR, r. 28(8)); the Committee must consult the Commission as to designating objects of outstanding interest (CCM 2011, s. 24(4)); Chapter must send the Commission the precinct plan (s. 25), the quinquennial report (s. 26(1)) and archaeologist's report (s. 28); and the Committee secretary must send its meeting agenda and minutes to the Commission (CCM 2011, Sch. 2, par. 15).
69 CCM 2011, s. 4(1)-(2); see also s. 4(3): Schedule 2 has effect with respect to these Committees.
70 CCM 2011, s. 5: i.e. determination of the Commission under s. 6(2) and of a Committee under s. 5(1)(a).

The fabric of the cathedral church 221

such person shall be entitled to vote. The cathedral architect or surveyor of the fabric and archaeologist must also attend Committee meetings unless the chair permits or directs otherwise. No-one who holds paid office in the Commission may be a Committee member. Members hold office for five years but are eligible for re-appointment. The Committee must appoint a secretary, whether or not a member; but, if that person is a Chapter member, employee or paid officer of the cathedral, the Committee must have particular regard to whether there is a conflict of interests which would make it inappropriate to appoint the person as secretary. Expenses properly incurred by a Committee member must be reimbursed by Chapter. If a casual vacancy occurs, the body which appointed the person whose place is to be filled may, with the same consultation as required in making the first appointment, appoint a person to fill the vacancy for the unexpired portion of the term of office of the person in whose place he/she is appointed.[71]

Quorum must be six members, if the Committee has a membership of ten; five if it has eight members; and four if it has six; but the Committee may act notwithstanding any vacancy in its membership. Committee business must be decided by a majority of members present and voting; the chair has a casting vote. The Committee must hold not less than two meetings each year; but if three or more members, by notice sent to its secretary, request a special meeting, this must be held within four weeks of the sending of that notice. The secretary must place on the agenda for the next meeting any matter requested by any committee member, before each meeting send to Chapter and Commission a copy of the agenda, and after each meeting send to the same a copy of the minutes. The Committee may regulate its own procedure.[72] Committee meetings must be held in private, but it may invite persons to attend.[73]

The Committee must each keep a register of applications made to it. This must be kept in the custody of its secretary but a copy must be held at the Chapter office where it must be available for inspection by any person free of charge by prior arrangement. On prior application a person must be supplied with one or more extracts of that part of the register relating to an application specified by that person; and on prior application a person may be supplied with parts of the register additional to such extracts or a copy or copies of the whole register.[74] A person applying for extracts or copies of further parts or of the register must pay such fee for each extract or copy as shall be fixed from time to time by the Committee and the list of fees payable must be made publicly available in the Chapter office.[75]

---

71 CCM 2011, Sch. 2, pars. 1–9.
72 CCM 2011, Sch. 2, pars. 10–16; CCR, r. 22(1): subject to CCM 2011, Sch. 2, pars. 10–14.
73 CCR 2006, r. 22(2)-(5): i.e. for the duration of consideration of a particular item; they may speak but not vote.
74 CCR 2006, r. 27(1)-(2); a person may apply for inspection by telephone or otherwise.
75 CCR 2006, r. 27(3): fees are fixed under CCM 2011, s. 10B(2).

Applications for the approval of the Fabric Advisory Committee

An application by Chapter for approval by the Fabric Advisory Committee must be in writing and accompanied by such detailed plans, drawings, specifications and other documents as describe the proposal or may be requested by the Committee.[76] The cathedral administrator must display a notice, in the prescribed manner and form,[77] specifying the place where details of the proposal are available for inspection and stating that written representations may be sent to the Committee secretary before the end of the period specified; and the administrator must send the notice to the Commission, and, if required, to English Heritage, the national amenity societies (or their appointees), and local planning authority.[78] The notice must be displayed for 28 days inside and outside the cathedral, and any written representations must be sent to the Committee secretary arriving no later than 28 days from the date of the notice.[79]

Immediately after expiry of the 28 days after display of the notice, the administrator must complete the certificate of publication and send/deliver it to the Committee secretary.[80] After receiving it and considering representations, the Committee determines whether to approve the proposal, either unconditionally or subject to such conditions as it may specify, or refuse to give its approval.[81] The decision must be in writing and, in the case of refusal or approval subject to conditions, reasons must be given in writing in the decision itself.[82] Within ten days of the decision, the Committee secretary must send/deliver a notice of it to the Chapter, Commission, and anyone to whom notice of the application was sent.[83] The administrator must also within seven days of receipt of the notice sent to Chapter, display a copy of it inside and outside the cathedral for not less than 28 days.[84] However, if at least three Committee members present and voting at a meeting at which an application is considered determine that the proposal gives rise to considerations of such special architectural, archaeological, artistic, or historic interest that it should be determined by the Commission, the Committee secretary must refer the application to the Commission and immediately notify Chapter accordingly.[85]

---

76 CCR 2006, r. 5(1).
77 CCM 2011, s. 30: all notices must be in writing and in the prescribed form; see also s. 13.
78 CCM 2011, s. 8(1); CCR 2006, r. 5(3); if the proposal would affect clergy housing, the Church Commissioners may need to be involved: r. 10; if the proposal affects listed building consent or scheduled monument consent, the administrator must also send a notice to the Commission: CCM 2011, s. 29; CCR 2006, r. 11.
79 CCR 2006, r. 5(2). See also CCM 2011, s. 30.
80 CCR 2006, r. 5(5).
81 CCM 2011, s. 8(2); CCR, r. 5(6).
82 CCR 2006, r. 5(3).
83 CCR 2006, r. 5(7).
84 CCR 2006, r. 5(8).
85 CCR 2006, r. 5(4): CCM 2011, s. 8 and CCR r. 7 then apply to that application.

Appeals to the Cathedrals Fabric Commission

If the Fabric Advisory Committee refuses to give approval or gives it subject to conditions, Chapter may appeal to the Cathedrals Fabric Commission.[86] The appeal must be made within three months of the day the Committee sent its decision.[87] The Commission may reverse, confirm or vary the Committee's decision or any part of it.[88] No member of the Commission who is also a member of the Committee may participate in the proceedings.[89] Similarly, if an application is not determined by the Committee within three months immediately following the making of the application, Chapter may, by notice given within the prescribed period, request that the application be dealt with by the Commission.[90] The application is then dealt with in the same way as the Fabric Advisory Committee would have dealt with it and the determination has effect as if given by that Committee – but there is no right of appeal to the Commission; the appeal is instead by way of request to the Commission of Review (see below).[91] Approvals lapse after ten years from the date on which notice of the decision was given to Chapter but may be extended by the body granting approval. In an appeal, time runs from the date of the decision of the Commission (or Commission of Review). When the works for which approval has been given have been completed, notification of completion must be given by the cathedral administrator to the Committee of the cathedral in question.[92]

The cathedral interviews

These disclose general satisfaction as to norms on the role of the Fabric Advisory Committee. Fabric matters are discussed regularly by Wells' Chapter, and the Fabric Advisory Committee operates well in terms of the skills and diligence of its members; any differences of views as between the Committee and Chapter are worked on and resolved.[93] Similarly, Winchester's Committee 'works well',[94] but at Chester, formerly the Committee 'drove the policy' as to cathedral fabric – as a result a 'clarifying of roles' was needed and undertaken so that today the Committee responds to Chapter 'more fully' and in general, therefore, it 'works well'.[95]

---

86 CCM 2011, s. 10(1). See also for appeals CFCE: PGN 1 (2012) 8.1–8.4 and PGN 2 (2012) II.3.
87 CCR 2006, r. 8.
88 CCM 2011, s. 10(3); CCR, r. 8.
89 CCM 2011, Sch. 1, par. 20.
90 CCM 2011, s. 10(2).
91 CCM 2011, s. 10(4).
92 CCM 2011, s. 12(1)-(3). See CCR 2006, r. 6: the process for requests by Chapter to the Commission when an application has not been determined by the Committee; r.8: the process for appeals to the Commission against a decision of the Committee; r. 9 deals with appeals to the Commission by Chapter or a tenant seeking approval.
93 Wells: Dean: Int. 12-8-2016.
94 Winchester: Acting Dean: Int. 16-8-2016.
95 Chester: Vice-Dean: Int. 19-8-2016.

224 *The fabric of the cathedral church*

The involvement of the cathedral architect or surveyor of the fabric is also critical. Various practices are used to implement the rules under national law that: each cathedral constitution must provide for the appointment of an architect or surveyor of the fabric for the cathedral;[96] the person must have such qualifications and expertise in matters relating to the conservation of historic buildings and other matters as Chapter, after consulting the Commission and such others as it thinks fit, considers appropriate to enable the architect or surveyor to function;[97] and Chapter must consult the Commission before appointing the person.[98] For example, at Carlisle, the Surveyor of the Fabric must be a qualified architect appointed on such terms in respect of tenure, remuneration and duties as Chapter may determine, to: exercise 'a vigilant oversight of the fabric ... and all other buildings' for which Chapter is responsible; render to Chapter a report thereon once a year or as Chapter requires; supervise repairs and alterations whensoever required by Chapter; and assist Chapter by advice and information in all matters relating to the office; the surveyor must if required attend meetings of Chapter, Council, and College of Canons.[99] Similar norms exist at other new foundations,[100] Henrician foundations,[101] and parish church cathedrals.[102] St Edmundsbury has particularly fulsome norms. The Architect must advise Chapter on 'the repair, maintenance and long term development of the ... fabric'; report 'at regular intervals on the state of the fabric', and 'supervise any works of reparation, extension and embellishment thereto'; if Chapter so decides, the Architect may be appointed as Surveyor to the Fabric of 'the Secular Properties of the Cathedral', so as to advise Chapter on 'the repair and maintenance of other Cathedral

---

96 CM 1999, s. 9(1)(f) (amended by the Care of Cathedrals (Amendment) Measure 2005, Sch. 3, par. 7(1)(a)).
97 CCM 2011, s. 32(1): 'architect' means a person registered under the Architects Act 1997; the surveyor must be a member of the Royal Institution of Chartered Surveyors and qualified as a chartered building surveyor.
98 CCM 2011, s. 23(1).
99 Carlisle: Con. Art. 15 and Stat. 24: the person must be qualified under the Architects Act 1997.
100 E.g. Winchester: Con. Art. 16: the architect is not styled 'Surveyor of the Fabric'.
101 E.g. Bristol: Con. Art. 12: architect or surveyor; Stat. 5(1) and 9: the Keeper of the Fabric must direct works of maintenance and repair necessary to the cathedral fabric or buildings in the Precinct or elsewhere, make applications for approval, have charge of 'all objects belonging to the Cathedral which are of architectural, archaeological, artistic or historic interest', and maintain the inventory (under CCM 1990, s. 13–14); Peterborough: Con. Art. 12(2): the architect 'may be styled Surveyor of the Fabric'; Chester: Con. Art. 15(x) and Stat. 14: the Architect and Surveyor of the Fabric must inspect the fabric every five years, periodically report to Chapter on it, and 'supervise all work ordered' by Chapter 'to be done upon the fabric and ornaments'; Chapter may appoint any other architect or qualified specialist as 'Consultant'; see also Con. Art. 15(xi): Chapter must appoint an Estate Manager 'on such terms in respect of tenure, remuneration and duties as the Chapter may determine'.
102 E.g. Birmingham: Con. Art. 16(2); St Albans: Con. Art. XII.2; Leicester: Con. Art. 15.2.

properties'; Chapter may also appoint a Consulting Architect in addition to the Architect and Surveyor to the Fabric.[103]

Indeed, some cathedrals, such as old foundation Chichester, have a Clerk of Works who is 'responsible for the oversight of the day-to-day restoration and maintenance of the Cathedral and its properties'.[104] And the Association of Cathedral Clerk of the Works exists to provide mutual support, encouragement and information for Cathedral Clerks of the Works, consider, debate and make suggestions on any matters affecting the fabric of cathedrals, and, if thought fit or requested by the Association of English Cathedrals, make recommendations to it.[105]

A Commission of Review

A Commission of Review may be constituted to review decisions of the Cathedrals Fabric Commission and to consider applications where the Cathedrals Fabric Commission has failed within the prescribed time limits to reach a decision either on an appeal or on an application to it for approval – including one made to the Cathedrals Fabric Commission where the Fabric Advisory Committee has failed to reach a decision within the prescribed time limits. In the case of an application for approval made to the Cathedrals Fabric Commission (including one where the application was made because the Fabric Advisory Committee failed to deal with it in the prescribed time limit), where the Cathedrals Fabric Commission refuses approval or has given approval subject to conditions, and in the case of an appeal to the Cathedrals Fabric Commission where that Commission refuses approval or refuses to reverse or vary conditions subject to which approval was given by the Fabric Advisory Committee, the review process is initiated by Chapter making a request by notice (in the prescribed form) given within the prescribed period to the registrar of the province in which the cathedral is situated that the decision be reviewed. Similarly, in a case where an application for approval or appeal is made to the Cathedrals Fabric Commission and that Commission fails to deal with the application or appeal within three months, Chapter may, by like notice, request that the application or the appeal be reviewed by a Commission of Review.[106]

Composition and procedure of a Commission of Review

A Commission of Review must consist of: the Dean of Arches and Auditor or appointee; one person appointed by the Archbishops of Canterbury and York, who is or has been a dean, provost or residentiary canon of a cathedral other than that to which the application or appeal relates; and one person appointed by the

---

103 St Edmundsbury: Stat. 24–25; see also Con. Art. 13(2): appointment.
104 Chichester: Stat. 21.e. See also e.g. Lincoln: Stat. 19; Salisbury: Stat. 6.
105 ACCW: Con. Art. 2. See also the ACCW Guide: An Introduction to the Role (2012).
106 CCM 2011, s. 11(1)-(2); CCR 2006, rr. 17, 19–20, 24, 26. See also HLE par. 366.

Secretary of State who has special knowledge of the architecture, archaeology, art (including history of art) or history of cathedrals; but, except the Dean of Arches and Auditor (or appointee), no person who has been a member of the Cathedrals Fabric Commission at any time during the preceding five years may be appointed.[107]

A Commission of Review must sit in public and may receive such representations, if any, as it thinks fit. Subject to this and to any directions as to procedure given by the General Synod, a Commission of Review may regulate its own procedure. The Dean of the Arches and Auditor (or appointee) may, whether or not an application has been made by any person, give directions on procedure, including directions fixing or varying the date or place of sittings. A Commission of Review may make such orders for: (a) for the payment of costs by any person, including administrative expenses in connection with the hearing of an appeal or the conduct of a review, expenses incurred by any of its members in the matter, and any fees as may be fixed by the Fees Advisory Commission of the Church of England; and (b) the giving of security for costs by any person concerned, as seem to the Commission of Review to be just. For the purposes of any application, appeal, request or other regulated matter, the Commission of Review (and Fabric Advisory Committee and Cathedrals Fabric Commission) may receive oral, documentary or other evidence of any fact or matter which appears to it to be relevant, and receive oral evidence which is not given upon oath or affirmation.[108]

The Commission of Review may reverse, confirm or vary the decision of the Cathedrals Fabric Commission or Fabric Advisory Committee or any part of it; or, where the application is one which arises out of a failure of the Cathedrals Fabric Commission to determine the matter, the Commission of Review may refuse or give its approval to the proposal either unconditionally or subject to such conditions as it may specify, and such determination has effect as if it had been given by the Cathedrals Fabric Commission.[109] Its decision is final.[110] When the Commission of Review gives approval, the approval will lapse after ten years from the date on which notice of the decision was given to Chapter, but it may extend that period by such time as it may specify, and as soon as possible after the completion of any work which has been approved, the cathedral administrator must notify the Fabric Advisory Committee or Cathedrals Fabric Commission, as appropriate, of the date of the completion.[111]

An irregularity or error of procedure does not invalidate any step in any application, appeal or review unless the Commission or Commission of Review decides otherwise. The chair of the Commission or Dean of the Arches and Auditor may

---

107 CCM 2011, s. 11(3).
108 CCR 2006, rr. 24, 26: fees may be fixed under the Ecclesiastical Fees Measure 1986; the Ecclesiastical Jurisdiction Measure 1963 ss. 60(3) and 61 apply to any order for the payment of costs which includes fees, charges, disbursements, expenses and remuneration.
109 CCM 2011, s. 11(4)-(6).
110 CCM 2011, s. 11(7).
111 CCM 2011, s. 12.

give directions to cure or to waive that irregularity or error.[112] At a meeting of the Commission or the Fabric Advisory Committee, a member who has a personal interest in an item to be discussed must (a) so declare before the item is to be discussed, and (b) withdraw from the meeting for the whole of the discussion and vote (if any). Nevertheless, if satisfied that it would assist the members present to be informed as to some matters of fact, the chair may permit the member with a personal interest to remain at the meeting at the commencement of the discussion on the item in order to provide factual information and thereafter that member must withdraw from the meeting.[113]

The cathedral interviews

These reveal no particular issues as to the Commission of Review. Several were of the view that the regime discussed throughout this chapter is not of itself too complicated.[114] Needless to say, the aim of the rules is in part to protect the national heritage, a value often expressed in cathedral strategic vision documents; for instance, Worcester provides: 'Implicit in the entire life and work of the cathedral is the need for the building to be in a good state of repair' for it 'to fulfil its calling to be the seat of the bishop and a centre of worship and mission, and the spiritual home of the cathedral community'; Chapter, thus, is committed 'to the continual task of conserving and repairing the fabric of the cathedral, its ancillary buildings and all the properties in the precinct', and 'to its environmental responsibility in all aspects of cathedral life. The funding of fabric repairs remains the first call on Chapter's fund-raising strategy'.[115]

Conclusion

Each cathedral must have a Fabric Advisory Committee to advise Chapter in the care and maintenance of the cathedral and to determine applications for approval of proposals in relation to prescribed works on the cathedral church and its ancillary buildings. However, some prescribed categories of work require the approval of the national Cathedrals Fabric Commission, which may also determine appeals against refusal to grant permission by the Fabric Advisory Committee. Refusals to give permission by the Commission may in turn be reviewed by the national Commission of Review. As seen in Chapter 2, contraventions of the system may be dealt with by a variety of means depending on the nature of the contravention and degree of urgency needed for intervention. The approvals

112 CCR 2006, r. 33.
113 CCR 2006, r. 25(1); similar rules apply to the chair and vice-chair: r. 25(2).
114 Ely: Dean: Email 17-1-2017; Carlisle: Dean: Email 17-1-2017; Liverpool: Dean: Email 21-1-2017; Wakefield: Dean: Email 24-1-2017. However, compare Southwark: Dean: Email 17-1-2017: greater 'simplification' is needed such as applies to Diocesan Advisory Committees in faculty cases.
115 Worcester: Renewal and Development: A Strategic Vision for Worcester Cathedral 2015–2020 (2015) par. 10.

required nationally are in addition to, and do not dispense with any consent or approval required under the constitution and statutes relating to the particular cathedral in question. In exercising their functions, the Fabric Advisory Committee, Cathedrals Fabric Commission, and Commission of Review must have regard to the fact that the cathedral is the seat of the bishop and a centre of worship and mission, and to the desirability of preserving: the fabric of the cathedral church and any of its features of architectural, archaeological, artistic or historic interest; the immediate setting of the cathedral church; any building within the cathedral precinct of architectural, archaeological, artistic or historic interest; any archaeological or human remains in or under the cathedral church or within its precinct; and any valuable objects held by the cathedral. The system provides a complex regime for care and conservation and continues and refines arrangements commended by the Archbishops' Commission 1994. The cathedral interviews underscore the value of the system and the role of the cathedral architect and other staff in its efficient operation, but some also express disquiet about its potential to become adversarial.

10 The cathedral close: the precinct, houses and security

The medieval monastic cathedral influenced the character of its setting, often surrounded as it was by a wall or close. That setting, collegiate, secluded and perhaps aloof, set slightly apart from the town,[1] 'constituted a distinct and exclusive *quartier*'; some secular cathedrals were similar, like Wells where the double staircase to the Chapter House leads to a bridge over the Chain Gate and to a hall (c. 1348) where the vicars choral dined and, beyond, to the Vicars' Close with terraced houses in an enclosed collegiate quadrangle completed by a library and chapel; thus: 'the cathedral close became an important formative element in the social and aesthetic character of our cathedrals, an element which has survived the dissolution of the monastic foundations and is still visible … today'; indeed, some consider that Salisbury Close with its 'large, magnificent and uncluttered collection of episcopal and canonical buildings' is 'the best of any English cathedral'.[2] Close buildings were regulated by numerous laws, and the close itself was presumed in law not to form part of any neighbouring parish.[3] This Chapter examines the precinct, the area surrounding the cathedral church: the designation, ownership, and regulation of the precinct (including any archaeological and human remains there); the regulation of housing for cathedral clergy and other staff, canonical houses, and 'close residence'; and cathedral security, including the use in some of cathedral constables.

The cathedral precinct

The Care of Cathedrals Measure 2011 provides for the process of designating the precinct of a cathedral church, the process by which a precinct boundary (once the precinct has been so designated) may be amended, the effects of the designation, and the operation of statutory controls in relation to the precinct.[4] For the purposes of the Measure, the precinct is a legally defined area designated as such by

---

1 A. Clifton-Taylor, *The Cathedrals of England* (1967) 105.
2 P. Johnson, *British Cathedrals* (1980) 14–15, 82–83; see 201 for the royal court accommodated in the close.
3 Gibson 174; Burn II.87: on Wells; Phillimore I.133.
4 CFCE: PGN 3 (2012, and due for revision).

the Cathedrals Fabric Commission on a plan prepared by Chapter which shows the land surrounding the cathedral church owned by the cathedral's corporate body.[5] Cathedral constitutions and/or statutes also sometimes define 'precinct' or 'close'.[6] As we have already seen (in Chapter 3), one of the legal incidents which may attach to a precinct (or close) is that the dean and/or the residentiaries must provide for the cure of souls for those resident within it; for example: at Exeter: 'The Dean shall have the cure of souls within the precincts of the Close'; at Lichfield: 'The Dean and the Residentiary Canons shall provide for the cure of souls in the Cathedral Close'; and at Peterborough, which is unusual, the statutes enumerate rights of residents of the precinct which have been possessed 'from ancient times'.[7] There are fewer references to the close at the modern cathedrals; in point of fact, Newcastle provides that the cathedral is 'distinct from ancient cathedrals with their residential closes, and this is recognised in the Constitution and Statutes'.[8] However, at Guildford, the cathedral community includes persons 'resident in the Cathedral Close'.[9]

The designation of the precinct

Under the Care of Cathedrals Measure 2011, Chapter must prepare a plan indicating the extent of the land surrounding the cathedral church of which the fee simple is vested in the cathedral's corporate body. The cathedral administrator must send the plan to the Cathedrals Fabric Commission. On receipt, the Commission must, after consulting Chapter, indicate on the plan the precinct of the cathedral church for the purposes of the Measure. The precinct consists of so much of that land as, in the opinion of the Commission, is necessary to preserve or protect: (a) the architectural, archaeological, artistic or historic character of (i) the cathedral church, (ii) any buildings of architectural, archaeological,

   5 CCM 2011, s. 32(1): "precinct" means 'the precinct for the time being indicated on the plan required for that cathedral church' by s. 25. See also CFCE: PGN 3 (2012), Glossary: for the Legal Advisory Commission (originally dealing with CCM 1990, s.13), 'the precinct' refers to 'land in the immediate environs of the cathedral church and of which the cathedral itself (including its historical and archaeological context) is the focus'; the extent of this area depends on the particular circumstances at each cathedral but might in practice be clarified by reference to artificial boundaries such as those constituted by buildings, walls and roads.
   6 E.g. Lichfield: Con. Art. 15(1): '"The Close" means the land and premises surrounding the Cathedral and commonly known by that name in so far as the same is vested in the Chapter'; Canterbury: Con. Art. 1(2): '"Vill of Christ Church" means the entirety of the area of land lying within the Precincts'; Durham: Con. Art. 1: 'precinct' means 'the area of the Cathedral's grounds, the College and the inner banks of the River Wear'; Gloucester: Con. Art. 2(1).
   7 Exeter: Stat. VI.3; Lichfield: Stat. III(3); Peterborough: Stat. 18. See also Worcester: Stat. 10.3(b): residentiaries must give pastoral care to precinct residents; Salisbury: Con. Art. 13.2: 'all who work for the Cathedral and within its precinct'; Durham: Stat. VII.3: prescribed elections must be held 'in the Precinct'.
   8 Newcastle: Con. Preamble.
   9 Guildford: Con. Art. 15.

artistic, or historic interest associated with it, (iii) any archaeological or human remains associated with or situated in, under or near the cathedral church or any such buildings; and (b) the setting of the cathedral church and any such buildings and remains. In implementing these requirements, the Commission must have regard to the context in which the cathedral church and buildings have developed over time. Chapter must keep its plan up-to-date and notify the Commission of changes to it. When so notified, the Commission must, after consulting Chapter, make alterations to the precinct indicated on the plan as it considers appropriate. In doing so, it must have regard to what is necessary to preserve or protect the matters in (a) and (b) above and the context in which the cathedral church and buildings have developed. Also, the Commission may, after consulting Chapter, make alterations to the precinct indicated on the plan prepared by Chapter as it considers appropriate, having regard to the same matters.[10]

The precinct boundary is marked on the plan in green and is known customarily as the 'green line' plan; the Commission and Chapter both hold copies of the plan.[11] The area may (but not necessarily) coincide with the area of the cathedral 'Close' as it is traditionally understood.[12] Within the broader area of the precinct, a more restricted area is designated within which secular listed building control (see below) does *not* apply to any ecclesiastical building for the time being used for ecclesiastical purposes. This area is marked with a red line; this plan is known customarily as the 'red line' plan.[13] In practice, the 'red line' usually encompasses the cathedral church, its side chapels, vestries, cloisters and chapter house. The Department for Culture, Media and Sport, Commission, Chapter and local planning authority each retain a copy of this plan. The 'red line' plan, and the area in it, is distinct from the cathedral precinct and the 'green line' plan on which the precinct is marked. There is no mechanism for altering the 'red line'.[14] Any other church building (e.g. whose primary use is as a place of worship) outside the 'red line' but within the designated 'green line', together with certain monuments outside the 'red line' but within the precinct, are also exempted from listed building control.[15]

The Cathedrals Fabric Commission must advise Chapter and the Fabric Advisory Committee on the care, conservation, repair and development of buildings or archaeological remains in its precinct; and promote, consulting Chapters, Committees and others, good practice as to the care, conservation, repair and

10 CCM 2011, s. 25(1)-(5). See also CFCE: PGN 2 (2012) I.5.10.
11 CFCE: PGN 1 (2012) 9.3; see also PGN 3 (2012) 2.2.
12 CFCE: PGN 3 (2012) 2.3.
13 This area was marked with a red line on an official plan prepared for each cathedral by the Department of National Heritage (whose successor is the Department of Culture, Media and Sport) and was referred to in the Ecclesiastical Exemption (Listed Buildings and Conservation Areas) Order 1994. This Order has been superseded by the 2010 Order, for which see above Chapter 9 n. 7.
14 CFCE: PGN 3 (2012), 2.4: as from 1 January 2008.
15 CFCE: PGN 1 (2012) 4.4. This cites PGN 3 (2012).

232 *The cathedral close*

development of precincts and the compilation, maintenance and dissemination of information on buildings and archaeological remains in the precinct.[16]

The application of statutory controls to the precinct

Some works in the precinct are placed by the ecclesiastical exemption under civil law (see Chapter 9) outside secular controls and so fall under the ecclesiastical regime of the Care of Cathedrals Measure 2011; other works are subject to secular controls; and some are subject to both.[17] Thus, Chapter must not, without approval from the relevant body, implement or consent to implement any proposal to carry out works, including repair or maintenance, on, above or below land the fee simple in which vests in the corporate body, being works which would materially affect: (i) the architectural, archaeological, artistic, or historic character of any building within the precinct which is being used for ecclesiastical purposes, or (ii) the immediate setting of the cathedral church, or (iii) archaeological remains in the precinct.[18]

Whether Chapter must seek approval from the Commission or the Committee depends on the nature of the proposed work. Chapter must apply to the Commission if it proposes: (a) to carry works, including repair or maintenance, which would permanently alter the fabric of any building within the precinct used for ecclesiastical purposes; (b) the demolition of any part of such a building; and (c) the disturbance or destruction of archaeological or human remains within its precinct.[19] Otherwise approval must be sought from the Committee.[20]

However, after a written request by Chapter, and after consulting the local planning authority, Fabric Advisory Committee and English Heritage, the Commission may make a written declaration that no approval is required, if it is satisfied that: (a) the proposal, while involving the immediate setting of the cathedral church or any archaeological remains in or under it or within its precinct, does *not* involve human remains;[21] or (b) the proposal does *not* relate to a building within its precinct used for ecclesiastical purposes; or (c) planning permission, listed building consent or scheduled monument consent *is* required for the works; and (d) any considerations relevant to preserve the setting of the cathedral and remains will be adequately taken into account by the person or body responsible for granting permission or consent.[22]

---

16 CCM 2011, s. 3(2); CFCE: PGN 3 (2012) 5.6–7; PGN 6 (2012) I.1.1.
17 CFCE: PGN 3 (2012) 3.1–3.2.
18 CCM 2011, s. 2(1). See above Chapter 9 for the exceptions under s. 2(2) and definitions under s. 32.
19 CCM 2011, s. 6. See above Chapter 9 for the procedure.
20 CFCE: PGN 3 (2012) 3.8.
21 That is, if it falls within s. 2(1)(a)(ii) or (iii) but not within s 2(1)(a)(iv).
22 CCM 2011, s. 6; 'planning permission', 'listed building consent' and 'scheduled monument consent' are as defined in: the Town and Country Planning Act 1990, s. 336(1); Planning (Listed Buildings and Conservation Areas) Act 1990, s. 8(7); Ancient Monuments and Archaeological Areas Act 1979, s. 2(3)(a).

In turn, buildings and monuments within the precinct not used for ecclesiastical purposes *are* subject to secular listed building control or scheduled monument control. If Chapter proposes to apply for Listed Building Consent, or Scheduled Monument Consent,[23] in respect of any such building or monument within the precinct, the cathedral administrator must send a notice to the Commission informing it and stating that the Commission may send written representations to him within 28 days for the purposes of processing that application.[24] Moreover, any proposal for works by a tenant of Chapter (domestic or otherwise) or another person or body other than Chapter (such as a local authority or public utility) are also subject to the controls under the Care of Cathedrals Measure 2011 *if* they are of a type requiring approval under that Measure and *if* the tenant or other person or body requires Chapter's consent to implement the proposal in question; in these cases, Chapter must obtain approval from the Commission/Committee as appropriate in the usual way before giving its consent.[25]

Archaeological remains within the precinct

Under the Care of Cathedrals Measure 2011, Chapter must obtain approval from the relevant body for a proposal to carry out works which would materially affect archaeological remains within the precinct.[26] Chapter must apply to the Commission if the works would involve disturbance or destruction of archaeological remains there.[27] Archaeological remains are the remains of any building, work or artefact and any trace or sign of their previous existence.[28] To this end Chapter must, after consulting the Commission, appoint a cathedral archaeologist, unless the Commission notifies Chapter that in its view the archaeological significance of the cathedral church does not justify such appointment.[29] The archaeologist (by whatever name called) must be a person who possesses such qualifications and expertise in archaeological matters as the Commission may recognise as appropriate (see below).[30] The Commission has issued standards endorsing Government policy in planning guidance; this policy establishes a

---

23 Listed building consent (LBC) is granted by the local planning authority for specified works under the Planning (Listed Buildings and Conservation Areas) Act 1990, s. 8; this does not automatically mean that they will also require approval by the Commission or Committee (but these must be notified). Scheduled monument consent (SMC) is granted by the Secretary of State, advised by English Heritage, for specified works under the Ancient Monuments and Archaeological Areas Act 1979, s. 2(3)(a). This does not automatically mean that they will also require approval by the Commission or Committee (but these must be notified).
24 See also CCM 2011, s. 29; CCR 2006, r. 11.
25 CFCE: PGN 3 (2012), 3. For a tenant's right of appeal see CCM 2011, s. 14.
26 CCM 2011, s. 2(1): see above.
27 CCM 2011, s. 6: see above.
28 CCM 2011, s. 32(1).
29 CCM 2011, s. 23(2). See Chapter 8 for the involvement of the archaeologist in e.g. the quinquennial report.
30 CCM 2011, s. 32(1).

presumption in favour of preserving important archaeological remains without disturbance.[31]

If Chapter makes an application for a proposal that may involve disturbance or destruction of archaeological remains, the Commission expects Chapter to give an overview of the proposal and its context, including: (1) how it relates strategically to cathedral life, work and mission, the permanent benefits, and how these are desirable, necessary, and sustainable; (2) evidence that the resultant impact on the archaeology of the precinct and its buildings has been fully assessed and understood, and that this understanding has informed the proposals; and (3) an indication of how the proposals relate to the cathedral's Conservation Plan, if it has one.[32]

Therefore, the Commission expects Chapter to provide supporting information, including (as appropriate): (1) an assessment by the archaeologist, reviewing the existing archaeological information about the site, and analysing the likely impact upon it of the proposed works; (2) a statement of how to mitigate the archaeological impact, e.g. through preservation beneath the level of the works, recording and excavation, or other means; (3) an options appraisal detailing alternative sites and construction methods, such as might minimise still further the archaeological disturbance, and the reasons for rejecting these options; (4) a commitment by Chapter to provide adequate resources to see any archaeological project through from its inception to completion (including post-fieldwork analysis and archive deposition) and the dissemination of the results, in line with established good practice and published professional standards; and (5) such other written, drawn and photographic material as is necessary to give a sufficient account of the proposed works bearing in mind that such information should be proportionate to the particular project and provide a full understanding of what is proposed.[33]

If the assessment by the cathedral archaeologist does not provide sufficient archaeological information about the site to analyse the likely impact on it of the proposed work, the Commission may request that further information be obtained through a field evaluation. Such an evaluation may involve geophysical survey, trial excavation, or the opening up of sections of fabric (which may require the Commission's prior approval).[34] Moreover, if the application refers to an archaeological research excavation, the Commission will nevertheless presume in favour of preservation of important archaeological remains. This presumption, however, will not rule out the possibility of a research excavation where Chapter is able to demonstrate that the proposal is both directed towards clearly formulated and convincing academic aims, and backed by resources of finance, personnel, technology and time, such as will be fully adequate to see the project through from inception to appropriate conclusion.[35]

---

31 CFCE: GN (2012): Cathedrals and Archaeology: a Guide to Good Management.
32 CFCE: PGN 6 (2012) II.4.6.
33 CFCE: PGN 6 (2012) II.4.7.
34 CFCE: PGN 6 (2012) II.4.8.
35 CFCE: PGN 6 (2012) II.4.9.

For approval, the Commission requires additional documentation before work is put in hand, namely, in the case of: (i) an archaeological excavation, an archaeological Project Design; (ii) an archaeological monitoring project (e.g. a watching brief), an archaeological specification; (iii) as to an archaeological investigation and recording of standing buildings or structures, an archaeological Project Design or specification. Both the Project Design and specification should be drawn up in accordance with a brief provided by the cathedral archaeologist, or drawn up by another competent archaeologist and approved by the cathedral archaeologist.[36]

Human remains

It is frequently the case that there are Christian burials within and around a cathedral. Some precincts also include ancient sites which may contain pre-Christian burials. As a result, it is likely that below-ground works to cathedrals and their precincts will encounter and disturb human remains from a range of periods. Therefore, the underlying principles which apply are that: (1) human remains should always be treated with dignity and respect; (2) burials should not be disturbed without good reason, but it may be necessary to disturb them in advance of properly authorised development; (3) human remains and the archaeological evidence around them are important sources of scientific information; (4) particular weight should be given to the feelings and views of living family members if known; (5) decisions should be made in the public interest, and in an accountable way. Disarticulated bones (other than charnel deposits) can normally be carefully collected by general contractors for subsequent re-burial. However, if articulated human remains are discovered or predicted to be discovered, project teams should always include a professional archaeologist experienced in church archaeology, either the cathedral archaeologist or an archaeological contractor they brief and monitor.[37] Any work involving the disturbance or destruction of human remains within the precincts (or in or under the cathedral church) requires the approval of the Commission and more minor work needs the approval of the local Committee.[38] Until the end of 2014 the removal of human remains within the precincts also required a Ministry of Justice exhumation licence pursuant to the Burial Act 1857. However, since 1 January 2015, such a licence is no longer required, provided approval has been obtained under the Care of Cathedrals Measure 2011.[39]

36 CFCE: PGN 6 (2012) II.4.10.
37 Church Care, Cathedrals and Church Buildings Division, Archbishops' Council: Guidance.
38 That is, approval required by CCM 2011, s. 6: see above.
39 Church of England (Miscellaneous Provisions) Measure 2014, s. 2 (amending the Burial Act 1857, s. 25): it is an offence for a body or any human remains which have been interred in a place of burial to be removed unless the body or remains is or are removed in accordance with the approval of a proposal under the CCM 2011 by the Cathedrals Fabric Commission for England or a Fabric Advisory Committee; and

The Association of Diocesan and Cathedral Archaeologists

This Association, formed in 2000,[40] seeks to develop and promote the highest standards of practice in cathedral and church archaeology, which it defines as 'the complete study of the fabric and material remains of a church, above and below ground, in relation to its site, contents and historic setting, and to the community it has served'. Its objects are to: (1) serve as a forum for the development and dissemination of the highest professional standards in the conservation, recording, analysis and publication of all aspects of the archaeological remains of cathedrals and churches; (2) encourage, initiate or advise on programmes of research, training and education relating to cathedral and church archaeology; (3) provide a medium of communication amongst cathedral archaeological consultants through an annual conference; (4) maintain a register of them; and (5) form and maintain links with cathedral architects and other bodies responsible for the care of the ecclesiastical heritage.[41] Membership is open, *inter alia*, to persons holding the appointment of cathedral archaeological consultant and to other persons who are engaged in any professional archaeological capacity by a cathedral.[42]

The routine administration of the Association is carried out by a Committee consisting of a Chairman, Secretary, Treasurer, and up to two other Association members. The Committee is elected at an Annual General Meeting, held during the annual conference. Election to it is normally for three years, but retiring members are eligible for re-election. The Committee is to review policy about church archaeology, liaise with professional bodies, and organise conferences and meetings. All business must be reported to the Annual General Meeting and changes in policy submitted for approval. The Committee is responsible for the organisation of the annual conference and its programme. The conference may be open to non-members. The Annual General Meeting, open only to members, determines the annual subscription to assist with administrative costs. Association funds must be administered by the Treasurer.[43] Additions or amendments to the constitution may be proposed by the Committee or

    unless removal requires the approval of a proposal under the CCM 2011, the body or remains is or are removed under a licence from the Secretary of State and in accordance with any conditions attached to the licence. See also Historic England: Scheduled Monuments: A Guide for Owners and Occupiers (2013): this includes guidance on the Ancient Monuments and Archaeological Areas Act 1979 (as amended); and Church of England and English Heritage: Guidance for best practice for treatment of human remains excavated from Christian burial grounds in England (2005).
40 ADCA: Constitution (2000), Art. 1; it was formed through the enlargement of the Association of Cathedral Archaeologists to embrace Diocesan Archaeological Advisers and others working at churches.
41 ADCA: Con. Art. 2.
42 ADCA: Con. Art. 3; also, persons holding similar archaeological appointments to cathedrals and greater churches in England, Wales and Scotland may be invited to join; and others regularly engaged in a professional capacity in Church Archaeology may apply to join subject to approval by the executive committee.
43 ADCA: Con. Art. 5: archaeologist representatives of the Cathedrals Fabric Commission are invited to attend committee meetings and the Annual General Meeting *ex officio*.

by any two members of the Association and they must be approved by majority vote of those present at the Annual General Meeting.[44] The Association has issued several guidance documents.[45]

As seen above, the Care of Cathedrals Measure 2011 requires each cathedral to appoint an archaeologist,[46] and as we see below cathedral constitutions so provide; also, the constitution of the Association states that a cathedral archaeological consultant should in the discharge of functions meet the principles of good conduct and best practice which are to: (1) adhere to the highest standards of ethical and responsible behaviour in archaeological affairs; (2) hold responsibility for the conservation of the archaeological heritage; (3) conduct work in such a way that reliable information about the past may be acquired, and that the results be properly recorded; (4) inform the management, maintenance, and preservation of the cathedral, and ensure its sustainable future; and (5) make available the results of archaeological work with reasonable dispatch. In dispensing their roles and duties, cathedral archaeological consultants should also have due regard to the fact that churches are centres of worship and mission.[47]

The cathedral interviews

These reveal a number of different practices with regard to the precinct. At old foundation Hereford, there is a Close, but it is not gated, and it is called such on the precinct plan; moreover, the constitution requires the dean to provide pastoral care to the cathedral community and 'where appropriate' to visitors; in practice, the dean also provides pastoral care to Close residents.[48] At Exeter, similarly, whilst the constitution deals expressly only with the pastoral care of the cathedral community, in practice the dean provides such care in addition to residents of the Close.[49] At Wells, the 'Liberty' is roughly coterminous with the historic precinct.[50] St Paul's Amen Court (the location of canonical houses) is not treated as a Close nor is it within the official curtilage covered by the Fabric Advisory Committee.[51] Winchester precinct is 'open' but the Inner Close is 'shut at night'.[52] Henrician foundation Chester's constitution provides that the pastoral care of precinct residents must be committed by Chapter to its own ordained members or some other priest approved by the bishop; moreover, the cathedral

---

44 ADCA: Con. Art. 6: Rules of the Association come into effect on confirmation at an Annual General Meeting.
45 E.g. Guidance Note 1: Archaeological Requirements for Works on Churches and Churchyards (2004); Guidance Note 2: Archaeology and Burial Vaults (2010); and Guidance Note 3: Dealing with Architectural Fragments (2010).
46 That is, CCM 2011, s. 23(2) and s. 32(1).
47 ADCA: Con. Art. 4. The Association seeks to promote its 'The Role and Duties of the Cathedral Archaeological Consultant', which is revised from time to time.
48 Hereford: Dean: Int. 5–8-2016: see Con. Arts. 7(3) and 8(7).
49 Exeter: Dean: Int. 9–8-2016; there is also a Canon Pastor (not in the statutes).
50 Wells: Acting Dean: Int. 12–8-2016.
51 London: Dean: Int. 23–9-2016.
52 Winchester: Acting Dean: Int. 16–8-2016.

has about sixty-seven commercial tenants (offices, retail, and residents) within the green line and (like the cathedral shop) the red line; also, under its statutes, Chapter may appoint a custos to advise and recommend with regard to cathedral property, possessions and estate (on terms set by Chapter); in practice, however, the custos is the 'honorary gardener'.[53]

There are also various norm-making practices with regard to the statutory office of cathedral archaeologist.[54] Chichester's 'Consultant Archaeologist' must possess such qualifications and expertise in archaeological matters as may be 'recognized as appropriate' by the national Cathedrals Fabric Commission before appointment; the area of responsibility includes 'all Cathedral properties, walls and land within the Precinct'.[55] At Hereford: 'There shall be an archaeologist' appointed by Chapter, after consulting the Commission, 'on such terms in respect of tenure, remuneration, duties and otherwise' as Chapter may determine. Duties must include: advising Chapter on the history of the cathedral's fabric, material remains, site, contents and communities it has served; recording the buildings, fabric, fittings, ornaments and monuments as appropriate during any works on them and whenever the ground or floor levels are disturbed; organising excavations; co-operating closely with the architect where appropriate; and attendance at meetings of the Fabric Advisory Committee unless its chair permits or directs otherwise.[56] New and Henrician foundations and parish church cathedrals are similar.[57]

Canonical houses

That a dean and residentiaries must reside at the cathedral is an ancient rule but ownership and other rights over their residences was the subject of considerable legal activity.[58] Indeed, the Archbishops' Commission on Cathedrals 1994 recognised that: 'Patterns of ownership in Closes are often complex, with corresponding implications for responsibilities'; moreover: 'Disposal of properties for financial reasons are very often regretted by later generations, and a number of cathedrals have found it necessary or desirable to repurchase properties previously disposed'; and good practice includes sharing facilities with the diocesan office.[59]

Under the Cathedrals Measure 1999, Chapter may allocate for the use of anyone holding an office in connection with the cathedral any house, vested in the cathedral, as a residence from which to perform the duties of office.[60] The Church

---

53 Chester: Vice-Dean: Int. 19-8-2016; Con. Art. 16(ii): care; Stat. 12: custos.
54 See above for CCM 2011, ss. 23(2) and 32(1).
55 Chichester: Stat. 21.d.
56 Hereford: Con. Art. 19.
57 E.g. Canterbury: Stat. XXIII; Bristol: Con. Art. 12(6); St Albans: Con. Art. XII.3; Derby: Con. Art. 12.5.
58 Burn I.216, II.81–82: the dean's duty to reside; I. 262: prebendaries; Phillimore I.142 and II.1143–1146.
59 H&R 126, 251, Appendix 6.
60 CM 1999, s. 19; see also s. 35(1): a house of residence includes all buildings, gardens, and other land held therewith and a 'lease' includes a tenancy.

Commissioners may from their general fund make grants to a cathedral to secure better provision for houses for Clerks in Holy Orders holding office in the cathedral.[61] When a person is appointed as the dean or canon residentiary whose stipend is paid by the Commissioners, the Commissioners also may make out of their general fund a grant towards removal expenses incurred.[62] If such a house of residence is to be disposed of, Chapter must obtain the consent of the Church Commissioners, the consent of the dean or residentiary who normally occupies the house (except during a vacancy in these offices), and, where the house is allocated for the use of the holder of a dignity the right of presentation to which vests in Her Majesty, the consent of Her Majesty.[63] However, Chapter is not required to obtain the consent of the Commissioners to grant a lease to any cleric holding office in the cathedral or any person employed in connection with it.[64]

Moreover, under secondary legislation, if Chapter applies to the Fabric Advisory Committee or Cathedrals Fabric Commission for approval of prescribed proposals, and the proposal affects any house the whole or part of which is occupied or is to be occupied by a Clerk in Holy Orders holding office in the cathedral: (a) the cathedral Administrator must send the Church Commissioners a copy of the notice which must be displayed in respect of the proposal; (b) any observations made by the Church Commissioners to the Committee or Commission within the consultation period which must be treated as representations on the proposal; and (c) the Committee and Commission secretaries (or the Provincial Registrar in the case of a Commission of Review decision) must send the Commissioners a copy of notice of the decision/determination by the Committee, Commission or Commission of Review.[65]

The Deanery and Canons' Houses

By canon law, the dean and residentiaries must be resident 'in' the cathedral church 'for the time prescribed by law and by the statutes of the cathedral ... except they shall be otherwise hindered by weighty and urgent cause'.[66] The matter is treated at some length by the statutes of cathedrals. These deal with the periods of residence required, relaxation (usually by the bishop) of the residence requirement, and provision and maintenance of houses. There is considerable diversity between cathedrals as to the norms used to regulate these matters, particularly in terms of the subjects regulated as well as the depth and detail of these norms.

Some old foundations have few norms on the matter; for example, at Exeter the dean must reside in the house designated by Chapter 'as the Deanery',[67] and

---

61 CM 1999, s. 24.
62 CM 1999, s. 22.
63 CM 1999, s. 15(1).
64 CM 1999, s. 15, proviso.
65 CCR 2006, r. 10. See also CFCE: PGN 2 (2012) II, 7. See Chapters 8 and 9 for works requiring approval.
66 Canon C21.3.
67 Exeter: Stat. VI.2.

residentiaries must reside 'in the precinct of the Close unless given permission by the Bishop [after consulting the dean] to reside in some other specified dwelling'.[68] However, Hereford has more detail:

> The Dean shall reside in the Deanery or, with the consent of the Bishop, in a suitable house approved by the Chapter but, with the advance agreement of the Bishop, may take periods of absence for special reason in addition to normal holidays. Only in very exceptional circumstances may such periods of absence total more than three months in any three years.[69]

Each residentiary 'shall reside within the precinctual boundary of the Cathedral' unless permitted by the bishop, consulting the dean, 'to reside elsewhere in some other specified dwelling'; and Chapter may (with episcopal consent) grant in a three-year period one period of leave of absence of up to three months for specific reasons in addition to normal holidays; only exceptionally is this to be granted in respect of a period(s) totalling over three months in any three-year period.[70]

Some old foundations provide for 'close residence' allocated among clergy who then function as 'canons-in-residence'. Wells has these simple norms on the matter: 'Chapter shall allocate to each Residentiary Canon a period or periods of close residence in such manner that equal aggregate periods of close residence are allocated to each residentiary canon unless all the residentiary canons consent to some other arrangement'; the periods must cover the whole year 'save that the Dean may if he so desires fulfil such period or periods of close residence as may be agreed' with Chapter; a residentiary in close residence is 'canon-in-residence'.[71]

Some of the old foundations also deal with the administration of the house of residence; for example, at Lincoln the dean and residentiaries 'shall not pay rent and shall have council tax or any similar charge for the house assigned to them paid for out of cathedral funds'; the 'structure and internal repairs of the deanery and of the houses of residence', and such decorations to these houses as Chapter may 'specifically determine, shall be a charge upon the cathedral funds'; Chapter may also make 'a suitable contribution towards the cost of heating, lighting and cleaning these houses and for keeping the gardens in good condition'.[72]

Other old foundations provide for housing for persons in addition to dean and residentiaries. York is a good example: 'The Dean shall be entitled to occupy his house, and each holder of a major Dignity shall be entitled to have a house assigned' by Chapter. These houses must be occupied free of rent and council tax, the costs of building insurance and structural repairs, and such other services as may be deemed necessary for the performance of the duties of the dean,

---

68 Exeter: Stat. VII.1.b.
69 Hereford: Stat. V.3.
70 Hereford: Stat. VI.1–2.
71 Wells: Stat. 4(3): there is no reference to the canonical residences; see also Lichfield: Stat. III(5).
72 Lincoln: Stat. 22; see also Stat. 4(1) on Chapter's allocation of periods of 'official residence'.

residentiary or other dignitary. However, Chapter may also assign a house to 'any other person, in association with work in the service of the Cathedral Church', on such terms as Chapter may determine, and it may pay the costs of the external and internal decoration of a house occupied by a major dignity.[73] Moreover, the dean and residentiaries must be 'in residence either open or close during eight months of each year'. Periods of close residence must, after mutual agreement between dean and residentiaries, be declared by the Chancellor annually at the autumn Chapter meeting as follows: with his consent, the dean must be allotted and may undertake periods of residence to meet an emergency; a residentiary who does not hold a major dignity may be allotted a period in accordance with an agreement made with Chapter; the remainder of the year must be divided equally among the major dignities.[74]

Similar patterns are found at new foundations. Some have norms applicable to both the dean and the residentiaries, but others deal with these separately. Among the former, for example at Carlisle, the dean and residentiaries must dwell in the Abbey except for 90 days each year in the house assigned by Chapter unless the bishop and Chapter 'for some special reason' permit residence elsewhere or extend absence from residence beyond 90 days. The permission, reasons and period must be 'set down in writing'. Further: the dean 'shall occupy his allotted house of residence free of rent'. As to the deanery and residentiaries' houses, the cost of structural repairs, external decoration, council tax, and insurance 'must' be met from cathedral revenues; however, the cost of internal decoration or redecoration of the deanery and residentiaries' houses 'may' be met from cathedral revenues as Chapter may determine; in other cases, internal decoration 'shall be the responsibility of the occupant'.[75]

As to the latter, where the dean and residentiaries are treated separately, various matters are regulated. At Norwich: 'The Dean shall reside in The Close of the Cathedral Church in the house allocated' by the Chapter and on ceasing 'to hold the office of Dean … shall vacate the house'; each residentiary must reside similarly; and: 'Chapter may from time to time vary the allocation of the canonical houses to the Residentiary Canons, provided that no Residentiary Canon shall be required against his will to vacate the house previously allocated to him'.[76] At Winchester, the dean and two residentiaries engaged exclusively on cathedral duties 'shall be provided with suitable accommodation during the term of their appointment'; and other residentiaries are 'expected to live within a short distance of the Cathedral so as properly to fulfil their duties'.[77] Periods of residence are also prescribed. For example, at Worcester, the dean must reside in the house assigned

---

73 York: Stat. V.7: also, Chapter may pay the dean or a residentiary on retirement, or their personal representative on death, such sum as it thinks fit to assist with costs of removal and other expenses arising.
74 York: Stat. V.8.
75 Carlisle: Stat. 4(2) and 5(3).
76 Norwich: Stat. IV.7: dean; V.3: canon; see also V.6 and 8: the period of residence is determined by Chapter.
77 Winchester: Stat. 4: living accommodation.

for not less than 240 days in each year, but time spent in the service of Her Majesty, in attendance at or before any Royal or Statutory Commission, at meetings of Convocation or General Synod, or any of its Committees or Commissions, at Diocesan Synods or Conferences or on any duties approved by the bishop, 'shall be reckoned as part of such residence'. The same but separate provision is made for each residentiary.[78] However, Chapter may also, with the bishop's consent, grant 'special leave of absence' to a residentiary for 'theological study or other work for the Church at home or abroad' subject, as to residentiaries engaged exclusively on cathedral duties, to the discharge of those duties.[79]

Provision may also be made for costs associated with housing. Durham is typical: the dean and residentiaries occupy the allotted house free of rent; the cost of repairs and decoration is met from the cathedral revenues as Chapter may determine; and, unusually: 'All Cathedral property contained in the residences of the Dean and Residentiary Canons or elsewhere in the Precinct shall be itemised on lists prepared and deposited with the Chapter Clerk' who is to check them every seven years or as Chapter may direct.[80] Similarly, at Canterbury: 'The Deanery and the canonical houses are vested in the Body Corporate and the cost of structural repairs, annual outgoings of a statutory and recurring nature and maintenance and insurance are to be paid' by Chapter; moreover:

> Every Residentiary ... shall occupy the house assigned to him by the Chapter, with the gardens, garage and other appurtenances; and so long as he remains a Residentiary Canon he must occupy it, unless the Chapter and the Archbishop agree otherwise.

Further, no alteration of the deanery or canonical house, etc., may be made during a vacancy in the office of dean/canonry without the consent of the Archbishop and Chapter.[81] Much the same provisions are found in the statutes of Henrician foundations.[82]

---

78 Worcester: Stat. 2.10.
79 Worcester: Stat. 10.4.
80 Durham: Stat. IX.4; see also Stat. X: visitation of the cathedral lands. Compare Ely: Stat. 3(3): the dean must occupy the house appropriated by Chapter to the office (unless the bishop grants leave to live elsewhere) and may not sub-let or use the house or any part of it for business purposes except with Chapter's written authority.
81 Canterbury: Stat. XXVIII.
82 E.g. Chester: Stat. 2(vii) and 3(iii); Peterborough: Stat. 3(4): the Deanery must not be 'exchanged for another house' without the consent of Chapter; Stat. 5(3): residentiaries; Gloucester: Stat. 3: each residentiary must take periods of 'close residence' as determined by Chapter, and reside in property owned by Chapter unless the bishop with Chapter's consent decides otherwise; also: 'the Canon-in-Residence shall attend all services and represent Chapter at events in the Cathedral or find a deputy when unable to be present'.

Parish church cathedrals generally have less detailed norms.[83] However, at Manchester the dean must be in residence except for 100 days in each year and 'shall reside in the Deanery'; however, the dean may be absent to attend meetings of Convocation or General Synod, 'any provincial or diocesan council', or 'any royal or statutory commission' or any commission or committee of the General Synod. The bishop may, 'for reasons which seem to him good and sufficient, grant the dean a licence of non-residence for such period ... as to the bishop seems fit'. Each residentiary must likewise be in residence except for 100 days in each year and reside in the house allocated or failing such house in a house which may be approved by Chapter. The bishop may grant a licence of non-residence on the same terms as those applicable to the dean.[84] Newcastle's residentiaries must be in residence for at least nine months a year; absence is permitted, interestingly, 'for any purpose in connection with the work of the Church or the State undertaken without objection from the Visitor or the Chapter', or under licence granted by the Visitor with the approval of Chapter.[85] And Derby's residentiaries must reside 'within the City of Derby or within five miles of the Cathedral ... either in any house or residence as may be provided for him or, with the approval of the Bishop, in a house of his choosing'.[86]

Few parish church cathedrals make statutory provision to house other cathedral personnel. Chelmsford is unusual:

> Where the Dean, Residentiary Canons and any other Cathedral clergy, the Director of Music and Vergers are provided with a house of residence: any council tax, water charges and the cost of structural repair, external decoration and insurance relating thereto shall be paid from Cathedral funds; the cost of interior decoration may be met from Cathedral funds if the Chapter so determine.

Also, where any canon is not provided with a house, he may be paid such annual allowance in addition to his stipend as must be agreed by Chapter after considering the circumstances of each case.[87] And non-parish church cathedral Guildford provides: 'Chapter may allocate any house vested in the corporate body for the use of any person holding an office in connection with the Cathedral as a residence from which to perform the duties of that office'; in turn: 'The Dean shall reside in the Deanery' and the 'Residentiary Canons shall reside in The Close, unless permitted otherwise by the Chapter'.[88]

---

83 E.g. Southwell: Stat. 3.4: 'The Dean and the Residentiary Canons shall consult annually to determine the periods of residence for the ensuing year'; Coventry: Stat. 3.4: 'Each Residentiary Canon for whom a house is provided shall live in it'; Leicester: Stat. 3(4): each residentiary must 'live in the house provided'.
84 Manchester: Stat. II.4–6: dean; III.1: residentiaries; the reasons and the period must be stated in the licence.
85 Newcastle: Stat. 7.3: licensed absence counts as residence.
86 Derby: Stat. 3.4: licensed absence counts as residence.
87 Chelmsford: Stat. 19.
88 Guildford: Stat. VI.3: allocation; II.5: dean; II.7: residentiaries. For the same rules, see Truro: Stat. II.8, V.2.

The cathedral interviews

These disclose a variety of practices and views around norms on houses. For example: at Exeter three of the four residentiaries live in the close.[89] The Winchester statutes are very brief on housing for clergy (Stat. 4), and they do not address such matters as who pays for heating etc. – the reason for the absence of norms on this was not known but such absence is considered flexible and desirable when it comes to meeting changing HMRC requirements.[90] Whilst at Chester the dean and residentiaries must reside in the house allotted by Chapter (Stat. 2(vii) and 3(iii)), the statutes are silent on the care of canonical houses. However, there would be 'value' in making norms 'to make it clear that clergy have a tenancy-like agreement with mutual expectations from the tenant and of the [cathedral as] landlord'. As is the case with commercial and residential tenants in the precinct and elsewhere, clergy housing should be dealt with under the domestic law of the cathedral or ideally under common tenure.[91]

Cathedral security

Security has been a persistent theme in the history of cathedrals – and the precincts of many are still bounded by fortified walls and gates. It is also an issue today; for example, Peter Tatchell was convicted and fined under the Ecclesiastical Courts Jurisdiction Act 1860 for disturbing a service at Canterbury Cathedral (1998); and recent high profile incidents related to cathedral security include: the Occupy London protests outside St Paul's (2012); the use of guards carrying guns at Canterbury at Christmas after terrorist attacks in Berlin (2016); and fathers' rights protesters at St Paul's (2016).[92] As we have seen, one function of the verger is to care for the security of the cathedral (see Chapter 4), and at Liverpool, there are Cathedral Constables, York Minister has the Minster Police, and at Canterbury, Hereford, Chester, and Salisbury there are Close Constables. There is also a Cathedral Constables Association.

The Cathedral Constables Association

The aim of the Association is to promote the safeguarding of cathedrals through raising the professional profile of the Cathedral Constables and Yard Beadles employed by them.[93] Its objectives are to: (1) promote the role of the Cathedral Constable and Yard Beadle regardless of age, ethnic origin, ability, sex, belief or political affiliation; (2) work with members through the Association Leaders Council to identify training and development opportunities; (3) promote and

---

89 Exeter: Dean: Int. 9–8-2016.
90 Winchester: Dean: Int. 16–8-2016.
91 Chester: Vice-Dean: Int. 19–8-2016.
92 For a history of the subject, see J. Hobson, *Cathedral Bobbies* (Mirfield: Mirfield Publications, 3rd ed., 2015).
93 CCA: Con. Art. 2; see also Art. 1: Name.

share best practice through the Leaders Council, providing mutual support and where appropriate resources for a professional, highly regarded and cost-effective service to cathedrals; (4) develop and promote co-operation between the Association and statutory and non-statutory agencies; (5) raise funds and receive contributions where appropriate to finance its work; (6) publicise and promote its work and that of its member cathedrals; and (7) organise meetings, training courses and events, and work with similar groups for the exchange of information and advice so as to develop and improve the security of cathedrals.[94]

Membership is open to any cathedral which employs designated security teams, is interested in helping the Association to achieve its aim, and is willing to abide by the rules of the Association. Every member cathedral through the Leaders Council has one vote at general meetings. The Council may refuse membership to an applicant, where it is considered such membership would be detrimental to the aims, purposes, or activities of the Association. Any member cathedral may resign membership and any representative of a member organisation may resign by giving written notice to the Chief Officer. The Council may, by resolution passed at a meeting, terminate or suspend membership, if in its opinion the conduct of the member is prejudicial to the interests and objects of the Association. However, the individual member or representative of the member cathedral (as the case may be) has the right to be heard by the Council before the final decision is made. There is also a right of appeal to an independent arbitrator who is to be appointed by mutual agreement between the parties.[95]

The Association is controlled by the Leaders Council, which is made up of Head Constables, Chief Beadle, Chief Officer, and Honorary President. The Council must elect a Chief Officer as chief executive to manage day-to-day arrangements and to serve for an initial term of three years which may be extended. The Council must also elect an Honorary President to act as the figurehead of the Association for a term of three years which Council may extend for an additional three years. Council must meet at least twice each year. Quorum is four members. A Head Constable or Chief Beadle unable to attend may send a deputy who will have a proxy vote. Voting at Council is by show of hands on a majority basis; the Honorary President has a casting vote. The Council may set up subgroups and working parties as necessary and these are accountable to Council; its Management Committee meets at least twice yearly.[96]

The Association must hold an Annual General Meeting. Where possible members must be notified personally, otherwise notice will be deemed served by advertising the meetings in at least five public places giving at least 14 days' notice of the meeting. The business of the meeting must include: receiving a report from the Chief Officer of the activities over the previous period; receiving a report and

94 CCA: Con. Art.3.
95 CCA: Con. Art. 4.
96 CCA: Con. Art. 5; Art. 6: finance; Art. 7: the Council is accountable to the members at all times; all meeting decisions must be recorded and available to any interested party; all Council members must be given at least 14 days' notice of a meeting unless it is deemed an emergency meeting.

presentation of the financial year's accounts on the finances of the group; electing a new Chief Officer and Honorary President; and considering any other matter as may be appropriate. The quorum is at least five Council members.[97] A faithful service medal may be issued to officers for ten years of good service and conduct.[98]

Proposals to amend the constitution, or to dissolve the Association, must be delivered to the Chief Officer in writing. The Chief Officer with all other Leader Council members must then decide on the date of a forum meeting to discuss the proposals with at least twenty-eight days' notice. Any changes to the constitution must be agreed by at least two thirds of the members present and voting at any general meeting.[99] The Association may be wound up at any time if agreed by two thirds of the members present and voting at a general meeting. Assets must be returned to their providers, if they require it, or passed to another group with similar aims.[100]

The role of cathedral constables

The Association has issued a Manual to support Cathedral Constable Foundation Training. Minimum training for an attested constable is completion of the Initial Training for Special Constables. In addition to the training provided by the Association, further training may be available at a cathedral in, for instance, health and safety matters, lost and found property procedures, safeguarding, anti-terrorism, first aid, conflict management and self-defence.[101]

The cathedral constable is to maintain law and order, protect members of the public and their property and prevent, detect and investigate crime, serving as an integral part of the cathedral community in, around, and for that community, with responsibility for the safeguarding of the cathedral, its treasures, communities, and visitors. Each must be attested (sworn in) by a Justice of the Peace after being appointed as constable by the cathedral 'under common law' to exercise functions in the curtilage of the cathedral and not beyond.[102] Under the Attested Constable Code of Conduct, they must: be courteous and polite to all members of the public, staff, and visitors, and act impartially and professionally;[103] be prompt and

---

97 CCA: Con. Art. 9: the AGM must be held at not more than 36 monthly intervals.
98 CCA: Con. Art. 10: a commendation may be issued at any stage of an officer's service for a particular meritorious act; approval must be obtained from Council and agreement sought if appropriate from the officer's cathedral for a joint award; it is in the form of a framed citation and a medal ribbon with a bronze oak leaf.
99 CCA: Con. Art. 11.
100 CCA: Con. Art. 12; see also Art. 13: the constitution was adopted at the AGM held on 24 October 2013.
101 Cathedral Constables Association: Cathedral Constable Foundation Manual (undated) (CCA: CCFM).
102 CCA: CCFM, Introduction: the constable is to uphold 'the rule of law' and 'The Queen's Peace'.
103 CCA: CCFM, Attested Constable Code of Conduct (hereafter Code), 1.1: they must 'treat others as [they] would like to be treated'; respect, equality and diversity are paramount.

punctual at all assignments;[104] undertake all lawful orders and assignment instructions promptly, inform their relief of new orders or instructions given during the tour of duty, deal with outstanding entries in the incident log or pass them to the relief shift before going off duty, and comply with any Cathedral Operating Policies and Procedures.[105] They must also remain alert at all times; cooperate with colleagues and management; and safeguard the public image of the cathedral, preserve positive relationships with its visitors, congregation, volunteers, and clients, and ensure they do not behave in a discriminatory manner. They must not: conduct outside business of any kind at the assignment location; accept gifts or gratuities whilst on duty;[106] leave the precincts without obtaining permission;[107] knowingly associate or have dealings with any person or organisation advocating or fostering hatred or prejudice against any racial, ethnic, or religious group, or anyone engaged in unlawful activities; or consume on duty, or commence duties, if unfit to do so due to the consumption of alcohol or drugs.[108] Constables must only wear items of uniform as prescribed by the cathedral and as designated by the Head Constable; the full uniform of the day must be worn at all times unless a special dispensation has been given.[109] There are also norms on uniforms for special occasions.[110]

Any act, or omission, by which a constable brings discredit to the good order of the cathedral, may result in disciplinary action.[111] If a complaint is received by a constable, either in respect of himself, or a colleague, the officer should inform the complainant to contact the Head Constable who will discuss the complaint with the complainant and seek to resolve the matter informally. If the complaint is serious or cannot be resolved informally, the Head Constable will, with the support of the cathedral human resources manager, formally investigate the complaint using the procedure in the grievance procedure of the cathedral.[112]

The use of constable powers should be minimal and generally they should be exercised as a last resort; the 'normal practice' should be to manage a situation without recourse to them. However, where it is clear an incident cannot be safely

104 CCA: CCFM, Code 1.2: if unable to report for duty at the scheduled time, they must ensure the Head Constable or Supervisor is informed before duty; they must not leave their assigned post until properly relieved.
105 CCA: CCFM, Code 1.3.
106 The donor is invited to take the gift to the welcome desk; exceptions include e.g. sweets at Christmas.
107 CCA: CCFM, Code 1.4.
108 CCA: CCFM, Code 1.9: except prescribed drugs for any medical condition if these do not impair the performance of duties. Alcohol may be consumed if authorised by the cathedral.
109 CCA: CCFM, Code 1.6: the uniform must be neatly pressed and all accoutrements correctly displayed; the appropriate patrol jacket for the season must be worn displaying the constable's number; NATO style pullovers must be worn in cold or inclement weather; a constable should not walk or stand around with hands in pockets.
110 CCA: CCFM, Code 1.6: the tunic consists of jacket, whistle and chain; medals, if issued, may be worn. See also 1.7: personal protection equipment.
111 CCA: CCFM, Code 1.3.
112 CCA: CCFM, Code 1.5.

managed without using these powers, the constable should first inform the individual(s) that he holds the office of constable and has a power of arrest: 'Any abuse of the use of [any] constable powers will result in disciplinary action'. The constable's 'jurisdiction is limited to the cathedral and its precinct and cannot be used beyond this'. If a constable is asked to perform duties at another cathedral which attests constables, the use of such powers is limited to the curtilage of that cathedral; and such a constable must follow the instructions of the incumbent head constable and work within the policies and procedures of the Dean and Chapter of the host cathedral.[113]

Security under cathedral constitutions, statutes, and policies

Security is commonly dealt with at cathedrals by their own domestic policy documents, often in the context of norms on health and safety at the cathedral.[114] Those cathedrals which have constables also deal with the subject by means of basic norms in their constitutions and/or statutes. For example, Salisbury Chapter must appoint 'suitably qualified persons for the duties of Head Verger, Close Constable, Vergers and Constables'; their terms of employment and 'duties and authority in the Cathedral or in the Precinct' are as Chapter determines;[115] and York Chapter must appoint as many 'Minster Police as may ... seem necessary' on terms determined by Chapter; and: 'The Minister Police shall be concerned with the security of the Cathedral Church and shall carry out such necessary duties as the Chapter may determine'.[116]

Liverpool Cathedral has a handbook which echoes but also goes beyond the Manual of the Cathedral Constables Association.[117] For example, there are norms on security in relation to: buildings and their contents; personal property (staff and visitors); personal attack and threats of violence; car parking and vehicles; alarm systems (shop, tower, refectory, and workshop); incident reporting; keys (no keys, except personal drawers/filing cabinets, should leave the precinct); identity cards (all staff should wear one at all times); information technology; terrorist attacks; searching persons and vehicles (with consent); investigating allegations of fraud and bribery; lost property; handling cash (from e.g. weekly takings, donations, services, lectures, concerts, and other events, pay on entry and car parking); the

---

113 CCA: CCFM, Code 1.8: this provides guidance on the powers of arrest, issuing cautions, stop and search, and use of force, as to a wide range of crimes e.g. theft; making off without payment; assault; public order; violent disorder; intentional harassment, alarm or distress; breach of the peace; and drink or drug related crimes.
114 See e.g. Exeter: Staff Handbook (2015), Section 9: Health and Safety, 42: General Security.
115 Salisbury: Stat. 12.1.
116 York: Stat. XVII.
117 Liverpool: Liverpool Cathedral Constables' Handbook: The Cathedral and Precincts (2015): the handbook 'is the policy of the Dean and Chapter of Liverpool Cathedral' and constables are 'expected to work in accordance with it'; constables must also familiarise themselves with the additional policies and procedures in the Staff Handbook. It has separate policies on e.g. Health and Safety.

use of closed circuit television; and cathedral evacuation (in the event of fire, bomb, and terrorist threats).[118]

There is also guidance on disturbances.[119] In addition to civilian powers, cathedral constables may arrest or detain any person who commits an offence under the Ecclesiastical Courts Jurisdiction Act 1860 and associated legislation (for which see above Chapter 4),[120] and use reasonable force in so doing.[121] Whilst the cathedral doors are open for worship at all services and may not be locked or closed during services because of health and safety and evacuation considerations, in the event of a disturbance, constables, stewards and other staff/volunteers are not to attempt to restrain any demonstrators physically; this can aggravate a situation and risk injury to the staff/volunteers. Constables or stewards who sense that a disturbance or demonstration may be about to occur should immediately inform the vergers and through them the clergy.[122] The dean/senior cleric present will take immediate control, ask the congregation to sit, and invite the demonstrators to make a statement and either leave or join in the worship without further disruption. One verger must go immediately to the telephone to 'stand by', and another will remain at the public address system control desk.[123]

If demonstrators engage in criminal activity it is proper and lawful to use 'reasonable force' to restrain them and eject them from the building and precinct; this should be done by the cathedral constables (who may also arrest) but only as a last resort. If demonstrators refuse to cease their disturbance or proceed to attack anyone, the constables will call the police without further instruction from clergy (as this may be provocative). If there is any concern for the choristers' welfare, the organist may take them by the most discreet route to the education suite and then undercroft. Moreover, senior clergy should consider: having a short period of silence; inviting reflection on the vehemence and frustration which cause people to act in such a manner; praying for those who demonstrated and for those about whom they have demonstrated; and inviting the congregation to re-commence the service at the point prior to the disturbance (e.g. back to the last hymn and start again). The organ should not be played to drown out disturbances – and hymns should not be sung as a counter-demonstration.[124]

---

118 Ibid. ss. 5–12: which staff are responsible depends on the timing; the handbook refers to e.g. the Bribery Act 2010, Data Protection Act 1998, and Human Rights Act 1998, and Serious Crimes and Police Act 2005.
119 The handbook refers to the Serious Crimes and Police Act 2005; any citizen, including a cathedral constable, may arrest without a warrant if a suspect has committed or is committing an indictable offence.
120 Liverpool: Handbook, s. 8.3.
121 Liverpool: Handbook, s. 8.5: 'at Common Law' there is a right of self-defence 'if attacked using reasonable force'; any force used to prevent a crime or for an arrest must comply with Criminal Law Act 1967, s. 3(2).
122 Cards with 'Demonstration Procedure' will be placed at all times in the vestry and clergy stalls.
123 If e.g. the bishop is celebrant, it is for the dean or a canon to take control.
124 Liverpool: Handbook s. 8.6: the police are notified of all visits by the Archbishop and other notables; on such occasions, there will be a police officer in the congregation,

250 *The cathedral close*

The cathedral interviews

These reveal common practices. The Dean of Salisbury explains that currently the office of constable (under Statute 12) is vacant, but the cathedral contracts out security (and it employs car-park attendants); in practice, the vergers are responsible for security within the cathedral building (but the cathedral statutes do not expressly provide for this).[125] At Winchester, where the Inner Close is shut at night, the vergers are responsible for security, but the cathedral employs a security service during the summer and for special events.[126] And at Chester, under its statutes, the vergers are appointed by Chapter 'to uphold the dignity of worship in the Cathedral, to ensure good order and to welcome all who enter it' (Stat. 15); in practice, the maintenance of security is included in the 'job description' of each verger; the cathedral has also recently appointed a 'cathedral constable' who has the power of arrest.[127]

Conclusion

National law provides for the process of designating the precinct of a cathedral church and the process by which a precinct boundary may be amended: Chapter prepares the plan and the Cathedrals Fabric Commission effects the designation. The precinct consists of so much of that land as, in the opinion of the Commission, is necessary to preserve or protect the cathedral and its surrounding area. National law also provides for the operation of statutory controls over the precinct, particularly on works to buildings in the precinct and in relation to archaeological and human remains there; a large volume of national guidance exists on these matters, and the interviews highlight the important role of the cathedral archaeologist in this regard. The Association of Diocesan and Cathedral Archaeologists promotes professional standards. Cathedral constitutions and/or statutes sometimes define the precinct and make provision for the pastoral care of its residents; but normative coverage of this is inconsistent.

National law regulates the allocation by Chapter of houses for those who hold offices in connection with the cathedral, and the Church Commissioners hold funds for the better provision of housing for cathedral clergy. Chapter cannot dispose of such houses without the consent of the Church Commissioners and their clerical occupants. However, cathedral statutes are the primary means used to regulate housing for cathedral clergy. These deal with the periods of residence required of the dean and residentiaries, relaxation of the requirement (usually by

---

who may only act within the church at the request of the dean and Chapter member. If there is advance warning of any demonstration, the police will be notified and all staff and stewards briefed before the service. If staff or volunteers hear of plans or become suspicious of people planning a disturbance, they should contact the dean or sub-dean directly and immediately.
125 Salisbury: Dean: Int. 20-9-2016.
126 Winchester: Acting Dean: Int. 16-8-2016.
127 Chester: Vice-Dean: Int. 19-8-2016.

the bishop), and provision for and the maintenance of houses. Generally, the financial costs associated with their upkeep are met from cathedral revenues as determined by Chapter. Some cathedrals have norms on housing other cathedral dignitaries and officers. The interviews disclose some concerns about the absence of norms requiring such houses to be kept in a tenant-like manner; they also indicate that precincts may be used commercially.

Cathedral security has recently become the object of very detailed national guidance from the Cathedral Constables Association. Cathedrals too produce policies on cathedral security, including what to do in the event of disturbances and demonstrations. However, the statutes of few cathedrals expressly provide for the appointment and functions of cathedral or close constables. Rather, security is assigned by statute to vergers. The interviews also reveal the growing practice of cathedrals contracting out cathedral security to external service providers.

Conclusion

The cathedral as a normative space: conception and experience

Over the centuries, many images of a cathedral have been developed. A persistent image has been that of a cathedral as 'theology in stone'. This finds an echo conceptually in church law which too is often understood as 'theology in action', or applied theology: the translation of theology into norms of conduct. Theology articulates Christian belief (the primary stimulus for law), it proposes values (the primary source of law), it contemplates action (the primary focus of law), and it animates these values in norms of conduct (the primary character of law).[1] Theology stimulated the design of medieval English cathedrals: as representations of heaven on earth; sacred spaces with spiritual-symbolical importance attached to their various architectural features (like the font, altar, presbytery, and nave);[2] and as cruciform in ground-plan perhaps symbolising the cross of Christ in adaptation of early Roman basilica churches.[3]

These physical features, themselves products of theology translated into architectural norms used to shape cathedral design,[4] accommodated ecclesial activities which, in turn, became the subject of legal regulation in medieval England. As seat of the bishop, for both secular and monastic foundations, rules developed on the functions of clergy (such as deans, canons and chapters), cathedral worship and music, and the property of the cathedral. The Reformation of the sixteenth century changed cathedrals more in terms of status than substance: the secular old foundations and the secularised re-foundations and Henrician new foundations were creatures of law, each with their statutes and customs. Until the twentieth century, there was little radical reform of cathedral law: the legal categories developed before and at the Reformation continued to mould the conduct of cathedral governance and life. This legal continuity continues today to be valued

---

1 N. Doe, *Christian Law: Contemporary Principles* (Cambridge: Cambridge University Press, 2013) 29–41.
2 See e.g. N. Temple, J.S. Hendrix, C. Frost (eds.), *Bishop Grosseteste and Lincoln Cathedral: Tracing Relationships between Medieval Concepts of Order and Built Form* (Aldershot: Ashgate, 2014).
3 H&R 188–189.
4 See e.g. E.D. Hehl, 'The legal organisation of church construction, especially cathedral construction, in the Middle Ages', 24 *Philosophy and History* (1991) 108.

by cathedrals whose constitutional preambles often present their historical legal antecedents; this is also important for the identity of a cathedral.

It was not until the Archbishops' Commission on Cathedrals in 1994 that a comprehensive review was undertaken of the purposes, practices and laws applicable to English cathedrals. This Commission – more than any other – proposed radical changes for cathedral governance and management. Its recommendations of good practice are today found time and time again in the constitutions, statutes and policy documents of cathedrals. They have been influential with regard, for example, to the adoption by cathedrals of clear vision statements about their purposes, provision for their employees, volunteers and visitors, the ministry of preaching, outreach and civic engagement, and the promotion of the educational and associated work of cathedrals. Equally important, the Commission made recommendations designed to reform national cathedral law: this led directly to the enactment of new legislation by General Synod.

The Cathedrals Measure 1999, building on earlier legislation, was enacted 'to make further provision with respect to the constitution, statutes and administration of cathedrals'. Its requirement for each cathedral to have a Council, Chapter, and College of Canons (the body corporate) fosters a system of structured governance, of mutual accountability, and of defined responsibilities within a cathedral. Its treatment of the domestic constitution and statutes of each cathedral has also acted as a unifying force in the creation, content and consistency of cathedral constitutions and statutes, requiring these, as it does, to have norms on a range of matters critical to the efficient administration of the cathedral. The Measure also protects the autonomy of a cathedral, subject to oversight by the bishop as visitor, its service to the wider diocese as a centre of worship and mission, and its responsibility through the corporate body to review and amend its own constitution and statutes in order to meet local circumstances.

The constitutions and statutes of English cathedrals are the primary vehicles which are used to implement the strategic vision lying behind the Measure and to regulate cathedral life on a day-to-day basis. Examination of these demonstrates widespread compliance with the terms of the Measure. However, where national law confers discretion on a cathedral to legislate freely, or when national law is silent on a matter, cathedral constitutions and statutes exhibit profound differences in their substantive rules. Sometimes, here, the differences are related to the cathedral types: for example, cathedrals of the old and new foundations have norms on the cathedral close, library or school, but parish church cathedrals may not; or else, parish church cathedrals by virtue of their additional parochial status have more developed norms on the rites of passage, baptism, marriage, and funerals at the cathedral. In point of fact, most juridical diversity is in the form of difference in the topics addressed, the breadth or coverage of these topics, or the depth at which they are regulated – that is, in the details of the rules. Further research is needed on the reasons for this, for instance whether some differences are a product of the historical ministry of the cathedral in its particular area or its own traditions. This is especially so as constitutions and statutes do not present reasons for their own norms.

Nevertheless, in spite of legal differences, it is still possible to articulate principles of law induced from the similarities of cathedral constitutions and statutes (principles which are not found in national law). For example, it is a principle of law that: cathedrals should engage with local civic and educational institutions; the dean and residentiaries must on appointment take the customary oaths; they must also reside at the cathedral but may be absent in the service of the church if the bishop permits this; Chapter or College must be convened on the requisition of a prescribed number of members; cathedral officers (such as the administrator) are engaged on such terms in respect of tenure, remuneration, and functions as are determined by Chapter; the director of music should heed the advice of the precentor; the library is in the keeping of Chapter; a cathedral should engage in educational work to promote Christian faith.

The cathedral interviews reveal the jurisprudence which underlies cathedral law not only in terms of the wisdom of its legislators (national and cathedral) but also how the law is both perceived and experienced in practice. National law and constitutions and statutes are valued by cathedral clergy as important to facilitate and order the mission or ministry of a cathedral. Cathedrals also give new life to the ancient category of cathedral custom: each cathedral has developed its own practices alongside or within the interstices of the formal law; and commonly these practices – such as those roles of cathedral staff which are not defined in the constitution or statutes, or making decisions in Chapter on the basis of consensus, and the non-use of casting votes – are understood by cathedral clergy as the 'custom' of the cathedral. There is also general satisfaction with a host of legal norms studied in the course of this book.

However, the interviews also disclose areas of concern. These include: (1) whether policies should be put on the footing of by-laws; (2) the freedom of the College of Canons in episcopal elections; (3) the lack of norms about how a visitation is to be conducted; (4) whether rules on the cathedral community, roll and committee work well, and the usefulness of the parish electoral roll in parish church cathedrals; (5) the propriety of arrangements for ministerial development review of cathedral clergy; (6) the persons for whom deans and residentiaries have a cure of souls; (7) the perceptions of Councils about their powers to intervene in the business of Chapter; (8) the value of the College of Canons and the bishop's role in it; (9) the relationship between a cathedral and its school; and (10) how requirements as to approval for work to property tend to bureaucracy. Further research should be carried out into people's experiences as to how the law enables or frustrates cathedral ministry in areas such as these.

A notable innovation in the regulatory life of cathedrals in recent years has been the dramatic increase in the volume of national or local cathedral quasi-legislation, or soft law, in the form of guidelines, policy documents, or codes of practice. This exists today in relation to a wide range of issues. At national level, a great deal of quasi-legislation has been issued by, for instance, the Cathedrals Fabric Commission for England (in pursuance of functions allocated to it by the Care of Cathedrals Measure 2011) on works to the cathedral fabric, objects, and precinct buildings. The Church of England has issued a raft of documents for the better protection and safeguarding of children and vulnerable persons. The Association of English Cathedrals has issued guidance on for example the welfare of choristers; and other Associations too are active in the production of guidance, such as the Cathedral Libraries and Archives Association. Some of these national guidelines are echoed in cathedral statutes – such as those on the respective roles of precentors, directors of music and others responsible for cathedral music. The cathedrals themselves also produce policy documents, such as on admission to the sacraments, health and safety, volunteers, employment matters, or cathedral security. Sometimes such instruments are declaratory of national guidance, or they add to it. Unlike cathedral constitutions and statutes, quasi-legislation gives reasons for its own norms.

This raises socio-legal questions about the extent to which cathedrals today are influenced by developments in secular society and civil law. There is evidence that cathedrals accept and often incorporate in their regulatory instruments secular standards such as: consultation, particularly in matters of clerical appointments (usually consultation with the bishop or if appointments are made by the bishop with the dean and/or Chapter); giving reasons for decisions (such as a refusal by the Fabric Advisory Committee to approve proposals for works); the professionalisation of cathedral management (including the training of staff and volunteers, the use of job descriptions for staff, and the proliferation of the number of Associations for cathedral staff to promote standards); the application of equality standards in the choral activities of a cathedral; and the use of secular budget and accounting standards. These may suggest such themes in the sociology of religion as the 'internal secularisation' of cathedrals, their: attachment to social institutions e.g. tourism; pluralisation, e.g. as market-places for consumer commodities; bureaucratisation, e.g. professionalism; moderation, e.g. watering down their historical functions; and adaptation (to social change). Further research is needed to determine precisely the relationship between sociology and cathedral law.

The relation between church architecture and liturgy is well-known.[5] The word 'architecture' (Latin *architectura*) comes from the Greek word for 'architect' (ἀρχιτέκτων, or arkhitekton), which in turn is from 'chief' (ἀρχι) and 'builder' (τέκτων); today architecture is understood as the process and the product of planning, designing, and constructing buildings and other structures. Liturgy too is normative: it consists of prescribed ceremonies (actions) and rites (words); and it shapes church architecture, and *vice versa*. It is commonly understood that a cathedral building (and its internal geography) strongly influences the way in which liturgy is conducted: the spaces of a cathedral, its 'rooms', relate to one another physically and liturgically; there is a relationship between key liturgical furnishings, like the altar and font; visitor or pilgrim routes are shaped by the liturgical use of the cathedral; and liturgical ordering must be appropriate to the spaces it occupies and the purposes for which it is used.[6]

---

5 See e.g. N. Yates, *Buildings, Faith and Worship: The Liturgical Arrangement of Anglican Churches 1600–1900* (Oxford: Oxford University Press, 2001).
6 See e.g. CFCE: Guidance Note: A Liturgical Plan for Cathedrals (2013): see above Chapter 3.

The relationship between cathedral architecture and cathedral law is also significant, but somewhat elusive. Both are normative: both enable, direct and restrict the use of space. Importantly, the constitution and more often the statutes identify cathedral features/locations for required or permitted actions. For example: the diocesan bishop should be enthroned in the episcopal seat; baptisms must be administered at the font which (by canon law) must be near the principal entrance; a dean is instituted by the bishop and admitted and installed by Chapter in the quire; the stalls of residentiaries and other canons are often prescribed (and sometimes the law prescribes their location); morning prayer is conducted in a chapel and choral evensong in the quire; Chapter meetings must (sometimes) occur in designated rooms; there must be (in many cathedrals) a cathedral library; and the precinct exists to protect the character/setting of the cathedral. The law also often defines architectural features. Whether it is theology, law, the building, pure practicality, or combinations of these, which require(s) the use of these features is difficult to ascertain. It is also difficult to establish whether legal norms shape or are shaped by cathedral architecture (or both). Certainly, cathedral elements have legal significance or required/restricted use (such as the entrance for legal notices, the font for baptisms, the pulpit for preaching, and so on). It may indeed be that a cathedral is normative, with its various segmented spaces, its private spaces within (basically) a public building, and its architecture itself eliciting or directing the conduct of its users. As a cathedral is imagined as 'theology in stone', so it might be worth exploring the cathedral as a form of 'juristecture' – the cathedral as a 'builder of law', a 'law-building', or 'built law'.

Indeed, the cathedral interviews reveal a range of such ideas about the cathedral building as itself normative. At Wells the opinion was given that any 'church building does not describe our understanding of God; it *is* our understanding of God'.[7] For the Dean of St Paul's, there is 'an analogy between the building and law: the setting has influence'; 'the building itself constrains not just in terms of community but also individuality' – 'the more space, the more the sense of liberation and flexibility'; and 'the building, like law, provides boundaries to action' and 'is influenced by context, space and time'.[8] The Dean of Worcester, similarly, explains that: 'Like law, the building preserves the cathedral memory'; it both 'shapes and reflects customs' – 'what we do is shaped by the building'; that 'the nave is not chaired' (except for events) means the area is 'a permissive space'.[9] The Acting Dean of Winchester considers that: 'The building heavily shapes how we worship, but innovation is possible': historically, the nave is a 'processional space, not a gathering space'; but since the 1960s Sunday morning worship has been conducted there; this has led to 'a tradition'.[10] The Dean of Bristol also agreed that while a cathedral is 'a product of theological vision', there is too 'a fundamental connection' between what is done there and the building itself.[11] In

7 Wells: Acting Dean: Int. 12–8-2016.
8 London: Dean: Int. 23–9-2016.
9 Worcester: Dean: Int. 28–7-2016.
10 Winchester: Acting Dean: Int. 16–8-2016.
11 Bristol: Dean: Int. 3–8-2016.

similar vein, according to the Canon Precentor of Rochester: the cathedral 'is not a morally neutral space', but rather one which 'unites and asks questions' of those who live, work and visit there.[12]

History, reform proposals, national law, cathedral constitutions and statutes, and practical experiences, each, articulate the legal architecture of English cathedrals: their juristecture.[13]

---

12 Rochester: Precentor: Int. 30–9-2016; he develops these ideas in N. Thompson, 'Rochester Cathedral: a window onto eternity' (unpublished paper, January 2016).
13 H&R 199: in 1934, Giovanni Battista Montini, the future Pope Paul VI, wrote after visiting nine cathedrals of the Church of England: 'They are monuments on a vast scale, very well preserved, rather austere, with huge fantastic spaces, full of history, mystery and piety, veritable ships of the spirit where matter has not only a use but a meaning', and 'where glorious and sorrowful memories of the past are brought into living contact with the present'. To this we might add, as did lawyers in the centuries following the Reformation, that a cathedral, in which the Consistory Court was often held, was a 'place of judicature'; see e.g. A. Tarver, *Church Court Records* (Chichester: Phillimore and Co. Ltd., 1995) 8: Lichfield Consistory Court, Citation, 1734, for Thomas Fox to appear 'in the Cathedral Church of Lichfield and place of judicature there.' A splendid Consistory Court survives at Chester Cathedral.

Bibliography

Primary sources

Archbishops' Commission on Cathedrals: Report, *Heritage and Renewal* (1994)
Archbishops' Consultants on Interfaith Relations: *Interfaith Services and Worship* (1980)
Association of Cathedral Clerk of the Works: *Guide: An Introduction to the Role* (2012)
Association of Diocesan and Cathedral Archaeologists: *Constitution* (2000); *Guidance Note 1: Archaeological Requirements for Works on Churches and Churchyards* (2004); *Guidance Note 2: Archaeology and Burial Vaults* (2010); and *Guidance Note 3: Dealing with Architectural Fragments* (2010)
Association of English Cathedrals: *Dean: Responsibilities of the Role* (2013); *Pastoral Care of Choristers* (2014); *Executive Note on Cathedral Councils* (2016)
Birmingham Cathedral: *Constitution and Statutes of the Cathedral Church of Saint Philip Birmingham* (2000, as amended)
Blackburn Cathedral: *Constitution and Statutes of the Cathedral Church of Saint Mary the Virgin Blackburn* (2000, as amended)
Bradford Cathedral: *Constitution and Statutes of the Cathedral Church of Saint Peter Bradford* (2000, as amended)
Bristol Cathedral: *Constitution and Statutes of the Cathedral Church of the Holy and Undivided Trinity in Bristol* (2000, as amended)
Canons Ecclesiastical of the Church of England 1603/1604. Available at http://www.anglican.net/doctrines/1604-canon-law/
Canons Ecclesiastical of the Church of England 2017. Available at https://www.churchofengland.org/about-us/structure/churchlawlegis/canons/canons-7th-edition.aspx
Canterbury Cathedral: *Constitution and Statutes of the Cathedral and Metropolitical Church of Christ, Canterbury* (2002, as amended); *Policy of Child Protection; and Safeguarding Public Policy* (2016)
Care of Cathedrals Measure 2011. Available at http://www.legislation.gov.uk/ukcm/2011/1/pdfs/ukcm_20110001_en.pdf
Cathedral Constables Association: *Cathedral Constable Foundation Manual* (undated)
Cathedral Libraries and Archives Association: *Chapter and Verse: The Care of Cathedral Records*, Church of England Record Centre, Records Management Guide No. 4 (2013); 'Personal Files Relating to Clergy: Guidance for Bishops and Their Staff' (2013)
Cathedral Organists Association: *Rules and Constitution* (as amended 2012)
Cathedrals Administration and Finance Association: *Articles of Association* (2012); *Accounting and Reporting Regulations for English Anglican Cathedrals*, prepared by the

Cathedrals Administration and Finance Association with the Association of English Cathedrals (2015)

Cathedrals Fabric Commission for England: *Directions: The Form of the Inventory* (2001, due for revision); *Advisory Guidelines: The Form of an Inventory* (2001, due for revision); *The Role and Duties of the Cathedral Architect or Surveyor of the Fabric* (2008, due for revision); *The Roles and Duties of the Cathedral Archaeologist* (2010, due for revision); *Procedural Guidance Notes: PGN 1: The Care of Cathedrals Measure: A General Introduction and Context* (2012); *PGN 2: Proposals Requiring Approval and Making an Application* (2012); *PGN 3: Cathedral Precincts: Their Definition, Designation and Effect under the Care of Cathedrals Measure* (2008, due for revision); *PGN 4: Cathedral Inventories: Their Purpose, Scope and Compilation* (2001, due for revision); *PGN 5: Cathedral Inventories: Designation of Outstanding Items* (1996, due for revision); *PGN 6: The Cathedral Fabric Commission for England: Its Role and Function and Determining an Application: Procedures for the Commission* (2012); *PGN 7: Fabric Advisory Committees: Their Role and Function and Determining an Application: Procedures for Fabric Advisory Committees* (2012); *PGN 8: The Care of Cathedrals Measure and the Public Interest: The Role of Planning Authorities, English Heritage, the National Amenity Societies and the Public* (2012); *PGN 9: The Archaeological Assessment and Report for Cathedrals and their Precinct* (2009, due for revision); *PGN 11: Major New Developments at Cathedrals* (2008, due for revision); *Guidance Note: Cathedrals and Archaeology: A Guide to Good Management* (2012); *Policy and Practice Notes: Access Works in Cathedrals* (2012); *Lighting and Sound Equipment in Cathedrals* (2012); *Microgeneration in Cathedrals* (2012); *New Art in Cathedrals* (2012); *Loans of Objects for Cathedrals* (2015); and *Guidance Note: A Liturgical Plan for Cathedrals* (2013)

Cathedrals Liturgy and Music Group: *Disaster and Bereavement Liturgies*, Occasional Paper 13 (2003); *Producing a Cathedral Music Policy*, Occasional Paper (2006); *Music in English Cathedrals 2001–2011*, Occasional Paper (2012); *Suggested Guidelines for Appointing Directors of Music in Cathedrals* (2012); *Formation for Sacramental Liturgy and Music in Cathedrals*, Occasional Paper (2004)

Cathedrals Measure 1999. Available at http://www.legislation.gov.uk/ukcm/1999/1/pdfs/ukcm_19990001_en.pdf

Cathedrals Plus: A Network for Engagement with Visitors: *Volunteers – Standards Document* (2014); *Engaging Visitors in Places of Christian Worship: Standards for those Working with Young People in Education and Learning* (2014)

Carlisle Cathedral: *Constitution and Statutes of the Cathedral Church of the Holy and Undivided Trinity of Carlisle* (2001, as amended)

Chelmsford Cathedral: *Constitution and Statutes of the Cathedral Church of Saint Mary the Virgin, Saint Peter and Saint Cedd Chelmsford* (2000, as amended)

Chester Cathedral: *Constitution and Statutes of the Cathedral Church of Christ and the Blessed Virgin Mary in Chester* (2000, as amended)

Chichester Cathedral: *Constitution and Statutes of the Cathedral Church of the Holy Trinity in Chichester* (2000, as amended)

Church of England: *Child Protection Policy Statement of the Church of England – Promoting a Safe Church: Safeguarding Policy for Adults* (2006); *Protecting All God's Children: Policy for Safeguarding Children and Young People in the Church of England* (4th ed., 2010); *Responding to Domestic Abuse: Guidelines for those with Pastoral Responsibility* (2006); *Responding Well: Policy and Guidance* (2011); *Learning and Development Practice Guidance: Responding to Serious Safeguarding Situations* (2015); *Risk Assessment for Individuals who may pose a risk to Children or Adults* (2015); *Safer Recruitment* (2015); *Safeguarding in Religious Communities* (2015); *Safeguarding*

260 *Bibliography*

Records: Joint Practice Guidance for the Church of England and the Methodist Church (2015); *Safeguarding Guidance for Single Congregations in Local Ecumenical Partnerships* (2015); and, with English Heritage: *Guidance for best practice for treatment of human remains excavated from Christian burial grounds in England* (2005)

Coventry Cathedral: *Constitution and Statutes of the Cathedral Church of Saint Michael, Coventry* (2000, as amended)

Derby Cathedral: *Constitution and Statutes of the Cathedral Church of All Saints, Derby* (2000, as amended)

Durham Cathedral: *Constitution and Statutes of the Cathedral Church of Christ, Blessed Mary the Virgin and Saint Cuthbert of Durham* (2000, as amended)

Ely Cathedral: *Constitution and Statutes of the Cathedral Church of the Holy and Undivided Trinity of Ely* (2000, as amended)

Exeter Cathedral: *Constitution and Statutes of the Cathedral Church of Saint Peter in Exeter* (2000, as amended); *Staff Handbook* (2015); *Development Plan 2014–2019* (2014)

Gloucester Cathedral: *Constitution and Statutes of the Cathedral Church of Saint Peter and the Holy and Indivisible Trinity, Gloucester* (2000, as amended); *Volunteers' Welcome Handbook* (undated)

Guildford Cathedral: *Constitution and Statutes of the Cathedral Church of the Holy Spirit, Guildford* (2002, as amended); *Policies including Education Policy: Pursuing the Spirit's Gift of Wisdom*; *Policy Statement for the Safeguarding of Children and Adults at Risk of Harm* (2012–2016)

Hereford Cathedral: *Constitution and Statutes of the Cathedral Church of Saint Mary the Virgin and Saint Ethelbert the King in Hereford* (2000, as amended); *Hereford Cathedral Perpetual Trust: Memorandum and Articles of Association* (2008)

Historic England: *Scheduled Monuments: A Guide for Owners and Occupiers* (2013)

House of Bishops of the General Synod of the Church of England: *Advice to Clergy Concerning Marriage and Divorce* (2002); *Civil Partnerships: A Pastoral Statement of the House of Bishops of the Church of England* (2005)

Leicester Cathedral: *Constitution and Statutes of the Cathedral Church of Saint Martin, Leicester* (2000, as amended)

Lichfield Cathedral: *Constitution and Statutes of the Cathedral Church of Saint Mary and Saint Chad in Lichfield* (2000, as amended)

Lincoln Cathedral: *Constitution and Statutes of the Cathedral Church of the Blessed Virgin Mary of Lincoln* (2002, as amended)

Liverpool Cathedral: *Constitution and Statutes* (2002, as amended); *Cathedral Constables' Handbook: The Cathedral and Precincts* (2015)

London, St Paul's Cathedral: *Constitution and Statutes of the Cathedral Church of Saint Paul in London* (2000, as amended); *Additional Safeguarding Procedures Pertaining to the Schools and Families Department* (2014); *Safeguarding (Child Protection) Policy and Procedures and Additional Safeguarding (Child Protection) Procedures Pertaining to the Music Department* (2014)

Manchester Cathedral: *Constitution and Statutes of the Cathedral, Collegiate and Parish Church of Saint Mary, Saint Denys and Saint George in Manchester* (2000, with amendments to 2014)

Newcastle Cathedral: *Constitution and Statutes of the Cathedral Church of Saint Nicholas Newcastle upon Tyne* (2001)

Norwich Cathedral: *Constitution and Statutes of the Cathedral Church of the Holy and Undivided Trinity of Norwich* (2001, as amended)

Bibliography 261

Oxford, Christ Church (The House): *Statutes of Christ Church Oxford* (approved by Her Majesty in Council 2011)
Peterborough Cathedral: *Constitution and Statutes of the Cathedral Church of Saint Peter, Saint Paul and Saint Andrew in Peterborough* (2001)
Portsmouth Cathedral: *Constitution and Statutes of the Cathedral Church of Saint Thomas of Canterbury Portsmouth* (2000)
Review of the Cathedrals Measure 1999: Report by John W. Bullimore, commissioned by the Deans of the Cathedrals of the Province of York (2012)
Ripon Cathedral: *Constitution and Statutes of the Cathedral Church of Saint Peter and Saint Wilfrid at Ripon* (2001, as amended 2014)
Rochester Cathedral: *Constitution and Statutes of the Cathedral Church of Christ and the Blessed Virgin Mary, Rochester* (2000, as amended); *Customary* (2008)
St Albans Cathedral: *Constitution and Statutes of the Cathedral and Abbey Church of Saint Alban in the City of St. Albans* (2000, as amended)
St Edmundsbury Cathedral: *Constitution and Statutes of the Cathedral Church of Saint James and Saint Edmund, Bury St Edmunds* (2000, as amended)
Salisbury Cathedral: *Constitution and Statutes of the Cathedral Church of the Blessed Virgin Mary of Salisbury* (2001, as amended); *Good Governance* (2013)
Sheffield Cathedral: *Constitution and Statutes of the Cathedral Church of Saint Peter and Saint Paul, Sheffield* (2001, revised 2009 and 2013)
Southwark Cathedral: *Constitution and Statutes of the Cathedral and Collegiate Church of Saint Saviour and Saint Mary Overy, Southwark* (2000, as amended)
Southwell Minster: *Constitution and Statutes of the Cathedral and Parish Church of the Blessed Virgin Mary (Southwell Minster)* (2000, revised 2012)
Spiritual Capital: The Present and Future of English Cathedrals (2012), Commissioned by the Foundation for Church Leadership and the Association of English Cathedrals
Talent and Calling: A Review of the Law and Practice regarding Appointments to the Offices of Suffragan Bishop, Dean, Archdeacon and Residentiary Canon (General Synod Paper 1650: 2007)
The Appointment Process for Deans: issued by the Archbishops' Secretary for Appointments on behalf of the House of Bishops (July 2011)
The Appointment Process for Residentiary Canons: issued by the Archbishops' Secretary for Appointments on behalf of the House of Bishops (January 2009)
The Economic and Social Impacts of England's Cathedrals: A Report to the Association of English Cathedrals, written by Ecorys and commissioned by the Association and English Heritage (September 2014)
The Society of Friends of Cathedral Music: *Constitution* (2007)
Truro Cathedral: *Constitution and Statutes of the Cathedral Church of the Blessed Virgin Mary in Truro* (2000, as amended)
Wakefield Cathedral: *Constitution and Statutes of the Cathedral Church of All Saints Wakefield* (2000, as amended)
Wells Cathedral: *Constitution and Statutes of the Cathedral Church of Saint Andrew in Wells* (2000, as amended)
Winchester Cathedral: *Constitution and Statutes of the Cathedral Church of the Holy Trinity and of Saint Peter and Saint Paul and of Saint Swithun in Winchester* (2000, as amended)
Worcester Cathedral: *Constitution and Statutes of the Cathedral Church of Christ and the Blessed Mary the Virgin of Worcester* (2001, as amended); *Renewal and Development: A Strategic Vision for Worcester Cathedral 2015–2020* (2015); *Henrician Statutes: Translated from the privately printed Latin edition of 1879 by R.J.W. Bryer* (1994)

York Minster: *Constitution and Statutes of the Cathedral and Metropolitical Church of Saint Peter in York* (York Minster) (2000, as amended)

Secondary sources

Atherton, I., 'Cathedrals and the British Revolution', in M.J. Braddick and D.L. Smith (eds.), *The Experience of Revolution in Stuart Britain and Ireland* (Cambridge: Cambridge University Press, 2011)

Backhouse, J. (ed.), *The Medieval English Cathedral* (Donington: Harlaxton Medieval Studies, 2003)

Bannister, A.T., *The Cathedral Church of Hereford: Its History and Constitution* (London: SPCK, 1924)

Bray, G. (ed.), *The Anglican Canons: 1529–1947* (London: Boydell Press: Church of England Record Society, 1998)

Briden, T. (ed.), *Moore's Introduction to English Canon Law* (London: Bloomsbury, 4th ed., 2013)

Bruce, S., *Religion in the Modern World: From Cathedrals to Cults* (Oxford: Oxford University Press, 1996)

Burn, R., *Ecclesiastical Law* (1763, 5th ed., 1788)

Clifton-Taylor, A., *The Cathedrals of England* (London: Book Club Association, 1967)

Coke, E., *Institutes of the Lawes of England* (1628–1644)

Colton, P., 'The rise of ecclesiastical quasi-legislation', in F. Cranmer, M. Hill, C. Kenny and R. Sandberg (eds.), *The Confluence of Law and Religion: Interdisciplinary Reflections on the Work of Norman Doe* (Cambridge: Cambridge University Press, 2016) 81–95

Cross, F.L., and E.A. Livingstone (eds.), *The Oxford Dictionary of the Christian Church* (Oxford: Oxford University Press, 3rd ed., 1997, rev. 2005)

Curthoys, J., *The Cardinal's College: Christ Church, Chapter and Verse* (London: Profile Books, 2012)

Davie, G., *Religion in Modern Europe: A Memory Mutates* (Oxford: Oxford University Press, 2000)

Doe, N., *The Legal Framework of the Church of England* (Oxford: The Clarendon Press, 1996)

Doe, N., *Canon Law in the Anglican Communion* (Oxford: The Clarendon Press, 1998)

Doe, N., *Christian Law: Contemporary Principles* (Cambridge: Cambridge University Press, 2013)

Edwards, K., *The English Secular Cathedrals in the Middle Ages: A Constitutional Study with Special Reference to the Fourteenth Century* (Manchester: Manchester University Press, 1949)

Edwards, O., and T. ap Siôn, 'Cathedral engagement with young people', in L.J. Francis (ed.), *Anglican Cathedrals in Modern Life: The Science of Cathedral Studies* (London: Palgrave Macmillan, 2013) 29–49

Escott, M., *Around the Cloisters* (Bristol: Silver Wood Books Ltd., 2011)

Francis, L.J. (ed.), *Anglican Cathedrals in Modern Life: The Science of Cathedral Studies* (London: Palgrave Macmillan, 2015)

Francis, L.J., J. Annis, and M. Robbins, 'The spiritual revolution and the spiritual quest of cathedral visitors', in L.J. Francis (ed.), *Anglican Cathedrals in Modern Life: The Science of Cathedral Studies* (London: Palgrave Macmillan, 2015) 171–187

Gibson, E., *Codex Juris Ecclesiastici Anglicani, or, The Statutes, Constitutions, Canons, Rubrics and Articles of the Church of England* (1713)

Godolphin, J., *Repertorium Canonicum or Abridgement of the Ecclesiastical Laws of this Realm* (1678)
Goodman, A.W., and W.H. Hutton (eds.), *The Statutes Governing the Cathedral Church of Winchester* (Oxford: The Clarendon Press, 1925)
Greatrex, J., *The English Benedictine Cathedral Priories: Rule and Practice, c. 1270–1420* (Oxford: Oxford University Press, 2011)
Halsbury's Laws of England, Volume 34, Ecclesiastical Law (London: Butterworths/Lexis/Nexis, 5th ed., 2011)
Harvey, J., *English Cathedrals* (London: B.T. Batsford, 2nd ed., 1956)
Hehl, E.D., 'The legal organisation of church construction, especially cathedral construction, in the Middle Ages', *Philosophy and History* 24 (1991) 108–109
Hill, M., *Ecclesiastical Law* (Oxford: Oxford University Press, 3rd ed., 2007)
Hill, M., R. Sandberg, and N. Doe, *Religion and Law in the United Kingdom* (Hague: Wolters Kluwer, 2nd ed., 2014)
Hislop, M., *How to Build A Cathedral* (London: Bloomsbury, 2012)
Hobson, J., *Cathedral Bobbies* (Mirfield: Mirfield Publications, 3rd ed., 2015)
Hooker, R., *Of the Laws of Ecclesiastical Polity* (1593)
Jeffrey, P., *England's Other Cathedrals* (Stroud: The History Press Ltd., 2012)
Jenkins, S., *England's Cathedrals* (London: Little Brown, 2016)
Johnson, J., *A Collection of All the Ecclesiastical Laws* (1720)
Johnson, P., *British Cathedrals* (London: Weidenfeld & Nicolson, 1980)
Kieckhefer, R., *Theology in Stone: Church Architecture from Byzantium to Berkeley* (Oxford: Oxford University Press, 2004)
Kilde, J.H., *Sacred Power – Sacred Space: An Introduction to Christian Architecture and Worship* (Oxford: Oxford University Press, 2008)
Kitchen, M., J. Halliburton, and K. Walker (eds.), *Cathedrals and Society: A Theological Appraisal* (London: Tiltman Desktop Publishing, 1995)
Lehmberg, S.E., *English Cathedrals: A History* (London: Hambledon Contiuum, 2005); and 'Henry VIII, the Reformation and the cathedrals', *Huntington Library Quarterly* 49 (1986) 261–270
MacKenzie, I.M. (ed.), *Cathedrals Now: Their Use and Place in Society* (Norwich: Canterbury Press, 1996)
Maltby, J., 'Suffering and surviving: the civil wars, the Commonwealth and the formation of "Anglicanism", 1642–1660', in C. Durston and J. Maltby (eds.), *Religion in Revolutionary England* (Manchester: Manchester University Press, 2006) 158–180
Mulcahy, L., *Legal Architecture: Justice, Due Process and the Place of Law* (Abingdon: Routledge, 2011)
Nelson, W., *The Rights of the Clergy of Great Britain* (1710)
Phillimore, R., *Ecclesiastical Law* (1873) (London: Sweet and Maxwell, 2nd ed., 1895)
Platten, S., and C. Lewis (eds.), *Dreaming Spires? Cathedrals in a New Age* (London: SPCK, 2006)
Sandberg, R., *Religion, Law and Society* (Cambridge: Cambridge University Press, 2013)
Saunders, J., 'The limitations of statutes: Elizabethan schemes to reform new foundation cathedral statutes', *Journal of Ecclesiastical History*, 48:3 (1997) 445–467
Smith, K.E., 'An old cathedral for a new Russia: The symbolic politics of the re-constructed Church of Christ the Saviour [Moscow]', *Religion, State and Society* 25 (1997) 163–175

Tarver, A., *Church Court Records* (Chichester: Phillimore and Co. Ltd., 1995)

Temple, N., J.S. Hendrix, and C. Frost (eds.), *Bishop Grosseteste and Lincoln Cathedral: Tracing Relationships between Medieval Concepts of Order and Built Form* (Aldershot: Ashgate, 2014)

Thompson, N., 'Rochester Cathedral: a window onto eternity' (unpublished paper, January 2016)

Tracy, C., with A. Budge, *Britain's Medieval Episcopal Thrones* (London: Oxbow Books, 2015)

Watson, W., *Clergyman's Law* (1701)

Yates, N., *Buildings, Faith and Worship: The Liturgical Arrangement of Anglican Churches 1600–1900* (Oxford: Oxford University Press, 2001)

Index

accountability 90
Acts of Parliament 17, 24, 36
administrators 26, 131–2, 140, 144–8, 154–5, 163, 192–4, 218, 220, 223–4, 226
aisles 79
albs 72
Anglican Communion 17, 45
Appointment of Bishops Act 1533 38, 39, 41
archaeological remains 212, 216, 232, 233–5
Archbishop of Canterbury 17, 21, 38, 100, 109, 213–14, 225
Archbishop of York 17, 38, 213–4, 225
archbishops 77; *see also* Archbishop of Canterbury; Archbishop of York; Archbishops' Commission on Cathedrals 1994; Archbishops' Council
Archbishops' Commission on Cathedrals 1994 2, 3, 8, 9, 16, 253; on appointment to cathedral posts 106–7; on bishops' visitations 46; on by-laws 29; on canonical houses 238; on care and conservation 210; on cathedral constitutions and statutes 25; on cathedral culture and arts 172; on cathedral employees 89; on cathedral finances 196; on cathedral governance 132; on cathedral libraries 157; on cathedral music 123; on cathedral schools 175; on confirmation 61; on educational work 166; on preaching 74; on the bishop's role 45; on the cathedral community 79; on the purpose of cathedrals 18–20; on tourism 92; on volunteers 89; on worship 68
Archbishops' Council 17, 45, 214
archdeaconries 17
archdeacons 13, 49, 65–6, 71, 76–7, 97, 107–8, 150

archives 157–66
arts 172–3
assistant bishops 45, 71, 150, 152
Association of Diocesan and Cathedral Archaeologists 236–7
Association of English Cathedrals 1, 25, 32, 111, 123–4, 133, 139, 166, 184, 196, 201, 225, 255
auditor 200-1

baptism: administration of 58–60; cathedral interviews 66–7; policy 66–7
Bath 12
bedesmen 88
bellringers 195-6
Benedictine abbeys 12
Birmingham Cathedral 13; and bishop's visitations 52; baptismal policy 67; canons of 117, 122; Chapter 150; College of Canons 154; community 84, 86; Council 139; educational work 175; finances 208; Holy Communion 65, 66; interviews 35; law 35; objects 21, 23; outreach 94, 104; role in the appointment of bishops 44; theological studies 169
Bishop of Bath and Wells 12
Bishop of Canterbury 12; *see also* Archbishop of Canterbury
Bishop of Coventry 12
Bishop of Hereford 109
Bishop of Lichfield 12
bishops 4; and cathedral liturgy 50–1; and cathedral ministry 49–50; and cathedral worship 68–71; and educational work 167–9; and enforcement of cathedral care standards 52–5; and Holy Communion 64–5; and the Chapter 149–50; and the College of Canons

150–3; confirmation of 40–1; consecration of 41; election of 39–40; enthronement of 37–44; functions of 6, 7, 44–52; installation of 41–2; nomination 39; preaching at cathedrals 75; teaching seat of 4, 17–19; visitations 46–9, 51, 53–4; *see also* assistant bishops; suffragan bishops

Blackburn Cathedral 13; altar and corona 57; cathedral community 81, 85; cathedral funds 200; cathedral worship 71; ecumenical activity 98; Holy Communion 65; lay canons 96; preaching 76–7

block grants 7

Book of Common Prayer 1662 50

Bradford Cathedral 13; bishop 46; College of Canons 151–2; community 85; deans of 110; outreach 97; vesture worn during worship 72

Bristol Cathedral 12, 16; and bishop's visitations 52; baptismal policy 66–7; buildings 256–7; canons of 122; chapter houses 131; College of Canons 153; community 81, 82, 84, 86; Council 138; customs 31; deans of 114; ecumenical activity 99; educational work 174; finances 201, 207; Holy Communion 61, 64, 66; law 34–5; library 161; liturgical custom 73; music 128–9; outreach 103; worship 69–72

British Empire Medal 100

British Museum 194

Burial Act 1857 235

burials 17

Burn, Richard 4

by-laws 29–31, 34–35

Cambridge University 74, 160

canonical houses 238–44, 250–1

canon law 6, 24, 37, 60; as a source of cathedral law 24; on baptism 58; on canons 74, 117, 239; on cathedral customs 29; on cathedral worship 68, 69; on deans 74, 239; on Holy Communion 61, 63; on preaching at cathedrals 74; on safeguarding issues 29, 181

canonry 98, 115–16, 118, 122, 149, 168; *see also* canons

canons 113–14; and Holy Communion 65–6; appointment of 115–16, 129–30; cathedral interviews 120–3; ecumenical 98, 102–3, 105, 150, 153; honorary 66, 70, 76–7, 95–6, 99, 102–3, 120, 122; lay 70, 72, 96, 102–5, 115, 120, 150, 168–9, 174, 207; ministerial development review of 120–3; non-residentiary 115, 118–20; preaching at cathedrals 76, 77; 'prebendaries' 12; residentiary 6, 7, 9, 67, 70, 115–18, 120–3, 130, 240–4; stipendiary 115; *see also* canonry; canon's house

Canons Ecclesiastical 1603/4 123

canon's house 239–43

Canterbury Cathedral 12; and Cathedrals Fabric Commission 219; as the 'mother church' 17; by-laws 30–1; canonical houses 242; canons of 116; Chapter 54, 140, 147; community 81, 85; constitution and statutes 28; Council 134–5; deans of 112; ecumenical activity 98; finances 201; Holy Communion 64, 65; hospitality 87; library 156, 160; music 126–7; objects 21; position of the bishop 45; preaching at 77; property 190–1; pulpit 57; School 178, 179; security incidents 244; worship 70, 71, 72; University of Kent at Canterbury 161

Care of Cathedral Rule 2006 210

Care of Cathedrals Measure 1990 7, 210

Care of Cathedrals Measure 2011 1, 8, 24, 47, 52; appointing archaeologists 237; as a source of cathedral law 24; on care and conservation 187, 211; on cathedral precincts 229–30, 232, 233; on record keeping 165

Carlisle Cathedral 8–9, 12; bishop's visitations 47–8; by-laws 30; canonical houses 241; canons of 116; Chapter 142; community 81; constitutions and statutes 28; Fabric Advisory Committee 224; funds 199–200; library 160; preaching at 75; property 191; volunteers and employees 91

cassocks 72

cathedral accounts 201–3; *see also* cathedral finances

cathedral architecture: and images of power 3; and law 256; and liturgy 255; regulation 3; *see also* cathedral buildings

cathedral buildings 212, 255–6; listed 8; *see also* cathedral architecture

cathedral close 229, 230; *see also* cathedral precincts

cathedral community 79–80, 104; and baptism 59, 60, 66; annual meetings

82–3; cathedral interviews 85–6; committees 26, 80, 82–3, 85–6, 104; pastoral care of 83–5; roll 80–2, 85–6
cathedral constables 244–6; role of 246–8
Cathedral Constables Association 244–6
cathedral constitutions 26, 253–4; as sources of cathedral law 25–9; on cathedral property 190–1; on role of cathedrals 20–2; on security 248–9; on worship 68–73; revision of 26–8, 32–3
cathedral finances 7, 196–208; annual report 204–5; *see also* cathedral accounts; cathedral funds; cathedral investments
Cathedral Friends 81, 142
cathedral funds 199–200; *see also* cathedral finances
cathedral investments 205–6; *see also* cathedral finances
cathedral law 2–4, 8, 10, 16; sources of 23–36
Cathedral Libraries and Archives Association 156, 162–5, 184
Cathedral Organists' Association 124
cathedral precincts 229–38, 250; designation of 230–2
cathedral property 186–91; inspections of 189–90; interviews 190–1; records 189–90; reports 189–90
cathedrals: and politics 4; as a form of European museum 3; as a seat of the bishop 17–19; as centres of mission and worship 18–19; as charities 14; as embodiments of memory 3; as normative spaces 252–7; as social phenomena 3; auditors 200–1; care and conservation of 52–5, 210–28; classification of 11–16, 35–6; corporate structure 14; customs 29–31; ecumenical activity 98–9; history of 4; independence of 5, 19, 25; institutions 96–7, 102–4; interdependence of 19, 25; in the national church and legislation 16–18; inventories 188–91; legal self-identity 12; ministry 2, 49–50, 114, 150, 154, 175, 199, 202; monastic, 4–5, 10; ownership of land 7; pre-Reformation 12; purposes 6–8, 16–23, 36; Registrars 48, 110; secular 4, 5, 12; treasures 185, 191–6; wardens 79, 89; *see also* cathedral accounts; cathedral architecture; cathedral buildings; cathedral close; cathedral communities; cathedral constables; cathedral constitutions; cathedral finances; cathedral funds; cathedral investments; cathedral law; cathedral precincts; cathedral property; cathedral schools; cathedral security; cathedral statutes
Cathedrals Administration and Finance Association 206–7
Cathedrals Advisory Commission 7
cathedral schools 175–84; interviews on 182–3; relationship with cathedrals 175–80
Cathedrals Commission 6–7
cathedral security 244–50; interviews on 250; under cathedral constitutions and statutes 248–9
Cathedrals Fabric Commission for England 8, 18, 32, 52, 173, 187, 210, 212, 225–8; application to 216–19; cathedral interviews 219; composition and procedure of 213–15; functions of 213–15; on cathedral precincts 230–5, 238; on educational and research projects 156–7; on liturgy 72–3; on valuable objects 191–5
Cathedrals Measure 1931 7, 8
Cathedrals Measure 1934 8
Cathedrals Measure 1963 7, 8, 18
Cathedrals Measure 1976 7
Cathedrals Measure 1999 1–3, 10, 13, 15, 18, 20, 253; as a source of cathedral law 24–5; on accounts 201; on appointment to cathedral posts 107; on bishops 45–8; on body corporate of the cathedral 131–2; on canonical houses 238; on canons 115, 118; on cathedral auditors 200; on cathedral community 80, 83–4, 104; on deans 111; on ecumenical activity 98–9; on finances 196; on investments 205; on libraries 157, 183; on liturgy 50; on maintaining order 92–3; on outreach to the wider community 96–7, 105; on statutes and constitutions 25–6; on the Chapter 140–1, 143, 145, 154–5; on the College of Canons 150–2, 154–5; on the Council 133, 135–7, 154; on worship 69
Cathedrals Plus 91
cathedral statutes 4–9, 253–4; as sources of law 25–9; on new foundations 5, 23–4; on property 190–1; on role of cathedrals 20–2; on security 248–9; on worship 68–73; revision of 26–8, 32–3
Cathedral Statutes Commission 7, 25
cathedral studies 3–4

268 *Index*

Chapter Clerks 145–8
Chapter Finance Committee 134, 207, 208
Chapter 7, 13, 142, 149, 158, 214; and by-laws 34–5; and cathedral law 26–7, 32–3; and College of Canons 152, 153; and the Council 137; as the 'administrative powerhouse' 139; cathedral interviews 148–50; composition of 140; functions of 141–3; meetings of 143–5; officers of 145–8
Chapter Stewards 146, 147
charities 14, 24–5
Charities Act 1993 187
Charities Act 2011 14, 200
Charity Commission 24, 162
Charles I 9
Charles II 5
Charter and Royal Licence 9
chasubles 72
Chelmsford Cathedral 13; canonical houses 243; deans of 110; vesture worn during worship 72
Chester Cathedral 12; and Cathedrals Fabric Commission 219; appointment of bishops 44; bishop's visitations 52; canonical houses 244; canons of 122; Chapter 147, 150; Chapter houses 131; community 81, 82, 84, 86; deans of 114; educational work 171, 174–5; Fabric Advisory Committee 223; Holy Communion 63, 66; library 161; objects of 23; outreach 97, 103; preaching at 76; security 250; visitors 93; worship 68–9, 71; University of Chester 97
Chichester Cathedral 12; and Cathedrals Fabric Commission 219; by-laws 30; canons of 116–18; Chapter 140–2, 144, 145, 148; College of Canons 151, 152; community 80, 82–3; Council 135, 136; deans of 112; customs 29; educational work 171; enthronement of the bishop 42; Fabric Advisory Committee 225; finances 200; Holy Communion 64; library 158; outreach 96; preaching at 76; precinct 238; School 176–7; theological studies 167–8; treasures 185; vergers 88
children: baptism 58–60; Holy Communion 62–3; of same-sex couples 60; protection of 180–2
choirs 19, 106; boys' 123, 129; girls' 123, 129; habits 72; inclusiveness 129; liturgical 106; ritual 106; *see also* choir schools; choristers

choir schools 123
Choral Evensong 68
choristers 125–9; education 123; pastoral care 124
Church Buildings Council 157, 213, 214
Church Commissioners 7, 32, 36, 46, 54, 110; and cathedral finances 197–8, 205, 208–9
Church Dignitaries (Retirement) Measure 1949 49, 129
Church of England 16–17; organisation of 17–18; Record Centre 157, 162; territorial units 17
Church of England (Ecumenical Relations) Measure 1988 98
church wardens 9, 104
church wealth 6
civic life 21, 94, 97
civil partnerships 100
Clergy Discipline Measure 2003 130, 181
cloisters 156
College of Canons 13, 15, 150–2; appointment of the bishop 39–41, 43–4; cathedral interviews 153–4
Commission of Review 225; cathedral interviews on 227; composition and procedure of 225–6
Common Prayer 50, 67
Communars 140, 144, 145, 152
confirmation 61, 62
congé d'élire 39
consultation 132
corporate body 13–14, 26, 31, 36, 131–33, 154, 242; *see also* Chapter; Council; College of Canons
corporate governance 13
Council 13, 133; cathedral interviews 137–9; functions and meetings 135–7; membership of 133–5; revision of constitution and statutes by 26–8
Council for British Archaeology 214
Coventry Cathedral 13; and Cathedrals Fabric Commission 219; bishops and 12; community 82–4; customs 31; cultural events 172–3; funerals 101; Holy Communion 63, 65, 66; outreach 94; theological studies 169; worship 70
criminal activity 249
crossings 79
Crown Nominations Commission 38
cultural events 172–3
customs 29–31

daily chaplaincy 93, 94, 122
Data Protection 165
deacons: and cathedral worship 67–8; ordination of 71
Dean and Chapter 9, 13, 24, 73, 80, 115–16, 123, 141, 152, 179; cathedrals 13, 36, 132; of St Paul's 187; relationship with the bishop 46, 64
deaneries 17, 239–43
Deanery Synods 17, 83
Dean of Birmingham 35, 44, 86, 122, 133, 138, 139, 154
Dean of Bristol 34, 103, 114, 256
Dean of Canterbury 112
Dean of Coventry 84
Dean of Derby 35, 44, 86, 114
Dean of Exeter 33, 34, 43, 51, 84, 207
Dean of Hereford 43, 84, 113, 137, 149
Dean of Salisbury 33, 43, 113, 121, 138, 182, 250
Dean of St Albans 122
Dean of St Paul's 33, 43, 73, 85, 113, 256
Dean of the Arches 225–6
Dean of Wells 138
Dean of Worcester 34, 44, 85, 256
deans 108–14: and cathedral worship 67–7, 69–70; and Holy Communion 65–6; and pastoral care 84; appointment of 108–9; cathedral interviews on 113–14; duties of 112–13; functions of 111–12; preaching at cathedrals 74, 76, 77; rights of 112
demolition 216
Derby Cathedral 13; and appointment of the bishop 44; and bishop's visitations 54; baptismal policy 67; canonical houses 243; canons of 122; Chapter 148, 150; community 81, 86; constitutions and statutes 23, 28; Council 138–9; deans of 114; educational work 171, 175; finances 207; Holy Communion 64–5; interviews on 16, 35; law 35; liturgical custom 73; objects 21–2; outreach 94–5, 103–4; School 183; vergers 88–9; worship 68
Devon 95
diocesan officers 149
diocesan offices 7, 238
Diocesan Synods 17, 45, 83, 97, 111, 113, 242
dioceses: and cathedrals 16; definition 17; 'mother church' of 18; regulations 14–15
Directors of Music 123–5, 128, 130

disciplinary proceedings 58, 120, 128, 130, 181, 247–8
disputes 48
disturbances 249, 251
domestic law 24, 29, 36; *see also* cathedral constitutions; cathedral statutes
Duke of Lancaster's Regiment 60
Durham Cathedral 12; baptismal policy 59; by-laws 31; canonical houses 242; canons of 117, 119; Chapter 140, 146–7; community 81, 82; Council 134; customs 31; ecumenical activity 98; employees 90; finances 201; font 57; funerals 101; Holy Communion 64; library 160, 161; outreach 96; preaching at 76; property 191; School 178–9; theological studies 168; University of Durham and 98, 168; vergers 88; volunteers 90; worship 69, 72

Ecclesiastical Architects and Surveyors Association 214
Ecclesiastical Commission 1835 6
Ecclesiastical Commissioners Act 1840 9
ecclesiastical courts 24
Ecclesiastical Courts Jurisdiction Act 1860 244, 249
Ecclesiastical Duties and Revenues Act 1840 6
ecclesiastical law 1, 3, 4, 17, 24, 100, 139
Ecclesiastical Offices (Terms of Service) Measure 2009 129
ecumenical activities 98–9
ecumenical canons 98, 102–3, 105, 150, 153
ecumenical prebendaries 99, 103
education officers 169–72
educational policy 169–72
educational work 156, 166–75, 184; cathedral interviews on 173–5; protection of children and vulnerable adults 180–2; *see also* cathedral schools
Edward VI 9
Elizabeth I 5, 9
Ely Cathedral 12; community 83; Chapter 147; ecumenical activity 98; library 160; outreach 97; position of the bishop at 45; School 178
employees 89–91, 104
English Heritage 7, 214, 216–18, 222, 232
enquiry centres 92
episcopal offices 5
episcopal throne 37, 55, 106
Eucharist 61; *see also* Holy Communion

Exeter Cathedral 12; and bishop's visitations 51; and election of the bishop 43; appointment to cathedral posts 107; baptismal policies 66; bishop's throne 37; canons of 95–6, 116, 120–1; community 80, 84, 85; finances 207; interviews on 22, 33; objects 22; precinct 237; School 177, 182; University of Exeter and 158; worship 69, 70

Fabric Advisory Committees 32, 52, 134, 187–90, 208, 210, 212–19, 225–8; appeals to 223; applications for approval of 222; cathedral interviews on 223–5; composition and procedure of 220–1; functions of 220–1; on cathedral precincts 231–2, 237
female clergy 107
Finance and Investment Advisory Committee 196, 207
Finance and Property Committee 196
Foundation for Church Leadership 1
foundations 14
funerals 100–1

General Synod 17; Crown Nominations Commission 38; Secretary-General of 27, 28
Gibson, Edmund 4
Gift Aid 14, 60
Gloucester Cathedral 12; and bishop's visitations 52; canons of 117; community 85; chapter house 131; College of Canons 153–4; constitution and statutes 28, 35; Council 138; deans of 114; educational work 174; library 166; monastic cloisters 156; music 129; outreach 103; School 179, 183; vergers 88; visitors 93; volunteers 91
Godolphin, John 4
good practice 19
gowns 72
grants 7, 198
Great Seal 39–40
'green line' plans 231
Guildford Cathedral 10, 13; cathedral close 230; Chapter 148; Council 137; dispute resolution 48; ecumenical activity 99; educational work 171–2; enthronement of the bishop 43; finances 198; protection of children and vulnerable adults 181; quasi-legislation 32
guilds 91

Henrician foundations 10, 15, 31
Henry V 9
Henry VIII 5, 8–10, 12
Hereford Cathedral 12, 15; and the appointment of the bishop 43; as the 'mother church' 22; baptismal policies 66; bishop's visitations 51; by-laws 30; canonical houses 240; canons of 119; Chapter 142, 144, 146, 149; community 84, 85; Council 137; customs 32–3; deans of 109, 112, 113; ecumenical activity 98–9; educational work 173; enthronement of the bishop 42; finances 200; Holy Communion 64, 65; law 32–3; library 156, 158–9; liturgical custom 73; music 125–6, 128; objects 20, 22; outreach 95, 102; preaching at 75; precinct 237; School 177; theological studies 167; vergers 88; visitors 92; worship 70
Heritage and Renewal 2, 3, 8, 9. See also Archbishops' Commission on Cathedrals 1994
High Steward 95, 134
Holy Communion 58, 59; administration of 61–6, 78; admitting children to 62–3; cathedral interviews on 66
Hooker, Richard 4
hospitality 87, 92, 104
House of Bishops 45
housing *see* canonical houses
human remains 216, 232, 235

Imperial Society of Knights Bachelor 100
incapacity 28, 49, 115
Incumbents (Vacation of Benefices) Measure 1977 49
infirmity 49
inspections 189–90
Institution of Civil Engineers 214
Institution of Structural Engineers 214
interviews 15–16; on areas of concern 254; on baptism 66–7; on bishop's role and functions 43–4, 51–2; on canonical houses 244; on canons 120–3; on cathedral buildings 256–7; on cathedral community 85–6; on cathedral finances 207–8; on cathedral law 32–5; on cathedral libraries and archives 166; on cathedral music 128–9; on cathedral objects 22–3; on cathedral precinct 237–8; on cathedral property 190–1; on cathedral schools 182–3; on cathedral security 250; on Chapter 148–50; on

Cathedrals Fabric Commission 219; on Colleges of Canons 153–4; on Commission of Review 227; on deans 113–14; on educational work 173–5; on Fabric Advisory Committees 223–5; on Holy Communion 66–7; on outreach to the wider society 102–4; on preaching 77; on the Council 137–9; on visitors 93–4; on worship and liturgy 73–4
inventories 188-91

land ownership 7
Latin 51
Law Courts 3
lay canons 70, 72, 96, 102–5, 115, 120, 150, 168–9, 174, 207
lay clerks 124-8
lay vicars 125
Leicester Cathedral 13; baptismal policy 60; community 82; funerals 101; Holy Communion 65, 66; hospitality 87; theological studies 169; vergers 89; volunteers and employees 91
libraries 156; cathedral interviews on 166; in new foundations 159–61; in old foundations 157–9; in parish church cathedrals 162
Lichfield Cathedral 12; bishop's visitations 48; by-laws 30; cathedral close 230; Cathedral School 177; Chapter 140, 141, 143–4; College of Canons 150–2; Council 134, 136; dean 110; enthronement of the bishop 42; funds 200; library 159, 161; role of the bishop 45
Lincoln Cathedral 12; appointment to cathedral posts 107; by-laws 30; canonical houses 240; Chapter 146; community 84; constitution and statutes 28; educational work 156; enthronement of the bishop 42; hospitality 87; library 158; music 124–5; volunteers 90
Listed Building Consent 233
listed buildings 8
Litany 67
Liturgical Commission 214
Liturgical Plan 72–3, 78
liturgical texts 67
liturgy 50–1, 67–74; and church architecture 255; cathedral interviews on 73–4; Cathedrals Fabric Commission for England on 72–3
Liverpool Cathedral 10, 13; constitution and statutes 35; customs 31; employees 90; security 248–9
London 12; *see also* St Paul's
London Gazette 39

maintenance 211, 216
Manchester Cathedral 9, 13; baptismal policy 59–60; canonical houses 243; College of Canons 152; community 82; enthronement of the bishop 43; foundation of 12; outreach 97; role of the bishop 48–9; theological studies 169; volunteers and employees 91
marriage 17, 100–1
Mary I 5, 9
Measures of the General Synod of the Church of England 1, 24
medieval England 4
memory 3
mental incapacity 49
ministerial development review 120-3
ministers: cathedral worship 68; preaching at cathedrals 74–5
minor canons 120, 125, 127
monastic cathedrals 4–5, 10
monastic foundations 12
Morning and Evening Prayer 67, 68, 70, 72, 78
multi-faith worship 101
music 123–9, 130; cathedral interviews on 128–9; *see also* choirs

national celebrations 101
national mourning 101
naves 79
Newcastle Cathedral 13; by-laws 30; canonical houses 243; cathedral close 230; community 82; educational work 171; funds 200; objects 21; role of the bishop 46
new foundations 5, 8, 10–15, 35–6, 67, 69, 83–4, 96–7, 108, 127, 137, 146, 151–2, 241; libraries 159–61; statutes of 23–4
non-residentiary canons 115, 118-20
Norwich Cathedral 8, 12; by-laws 30; canonical houses 241; canons of 96, 116, 118; Chapter 140, 147; Council 134; deans of 110, 112; educational work 171; enthronement of 42–3; library 159–60; objects 21; preaching at 75; role of the bishop 45; School 178

oaths 29, 109, 110, 116
old foundations 5, 8, 10, 12, 15, 35, 84, 108–9, 124, 134–5, 137, 145, 150–2, 158, 239–40; libraries 157–9

Order in Council 8, 9, 14, 36
Order of St George 59, 100
Order of St Michael 59, 100
Order of the British Empire 100
Order of William Temple 91
ordinations 44, 45, 50, 70, 71, 75, 78
organists 123–4, 127–8, 249
organs 106
outreach 94, 96–104; responsibility for 94–6
Oxford Cathedral (Christ Church) 12; College of Canons 152; law 24; School 179–80
Oxford University 74, 180

parish church cathedrals 7, 10, 13, 15, 21, 35–6, 69–71, 75–6, 81–6, 93, 127, 130, 132, 137, 243, 253; libraries of 162
parishes 17
Parish of Manchester Division Act 1850 9
Parish of Manchester Revenues Measure 1933 9–10
Parochial Church Council 17
pastoral ministry 6
Patronage of Benefices Measure 1986 141
pension arrangements 198
Peterborough Cathedral 12; cathedral close 230; community 81, 82, 83; customs 31; funerals 101; Holy Communion 65; library 161; outreach 97; volunteers 90; worship 68
Phillimore, Robert 4
planning permission 217, 232
politics 4
Portsmouth Cathedral 13; body corporate of 132; customs 31; preaching at 77
power 3
preaching 74–7
prebendaries 12, 114–15, 118–19; ecumenical 99, 103
prebends 6, 114–15
precentors 12, 66, 69, 71, 72, 88, 110, 124-8
presbytery 106
priests 37, 45, 50: cathedral worship 67–8; ordination of 71; secular 35
priest vicar 125
Prime Minister 38
Privy Council 25
pro-cathedrals 14–15
public order 92–3
pulpits 74

quasi-legislation 31–2, 254–5
Quattuor Personae 107

reasonable force 249
Receiver General 140, 147, 149, 207
rectories 6
'red line' plans 231
Reformation 4, 5; and classification of cathedrals 11–12
registrar 48, 110
relics 4
religious orders 4
repairs 211, 216
residentiary canons 6, 7, 9, 67, 70, 115–18, 120–3, 130, 240–4
restoration order 54–5
retirement 49; *see also* pension arrangement
Ripon Cathedral 13; canons 122; foundation of 12; honorary canons 120; liturgical custom 73–4; visitors 93–4
robes 72
Rochester Cathedral 12; and the appointment of the bishop 43–4; baptismal policy 59; bishop's visitations 51–2; buildings 257; canons of 96, 121; Chapter 150; College of Canons 153; community 86; constitution and statutes 34; Council 138; customs 31; deans of 114; ecumenical activity 98; educational work 170; finances 207; Holy Communion 65; library 156; liturgical custom 73; music 129; outreach 95, 97, 102; School 178, 183; worship 72
Royal Institute of British Architects 214
Royal Institution of Chartered Surveyors 214
Royal School of Church Music 214
Rule of St Benedict 73

sacraments 57–67
sacrists 12, 66, 72, 118
Safeguarding and Discipline Measure 2016 180
safeguarding officers 129, 182, 184
saints 4
Salisbury Cathedral 12; and appointment of the bishop 43; and Cathedrals Fabric Commission 219; appointment to cathedral posts 107; bishops' visitations 51; canons of 96, 116, 121; Chapter 146, 149; chapter houses 131; College of Canons 151, 153; constitution and statutes 33; Council 135, 137; customs 29; deans of 113; educational work 170–1; employees 90; finances 207; library 156, 159; monastic cloisters 156; music 128; objects 20, 22;

quasi-legislation 32; School 177, 182–3; security 248, 250; theological studies 167; visitors 92, 93; volunteers 90; worship 69, 70
Salisbury Close 229
Salisbury's Foundation 14
same-sex couples 60
Scheduled Monument Consent 233
schools 175-83
secular cathedrals 4, 5, 12
secularisation 255
security 244-50
Sheffield Cathedral 28, 110–11, 195-6
shrines 4, 5
Society of Antiquaries of London 214
Society of Friends of Cathedral Music 124
sociology of religion 3
soft law 254; *see also* quasi-legislation
Southwark Cathedral 13; baptismal policy 60; by-laws 31; Chapter 148; dispute resolution 48; funerals 101; Holy Communion 63, 66; marriage policy 100; music 127–8; vergers 88
Southwell Cathedral 13, 131
Spiritual Capital 1
St Albans Cathedral 13; canons 95, 122–3; Chapter 147; foundation of 13
standing orders 31, 152
Statement of Financial Activities (SOFA) 202
Statement of Recommended Practice (SRP) 202, 203
statement of vision 20, 22, 91
St Edmundsbury Cathedral 13; by-laws 31; Chapter 147–8; community 85; Fabric Advisory Committee 224–5; funerals 101; Holy Communion 64, 66; library 162; music 127–8; outreach 95, 97; theological studies 169; vergers 88
stoles 72
St Paul's Cathedral 12; and appointment of the bishop 43; baptismal policy 59; buildings 256; canons of 120; Chapter 149; College of Canons 153; community 85; constitution and statutes 28, 33; Council 138; customs 29; deans of 113; educational work 174; finances 207; liturgical custom 73; marriage 100; outreach 102; precinct 237; protection of children and vulnerable adults 181–2; purposes 22–3; quasi-legislation 32; School 176; security incidents 244; statement of vision 22; worship 68
Stuart England 4

succentor 72, 125, 128
suffragan bishops 45, 63, 71, 76–7, 97, 107, 150
Synod 1070 4

Tatchell, Peter 244
tax 14
team-work 90
terrorism 244, 246, 248, 249
theological studies 167–9
theology 252
tourism 7, 92
Treasure Act 1996 193
treasures 185, 191-6
Truro Cathedral 13; canons 117, 119–20; Chapter 148; foundation of 12–13; theological studies 169
Tudor England 4

Vacancy in See Committee 38
valuable objects 191–6; exhibition 191–2; loan 192; sale 192–3; work on 193
vergers 87–9
vesture 72, 119
Vicar General 40, 52, 54, 194-5, 213
vicars choral 124
virgers 87–8; *see also* vergers
visitation: *see* bishops
visitor centres 92
visitors 92–4; cathedral interviews 93–4; pastoral care of 93
volunteers 89–91, 104; care for visitors 93–4
Volunteers Handbook 91

Wakefield Cathedral 13; allocation of seats 113; Chapter 144
Wells Cathedral 12; baptismal policy 66; buildings 256; canons of 121; Chapter 140, 141, 144, 145, 149; chapter house 131; College of Canons 153; community 84; Council 134–7; deans of 112, 113; Fabric Advisory Committee 223; finances 207; library 157–8; outreach 102; precinct 237; purposes of 22; School 177, 182; theological studies 167
wardens 79, 89
Winchester Cathedral 9, 12; and appointment of the bishop 43; bishop's visitations 51; buildings 256; canonical houses 241, 244; canons of 95–6, 121; Chapter 142–3, 147, 148, 149; community 86; constitution and statutes

34; Council 138; deans of 113–14; educational work 171, 174; employees 90; Fabric Advisory Committee 223; finances 207; hospitality 87; library 160, 161; liturgical custom 73; objects 21; outreach 95, 102–3; precinct 237–8; purposes 23; School 183; security 250; theological studies 168; visitors 92; volunteers 90

wine 61, 66

Worcester Cathedral 5, 12, 15; and appointment of the bishop 44; baptismal policy 66; bishop's visitations 51; buildings 256; canonical houses 241–2; Chapter 147; community 82, 83, 85–6; constitution and statutes 34; finances 207; funds 200; objects 23; property 191; visitors 92, 93; worship 68

worship 67–74; cathedral interviews 73–4; multi-faith 101; under cathedral constitutions and statutes 67–73

Yard Beadles 244

York Cathedral 8, 12, 17; Archbishop and 17, 38, 213–4, 225; canonical houses 240–1; canons 116; Cathedrals Fabric Commission 219; Chapter 54, 145–6; constitution and statutes 28; dean 109; library 156, 159; School 177–8; security 248; theological studies 167; University of York 159